IDENTIFYING THE ENEMY

Identifying the Enemy

Civilian Participation in Armed Conflict

EMILY CRAWFORD

OXFORD
UNIVERSITY PRESS

OXFORD
UNIVERSITY PRESS

Great Clarendon Street, Oxford, OX2 6DP,
United Kingdom

Oxford University Press is a department of the University of Oxford. It furthers the University's objective of excellence in research, scholarship, and education by publishing worldwide. Oxford is a registered trade mark of Oxford University Press in the UK and in certain other countries

First Edition published in 2015

Published in the United States of America by Oxford University Press
198 Madison Avenue, New York, NY 10016, United States of America

British Library Cataloguing in Publication Data
Data available

Library of Congress Control Number: 2015940870

ISBN 978–0–19–967849–5

For James, for setting the bar
For Graham, for his determination
And for Red, for always making everything better

Preface

For as long as there have been armed conflicts, civilians—persons we can colloquially define as those who are not part of the armed forces of their State or governing authority—have been involved in those conflicts. Civilians have been subjected to siege warfare,[1] to starvation tactics,[2] and to enslavement at the hands of occupying powers.[3] Civilians have taken up arms to defend their homelands from invasion: in post-revolutionary France, the Republican government, facing possible invasion by European neighbours, called on its citizenry to defend France. This was the *levée en masse*, the mass uprising of the entire populace of a threatened nation, as outlined in the Decree of 23 August 1793:

> from this moment until the enemies are driven out from the territory of the Republic, all Frenchmen are in permanent requisition for service in the army. Young people will go to combat; married men will forge weapons and transport supplies; women will make tents and clothes and serve in hospitals; children will shred old clothes; the elderly will get themselves carried to public squares in order to excite the courage of the warriors, to preach hate of the kings and unity of the Republic.[4]

Indeed, the event generally considered to be the origin of modern international humanitarian law—the Battle of Solferino[5]—involved civilians from the township of Castiglione delle Stiviere providing medical aid and relief to the wounded and sick of the armies of France, Austria, and Piedmont–Sardinia who had been left behind on the battlefield.[6] Civilians have always had 'a role to play in military strategies.'[7]

[1] See generally Alexander Gillespie, *A History of the Law of War: Volume 2—The Customs and Laws of War with Regards to Civilians in Times of Conflict* (Hart, 2011), at 52–63.

[2] Alexander Gillespie, *A History of the Law of War*, at 52–63.

[3] Alexander Gillespie, *A History of the Law of War*, at 103–41.

[4] Decree of the National Convention of 23 August 1793, reprinted in Thomas Hippler, *Citizens, Soldiers and National Armies: Military Service in France and Germany, 1789–1830* (Routledge, 2008), at 82.

[5] Simon Chesterman, 'Global Norms, Local Contexts', in Simon Chesterman (ed.), *Civilians in War* (Lynne Rienner, 2001), at 1; see also, Marco Sassòli, Antoine Bouvier, and Anne Quintin, *How Does Law Protect in War? Cases, Documents, and Teaching Materials on Contemporary Practice in International Humanitarian Law* (3rd edn, ICRC, 2012, hereinafter *How Does Law Protect in War*), at 195.

[6] See generally Jonathan Crowe and Kylie Weston-Scheuber, *Principles of International Humanitarian Law* (Elgar, 2013), at 29–30, and Gary Solis, 'An Introduction to the 1949 Geneva Conventions', in *Geneva Conventions* (Annotations by Fred Borch, Kaplan, 2010), at 3–6, on Dunant and his early humanitarian work.

[7] Anicée van Engeland, *Civilian or Combatant? A Challenge for the 21st Century* (OUP, 2011), at xi.

This book focuses on one particular aspect of how civilians are involved in armed conflict, specifically, when they take direct and active part in the hostilities. It examines the increasingly difficult task of identifying when civilians take direct part in hostilities, and how such direct participation influences the conduct of parties to the conflict and affects the law that governs the conduct of parties to armed conflicts: the law of armed conflict, also known as international humanitarian law (IHL).[8]

The scope of this book is limited to a few unique but interconnected areas that have been of particular concern in the last ten to twenty-five years: the practice of targeted killing, the emergence of cyber warfare as a nascent method of warfare, the growth of the private military and security company, and the problems that arise from high-level criminal activity that often occurs alongside existing military engagements. As such, certain categories of civilians who take direct part, such as child soldiers, are excluded from the scope of this book. This is not because the question of child soldiers bears no connection to questions of direct participation, but rather that an appropriate examination of the issue of child soldiers is beyond the scope of this book.[9] Instead, this book looks at the emerging trend towards increased civilian involvement and participation in armed conflict, and what issues that raises for the current law of armed conflict, and those who must observe the law. The research is current to January 2015.

A work such as this is never done in isolation. This book is the result of the post-doctoral fellowship I was fortunate enough to receive from the University of Sydney, which gave me the luxury of three years to investigate this particular area of IHL. Furthermore, I could not have finished this without the help of a number of colleagues and friends who provided invaluable and unceasing support, guidance, feedback, and encouragement. At the University of Sydney, my thanks go to my office neighbours and mentors, Professor Ben Saul and Professor Tim Stephens, who were always available with a kind word and an expert eye. Professor Margaret Harris at the Faculty of Arts and Social Sciences was also invaluable in helping me craft the proposal that became the post-doctoral study; this work would not exist were it not for her gracious and patient supervision and support. At Oxford University Press, thanks go to my commissioning editor Merel Alstein, who helped me shepherd the proposal from its earliest stages to its current form, and to the editorial team of Anthony Hinton, Emma Endean,

[8] The terms law of armed conflict and IHL are used interchangeably in this text.

[9] And is indeed worthy of its own standalone examination: see, eg, Matthew Happold, *Child Soldiers in International Law* (Manchester University Press, 2005), and Ilene Cohn, *Child Soldiers: The Role of Children in Armed Conflict* (OUP, 1994).

and Jamie Berezin, who helped me get the manuscript to print; also invaluable were my reviewers, especially Professor Stephen Haines, all of whom were unstinting in their expert advice. My colleagues and friends, Professor Helen Irving, Dr Rayner Thwaites, Dr Alison Pert, Ms Elisa Arcioni, Dr Jacqueline Mowbray, Professor Chester Brown, and Ms Irene Baghoomians at the Sydney Law School, Dr Catherine Renshaw at University of Western Sydney, and Professor Michael Lewis at Ohio Northern University were also a constant source of friendship and good humour. Professor Lewis especially was of invaluable help in honing my arguments and perspectives on the questions raised by drone warfare. Thanks must also go to my family—Marisa, Rebecca, Graham, James, Daniel, Sofia, Stella, Sadie, Lynn, Philip, Liv, Deme, and Lachlan—who always believed in me, even if some of them were too young to understand. Finally, thanks and more go to James Ryan, who never complained when I took over the dining table, who appreciates a good anagram, and who always makes everything better.

Emily Crawford

Sydney
January 2015

Contents

II: CURRENT CHALLENGES TO THE LAW ON CIVILIANS AND ARMED CONFLICT

III: CIVILIAN PARTICIPATION IN ARMED CONFLICT AND THE LAW IN THE TWENTY-FIRST CENTURY

Table of Cases

INTERNATIONAL CASE LAW

The International Court of Justice

The International Criminal Court

The International Criminal Tribunal for Rwanda

The International Criminal Tribunal for the Former Yugoslavia

Table of Treaties, Legislation, and Other International Instruments

TREATIES

DECLARATIONS, MANUALS, AND OTHER SOFT LAW INSTRUMENTS

List of Abbreviations

ACLU	American Civil Liberties Union
AJIL	American Journal of International Law
ANSA	armed non-State actor
API	Protocol Additional to the Geneva Conventions of 12 August 1949, and Relating to the Protection of Victims of International Armed Conflicts, of 8 June 1977
APII	Protocol Additional to the Geneva Conventions of 12 August 1949, and Relating to the Protection of Victims of Non-International Armed Conflicts, of 8 June 1977
AP Commentary	Yves Sandoz, Christophe Swinarski, and Bruno Zimmerman (eds), *Commentary on the Additional Protocols of 8 June 1977 to the Geneva Conventions of 12 August 1949*, ICRC/Martinus Nijhoff, Geneva, 1987
AQAP	al-Qaeda in the Arabian Peninsula
ATF	US Bureau of Alcohol, Tobacco and Firearms
ATM	automated teller machine
AUC	Autodefensas Unidas de Colombia
AULR	American University Law Review
BACRIM	*bandas criminales*
BYBIL	British Yearbook of International Law
CAAF	contractors authorized to accompany the force
Case W Res J Int'l L	Case Western Reserve Journal of International Law
CDDH	Diplomatic Conference on the Reaffirmation and Development of International Humanitarian Law Applicable in Armed Conflicts (Geneva, 1974–77)
CIA	Central Intelligence Agency
CNA	Computer Network Attack
CNE	Computer Network Exploitation
Colum J Transnat'l L	Columbia Journal of Transnational Law
Convention I	Geneva Convention (I) for the Amelioration of the Condition of the Wounded and Sick in Armed Forces in the Field, of 12 August 1949

Convention II	Geneva Convention (II) for the Amelioration of the Condition of the Wounded, Sick in Armed Forces at Sea, of 12 August 1949
Convention III	Geneva Convention (III) Relative to the Treatment of Prisoners of War, of 12 August 1949
Convention IV	Geneva Convention (IV) Relative to the Protection of Civilian Persons in Time of War, of 12 August 1949
COW	Correlates of War
CTS	Consolidated Treaty Series
CUP	Cambridge University Press
DDoS	Distributed Denial of Service Attack
Doc.	Document
DoD	Department of Defense (US)
DoS	denial of service
DPH	Direct Participation in Hostilities
DPHIG	Direct Participation in Hostilities Interpretive Guidance (ICRC)
ECOSOC	Economic and Social Council (UN)
ECtHR	European Court of Human Rights
Edn	Edition
EJIL	European Journal of International Law
ELN	Ejército de Liberación National
EMP	electromagnetic pulse
EW	Electronic Warfare
FARC	Fuerzas Armadas Revolucionarias de Colombia
FBI	Federal Bureau of Investigation
Final Record	*Final Record of the Diplomatic Conference of Geneva of 1949*
FMLN	Farabundo Martí National Liberation Front
GA Res	United Nations General Assembly Resolution
GC	Geneva Convention
GCI Commentary	Pictet (ed.), *Commentary to Geneva Convention I for the Amelioration of the Condition of the Wounded and Sick in Armed Forces in the Field*, ICRC, Geneva, 1952
GCII Commentary	Pictet (ed.), *Commentary to Geneva Convention II for the Amelioration of the Condition of the Wounded and Sick in Armed Forces in the Field*, ICRC, Geneva, 1960

GCIII Commentary	Pictet (ed.), *Commentary to the Third Geneva Convention Relative to the Treatment of Prisoners of War*, ICRC, Geneva, 1960
GCIV Commentary	Pictet (ed.), *Commentary to Geneva Convention IV Relative to the Protection of Civilian Persons in Time of War*, ICRC, Geneva, 1958
Hague Regulations	Regulations concerning the Laws and Customs of War on Land, Annex to Convention (IV) Respecting the Laws and Customs of War on Land, of 18 October 1907
Harvard Manual	*Manual on International Law Applicable to Air and Missile Warfare* 2009
HPCR	Humanitarian Policy and Conflict Research
ICC	International Criminal Court
ICCPR	International Covenant on Civil and Political Rights
ICJ	International Court of Justice
ICJ Rep	International Court of Justice, Reports of Judgments
ICRC	International Committee of the Red Cross
ICRC CIHL Study	Jean-Marie Henckaerts and Louise Doswald-Beck (eds), *International Committee of the Red Cross: Customary International Humanitarian Law*, Volume I: Rules, Volume 2: Practice (in two parts), Cambridge University Press, Cambridge, 2005
ICTR	International Criminal Tribunal for Rwanda
ICTY	International Criminal Tribunal for the former Yugoslavia
IDF	Israeli Defence Force
IED	improvised explosive device
IHL	International Humanitarian Law
IHRL	International Human Rights Law
ILA	International Law Association
IMDC	Internal Displacement Monitoring Centre
IRRC	International Review of the Red Cross
ISAF	International Security Assistance Force (in Afghanistan)
IW	Information Warfare
J Conf & Sec L	Journal of Conflict and Security Law
JEM	Justice and Equality Movement (in Sudan)
JICJ	Journal of International Criminal Justice

Lieber Code	Instructions for the Government of Armies of the United States in the Field, Prepared By Francis Lieber, Promulgated as General Orders No. 100 by President Lincoln, 24 April 1863
LNTS	League of Nations Treaty Series
MCA	Military Commissions Act of 2009
Mil L Rev	Military Law Review
Montreux Document	The Montreux Document on Pertinent International Legal Obligations and Good Practices for States related to Operations of Private Military and Security Companies during Armed Conflict 2008
MPRI	Military Professional Resources Incorporated
n.	note
NATO	North Atlantic Treaty Organization
New Rules	Michael Bothe, Karl Joseph Partsch and Waldemar Solf (eds), *New Rules for Victims of Armed Conflicts: Commentary on the Two 1977 Protocols Additional to the Geneva Conventions of 1949*, Martinus Nijhoff, The Hague/Boston/London, 1982
NIAC	Non-International Armed Conflict
NSA	National Security Agency
OAU	Organisation of African Unity
Official Records	*Official Records of the Diplomatic Conference on the Reaffirmation and Development of International Humanitarian Law Applicable in Armed Conflicts Geneva 1974–1977*
ONG	Organización Nueva Genaración
OUP	Oxford University Press
Para.	Paragraph
PCATI	Public Committee Against Torture in Israel
PMSC	Private Military and Security Contractor
POW	Prisoner of War
Protocol I	Protocol Additional to the Geneva Conventions of 12 August 1949, and Relating to the Protection of Victims of International Armed Conflicts, of 8 June 1977
Protocol II	Protocol Additional to the Geneva Conventions of 12 August 1949, and Relating to the Protection of Victims of Non-International Armed Conflicts, of 8 June 1977
PRT	Provincial Reconstruction Team

PSPHRE	Palestinian Society for the Protection of Human Rights and the Environment
Res.	Resolution
Rome Statute	Rome Statute of the International Criminal Court
ROTC	Reserve Officer Training Corps
Sassòli, Bouvier, and Quintin	Marco Sassòli, Antoine Bouvier, and Anne Quintin (eds), *How Does Law Protect in War? Cases, Documents and Teaching Materials,* 3rd edn, ICRC, Geneva, 2011
Schindler and Toman	Dietrich Schindler and Jïri Toman (eds), The *Laws of Armed Conflicts: A Collection of Conventions, Resolutions and Other Documents*, 4th edn, Martinus Nijhoff, Leiden, 2004
SMR	Standard Minimum Rules for the Treatment of Prisoners
SPLM/A	Sudan People's Liberation Movement/Army
SPLM–N	Sudan People's Liberation Movement–North
Tallinn Manual	Michael Schmitt (ed.), *The Tallinn Manual on the International Law Applicable to Cyber Warfare,* Cambridge University Press, New York, 2013
Targeted Killings	*The Public Committee against Torture in Israel et al. v the Government of Israel et al.*, HCJ 769/02, 13 December 2006
UAV	unmanned aerial vehicles
UN	United Nations
UK	United Kingdom
UNTS	United Nations Treaty Series
US/USA	United States/United States of America
USAF	United States Air Force
Va J Int'l L	Virginia Journal of International Law
Vol	Volume
WWI	First World War
WWII	Second World War
YBIHL	Yearbook of International Humanitarian Law

Introduction

Regulating the Irregular: International Humanitarian Law and the Question of Civilian Participation in Armed Conflicts

The law of armed conflict essentially revolves around a particular fulcrum: the principle of distinction. One of the 'fundamental and intransgressible principle[s]'[1] of international humanitarian law (IHL), the principle of distinction obliges parties to a conflict, when making targeting decisions, to distinguish between civilians and combatants, and between civilian objects and military objectives. Under IHL, only military objectives may be lawfully directly targeted, while civilians and civilian objects are immune[2] from direct targeting.[3] The principle of distinction is considered the cornerstone of the modern law of armed conflict.

However, the principle of distinction is itself based on a fundamental assumption: that one is able to make the distinction between a civilian and a combatant clearly and easily. What does one do then if a combatant looks like a civilian, or if a civilian acts like a combatant? How does one observe the principle of distinction if, in practice, making that distinction is difficult or impossible?

To understand the principle of distinction one must understand its historical origins. Starting with the first Geneva Convention of 1864, the modern laws of armed conflict were, for a long time, structured around the idea that

[1] *Legality of the Threat or Use of Nuclear Weapons* (Advisory Opinion) [1996] ICJ Rep 226, at 257 (hereinafter *Nuclear Weapons*).

[2] The term 'civilian immunity' in not a legal term; as discussed in Ch. 1, the relevant legal instruments indicate that civilians are protected from direct attack, rather than being immune from attack. As such, the term 'civilian immunity' is used in this book as a descriptive term of art.

[3] However, civilians and civilian objects will lose their immunity from targeting if they are deemed as having a military purpose. For civilian objects, immunity from targeting is lost if the object is considered as having a military purpose or use. For civilians, immunity is lost if the civilian takes direct part in the hostilities. Ch. 1 of this book explores the details of immunity and targeting in more detail.

only international armed conflicts warranted international regulation, and that such wars must be fought solely by States and their agents.[4] State armed forces tended to wear uniforms or other distinctive regalia or insignia. They would usually carry their weaponry openly. As such, it was (comparatively) easy to distinguish between a member of the armed forces and a civilian.[5]

Furthermore, in order to ensure that only members of the armed forces would take direct part in the hostilities, the law of armed conflict offered incentives to regular participation, that is, participation in the hostilities through regular outlets such as the armed forces. Certain rights and privileges attached to regular participation, such as the right to prisoner-of-war (POW) treatment on capture. The other significant privilege that came with combatant status was the combatant's privilege, the right to take direct part in hostilities. While regular participation in hostilities meant that a combatant was liable for direct targeting, the combatant's privilege meant that combatants could themselves lawfully directly target the armed forces of the adverse party. Moreover, combatants would not be held liable under domestic law for their warlike acts, provided such acts were carried out in accordance with the law of armed conflict. Thus, a combatant would be immune from domestic prosecution for property damage, the infliction of bodily harm, or for killing a member of the armed forces of the enemy, provided that such acts were done in accordance with the law of armed conflict, and in connection to the armed conflict, as lawful acts of war.[6]

The law of armed conflict also determined certain distinct disadvantages to those civilians who did participate in armed conflicts. Civilians were granted immunity from direct targeting, but that immunity was dependant on civilians refraining from taking a direct part in the hostilities.[7] Civilians

[4] See, for instance, the 1868 Declaration Renouncing the Use, in Time of War, of Explosive Projectiles under 400 Grammes Weight (hereinafter the St Petersburg Declaration), which states 'that the progress of civilization should have the effect of alleviating as much as possible the calamities of war; [t]hat the only legitimate object which *States* should endeavour to accomplish during war is to weaken the *military forces* of the enemy' (emphasis added).

[5] See generally Stephen Wood, 'Uniforms', in Richard Holmes, Charles Singleton, and Spencer Jones (eds), *The Oxford Companion to Military History* (OUP, 2001), who notes that historically combatants have always worn costumes to distinguish themselves from non-combatants, though the reasons for doing so have not always been for reasons of legal necessity; see also Toni Pfanner, 'Military Uniforms and the Law of War', 86 IRRC 93 (2004); and Paul Martin, *European Military Uniforms: A Short History* (Spring Books, 1967), who discusses how uniforms and insignia developed in Europe during the Middle Ages as a means by which to 'weld fighting forces together and clearly demarcate opposing sides'.

[6] For more on combatants rights and privileges, see further Emily Crawford, *The Treatment of Combatants and Insurgents under the Law of Armed Conflict* (OUP, 2010), specifically Ch. 2.

[7] See Art. 22 of the Instructions for the Government of Armies of the US in the Field, General Orders, 24 April 1863; promulgated as General Orders No. 100 (hereinafter the Lieber Code): 'Nevertheless, as civilisation has advanced during the last centuries, so has likewise steadily

who *did* choose to take direct part in hostilities would not enjoy any combatant rights or privileges, and they would also lose their immunity from direct targeting for as long as they took direct part in hostilities. Civilian participation in armed conflict was (and is) not internationally unlawful,[8] but neither was it protected in the same way as participation by combatants.

However, despite these disincentives, civilians have taken and continue to take direct part in hostilities, often in coordinated and systematic ways. As international law became more involved in regulating the conduct of non-international armed conflicts,[9] the question of civilian participation in armed conflict became more pressing, and one that needed to be addressed. However, throughout the last 150 years, when States have convened to discuss the question of widespread, systematic civilian participation in hostilities, they have essentially ignored a significant part of the issue. That is to say, rather than attempt to define the parameters of direct participation, States have instead chosen to amend the existing rules to incorporate certain categories of civilian direct participants into pre-existing categories of combatant—basically making the 'irregular' 'regular' combatants. Thus, homeland defenders in a *levée en masse* became combatants in 1899, partisan and resistance fighters in occupied territory became combatants in 1949, and guerrilla fighters against colonial occupiers and racist regimes became combatants under the law of armed conflict in 1977.[10]

The consequence, intended or not, of deeming the irregular participant to be a regular combatant has been that the question of defining the parameters of direct participation is something that has remained essentially unexamined in the treaty law. Furthermore, State practice on the issue has been somewhat unclear. Thus, in the twenty-first century, the process of correctly and lawfully identifying the enemy and observing the principle of distinction has become remarkably difficult.

The situation has only been made more complicated by developments in State practice over the last twenty-five years. As noted, the principle of distinction, at its most basic (if simplistic) level, places persons and objects

advanced, especially in war on land, the distinction between the private individual belonging to a hostile country and the hostile country itself, with its men in arms. The principle has been more and more acknowledged that the unarmed citizen is to be spared in person, property and honour as much as the exigencies of war will admit.'

[8] Except in the case of mercenaries. See further Ch. 2 of this book.

[9] For an overview of the development of the law of non-international armed conflict, and the increasing regulation of such conflicts under international law, see further Lindsay Moir, *The Law of Internal Armed Conflicts* (CUP, 2002), specifically Chs 1–2; and Sandesh Sivakumaran, *The Law of Non-International Armed Conflict* (OUP, 2012), specifically Chs 1–2.

[10] The provisions and treaties in which combatant status was granted to these participants in discussed in more detail in Ch. 2.

into categories—military or civilian, targetable or non-targetable. *Prima facie*, once such a categorization is made—once you fall into one category or another—certain consequences follow, and certain legal regimes activate, while others are closed off. Laudable in theory, implementing the principle of distinction and making determinations as to status is much more complicated, and the last quarter of a century has made the civilian/military parameters harder to ascertain and the distinctions harder to draw, if they were indeed ever particularly easy. Changes in technology and in military infrastructure and funding have put civilians in the battlefield in more ways than could have been imagined by the drafters of the Geneva Conventions in 1949. Alongside the more 'conventional' civilian participants such as non-State armed groups, civilians now directly participate in hostilities in manifold ways: they pilot drones undertaking so-called 'targeted killings';[11] they guard military convoys and sites, and operate infrastructure such as mess-halls;[12] they conduct computer network attacks and computer network exploitation;[13] they operate alongside and as part of drug cartels, or those trafficking in 'blood diamonds' or ivory, using the armed conflict to conceal or further their own criminal or insurgent acts.[14]

As these new participants push at the boundaries of the law, as more civilians behave like combatants or are put in quasi-combatant roles, those who must observe and implement IHL find themselves increasingly challenged to explain whether such irregulars can be adequately addressed under the existing law. The uncertain scope of the concept of direct participation under customary international law and the paucity of specific treaty rules sits uneasily with these new civilian participants and quasi-participants. The tension between these two forces is evident and possible resolutions, in the form of new treaties or the extension of combatant

[11] David Cloud, 'Civilian Contractors Playing Key Roles in U.S. Drone Operations', *Los Angeles Times*, 29 December 2011, available at: <http://articles.latimes.com/2011/dec/29/world/la-fg-drones-civilians-20111230>.

[12] Peter Singer, *Corporate Warriors: The Rise of the Privatized Military Industry* (Cornell University Press, 2003).

[13] Dan Evan, 'Hackers Paralyze Israeli Hospital Websites, As Cyber War Heats Up', *Haaretz*, 25 January 2012, available at: <http://www.haaretz.com/news/diplomacy-defense/hackers-paralyze-israeli-hospital-websites-as-cyber-war-heats-up-1.409190>.

[14] See Paul Orogun, "'Blood Diamonds" and Africa's Armed Conflicts in the Post-Cold War Era', 166 World Affairs 151 (2004); Richard Schiffman, 'Ivory Poaching Funds Most War and Terrorism in Africa', *New Scientist*, 14 May 2014, available at: <http://www.newscientist.com/article/mg22229692.700-ivory-poaching-funds-most-war-and-terrorism-in-africa.html>; and Johan Bergenas and Monica Medina, 'Break the Link between Terrorism Funding and Poaching' (Opinion), *Washington Post*, 31 January 2014, available at: <http://www.washingtonpost.com/opinions/break-the-link-between-terrorism-funding-and-poaching/2014/01/31/6c03780e-83b5-11e3-bbe5-6a2a3141e3a9_story.html>.

status to more irregulars, seem unlikely and indeed may not be the best response.

It is these questions that form the central focus of this book. At the heart of the issue is an apparently simple yet complex and controversial question: when is a civilian no longer a civilian, for the purposes of losing their immunity from targeting? It is a question that is of pressing concern for all persons who are engaged in armed conflict; for those who must make targeting decisions to those who must assess whether their own involvement in an armed conflict renders them targetable.

This book uses the term 'irregular' to cover all persons who take direct part in hostilities but who do not fall within the recognized categories of combatant as outlined in the Geneva Conventions[15] and Additional Protocols.[16] This book examines a number of current challenges to the framework of IHL presented by new irregular participants such as civilians who are deemed to be taking direct part in hostilities, as well as *sui generis* groups such as private military and security contractors (PMSCs). This book will also examine how technology has expanded the capacity for civilian participation, in the form of computer-based participation in armed conflict, including civilian pilots of unmanned aerial vehicles (UAVs) used in targeted killings and civilians conducting cyber-attacks. Finally, this book also examines one of the more vexing issues confronting the law of armed conflict: when high-level criminal activities become virtually indistinguishable from armed conflict, either due to their scope and the intensity of violence (as seen in the Mexico drug

[15] Comprising Geneva Convention for the Amelioration of the Condition of the Wounded and Sick in Armed Forces in the Field of 12 August 1949 (hereinafter Geneva Convention I or GCI) 75 UNTS 31 (1950); Geneva Convention for the Amelioration of the Condition of Wounded, Sick and Shipwrecked Members of Armed Forces at Sea of 12 August 1949 (hereinafter Geneva Convention II or GCII) 75 UNTS 85 (1950); Geneva Convention Relative to the Treatment of Prisoners of War of 12 August 1949 (hereinafter Geneva Convention III, GCIII, or the POW Convention) 75 UNTS 135 (1950); and Geneva Convention Relative to the Protection of Civilian Persons in Time of War of 12 August 1949 (hereinafter Geneva Convention IV, GCIV, or the Civilians Convention) 75 UNTS 287 (1950). Art. 4A of Geneva Convention III outlines the provisions for combatant status.

[16] The Additional Protocols comprise Protocol Additional to the Geneva Conventions of 12 August 1949, and relating to the Protection of Victims of International Armed Conflicts of 8 June 1977 (hereinafter Protocol I or API), 1125 UNTS 3, and Protocol Additional to the Geneva Conventions of 12 August 1949, and relating to the Protection of Victims of Non-International Armed Conflicts of 8 June 1977 (hereinafter Protocol II or APII), 1125 UNTS 609. Additional Protocol III (Protocol Additional to the Geneva Conventions of 12 August 1949, and relating to the adoption of an additional distinctive emblem, 8 December 2005, 2404 UNTS 261) was adopted in 2005 and adds an additional protected emblem—that of the Red Crystal—to the existing Red Cross and Red Crescent emblems. However, in discussing the Additional Protocols in this book, reference is intended to the 1977 Protocols only. Arts 43 and 44 of Additional Protocol I outline the rules on combatant status in Additional Protocol I.

wars), or else due to the co-mingling of criminal activities with 'conventional' armed conflict (as seen in Colombia and Afghanistan).

Chapter 1 outlines the general law that relates to civilians in armed conflict, the principle of distinction, which provides that civilians are immune from targeting as long as they refrain from taking direct part in hostilities, and that only military objects are lawfully targetable. In order to make distinction-compliant targeting assessments, it is necessary to be able to determine whether something or someone is civilian or military. Therefore, this chapter also examines how civilians are defined under the law of armed conflict, and how that definition is constructed in opposition to the definition of combatant. Finally, this chapter also examines the general rules on when people may be targeted under the law of armed conflict, both due to status (as a combatant) and due to behaviour (as a civilian taking direct part).

Chapter 2 then explores how the law of armed conflict has historically responded to civilians who lose their immunity by taking direct part in hostilities. This chapter offers a brief history of irregular participation in armed conflict and examines how the law of armed conflict has granted combatant status to some participants while excluding other civilian participants. This chapter demonstrates that States have avoided attempting to define direct participation and chosen instead to grant combatant status to certain types of civilians, and thus deeming to be regular certain kinds of civilian participation. However, State practice over the last 150 years has demonstrated that expanding the categories of combatant can only go so far; certain groups of civilians are always excluded from combatant status. The targeting of such civilians is thus still informed by the general principles of distinction in targeting and the notion of 'direct participation in hostilities (DPH)'.

In order to complete the picture regarding the law governing civilian participation in hostilities, Chapter 3 examines in detail the concept of DPH. This issue is pivotal for an analysis of irregular participation in hostilities as it is when civilians direct participate in hostilities that they lose their non-combatant immunity and render themselves liable for targeting. As so many of these new irregular participants are of uncertain status, an analysis of DPH is vital. This chapter will look at the history and development of the concept of DPH as an exception to non-combatant immunity. This chapter will also analyse the attempts to determine the parameters of DPH from before its first explicit iterations in the Additional Protocols to the Israeli Supreme Court Case on targeted killings. The chapter will culminate with an analysis of the most recent attempt to define DPH—the International Committee of the Red Cross Interpretive Guidance on Direct Participation in Hostilities—and examine the international legal and political reception to the Interpretive Guidance.

The remaining chapters of the book comprise case studies on specific irregular participants currently challenging the contours of IHL and the principle of distinction, the principle of non-combatant immunity, and the loss of immunity due to direct participation. These new challenges include the practice of using civilians to pilot drones in targeted killings, directed against civilians who are deemed to be taking direct part in hostilities; the use of PMSCs in armed conflict zones providing ancillary and quasi-military services to regular armed forces; high-scale and high-intensity criminal violence; and the conduct of cyber warfare by civilians. These chapters will analyse exactly what status such irregular participants have under IHL, whether the current law deals with these situations appropriately, and what challenges these new forms of civilian participation present for States under IHL. Chapter 4 will look at the practice of targeted killings, examining the criteria that are used to select irregulars for targeted killing. Chapter 5 builds on this, examining the problems raised by the employment of civilians to pilot the UAVs used to carry out targeted killings. This chapter will also examine the nascent area of computer network attacks (CNA) and computer network exploitation (CNE) in armed conflict, examining the status of civilians who directly participate in cyber warfare. Chapter 6 examines the employment of PMSCs in armed conflict situations, with Chapter 7 exploring the issue of high-intensity sustained violence in criminal endeavours that are indistinguishable or else coexistent and intermixed with existing armed conflict, and whether it can, and should, fit into the rubric of armed conflict.

Finally, this book will conclude with an assessment of the law as it stands in relation to current State practice, and will assess the prospects for the future of the law of armed conflict and irregular participants, whether the law as its stands is flexible enough to incorporate these new irregulars, and whether such incorporation is necessary or likely. Chapter 8 looks at how the question of DPH might be best addressed through unconventional means, such as soft law instruments, which offer the promise of flexibility and rapidity of response that treaties and customary law may not offer, and allow for a more nuanced and holistic approach to regulating the irregular in armed conflict.

PART I

THE DEVELOPMENT OF THE LAW RELATING TO CIVILIANS AND ARMED CONFLICTS

1

The General Rules on Civilians in Armed Conflicts

Civilian Immunity and the Principle of Distinction

Introduction

Since its earliest incarnations over 150 years ago, the modern law of armed conflict has developed according to a fundamental axiom: only military objects may be lawfully targeted while civilian objects remain immune. Translated to the 'personal' level, only combatants may be lawfully targeted (unless rendered *hors de combat* due to injury, illness, or capture);[1] civilians are immune from being targeted unless they directly participate in the hostilities.[2] When civilians take direct part in the hostilities, they lose their civilian immunity and become targets.[3] In the law of armed conflict, this dyad of immunity and targeting is known as the principle of distinction.[4]

In order to comply with the principle of distinction, parties to an armed conflict must therefore take steps to identify combatants and civilians and distinguish between them. On a macro level, this means that direct attacks may only be launched against military objectives, with civilian objects being immune from attack.[5] On a micro level, observing the principle of distinction means that those persons who are duly recognized combatants under the law of armed conflict must distinguish themselves from the civilian population and be identifiable as combatants.[6]

The benefits of combatant status include the right to take direct part in the hostilities, combatant immunity for their war-like acts if undertaken

[1] Art. 48, API. [2] Art. 51(3), API. [3] Art. 51(3), API.

[4] See generally Esbjörn Rosenblad, *International Humanitarian Law of Armed Conflict: Some Aspects of the Principle of Distinction and Related Problems* (Henry Dunant Institute, 1979), specifically 53–72, on the principle of distinction.

[5] Art. 52(2), API. [6] Art. 4A, GCIII; Art. 44(3), API.

in compliance with the laws of armed conflict, and prisoner-of-war (POW) rights if captured.[7] However, combatant status brings with it an additional status—that of target. Lawful combatants are liable to be targeted at all times during the armed conflict by virtue of their status as combatants.[8] Civilians are not targets by virtue of their status as civilians, that is, as persons not taking up arms against the enemy.[9]

In order to retain such targeting immunity, civilians must not take direct part in the hostilities. However, as noted in the Preface, civilians have participated and continue to participate in armed conflicts in manifold ways—from providing the labour for the production of munitions, to maintaining the 'home front', to fending off invaders and occupiers in their own territory. While all of these activities can be seen as war-sustaining and playing a 'part' in the hostilities, only a certain *type* of participation will be considered 'direct', warranting the loss of civilian immunity and rendering a civilian liable to be lawfully attacked. Thus, in order to comply with the principle of distinction, it is paramount for parties to the conflict to be able to determine accurately who is a civilian, who is a combatant, and what kinds of direct participation warrant the loss of civilian immunity and allow for lawful targeting of such a civilian.

This chapter will examine the principle of distinction and how it is applied in practice, exploring how international humanitarian law (IHL) defines civilians and combatants. It will also examine *why* the law developed as it did, marking out civilians as *prima facie* immune from targeting, and combatants *prima facie* always targetable. This chapter will establish the background framework for Chapter 2 which explores how the law of armed conflict has developed in line with the principle of distinction, and how a reluctance on the part of the international community to address the parameters within which civilians lose their immunity from targeting has shaped the evolution of the law in the twentieth century. This will then lead to the examination in Chapter 3 of what the law on participants has not yet fully explored—the concept of direct participation and the loss of civilian immunity.

[7] See Emily Crawford, *The Treatment of Combatants and Insurgents under the Law of Armed Conflict* (OUP, 2012), specifically Ch. 2 on combatant and POW rights under the law of armed conflict.

[8] Marco Sassòli and Laura Olson, 'The Relationship between International Humanitarian and Human Rights Law Where it Matters: Admissible Killing and Internment of Fighters in Non-International Armed Conflicts', 90 IRRC 599 (2008), at 605–06.

[9] Art. 51(1)–(2), API.

The Principle of Distinction and Civilian Immunity in Armed Conflicts

The principle of distinction developed out of a need to balance two seemingly incongruous ideas: that States want to prosecute their military endeavours effectively but at the same time be able to protect their own citizens. As Schmitt puts it:

> States have an interest in protecting civilians, especially their own . . . states have an equally compelling interest in being able to effectively prosecute military operations . . . as a result, IHL represents the synthesis in a dialectical process involving the balancing of two seemingly contradictory concerns: military necessity and humanity. The purpose of IHL is not solely to extend protections to civilians and their property. It is instead to find a rational equipoise between that goal and the equally valid objective of conducting effectual military operations in pursuit of national interests.[10]

The principle of distinction encompasses this dichotomy of balancing military needs with humanitarian objectives. In the modern laws of armed conflict, we can see this balancing of needs and interests in nearly all the legal instruments in the field, dating back to the preamble to the 1868 St Petersburg Declaration, which states that:

> the progress of civilization should have the effect of alleviating as much as possible the calamities of war; [t]hat the only legitimate object which States should endeavour to accomplish during war is to weaken the *military forces* of the enemy.[11]

As a practical matter, the principle of distinction obliges parties to a conflict to distinguish at all times between military and civilian objects and objectives, and between civilian persons and combatants (or persons taking direct part in the hostilities), and to direct attacks only against military targets.

[10] Michael Schmitt, 'Discriminate Warfare: The Military Necessity-Humanity Dialectic of International Humanitarian Law', in *Protecting Civilians During Violent Conflict: Theoretical and Practical Issues for the 21st Century* (David Lovell and Igor Primoratz eds, Ashgate, 2012), at 87–88.

[11] Emphasis added. See also Art. 22, Lieber Code which states that there exists a 'distinction between the private individual belonging to a hostile country and the hostile country itself, with its men in arms', although it adds the qualification that the 'unarmed citizen is to be spared in person, property, and honor *as much as the exigencies of war will admit*' (emphasis added). Thus, Lieber's concept of the principle of distinction was conditional, and he considered that there were limits to the protection of civilians under the Code. See further Sibylle Scheipers, 'Fighting Irregular Fighters: Is the Law of Armed Conflict Outdated?', 43 Parameters 45 (2013), at 46–49.

This is enunciated in treaty law in Article 48 of Additional Protocol I,[12] which states that:

> In order to ensure respect for and protection of the civilian population and civilian objects, the Parties to the conflict shall at all times distinguish between the civilian population and combatants and between civilian objects and military objectives and accordingly shall direct their operations only against military objectives.[13]

The principle of distinction thus has a number of layers—first, there is the obligation for parties to a conflict to distinguish between combatants and civilians. Combatants must distinguish themselves from civilians; that is to say, they must be visually identifiable as combatants.[14] Secondly, they must distinguish between combatants and civilians when directing their attacks; that is, only combatants (or other lawful military objects and objectives) may be targeted. Civilians are immune from targeting, unless they take direct part in hostilities. This is enunciated in treaty law in Article 51 of Additional Protocol I which states that:

> 1. The civilian population and individual civilians shall enjoy general protection against dangers arising from military operations.
> 2. The civilian population as such, as well as individual civilians, shall not be the object of attack. Acts or threats of violence the primary purpose of which is to spread terror among the civilian population are prohibited.
> 3. Civilians shall enjoy the protection afforded by this Section, unless and for such time as they take a direct part in hostilities.[15]

[12] See also Art. 25, Hague Regulations of 1899 (annexed to Convention (II) with Respect to the Laws and Customs of War on Land (187 CTS 429)) and the Hague Regulations of 1907 (annexed to Convention IV Respecting the Laws and Customs of War on Land (205 CTS 277)), which prohibits 'the attack or bombardment of towns, villages, habitations or buildings with are not defended'. The 1907 regulations add 'by whatever means' after the words 'attack or bombardment' to the prohibition. Although the Regulations do not expressly prohibit attacking civilians, the principle can be inferred from the instruments; the Commentary to the Protocols supports such an inference (see Yves Sandoz, Christophe Swinarski, and Bruno Zimmerman (eds), *Commentary on the Additional Protocols of 8 June 1977 to the Geneva Conventions of 12 August 1949* (ICRC, 1987, hereinafter *AP Commentary*), at 598, paras 1863–64), which states that the 'entire system established in The Hague in 1899 and 1907 and in Geneva from 1864 to 1977 is founded' on the principle of distinction). However, as Solis notes, the failure to proscribe deliberate attacks on civilians was not a failing in the law or an acknowledgement of the acceptability of targeting civilians, but rather a reflection of the realities of warfare in the late nineteenth and early twentieth centuries: 'before the First World War there was little need for statement of the rule [of distinction] because the civilian population and its objects suffered relatively little from the combatant's use of weapons, unless civilians were actually in the combat zone (Gary Solis, *The Law of Armed Conflict: International Humanitarian Law* (CUP, 2010), at 252).

[13] Art. 48, API.

[14] William Ferrell, 'No Shirt, No Shoes, No Status: Uniforms, Distinction, and Special Operations in International Armed Conflict', 178 Mil L Rev 94 (2003), at 105.

[15] Art. 51(1)–(3), API.

Thus, civilian immunity is interconnected with, and is a pivotal part of, the principle of distinction in armed conflict.

The principle of distinction is applicable in both international and non-international armed conflicts.[16] However, there is no concept of 'combatant' in non-international armed conflicts; there is no combatant status for non-state actors who take direct part in hostilities in non-international armed conflicts, no combatant immunity or POW rights that attach when a civilian takes direct part in a non-international armed conflict.[17] As such, the instruments that govern conduct in non-international armed conflicts cannot, logically, make reference to distinguishing between combatants and civilians. Rather, the principle of distinction in non-international armed conflicts is affirmed as a prohibition on targeting civilians who take no direct part in hostilities. Article 13(2)–(3) of Additional Protocol II provides that:

> The civilian population as such, as well as individual civilians, shall not be the object of attack. Acts or threats of violence the primary purpose of which is to spread terror among the civilian population are prohibited. Civilians shall enjoy the protection afforded by this Part, unless and for such time as they take a direct part in hostilities.[18]

The principle of distinction is considered customary international law.[19] It has been affirmed by the International Court of Justice (ICJ) as one of the 'cardinal'[20] and 'intransgressible'[21] principles of international law. Courts from the International Criminal Tribunal for the former Yugoslavia (ICTY)[22] to the Inter-American Commission on Human Rights[23] to the national courts of Israel,[24] Australia,[25]

[16] Jean-Marie Henckaerts and Louise Doswald-Beck (eds), *International Committee of the Red Cross: Customary International Humanitarian Law* (CUP, 2005; hereinafter *ICRC CIHL Study*), available at: <http://www.icrc.org/customary-ihl/eng/docs/home>; accessed 4 April 2015, Rule 1.

[17] Crawford, *The Treatment of Combatants and Insurgents under the Law of Armed Conflict*, at 68.

[18] Art. 13(2)–(3), APII.

[19] Rule 1, *ICRC CIHL Study*.

[20] *Nuclear Weapons*, at 257, para. 78.

[21] *Nuclear Weapons*, at 257, para. 79.

[22] *Prosecutor v Blaškić*, Case No. IT-95-14, Judgment, 3 March 2000, at § 180; *Prosecutor v Martić*, Case No. IT-95-11, Review of the Indictment under Rule 61, 8 March 1996, at § 10; *Prosecutor v Kordić and Čerkez*, Case No. IT-95-14/2-A, Appeals Judgment, 7 December 2004, at § 54; *Prosecutor v Kupreškić et al.*, Case No. IT-95-16-T, Judgment, 14 January 2000, at § 521; *Prosecutor v Strugar*, Case No. IT-01-42-T, Judgment, 31 January 2005, at §§ 220–221; *Prosecutor v Tadić*, Case No. IT-94-1-AR72, Decision on the Defence Motion for Interlocutory Appeal on Jurisdiction, 2 October 1995, at § 127; *Prosecutor v Galić*, Case No. IT-98-29-T, Judgment, 5 December 2003, at §§ 27, 45.

[23] *Juan Carlos Abella v Argentina*, Case No. 11.137, Report No. 55/97, Inter-Am. C.H.R., OEA/Ser.L/V/II.95 Doc. 7 rev. at 271 (1997), at § 177.

[24] *The Public Committee against Torture in Israel et al. v the Government of Israel et al.*, HCJ 769/02, 13 December 2006 (hereinafter *Targeted Killings*), at §§ 23, 26.

[25] *SZAOG v Minister for Immigration & Multicultural & Indigenous Affairs* [2004] FCAFC 316, 26 November 2004, at para. 17.

Colombia,[26] and Peru[27] have also affirmed the centrality of the principle of distinction to the law of armed conflict, either through affirmations of the principle in general or through statements confirming the prohibition on the targeting of civilians.[28] Violation of the principle of distinction is a war crime in both international[29] and non-international armed conflicts.[30]

Defining 'Civilian' and 'Combatant' in the Law of Armed Conflict

The principle of distinction is premised on the dyad of military and civilian, targetable and non-targetable. Implementing the principle of distinction thus requires parties to the conflict to distinguish between civilians and combatants—for example, the wearing of a uniform or fixed distinctive emblem[31] is one method by which parties to a conflict may distinguish themselves from the civilian population; the carrying of arms openly while engaged in hostilities is another.[32] At a macro level, applying the principle of distinction requires a definition of the concept of 'civilian' and 'combatant'. Thus, in order to understand the principle completely it is therefore necessary to understand how the law defines the terms 'combatant', 'military', and 'civilian'.

[26] Colombia Constitutional Court, Criminal Chamber, Constitutional Case No. C-037/04, at §§ 35–6; Colombia Constitutional Court, First Appeals Chamber, Constitutional Case No. T-165/06, at §§ 7–8; Colombia Constitutional Court, Plenary Chamber, Constitutional Case No. C-291/07, at § 78, where the Court stated that the principle of distinction 'forms part of customary international humanitarian law and has attained ius cogens status'.

[27] Peru Constitutional Court, *Gabriel Orlando Vera Navarrete*, Case No. 2798-04-HC/TC, 9 December 2004, at § 15.

[28] *Military Prosecutor v Omar Mahmud Kassem et al.*, Israel Military Court, Ramallah, 13 April 1969, 42 ILR 470 (1971), at 480.

[29] Art. 8(2)(b)(i)–(ii), Rome Statute of the International Criminal Court, 2187 UNTS 90 (1998) (hereinafter Rome Statute).

[30] Art. 8(2)(e)(i), Rome Statute.

[31] The Conventions specifically, and the law of war more generally, do not prescribe the wearing of a uniform as a requirement for combatant status; the need to wear a fixed, distinctive sign visible at a distance (under Art. 4A(4) of Convention III) does not mean one must wear a 'complete head-to-toe outfit that one normally associates with regular armed forces . . . states are free to choose their armed forces uniform, so long as it is readily distinguishable from the enemy and civilians' (Ferrell, 'No Shirt, No Shoes, No Status', at 106).

[32] Art. 4A(2)(c), GCIII; see also Art. 44(3), API, and Ch. 2 of this book on rules for guerrillas regarding the open carriage of arms.

Combatants

Under the law of armed conflict, combatants are any person who, in an international armed conflict, falls into the following categories:

(1) Members of the armed forces of a Party to the conflict as well as members of militias or volunteer corps forming part of such armed forces.
(2) Members of other militias and members of other volunteer corps, including those of organized resistance movements, belonging to a Party to the conflict and operating in or outside their own territory, even if this territory is occupied, provided that such militias or volunteer corps, including such organized resistance movements, fulfil the following conditions:
    (a) that of being commanded by a person responsible for his subordinates;
    (b) that of having a fixed distinctive sign recognizable at a distance;
    (c) that of carrying arms openly;
    (d) that of conducting their operations in accordance with the laws and customs of war.
(3) Members of regular armed forces who profess allegiance to a government or an authority not recognized by the Detaining Power.

...

(6) Inhabitants of a non-occupied territory, who on the approach of the enemy spontaneously take up arms to resist the invading forces, without having had time to form themselves into regular armed units, provided they carry arms openly and respect the laws and customs of war.[33]

Article 43 of Protocol I adds guerrilla and national liberation fighters to the categories of combatant.[34] Taken together, Article 43 of Protocol I and Article 4A of the Third Geneva Convention outline who is entitled to POW status and, by extension, combatant status. Combatants are entitled to take direct part in hostilities and are not held criminally responsible for any war-like acts committed in wartime, so long as such acts are in compliance with the laws of armed conflict. This is known as the combatant's privilege (or combatant immunity), 'in essence a licence to kill or wound enemy combatants and destroy other enemy military objectives'.[35] There is no combatant status in non-international armed conflicts.[36]

[33] Art. 4A(1)–(3), (6), GCIII.

[34] The inclusion of guerrillas and national liberation fighters as combatants, and the controversy around their inclusion, is discussed in more detail in Ch. 2 of this book.

[35] Inter-American Commission on Human Rights, *Report on Terrorism and Human Rights*, OEA/Ser.L/-V/II.116, Doc. 5, rev. 1, corr., 22 October 2002.

[36] See Ch. 2 of this book on the absence of combatant status in non-international armed conflicts; see also Crawford, *The Treatment of Combatants and Insurgents under the Law of Armed Conflict*, at 68; and Jann Kleffner, 'From "Belligerents" to "Fighters" and Civilians Directly Participating in Hostilities—On the Principle of Distinction in Non-International Armed

Civilians

Given the centrality of the concept of civilian status to the law of armed conflict, it is noteworthy that civilians do not have their own discrete definition; rather, civilians are defined in the negative in relation to combatants in the treaty law of armed conflict. Thus, in Article 50(1)–(2) of Additional Protocol I:

> A civilian is any person who does not belong to one of the categories of persons referred to in Article 4 A (1), (2), (3) and (6) of the Third Convention and in Article 43 of this Protocol. In case of doubt whether a person is a civilian, that person shall be considered to be a civilian.
>
> The civilian population comprises all persons who are civilians.

All persons who do not fall into the categories outlined in Article 4A(1)–(3) and 4A(6) of Geneva Convention III and Article 43 of Protocol I are considered civilians under the law of armed conflict. Additional Protocol I is the first IHL instrument to define civilian; no definition of 'civilian' is contained in either the Hague Regulations or the Geneva Conventions, even though Geneva Convention IV relates to the treatment of civilians in times of armed conflict. If there is any doubt as to the status of a person, the Protocol obliges parties to the conflict to designate such a person as a civilian.[37]

Targeting Combatants, not Targeting Civilians

At the core of the definitions of combatant and civilian, and indeed the principle of distinction itself, is the idea that civilians are immune from being directly targeted, but combatants do not enjoy such immunity. Combatants may be lawfully targeted at all times by virtue of their status as combatants. As Sassòli and Olson note: 'combatants are part of the military potential of the enemy and it is therefore always lawful to attack them for the purpose of weakening that potential.'[38]

However, the right to target combatants can only be inferred from the laws of armed conflict; it is not expressly stated in the Conventions or

Conflicts One Hundred Years after the Second Hague Peace Conference', 54 Netherlands Int'l L Rev 315 (2007), at 321–23.

[37] The Protocol also makes it clear that the presence of combatants intermingled within a civilian population does not deprive the civilian population of its civilian status. This was affirmed in the ICTY case of *Blaškić* (*Prosecutor v Blaškić*, Case No. IT-95-14-A, Appeals Judgment, 29 July 2004, at para. 113).

[38] Sassòli and Olson, 'The Relationship between International Humanitarian and Human Rights Law', at 606.

Protocols. Additional Protocol I only refers to military objectives,[39] defining such objectives as 'those objects which by their nature, location, purpose or use make an effective contribution to military action and whose total or partial destruction, capture or neutralisation, in the circumstances ruling at the time, offers a definite military advantage.'[40] Read in conjunction with the basic rule in Article 48, which allows only for targeting of military objectives, it would seem that only objects, and not persons, may be lawfully targeted. Nevertheless, as the Bothe Commentary to the Additional Protocols notes, 'it would, of course, be manifestly absurd to conclude from this somewhat imprecise drafting, that combatants are not a legitimate object of attack.'[41] This anomaly is attributed to misgivings held by delegates during the Diplomatic Conferences for the Additional Protocols that 'affirmatively suggesting violence even against combatants is not appropriate in a humanitarian instrument.'[42] As such, a reading of the other articles of the Protocols—such as Articles 37, 41, 42, 43(2), 44(3), 51(3), and 52(2)—support an interpretation of military objectives as including combatants.

While combatants are, *prima facie*, targetable at all times due to their status as combatants, there are exceptions to this: namely, when combatants are *hors de combat*. Article 41 of Protocol I provides that:

1. A person who is recognized or who, in the circumstances, should be recognized to be 'hors de combat' shall not be made the object of attack.
2. A person is 'hors de combat' if:
   (a) he is in the power of an adverse Party;
   (b) he clearly expresses an intention to surrender; or
   (c) he has been rendered unconscious or is otherwise incapacitated by wounds or sickness, and therefore is incapable of defending himself;

   provided that in any of these cases he abstains from any hostile act and does not attempt to escape.

In contrast to combatants, civilians are *prima facie* immune from targeting. This idea can been found in the writings of some of the earliest publicists of

[39] In Arts 48 and 52, API. [40] Art. 52(2), API.

[41] Michael Bothe, Karl Joseph Partsch, and Waldemar Solf (eds), *New Rules for Victims of Armed Conflicts: Commentary on the Two 1977 Protocols Additional to the Geneva Conventions of 1949* (Martinus Nijhoff, 1982 (hereinafter *New Rules*)), at 285. *New Rules* was reissued as a second edition reprint in 2013; however, this edition was not a substantially re-edited or revised version of the first edition. As such, any reference to *New Rules* in this book is to the 1982 first edition.

[42] See *Official Records of the Diplomatic Conference on the Reaffirmation and Development of International Humanitarian Law Applicable in Armed Conflicts, Geneva 1974–1977* (hereinafter *Official Records*) *XV*; CDDH/50/Rev. 1, at para. 17; Official Records XIV, CDDH/III/SR.2, at para. 22; and CDDH/III/SR.3, at paras 2, 8.

international law[43] and was an integral part of the discourse relating to the law of armed conflicts throughout the nineteenth century, as seen in the writings of publicists[44] and in documents such as the Lieber Code, adopted by the United States (US) Union Army during the American Civil War.[45]

Questioning civilian immunity

Given this understanding of how the law categorizes civilians and combatants, it is interesting to question and examine the philosophical underpinnings of the principle of distinction between civilians and combatants, and civilian immunity. Is the principle of distinction designed to protect civilians, or is it meant for the benefit of the combatant? Are combatants targetable simply because they are combatants—that is, targetable due to status—or are they targetable because they cause direct harm to the enemy (or are capable of causing harm to the enemy)?

The capability for causing harm would seem to lie at the core of the principle of distinction and the reason for civilian immunity from targeting and the right to target combatants. This approach can be traced back to the writings of theorists such as Rousseau who argued that wars must be considered as conflicts between States and not a conflict between the men who fight for the State:

> Men, from the mere fact that, while they are living in their primitive independence, they have no mutual relations stable enough to constitute either the state of peace or the state of war, cannot be naturally enemies. War is constituted by a relation between things, and not between persons; and, as the state of war cannot arise out of simple personal relations, but only out of real relations, private war, or war of man with man, can exist neither in the state of nature, where there is no constant property, nor in the social state, where everything is under the authority of the laws. …

[43] Grotius argued that 'by the law of war armed men and those who offer resistance are killed … [it] is right that in war those who have taken up arms should pay the penalty, but that the guiltless should not be injured.' Hugo Grotius, *The Law of War and Peace*, Book III, Chapter III, Section IX, in Leon Friedman (ed.), *The Law of War: A Documentary History* (Random House, 1972).

[44] As argued in Wheaton's *Elements of International Law*: '[no] use of force against an enemy is lawful, unless it is necessary to accomplish the purposes of war. The custom of civilised nations, founded upon this principle, has therefore exempted … [all] public or private individuals engaged in the ordinary civil pursuits of life, from the direct effect of military operations, unless actually taken in arms, or guilty of some misconduct in violation of the usages of war, by which they forfeit their immunity.' Henry Wheaton, *Elements of International Law*, Richard Dana (ed.) (Clarendon Press, 1936), at 362, § 345.

[45] Art. 22, Lieber Code.

> War then is a relation, not between man and man, but between State and State, and individuals are enemies only accidentally, not as men, nor even as citizens, but as soldiers; not as members of their country, but as its defenders. Finally, each State can have for enemies only other States, and not men; for between things disparate in nature there can be no real relation.
>
> ...
>
> The object of the war being the destruction of the hostile State, the other side has a right to kill its defenders, while they are bearing arms; but as soon as they lay them down and surrender, they cease to be enemies or instruments of the enemy, and become once more merely men, whose life no one has any right to take.[46]

As such, it is only a person's ability to cause harm, or their actually causing harm, that gives rise to the right to target such a person lawfully.

Rousseau's argument drew on similar philosophies found in religions and cultures through history, all of which held that 'not all persons constitute an enemy to be killed.'[47] The idea that civilians should be spared from the effects of the armed conflict can be found in texts from Islam,[48] Christianity,[49] and Hinduism.[50] However, these edicts often only sanctioned sparing certain kinds of civilians—women and children, for example[51]—while all adult

[46] Jean-Jacques Rousseau, *The Social Contract, Or Principles of Political Right* (1762, translated by GDH Cole, available at: <http://www.constitution.org/jjr/socon_01.htm> accessed 30 March 2015). However, see comments by Geoffrey Best, who called Rousseau's maxim 'pretentious and imprudent', 'defective and disadvantageous', and a 'well-meaning but practically useless maxim [which] merely encouraged self-deception among the French' (in *Humanity in Warfare: The Modern History of the International Law of Armed Conflicts* (Weidenfeld and Nicholson, 1980), at 55–59).

[47] Laurie Blank and Gregory Noone, *International Law and Armed Conflict: Fundamental Principles and Contemporary Challenges in the Law of War* (Wolters Kluwer, 2013), at 277.

[48] See comments by Abu Bakr, first successor to the Prophet: 'when you fight for the glory of God, behave like men, do not run away, nor let the blood of women or children and old people stain your victory.' Quoted in Marco Sassòli, Antoine Bouvier, and Anne Quintin, *How Does Law Protect in War? Cases, Documents and Teaching Materials on Contemporary Practice in International Humanitarian Law* (3rd edn, ICRC, 2011), at 143–44.

[49] See, eg, the writings of St Augustine, who espoused protecting women, children, and the aged from the effects of the conflict, as noted by GIAD Draper, 'The Interaction of Christianity and Chivalry in the Historical Development of Law of War', 7 IRRC 3 (1965).

[50] The *Mahabharata*, an epic poem in Sanskrit, stated that one should not attack a disabled opponent; that wounded men and persons who surrender should not be killed; and that non-combatants not directly engaged in the fighting should not be attacked. Cited in Solis, *The Law of Armed Conflict*, at 4; see also Leslie Green, *The Contemporary Law of Armed Conflict* (3rd edn, Juris, 2008), at 21.

[51] See, eg, comments by the prophet Elisha, who said 'when thou comest nigh unto a city to fight against, thou shalt smite every male thereof with the edge of the sword. But the women and the little ones... thou shalt take unto thyself.' Cited in Green, *The Contemporary Law of Armed Conflict*, at 26.

males were permitted to be killed or enslaved.[52] This again ties back to the idea of distinction existing relative to the capacity for harm, which justifies the targeting of all adult males who are able to engage in hostilities but spares women and children as being persons incapable of taking up arms.

These historical texts did not have the force of law; they were frequently tactical pronouncements or moral declarations. It was only with the development of the laws during the nineteenth century that the principle of distinction was codified as law. However, the principle of distinction, and the idea that civilians should be spared as far as possible from the effects of the hostilities, has not always been an incontrovertible axiom. As Kalshoven asks:

> why should this principle be respected at all? A reading of [Protocol I] clearly shows that the term 'civilian population' refers to the *enemy* civilian population. One may ask why a belligerent party should be required to respect those people who constitute a major component of the enemy state. In particular, one wonders how a state can be expected to observe this principle in situations involving highly polarized ideologies, in which the enemy civilian population is probably just as strongly identified with the 'evils' attributed to the enemy state as are its leaders and armed forces.[53]

Indeed, the idea that civilians should be categorically immune from targeting has been questioned by some who challenge the artificially neat distinction between military and civilian inherent to the principle of distinction. One particular argument posits that if the only valid and lawful objective of an armed conflict is to weaken the military capacity of the enemy, then surely logically, any object or person contributing in a meaningful way to the war effort should be targeted.[54] This is especially true when one considers the expansive and encompassing nature of modern warfare where civilians are integral to the maintenance of the war effort:

> Civilians and civilian infrastructure perform an indispensable role in the success of the armed forces, providing funds, power generation, food, clothing, supplies,

[52] See, eg, Sun Tzu's *The Art of War*, which urged that all soldiers taken captive should be cared for, but only so they could be 'used' by their enemies (quoted in Sassóli, Bouvier, and Quintin, *How Does Law Protect in War*, at 143).

[53] Frits Kalshoven, 'Civilian Immunity and the Principle of Distinction', 31 AULR 855 (1982), at 855.

[54] For arguments that not all non-participating civilians should be immune from targeting, see Seumas Miller, 'Civilian Immunity, Forcing the Choice, and Collective Responsibility', in Igor Primoratz (ed.), *Civilian Immunity in War* (OUP, 2007), who argues that civilians who benefit from an unjust or oppressive regime might be justifiably targetable (at 113); and Jeff McMahon, who suggests that civilians of a State which fights an unjust war might be considered morally responsible for the conflict, and could therefore be targeted (Jeff McMahon, 'The Ethics of Killing in War', 114 Ethics 693 (2004)), while Michael Walzer canvasses the argument that situations of 'supreme emergency' may warrant a broader targeting rationale (Michael Walzer, *Just and Unjust Wars: A Moral Argument with Historical Illustrations* (4th edn, Basic Books, 2006), at 251–62).

armaments, and ammunition to the armed forces. Civilians such as miners, farmers, transportation providers, or software engineers may encourage or support the armed conflict actively through the provision of goods, technology or services. Journalists, novelists, and television news anchors may discourage peace by actively fomenting jingoism or merely by whitewashing the horrors of the conflict. Even apparently innocuous entertainers, who visit war camps to raise military morale, may thereby prolong or intensify the conflict. The harm-causing distinction between civilians and military persons and objects blurs yet more as traditional military functions, such as aircraft maintenance, troop transportation, security and combat training are contracted out to civilian corporations, as the United States has increasingly done.[55]

Indeed, this very point was acknowledged by the US Supreme Court in the 1952 case of *Kawakita*,[56] where Justice Douglas noted that '[i]n these days of total war, manpower becomes critical, and everyone who can be placed in a productive position increases the strength of the enemy to wage war.'[57] If one views the principle of distinction through the lens of protecting those who are not causing harm or damage, it is possible to understand arguments that propose that civilians may be as capable of causing harm as combatants in an armed conflict—oft-times more so. Indeed, as noted by Fellmeth:

> if the litmus test...for justified killing is based on the capacity of combatants to harm the enemy, this raises the more general question of how to define the 'harm' that justifies drawing the line between legitimate targets of attack in one place rather than another. If one defines harm...to mean any causal and material contribution to the prosecution of the armed conflict in general, then a norm uniformly permitting intentional attacks on combatants and prohibiting such attacks on civilians is difficult to justify...to the extent that direct attacks on civilians would damage an opposing belligerent's military effort, such attacks seem more justifiable than attacks on military forces not hors de combat [*sic*] but presently in no position to harm the attacker or impede its military victory.[58]

Such an attitude would seem to advocate a 'total war' approach to armed conflict, that all aspects of the enemy—its people, its infrastructure, its economy—are legitimate targets. Total war is 'not only a war of annihilation but arises when annihilation takes as its "center" not only the enemy army or the enemy State, but the entire population and its economy.'[59] However,

[55] Aaron Fellmeth, 'Questioning Civilian Immunity', 43 Texas Int'l L J 453 (2008), at 469.

[56] *Kawakita v United States*, 343 US 717 (1952).

[57] *Kawakita v United States*, at 734.

[58] Fellmeth, 'Questioning Civilian Immunity', at 468–69.

[59] Gilles Deleuze and Félix Guattari, *A Thousand Plateaus: Capitalism and Schizophrenia* (Brian Massumi, trans., Athlone Press, 1988), at 421.

this approach runs contrary to over 150 years of treaty and customary international law. States have, since the earliest IHL instruments, consistently continued to enshrine the idea that civilians are immune from targeting by virtue of their status as non-participants.[60] As such, it seems untenable to suggest that civilians should be targeted for their tangential or incidental contribution to the war effort.

That said, the law does acknowledge that civilian immunity from attack exists only for as long as civilians refrain from taking an active part in the fighting. Thus Article 51(3) of Protocol I states that 'civilians shall enjoy the protection afforded by this Section, unless and for such time as they take a direct part in hostilities.'[61] This introduces a new element into the targeting framework, so that in addition to persons targetable due to their status, persons may become targetable due to their behaviour, namely, if they take direct part in hostilities. This aspect of the law is explored in more detail in Chapter 3.

Conclusion

The modern law of armed conflict has, from its outset, affirmed the centrality of civilian immunity and the principle of distinction. Civilians are all those persons who are not combatants. As such, they have no combatant's privilege, nor combatant's immunity. However, despite lacking such specialized protections, civilians have taken and continue to take direct part in hostilities. In the face of widespread and systematic civilian participation, the international community has attempted to regulate such conduct, not by outright prohibition of civilian participation in armed conflict,[62] but by instead 'regularizing' certain types of civilian participation, granting combatant status and rights to certain kinds of civilian participant so long as such participants comply with certain conditions. One perhaps unintended consequence of this has been that the question of how exactly civilian participants come to lose their civilian immunity has remained, until recently,

[60] These rules are described in more detail in Ch. 2.

[61] The remainder of Art. 51 deals with targeting obligations; see generally William Boothby, *The Law of Targeting* (OUP, 2012), specifically Ch. 6 on Art. 51.

[62] As Nathaniel Berman states: 'engagement in combat by those not covered by the combatants' privilege, assuming no war crimes have been committed, is not illegal per se under international law. Rather, since such acts are not immunised by international law, the contending parties are free to punish individuals engaged in such activities under their own law' (Nathaniel Berman, 'Privileging Combat? Contemporary Conflict and the Legal Construction of War', 43 Colum J Transnat'l L 1 (2004), at 14).

notably unexamined. In the next chapter, this book explores how legal responses towards irregular civilian participation have favoured this process and how the question of loss of civilian immunity for direct participation in hostilities remained, until the twenty-first century, an under-examined part of the law of armed conflict.

2

International Law and the History of Civilian Participation in Armed Conflict

Introduction

Chapter 1 of this book examined one of the foundational principles of the law of armed conflict: the principle of distinction and the related rule on civilian immunity. These principles were enshrined in the earliest written laws of armed conflict. Only combatants were entitled to take direct part in hostilities; in order to enjoy the benefits of civilian immunity, civilians must refrain from taking direct part in the hostilities. In order to give these principles practical effect, the law thus outlined that only certain persons could be considered combatants while others would remain classified as civilians. Civilians who took up arms and directly participated in hostilities would lose their civilian immunity and be liable to targeting due to their hostile acts. Additionally, such civilian participants would be denied the benefits that come with 'lawful' combatant status: immunity for their warlike acts and prisoner-of-war (POW) rights upon capture.

Despite the consequences that attach to civilian participation, civilians have nonetheless taken and continue to take direct part in hostilities. The response of the international community to such civilian participants has been interesting. Rather than offering a detailed test for what kinds of acts result in the loss of civilian immunity, thus re-emphasizing that civilians should not take direct part in hostilities, international law has instead chosen to 'reward' certain kinds of civilian participation by granting civilians combatant status.[1] Indeed, almost

[1] As noted by Scheipers, the progressive development of IHL in the twentieth century was almost entirely driven by attempts to respond to irregular fighters, but this development looked at how to deem as 'regular' such 'irregulars' rather than address them as discrete entities; as Scheipers argues 'major international actors in successive rounds of the law's codification had no interest in spelling out a detailed definition of unlawful belligerency... the law's exclusionary approach towards irregular fighters made it all too easy to marginalise them simply because they were perceived as an anomaly for which the law did not provide.' (Sybille Scheipers, 'Fighting Irregular Fighters: Is the Law of Armed Conflict Outdated?', 43 Parameters 45 (2013), at 53).

as soon as a set of criteria for who qualified as a combatant was proposed for inclusion in 1874 Brussels Declaration,[2] so too were exceptions to the category proposed. This pattern of inclusion and rejection has been a hallmark of the law of armed conflict over the last 150 years; as conflicts change and evolve, involving new irregular participants, so too has the international community debated whether these new irregulars should be incorporated into the international law that regulates armed conflict. By deeming 'regular' certain irregular participants, the law of armed conflict has compelled civilian participants to behave in much the same ways as combatants, by the wearing of distinctive uniforms or other visible markers, and by carrying arms openly, and abiding by the laws of armed conflict.

The last international treaty to grant combatant status to 'irregular' participants was Additional Protocol I, which recognized national liberation and guerrilla fighters. In the thirty-seven years since the adoption of the Protocols, no new 'irregulars' have been recognized under international humanitarian law (IHL). However, the categories of combatant have come under intense pressures from whole new types of irregulars who are participating in armed conflict on a scale and in a way unimaginable by States when they adopted the Conventions and Protocols. Who these irregulars are and the challenges they present to the conventional regime of IHL will be analysed in detail in the latter half of this book. This chapter examines how the IHL regime has dealt with such irregulars before in order to see how IHL addressed these issues previously and to examine whether any lessons can be gleaned from past efforts. This chapter will therefore explore the history of the law of armed conflict with regards to the regulation of irregular participation in armed conflicts.

Early International Legal Regulation

The Lieber Code, the Brussels Declaration, and the first international laws relating to irregular participation in armed conflict

The earliest writings on the modern laws of war with regards to irregular participation in armed conflict were in large part shaped by the European experiences of land warfare during the nineteenth century. Resistance warfare carried out by civilians against foreign invaders was considered illegal;

[2] Project of an International Declaration Concerning the Laws and Customs of War, 27 August 1874, reprinted in 1 (Supp.) AJIL 96 (1907).

partisan fighters were essentially bandits who were not entitled to any form of protection or recognition under the laws and customs of war at that time.[3] In his 1836 text, *Elements of International Law*, American jurist Henry Wheaton commented on the legal position of resistance warfare, mindful of State practice in Europe following Napoleon's advances on Russia and Spain:

> The usage of nations has [legalised] such acts of hostility only as are committed by those who are authorised by the express or implied command of the State. Such as regularly commissioned naval and military forces of the nation and all others called in its defence, or spontaneously defending themselves in case of urgent necessity, without any express authority for that purpose... hence it is that in land wars, irregular bands of marauders are liable to be treated as lawless bandits, not entitled to the protection of the mitigated usages of war as practiced by civilised nations.[4]

Why were civilians discouraged from participating in hostilities? The consensus seemed to be that civilians comprised an 'unknown entity' in armed conflict. Civilians may fight with fervour for their homeland but they are, by definition, not members of the armed forces and thus lack the training and discipline that members of the armed forces possess. Indeed, as argued by Fyodor Fyodorovich von Martens at the Hague Conference of 1899,[5] civilian participation in armed conflict should not be sanctioned or encouraged:

> It is not hard to stir the people up to oppose the enemy, but it is not easy to direct its aroused forces and to oblige it to subordinate itself to the orders of the government. In the majority of cases people's wars lead to complete anarchy, which is equally undesirable for the state which is attacked and the attacker.[6]

Warfare was meant to be preserved as the sole domain of the State: a 'political instrument at the disposal of a government, which held ultimate and exclusive authority over military force.'[7] Civilians were thus to take no part in the

[3] During the Franco-Prussian War of 1870–71, the German practice was to execute summarily any foreign volunteers serving in the French forces. When 13,000 riflemen in the Garibaldi corps were captured, Bismarck stated '13,000 Francs-tireurs, who are not even Frenchmen, have been made prisoners—why on earth were they not shot?' (Moritz Busch (trans.), *Bismarck in the Franco-German War 1870–1871* (Scribners, 1879) Vol 2, at 7). *Francs-tireurs*—translated as 'free shooters'—were unofficial groups of riflemen who operated ad hoc throughout German-occupied territory during the 1870 war. See generally Walter Laqueur, 'The Origins of Guerrilla Doctrine', 10 Journal of Contemporary History 341 (1975), at 357–58.

[4] Henry Wheaton, *Elements of International Law* (Clarendon Press, 1936), at 473.

[5] Martens was also Russian delegate at the 1874 Brussels Conference which debated, but failed to adopt, an instrument regarding the laws of armed conflict.

[6] Fyodor Fyodorovich von Martens, *Contemporary International Law of Civilised People*, at 523, cited in IP Trainin, 'Questions of Guerrilla Warfare and the Law of War', 40 AJIL 534 (1946), at 537.

[7] Jann Kleffner, 'From "Belligerents" to "Fighters" and Civilians Directly Participating in Hostilities—On the Principle of Distinction in Non-International Armed Conflicts One Hundred Years after the Second Hague Peace Conference', 54 Netherlands Int'l L Rev (2007), at 316–17.

hostilities. Their 'reward' for refraining from participation was protection from direct targeting by the adverse party. In the law of armed conflict this became known as the principle of distinction.[8]

The Lieber Code

When the first[9] codified laws of war were drafted during the United States Civil War, published the form of the US Union Army manual known as the Lieber Code, the instrument reaffirmed the centrality of the State in authorizing the use of force by individual citizens. Under Article 57, only a man 'armed by a sovereign government... [who] takes the soldier's oath of fidelity' is entitled to the protections of the laws of armed conflict. Such persons were to be considered a 'public enemy'[10] and thus to be protected under the laws of war, not subject to punishment for their lawful participation in the hostilities,[11] and entitled to POW protections.[12]

However, the Lieber Code included two other categories of person within the scope of POW protections, expanding the categories of lawful combatant but affirming that such persons could only engage in the hostilities under State authorization. The first of these new authorized participants were 'partisans', defined in the Code as 'soldiers armed and wearing the uniform of their army, but belonging to a corps which acts detached from the main body for the purpose of making inroads into the territory occupied by the enemy.'[13] The second category of persons entitled to use force under the Lieber Code were civilians engaged in a duly authorized *levée en masse* under Article 51:

> if the people of that portion of an invaded country which is not yet occupied by the enemy, or of the whole country, at the approach of a hostile army, rise, under a duly authorised levy *en masse* to resist the invader, they are now treated as public enemies, and, if captured, are prisoners of war.[14]

Excluded from the protections of the Code were spies[15] and soldiers caught wearing civilian clothes or the uniform of the enemy while engaged in espionage or other information gathering.[16] Also excluded were armed squads who engaged in the hostilities without having been duly authorized or

[8] See further Ch. 1 of this book on the principle of distinction.

[9] See Richard R Baxter, 'The First Modern Codification of the Law of War: Francis Lieber and General Orders No. 100', 25 IRRC 171 (1963).

[10] Art. 49, Lieber Code. [11] Art. 56, Lieber Code. [12] Art. 49, Lieber Code.

[13] Art. 81, Lieber Code. This definition of partisan is somewhat different from that of partisans in the Second World War: see below for a discussion.

[14] Art. 51, Lieber Code. [15] Art. 88; see also Art. 83, Lieber Code.

[16] Art. 83, Lieber Code.

incorporated into the regular armed forces,[17] and 'armed prowlers' who engaged in acts of sabotage against the enemy.[18] Law of war protections were also denied to so-called 'war rebels', defined as:

> persons within an occupied territory who rise in arms against the occupying or conquering army, or against the authorities established by the same. If captured, they may suffer death, whether they rise singly, in small or large bands, and whether called upon to do so by their own, but expelled, government or not. They are not prisoners of war; nor are they if discovered and secured before their conspiracy has matured to an actual rising or armed violence.[19]

While the article does not use the term 'civilian', it clearly relates to the civilian population of the occupied territory and expressly excludes them from any protections under the Code, or the laws of war more generally.

The Brussels Declaration

This position on irregular participants was reaffirmed when moves towards adopting an international document regulating armed conflict were debated in 1874 at the Brussels Conference. On the initiative of Tsar Alexander II of Russia, delegates from fifteen European States met in Brussels to discuss the draft of an international agreement concerning the laws and customs of war.[20] One of the debated articles dealt with participation in *levées en masse*. Article 10 of the Declaration kept the Lieber requirement of non-occupied territory for the raising of a *levée*, but excluded the need for the *levée* to be 'duly authorised'.[21] However, Article 10 added additional criteria that had to be met for a *levée* to be lawful, specifically that the *levée* be conducted in accordance with the laws of armed conflict. Thus, under the Brussels definition:

> the population of a territory which has not been occupied, who, on the approach of the enemy, spontaneously take up arms to resist the invading troops without having has the time to organise themselves in accordance with Article 9, shall be regarded as belligerents if they respect the laws and customs of war.[22]

[17] Art. 82, Lieber Code. [18] Art. 84, Lieber Code. [19] Art. 85, Lieber Code.

[20] The draft was submitted to the States by the Russian Government; see Dietrich Schindler and Jïri Toman (eds), *The Laws of Armed Conflicts: A Collection of Conventions, Resolutions and Other Documents* (4th edn, Martinus Nijhoff, 2004), at 21.

[21] Art. 57, Lieber Code.

[22] Project of an International Declaration Concerning the Laws and Customs of War; Brussels Declaration, Schindler and Toman (eds), *The Laws of Armed Conflict*, at 28; see also *The Oxford Manual of the Laws of War on Land*, published by the Institute of International Law, 9 September 1880, at 35 which included *levée en masse* in Art. 2(4).

The Brussels rules reinforced in the requirement that the *levée* may only be raised 'on the approach' of the enemy; that is, in territory not yet occupied. Thus, international recognition and protection was still denied to civilians taking direct part in hostilities in the context of resistance warfare. However, in the end, not all governments at the Conference were willing to accept the declaration as a binding convention, and the Conference closed without adopting the instrument.[23]

The Oxford Manual on the Laws of War on Land

In response to the failure to adopt the Brussels Declaration, the Institute of International Law undertook its own evaluation of the Declaration that year, the stated aim being that 'although governments have not ratified the draft issue by the Conference at Brussels, because since 1874 ideas, aided by reflection and experience, have had time to mature, and because it seems less difficult that it did then to trace rules which would be acceptable to all peoples.'[24] The study eventually led to the production, in 1880, of the *Oxford Manual of the Laws of War on Land*.

The *Oxford Manual* defined lawful participants in armed conflicts as those who comprised the 'armed forces of belligerent States'[25] and set out the criteria for such armed forces in Article 2, as comprising:

1. the army properly so-called, including the militia;
2. the national guards, *landsturm*, free corps and any other body which fulfil the three following conditions:
   (a) That they are under the direction of a responsible chief;
   (b) That they must have a uniform, or fixed distinctive emblem recognizable at a distance, and worn by individuals composing such corps;
   (c) That they carry arms openly
3. The crews of men-of-war and other military boats;
4. The inhabitants of non-occupied territory, who, on the approach of the enemy, take up arms spontaneously and openly to resist the invading troops, even if they have not had time to organize themselves [*levée en masse*].

[23] Countries such as Spain, Belgium, Holland, and Switzerland were the main advocates for extending belligerent rights to irregular fighters. As countries without large standing armies and historically the subject of frequent incursions from neighbouring European nations, they were reluctant to limit the scope of permissible civilian participation in armed conflict. See generally JM Spaight, *War Rights on Land* (Macmillan, 1911), at 51–53.

[24] Preface, *The Oxford Manual of Laws of War on Land* (hereinafter *Oxford Manual*); Schindler and Toman (eds), *The Laws of Armed Conflict*, at 36.

[25] Art. 1, *Oxford Manual*.

An additional requirement was that every belligerent armed force was bound to conform to the laws of war.[26] Spies were excluded from treatment as prisoners of war if they engaged in espionage in enemy territory while in 'disguise'.[27]

As with the Brussels Declaration before it, the *Oxford Manual* had no binding force. However, regardless of the failure to adopt the Brussels Declaration or the *Oxford Manual* as a formally binding instrument, both instruments were highly influential and provided important starting points for a process that would eventually lead to the adoption of the 1899 and 1907 Hague Regulations.[28] Both the Brussels and Oxford instruments also began the process of entrenching the notion that civilians and other irregulars who took direct part in hostilities must look and behave like regular armed forces in order to receive the benefits of the law of armed conflict. This was only further entrenched in the next major international instrument that regulated conduct in armed conflict, the Hague Regulations.

The Hague Regulations of 1899 and 1907

Although primarily dealing with rules regarding the means and methods of armed conflict, the Hague Regulations of 1899 and 1907 included provisions regarding irregular participation in hostilities. These were first outlined during the 1899 Hague Peace Conference[29] where, drawing on the Brussels and Oxford formulations, lawful combatant status was provided for the regular army as well as militia and volunteer corps. These provisions were uncontroversial, and reflected accepted State practice.[30]

However, something of a diplomatic stalemate emerged at the Conference when the time came to discuss *levée en masse* and other forms of resistance warfare.[31] The British delegate, General Sir John Ardagh, proposed adding a new provision into the Regulations, that 'nothing in this chapter is to be considered as tending to modify or suppress the right

[26] Art. 3, *Oxford Manual*. [27] Art. 23, *Oxford Manual*.

[28] Indeed, the Brussels Declaration was used as the reference paper from which discussions originated during the 1899 Diplomatic Conference; see James Scott (ed.), *The Reports to the Hague Conferences of 1899 and 1907* (Clarendon Press, 1917) (hereinafter *Reports to the Hague Conferences*), at 137.

[29] Hague Convention II with Respect to the Laws and Customs of War on Law 1899, 187 CTS 429.

[30] Arthur Eyffinger, *The 1899 Hague Peace Conference: 'The Parliament of Man, The Federation of the World'* (Kluwer, 1999), at 304.

[31] See *Reports to the Hague Conferences*, at 139–42.

which a population of an invaded country possesses of fulfilling its duty of offering the most energetic national resistance to the invaders by every means in its power.'[32]

This sentiment was echoed by a number of other delegates who encouraged the Conference to include provisions in the final instruments to recognize the right of a State's population to resist an invading army. The Swiss delegate, Arnold Künzli, spoke in favour of the right of resistance, urging the Conference, 'do not punish love of country; do not adopt rigorous measures against peoples who rise in a mass to defend their soil . . . we are of opinion that love of country is a virtue which should be cultivated and not suppressed.'[33] Other delegates from smaller European countries concurred.[34]

However, the larger European States rejected such an approach. Their position was that persons who engaged in resistance warfare in occupied territory were *francs-tireurs* and should be subject to summary execution.[35] As argued by the German delegate, Colonel Gross von Schwarzhoff, such ardent patriots should be encouraged to join established armed forces and militia and actively discouraged from unilaterally taking direct part in the hostilities without following the rules that bound all other participants:

> nothing prevents patriots from entering the ranks of the army . . . is it then so difficult to find a man who will lead the movement? Crowds can accomplish nothing unless commanded. Is it so difficult, moreover, to hoist some distinctive sign? A mere arm badge will suffice. Is it too much to demand that they bear arms openly and that they observe the laws of war, a thing which they expect and of which they are assured on the part of their adversaries? . . . And since we are speaking of humanity, it is time to remember that soldiers are also men, and have a right to be treated with humanity. Soldiers who, exhausted by fatigue after a long march or battle, come to rest in a village have a right to be sure that the peaceful inhabitants shall not change suddenly into furious enemies.[36]

[32] *Reports to the Hague Conferences*, at 54.

[33] *Reports to the Hague Conferences*, at 550–51; see also A Eyffinger, *The 1899 Hague Peace Conference* , at 304.

[34] *Reports to the Hague Conferences*, at 141. See comments by the Belgian plenipotentiary, Auguste Beernaert, who remarked: 'is it not the first duty of a citizen to defend his country, and is it not to the fulfilment of this duty that we owe the most beautiful pages of our national history?' (*Reports to the Hague Conferences*, at 502–03; see also Eyffinger, *The 1899 Hague Peace Conference*, at 296).

[35] *Reports to the Hague Conferences*, at 142.

[36] *Reports to the Hague Conferences*, at 287; see also Eyffinger, *The 1899 Hague Peace Conference*, at 304–05.

The Martens Clause

The impasse at the Hague Conference over irregulars was overcome when the Conference agreed essentially to 'split' the issue.[37] Persons participating in a *levée en masse* could be considered legitimate only if the *levée* took place within strict parameters:

> Art. 2. The population of a territory which has not been occupied who, on the enemy's approach, spontaneously take up arms to resist the invading troops without having time to organize themselves in accordance with Article 1, shall be regarded as belligerent, if they respect the laws and customs of war.

Persons participating in ongoing partisan or resistance war in occupied territory were *not* to be granted combatant status but were instead to be treated according to 'certain minimum fundamental standards of behaviour', as understood by considerations of 'humanity' and 'public conscience'. Thus, the preamble to the Hague Regulations stated:

> Until a more complete code of the laws of war is issued, the High Contracting Parties think it right to declare that in cases not included in the Regulations adopted by them, populations and belligerents remain under the protection and empire of the principles of international law, as they result from the usages established between civilised nations, from the laws of humanity, and the requirements of the public conscience.

This clause came to be known as the Martens Clause for its progenitor, Russian delegate Fyodor Fyodorovich von Martens,[38] who devised the compromise in order to ensure that the Regulations did not go the way of the Brussels Declaration and fail to be adopted as a binding international instrument. Although the Martens Clause was essentially intended to break a diplomatic stalemate, the succinct eloquence with which the Martens Clause expressed some of the fundamental principles of modern humanitarian law meant that the Clause influenced humanitarian law beyond the Hague Regulations.[39] Thus, when the Hague Conference reconvened in 1907, the

[37] *Reports to the Hague Conferences*, at 287.

[38] For a more detailed analysis of the Martens Clause, see Antonio Cassese, 'The Martens Clause: Half a Loaf or Simply Pie in the Sky?', 11 EJIL 187 (2000); Rupert Ticehurst, 'The Martens Clause and the Laws of Armed Conflict', 317 IRRC 125 (1997); and Theodor Meron, 'The Martens Clause, Principles of Humanity, and the Dictates of Public Conscience', 94 AJIL 78 (2000).

[39] The Martens Clause is included in Arts 63(4), 62(4), 142(4), and 158(4) of the four Geneva Conventions of 1949, Art. 1(2) of Additional Protocol I, and in the preamble to Additional Protocol II. It is also found in para. 5 of the Convention on Prohibitions or Restrictions on the Use of Certain Conventional Weapons Which May be Deemed to be Excessively Injurious or to Have Indiscriminate Effects (1342 UNTS 137; known as the Conventional Weapons Convention). Furthermore, the Clause has also been utilized in pleadings before, and in the decisions of, the ICJ and the ICTY; see *Nuclear Weapons*, at 226; and the written statement of the United Kingdom,

Clause was reiterated in the Preamble to the 1907 Hague Convention IV. As in 1899, the intent was to ensure that the exigencies of military engagement did not leave room for States to arbitrarily determine courses of action without some consideration given to the existing rules of international law.[40]

Also reaffirmed in 1907 was the provision on *levée en masse*. However, in this iteration, Article 2 of Convention (IV) respecting the Laws and Customs of War on Land, and its Annex: Regulations concerning the Laws and Customs of War on Land, added the additional requirement that:

> [t]he inhabitants of a territory which has not been occupied, who, on the approach of the enemy, spontaneously take up arms to resist the invading troops without having had time to organize themselves in accordance with Article 1, shall be regarded as belligerents *if they carry arms openly* and if they respect the laws and customs of war.[41]

This new requirement (of the open carrying of arms) was a further and final narrowing of the criteria for a *levée en masse*.[42] However, as in 1899, resistance and partisan war was not included in the categories of lawful combatant.

The Geneva Conventions of 1949

Following the Second World War, the laws of armed conflict were revisited and reassessed.[43] Again, considerable debate centred on questions regarding who may legitimately participate in armed conflict; namely, when were civilians allowed to legitimately participate in armed conflict? There was little controversy over including *levée en masse* in the categories of legitimate combatant. Reaffirming the Hague Regulations and utilizing the formula laid down in the 1907 Regulations, the Geneva Conventions included *levée en masse* in Article 13(6) of Convention I, Article 13(6) of Convention II, and Article 4(A)(6) of Convention III.[44]

Nuclear Weapons, ICJ Pleadings 1996 (2 June 1994), reprinted in 66 BYBIL 712 (1995); also Compilation of Written Statements, UN AW/95/31, at 47–48, para. 3.58. See also the ICTY cases *Kupreškić*, Judgment, at para. 527; *Martić*, Review of the Indictment, at para. 13; and *Prosecutor v Furundžija*, Case No. IT-95-17/1-T, Judgment, 10 December 1998, at para. 137.

[40] See Frits Kalshoven and Liesbeth Zegveld, *Constraints on the Waging of War: An Introduction to International Humanitarian Law* (4th edn, ICRC, 2011), at 22; see also Cassese, 'The Martens Clause', at 195.

[41] Emphasis added; Art. 2, Hague Convention IV; see also JB Scott (ed.), *The Proceedings of the Hague Peace Conference: The Conference of 1907* (Clarendon Press, 1920), Vol I at 623.

[42] See *Reports to the Hague Conferences*, at 522, 528–29.

[43] *Levée en masse* was affirmed in the 1929 Geneva Convention on Prisoners of War (Geneva Convention Relative to the Treatment of Prisoners of War, 118 LNTS 343 (1929)) by way of reference to the Hague Regulations. The 1929 Convention was replaced by the 1949 Conventions.

[44] See also Jean Pictet (ed.), *Commentary to the Third Geneva Convention Relative to the Treatment of Prisoners of War* (Geneva, 1960), at 67–68 (hereinafter *GCIII Commentary*).

However, the experience and treatment of partisan and resistance fighters in occupied Europe was such as to again put the issue on the agenda for the 1949 Diplomatic Conference.[45] In the latter stages of the war, the International Committee of the Red Cross (ICRC) had addressed a memorandum to all belligerents, urging them to grant POW status to captured partisans provided these partisans complied with the basic rules of organized command, the wearing of a fixed, distinctive emblem, and the open carriage of arms.[46] However, the Axis powers routinely denied legal protection to captured partisans and other resistance fighters; such captives were either summarily executed or sent to concentration camps.[47] State practice of Allied States demonstrates similar attitudes: when Winston Churchill announced the unconditional surrender on 8 May 1945, he stated that:

> [h]ostilities will end officially at one minute after midnight tonight... [t]he Germans are still in places resisting the Russian troops, but should they continue to do so after midnight they will of course deprive themselves of the protection of the laws of war and will be attacked from all quarters by the allied troops.[48]

During the war-crimes trials conducted following the Second World War it was explicitly confirmed that partisan fighters had no protected status under international law.[49] However, only a few years later, at the 1949 Geneva Diplomatic Conference, States that had been subject to occupation by the Nazis argued that partisans and resistance fighters deserved to be included in the category of combatant under the new Geneva Conventions, and that they should enjoy including full POW recognition and protection upon capture.[50]

Debate at the conference was 'most lively'[51] and protracted but eventually all parties agreed that partisans and resistance fighters should enjoy international protections and rights, provided they fulfilled the criteria outlined in

[45] See further *GCIII Commentary*, at 49–50, and 52–64 regarding the debates which took place during the preparatory work and the Diplomatic Conference itself, regarding recognition of partisan and resistance fighters, and generally W Thomas Mallison and Sally Mallison, 'The Juridical Status of Irregular Combatants under the International Humanitarian Law of Armed Conflict', 9 Case W Res J Int'l L 39 (1977), at 52–54.

[46] See further the Memorandum of 17 August 1944, reprinted in *GCIII Commentary*, at 53.

[47] See François Bugnion, *The ICRC and the Protection of War Victims* (ICRC, 2003), at 192–94.

[48] 'Nazis Prostrate: Japs Next: Churchill's Broadcast', *The Argus*, 9 May 1945, p. 1.

[49] See *The United States of America v Wilhelm List et al.*, also known as the Hostages Trial. In that judgment, it was held that partisan fighters operating in south-eastern Europe could not be considered legitimate combatants under the Hague Regulations of 1907, as 'captured members of these unlawful groups were not entitled to be treated as prisoners of war. No crime can be properly charged against the defendants for the killing of such captured members of the resistance forces, they being franc-tireurs.' (United Nations War Crimes Commission, *Law Reports of Trials of War Criminals*, Vol VIII, 1949, at 57).

[50] See *GCIII Commentary*, at 52–55.

[51] *GCIII Commentary*, at 53.

Article 1 of the 1907 Hague Regulations. Thus, the Geneva Conventions recognize partisan and organized resistance movements, under Article 4(A)(2) of Convention III, providing for treatment as POWs for organized groups even if they operate in occupied territory. Resistance fighters are obliged to comply with the Hague Regulation requirements in that they must be under responsible command,[52] wear a fixed, distinctive sign recognizable at a distance,[53] carry their arms openly,[54] and conduct their operations in accordance with the laws and customs of war.[55]

Common Article 3 and non-international armed conflicts

The Diplomatic Conference also dealt with the issue of civilians taking direct part in hostilities of a non-international character. During the Diplomatic Conference, it was clear that States were unwilling to apply the Conventions in their entirety to non-international armed conflict;[56] however, it was acknowledged that some new regulations were required. To that end, Article 3 common to all four Conventions was adopted. Often called a 'mini-convention' or a 'convention within the conventions',[57] Common Article 3 provides some guarantees ensuring respect for the fundamental principles of IHL, stating that:

> [i]n the case of armed conflict not of an international character occurring in the territory of one of the High Contracting Parties, each Party to the conflict shall be bound to apply, as a minimum, the following provisions:
>
> (1) Persons taking no active part in the hostilities, including members of armed forces who have laid down their arms and those placed *hors de combat* by sickness, wounds, detention, or any other cause, shall in all circumstances be treated humanely, without any adverse distinction founded on race, colour, religion or faith, sex, birth or wealth, or any other similar criteria. To this end, the following acts are and shall remain prohibited at any time and in any place whatsoever with respect to the above-mentioned persons:
>   (a) violence to life and person, in particular murder of all kinds, mutilation, cruel treatment and torture;
>   (b) taking of hostages;

[52] Art. 4(A)(2)(a), GCIII. [53] Art. 4(A)(2)(b), GCIII.
[54] Art. 4(A)(2)(c), GCIII. [55] Art. 4(A)(2)(d), GCIII.
[56] On the drafting history of Common Art. 3, see *Final Record of the Diplomatic Conference of Geneva of 1949*, Vol IIB, at 9–15 (hereinafter *Final Record*); and Jean Pictet (ed.), *Commentary to Geneva Convention I for the Amelioration of the Condition of the Wounded and Sick in Armed Forces in the Field* (ICRC, 1952; hereinafter *GCI Commentary*), at 38–48.
[57] Kalshoven and Zegveld, *Constraints on the Waging of War*, at 69.

(c) outrages upon personal dignity, in particular humiliating and degrading treatment;

(d) the passing of sentences and the carrying out of executions without previous judgment pronounced by a regularly constituted court, affording all the judicial guarantees which are recognized as indispensable by civilized peoples.

(2) The wounded and sick shall be collected and cared for.

An impartial humanitarian body, such as the International Committee of the Red Cross, may offer its services to the Parties to the conflict.

The Parties to the conflict should further endeavour to bring into force, by means of special agreements, all or part of the other provisions of the present Convention.

The application of the preceding provisions shall not affect the legal status of the Parties to the conflict.

No further steps were taken to address the question of civilian participants, either in international or non-international armed conflicts, in the Geneva Conventions. However, almost as quickly as the Conventions were adopted, changes in the practice of armed conflict and a surge in frequency of non-international armed conflicts would place considerable pressures on the law, pressures that would ultimately result in the adoption of the Additional Protocols of 1977.

The Additional Protocols of 1977

Following the adoption of the Geneva Conventions, a number of significant changes were experienced, both in the international community and in the conduct of armed conflict, which will be noted briefly here. First, in the years following the Second World War, non-international armed conflicts became by far the more frequent type of armed conflict, eclipsing international armed conflicts significantly.[58] Secondly, these non-international armed conflicts were often taking place in the context of decolonization; that is to say,

[58] Between 1945 and 1970, there were forty-two internal or non-international armed conflicts; yet during that same time, only eleven armed conflicts were categorized as international. See further studies undertaken by James Fearon and David Laitin, in the Political Science Department at Stanford University and from statistics collated by the Correlates of War project (COW), at Pennsylvania State University. The Fearon/Laitin figures put the number of internal armed conflicts at forty-two; version 3.0 of the Correlates of War Intra-State War Data, 1816–1997, put the number at forty (COW v 3.0 did not include the UK–IRA conflict, or the post-WWII conflicts which took place in the USSR involving Latvia, Estonia, Lithuania, and Ukraine; however, COW included some conflicts, such as the Buganda Tribe conflict with Uganda, which the Fearon/Laitin study does not). See further J Fearon and D Laitin, 'Ethnicity, Insurgency and Civil War', 97 American Political Science Review 75 (2003); for their datasets and statistics, see <http://web.stanford.edu/group/ethnic/>, accessed 29 March 2015. For COW, see Meredith Sarkees, 'The Correlates of War Data on War: An Update to 1997', 18 Conflict Management and Peace

many of these non-international armed conflicts were being fought by armed groups in Africa and South-East Asia against European colonial rulers.[59] The proliferation of these conflicts, known as wars of national liberation, prompted increased attention from the international community, primarily at the United Nations (UN).[60] The result of this attention was to elevate 'wars of national liberation'—conflicts fought in pursuit of the international legal right of self-determination—to the stratum of an international armed conflict.[61]

As such, it was argued that the Geneva Conventions should be reaffirmed and expanded on in order to incorporate this new type of international armed conflict.[62] To that end, when Additional Protocol I was adopted in 1977 it extended the categories of legitimate combatant to include irregular and guerrilla fighters. Additional Protocol I provides for its application in situations that are deemed to be:

[a]rmed conflicts in which peoples are fighting against colonial domination and alien occupation and against racist regimes in the exercise of their right of

Science 123 (2000), available at: <http://www.correlatesofwar.org/>, accessed 29 March 2015. Version 4.0 of the COW study has since revised the typology of armed conflicts; according to version 4.0, there were sixty-four armed conflicts classifiable as non-international, and fifteen international armed conflicts. See further Meredith Reid Sarkees and Frank Wayman, *Resort to War: 1816–2007* (CQ Press, 2010).

[59] On national liberation wars generally see further Heather Wilson, *International Law and the Use of Force by National Liberation Movements* (Clarendon Press, 1988); and Antonio Cassese, 'Wars of National Liberation and Humanitarian Law', in Christophe Swinarski (ed.), *Studies and Essays on International Humanitarian Law and Red Cross Principles in Honour of Jean Pictet* (ICRC, 1984).

[60] The UN had adopted a number of declarations and resolutions regarding self-determination and national liberation movements. A complete list of the resolutions and other relevant documents is available at: <http://www.un.org/en/decolonization/ga_resolutions.shtml>, accessed 29 March 2015. See also Stephen Schwebel, 'Wars of Liberation—as Fought in UN Organs', in John Norton Moore (ed.), *Law and Civil War in the Modern World* (Johns Hopkins Press, 1974).

[61] As noted in UN General Assembly Resolution 3103 (XXVIII) on the Basic Principles of the Legal Status of the Combatants Struggling Against Colonial and Alien Domination and Racist Regimes, in 1973, armed conflicts 'involving the struggle of peoples against colonial and alien domination and racist regimes are to be regarded as international armed conflicts in the sense of the 1949 Geneva Conventions'. Furthermore, the resolution states that 'the legal status envisaged to apply to the combatants in the 1949 Geneva Conventions and other international instruments is to apply to the persons engaged in armed struggle against colonial and alien domination and racist regimes.' (UN Doc. A/9030, 12 December 1973). See also Anthony Cullen, *The Concept of Non-International Armed Conflict in International Humanitarian Law* (CUP, 2010), at 63, and Wilson, *International Law and the Use of Force by National Liberation Movements*, at 91–135.

[62] See, eg, comments by delegates to the Diplomatic Conferences, such as Mauritania's President Ould Dad, who stated that 'if...the Conference did not grant freedom fighters the same protection as the oppressors, it would be making a serious mistake, for it would be contravening the principles set out in the Charter of the United Nations, the United Nations Declaration of Human Rights, the Declaration on the Granting of Independence to Colonial Countries and Peoples...and in the Geneva Conventions of 1949 which the Conference was designed to supplement' (*Official Records V*, CDDH/SR.1, at 13–14). See also Cullen, *The Concept of Non-International Armed Conflict*, at 69–73.

self-determination, as enshrined in the Charter of the United Nations and the Declaration on Principles of International Law concerning Friendly Relations and Co-operation among States in accordance with the Charter of the United Nations.[63]

Under Article 43 of Protocol I, a person may be considered a member of the armed forces of a party to a conflict provided they belong to an organized force, group, or unit under responsible command, even if such command is represented by a government or authority which is not recognized by the adverse party to the conflict. Furthermore, all such forces must be subject to an internal disciplinary system providing for the enforcement of and adherence to the rules of IHL.[64]

Protocol I also recognized the methods by which such wars were usually waged; that is, through guerrilla tactics. The employment of guerrilla tactics was a hallmark of wars of national liberation.[65] Guerrilla tactics and strategy in national liberation wars was to wage many 'little wars' against the much larger and better-equipped enemy. Guerrilla fighters often chose to blend in with the civilian population, forgoing the wearing of uniforms or insignia, and concealing their weaponry, only producing arms immediately prior to use in combat.[66]

These strategies were considered necessary in national liberation wars as a way of 'levelling the playing field' between well-equipped colonial State armed forces, and the weaker national liberation movement. Protocol I acknowledged this, recognizing guerrillas as legitimate combatants, rather than 'marauders or bandits',[67] and granting full combatants rights and responsibilities, and concomitant POW rights, to guerrilla fighters in national liberation wars. Protocol I also recognized that 'there are situations in armed conflicts where, owing to the nature of the hostilities an armed combatant cannot so distinguish himself'.[68] As such, the Protocol provides that such a combatant will not lose his combatant status so long as he 'carries his arms openly (a) during each military engagement, and (b) during such time as he

[63] Art. 1(4), API. [64] See *AP Commentary*, at 506–18, paras 1659–83.

[65] Keith Suter, *An International Law of Guerrilla Warfare* (St Martin's Press, 1984), at 1–4, and Geoffrey Best, *Humanity in Warfare: The Modern History of the International Law of Armed Conflicts* (Weidenfeld and Nicholson, 1980), at 326–28.

[66] For a more thorough analysis of guerrilla tactics and ideology, see Walter Laqueur, *Guerrilla: A Historical and Critical Study* (Little, Brown and Co., 1976), specifically Ch. 8, 'Guerrilla Doctrine Today'; Robert Taber, *The War of the Flea: A Study of Guerrilla Warfare Theory and Practice* (Paladin, 1970), specifically Ch. 10, 'Principles of Guerrilla Strategy and Tactics'.

[67] Leslie Green, *The Contemporary Law of Armed Conflict* (3rd edn, Juris, 2008), at 108. See also George Aldrich, 'Guerrilla Combatants and Prisoner of War Status', 31 AULR 871 (1981–82).

[68] Art. 44(3), API.

is visible to the adversary while he is engaged in a military deployment preceding the launching of an attack in which he is to participate.'[69]

Controversy over Protocol I and the exception to the principle of distinction in Article 44

The provision of Article 44(3) and the exception to the principle of distinction that it contained—that 'there are situations in armed conflicts where, owing to the nature of the hostilities an armed combatant cannot so distinguish himself'—was one of the most controversial inclusions in an already controversial instrument. The intent of Additional Protocol I—and the equally controversial Articles 1(4) and 43—was to acknowledge and, more importantly, regulate wars of national liberation and those who fought in them under international law. This was noted in Commentary to Protocol I:

> guerrilla fighters will not simply disappear by putting them outside the law applicable in armed conflict, on the basis that they are incapable of complying with the traditional rules of such law. Neither would this encourage them to at least comply with those rules which they are in a position to comply with, as this would not benefit them in any way.[70]

The Diplomatic Conference was thus faced with a quandary: how could irregular participants be regulated in a way that was both in keeping with existing principles of the law of armed conflict but that also took into account the operational distinctiveness of national liberation wars and guerrilla fighters?

Extending Article 4A of the POW Convention to include guerrillas as part of the 'armed forces' of a party to a conflict was a possibility, but this was problematic in one major respect. Article 4A(2) of the POWs Convention granted combatant status to irregular fighters only if such irregulars carried their arms openly and wore a fixed, distinctive insignia, recognizable at a distance. Such provisions were transparently at odds with the very nature of resistance and guerrilla warfare, the hallmarks of which are stealth and secrecy.[71] The requirement of wearing a fixed, visible insignia seemed an

[69] Art. 44(3), API. However, this article does not extend to regular armies the right to engage in guerrilla tactics. Art. 44(7) specifies that the article is 'not intended to change the generally accepted practice of States with respect to the wearing of the uniform by combatants assigned to the regular, uniformed armed units of a Party to the conflict'. See further *AP Commentary*, at 542, para. 1723.

[70] *AP Commentary*, at 521, para. 1684.

[71] See generally Laqueur, *Guerrilla*, at 100–51; and Suter, *An International Law of Guerrilla Warfare*, at 1–4.

unfeasible provision to include in a treaty concerning guerrilla warfare.[72] The absurdity of such a provision was noted by Christopher Greenwood who argued that if, as the British Military Manual requires, all irregulars 'standing against the skyline should be at once distinguishable from the outline of a peaceful inhabitant, and this by the naked eye of an ordinary individual at a distance from which the form of an individual can be determined',[73] then the 'life expectancy of such an irregular would be short.'[74] Indeed, this sentiment is echoed in the Commentary to the Protocols:

> As a practical matter, it was recognised early...that the prerequisites that members of such movements bear fixed distinctive signs visible at a distance, and that they carry arms openly, virtually precludes the use of the provision. Only rarely have members of organised resistance movements...been able to comply with all of the conditions of Art 4A(2). In order to accomplish their mission, they must work secretly, wear no uniform or distinguishing sign, and withhold their identity prior to their attack. Realisation of the inadequacy of this provision to provide privileged combatant status for those who fight regular military forces in colonial wars and struggles for self-determination gave rise to strong initiatives to relax or abolish the 1949 Geneva Conventions standards for 'freedom fighters'.[75]

The Diplomatic Conference thus needed to find a suitable compromise between the customary principle of distinction, and the practical issues raised by guerrilla fighters. The compromise was Article 44(3), which stated that a guerrilla would retain combatant status so long as he 'carries his arms openly (a) during each military engagement, and; (b) during such time as he is visible to the adversary while he is engaged in a military deployment preceding the launching of an attack in which he is to participate.'[76]

The compromise position that the Diplomatic Conference took on the question of distinction, as outlined in Article 44(3), was much criticized. During and following the Diplomatic Conference, a number of States including the US, Israel, India, and Pakistan stated their concerns regarding the Protocol[77]

[72] For the debate at the Diplomatic Conference regarding the difficulty for guerrilla fighters to meet such standards regarding insignia and other identification, see *Official Records XV*, CDDH/III/SR.55–56, at 156, paras 6–70; see also the comments from the French delegation in Committee III regarding the unrealistic nature of distinction requirements for resistance fighters as outlined in the Art. 4A(2), GC III at *Official Records XIV*, CDDH/III/SR.33–36, at 537, 538. Similar comments were made by Norway (*Official Records XIV*, CDDH/III/SR.33–36, at 400, 537). See further *New Rules*, at 245.

[73] *British Manual of Military Law* (London, 1958), Part III at para. 92.

[74] Christopher Greenwood, 'The Laws of War (International Humanitarian Law)', in Malcolm Evans (ed.), *International Law* (OUP, 2003), at 795.

[75] *New Rules*, at 245.

[76] Art. 44(3), API.

[77] See comments in *Official Records VI*, CDDH/SR.40–41, at 121–55, 178–81, 183–86, 189–92; and *Official Records XV*, CDDH/III/SR.55–56, at 155–87.

and the extension of combatant status to guerrillas and national liberation fighters. Additional Protocol I and Article 44 specifically had, as Geoffrey Corn puts it, undermined one of the fundamental '*quid pro quos* of humanitarian law: in exchange for making yourself more easily distinguishable from the civilian population (and as a result facilitating the ability of the enemy to lawfully attack you), the law granted you the benefit of POW status with its accordant combatant immunity.'[78]

The objection to Article 44 was that such a provision 'would reduce the protection of civilians to vanishing point. Members of the opposing armed forces would come to regard every civilian as likely to be a combatant in disguise and, for their own protection, would see them as proper targets for attack.'[79] Indeed, it was this very concern that stopped US President Ronald Reagan from submitting Additional Protocol I to the Senate for ratification, stating concerns regarding an instrument which would:

> grant combatant status to irregular forces even if they do not satisfy the traditional requirements to distinguish themselves from the civilian population and otherwise comply with the laws of war. This would endanger civilians among whom terrorists and other irregulars attempt to conceal themselves. These problems are so fundamental in character that they cannot be remedied through reservations... we must not, and need not, give recognition and protection to terrorist groups as a price for progress in humanitarian law.[80]

Political and legal commentators denounced the Protocol as 'law in the service of terror',[81] arguing that the Diplomatic Conference had gone out of its way to accommodate radicals and terrorists rather than acting to compel radical groups to curtail their own behaviour to comply with the existing laws of armed conflict.[82] The predominant concern regarding the expansion of combatant status to include guerrillas was that, in attempts to accommodate the unique nature of guerrilla warfare, the Protocol would instead:

> seriously undermine the principle which is so important for the protection of the civilian population, namely the presumption that apparently unarmed persons in

[78] Geoffrey Corn, 'Thinking the Unthinkable: Has the Time Come to Offer Combatant Immunity to Non-State Actors?', 22 Stanford L Pol'y Rev 253 (2011), at 274.

[79] United Kingdom Ministry of Defence, *The Joint Service Manual of the Law of Armed Conflict*, JSP 383, (2004), at 4.5.1.

[80] Message from the President of the United States transmitting the Protocol II Additional to the Geneva Conventions of August 12, 1949, and Relating to the Protection of Victims of Noninternational Armed Conflicts, Concluded at Geneva on 10 June 1977 (29 January 1987).

[81] Douglas Feith, 'Law in the Service of Terror—The Strange Case of the Additional Protocol', 1 National Interest 36 (1985), at 36.

[82] Abraham Sofaer, 'Terrorism and the Law', 64 Foreign Affairs 901 (1985–86), at 912–15.

civilian clothes pose no threat and should not be attacked, leaving the regular forces to concentrate on attacking enemy combatants who should be identifiable as such.[83]

In attenuating the principle of distinction in Article 44(3), by allowing guerrillas to conceal their weapons in certain circumstances and not wear a fixed distinctive sign, Protocol I was, it was argued, putting civilians in danger and placing a difficult and onerous obligation on regular armed forces who would 'come to regard every civilians as likely to be a combatant in disguise and, for their own protection, would see them as proper targets for attack',[84] thus reducing if not effectively nullifying any meaningful protections for civilians in the law.

However, there was one inclusion in Protocol I regarding civilian irregular participants that met with little resistance: that of prohibiting the use of mercenaries in armed conflicts.

Prohibiting civilian participation: Mercenaries

Additional Protocol I included rules regarding another kind of irregular participant, this time not to include but rather prohibit them: mercenaries. The prohibition on the use of mercenaries came about in response to the frequent use of mercenary armies by colonial powers against national liberation movements during the decolonization wars of the 1960s and 1970s.[85] Indeed, the first international organization to attempt to define and prohibit the use of mercenaries was the Organisation of African Unity (OAU). In 1967, Resolution AHG/Res. 49 (IV), adopted by the Fourth Ordinary Session of the Assembly of Heads of State and Government, appealed 'urgently to all States of the world to enact laws declaring the recruitment and training of mercenaries in their territories a punishable crime and deterring their citizens from enlisting as mercenaries.'[86] This was followed in 1971 by the OAU Council of Ministers' Committee of Legal Experts (1971),[87] whose

[83] MHF Clarke, T Glynn, and APV Rogers, 'Combatant and Prisoner of War Status', in Michael Meyer (ed.), *Armed Conflict and the New Law: Aspects of the 1977 Geneva Protocols and the 1981 Weapons Convention* (BIICL, 1989), at 120.

[84] Clarke, Glynn, and Rogers, 'Combatant and Prisoner of War Status', at 122.

[85] See generally, Michael Lee Lanning, *Mercenaries: Soldiers of Fortune, From Ancient Greece to Today's Private Military Companies* (Presidio, 2005), at 152–75.

[86] Held in Kinshasa, Congo, 11–14 September 1967, available at: <http://webmail.africa-union.org/OAU%20Decision/Assembly/AHG%20Res%2049%20(IV)%20_E.pdf>, accessed 4 April 2015.

[87] OAU Doc CM/1/33/Ref. 1 (1972).

draft convention on mercenaries was eventually adopted by the OAU in 1977.[88] Under Article 1 of the Convention, a mercenary:

is classified as anyone who, not a national of the state against which his actions are directed, is employed, enrols or links himself willingly to a person, group or organisation whose aim is:
(a) to overthrow by force or arms or by any other means the government of that Member State of the Organisation of African Unity;
(b) to undermine the independence, territorial integrity or normal working of the institutions of the said State;
(c) to block by any means the activities of any liberation movement recognised by the Organisation of African Unity.[89]

In the context of the Additional Protocols, during the early meetings of the Diplomatic Conferences the Working Group of Committee III examined a proposal by the Nigerian delegation to define mercenaries and prohibit their use in armed conflicts under Additional Protocol I.[90] While that proposal failed, a 1977 debate on the issue resulted in the adoption of Article 47, which defined a mercenary as any person who:
(a) is specially recruited locally or abroad in order to fight in an armed conflict;
(b) does, in fact, take direct part in the hostilities;
(c) is motivated to take part in the hostilities essentially by the desire for private gain and, in fact, is promised, by or on behalf of a Party to the conflict, material compensation substantially in excess of that promised or paid to combatants of similar ranks and functions in the armed forces of that party;
(d) is neither a national of a Party to the conflict nor a resident of territory controlled by a Party to the conflict;
(e) is not a member of the armed forces of a Party to the conflict; and
(f) has not been sent by a State which is not a Party to the conflict on official duty as a member of the armed forces.

The test outlined in Article 47 is cumulative; if a person does not meet one of the requirements, he or she cannot be classified as a mercenary.[91]

[88] The Convention for the Elimination of Mercenarism in Africa, OAU Doc CM/433/Rev. L, Annex I (1972).

[89] It is noteworthy that the Convention does not include any mention of financial gain as a prerequisite for mercenary status.

[90] CDDH/III/GT 82, reproduced in *Official Records XV*, CDDH/236/Rev. 1, at 404, para. 95; see also debates on the question in *Official Records XV*, CDDH/236/Rev. 1, at 404, paras 95–108; CDDH/407/Rev.1, at 454, para. 23; and CDDH/III/SR.57, at 189–90, paras 4–7.

[91] Considerable debate took place regarding the inclusion of motive in Art. 47—that of financial gain. Debate was split between those who felt that motive was a pivotal element for determining mercenary status and others who felt that it would be difficult to ascertain a person's motive when trying to classify their status and thus such elements should be excluded from the definition of mercenary. As noted in the 1976 Diplock Report, 'any definition of mercenaries which required positive proof of motivation would...either be unworkable or so haphazard in its application as

Armed opposition groups under Protocol II

Along with extending the categories of legitimate combatant under Protocol I, the Diplomatic Conferences that debated and adopted the Protocols also looked, albeit briefly, at the possibility of extending combatant status, or at the very least POW treatment, to participants in non-international armed conflicts. The ICRC had proposed in the 1972 Draft Protocol that:

> [m]embers of regular armed forces or of insurgent armed groups fulfilling the conditions stipulated in Article 4A(2) of the Third Convention, who fall into the power of the adversary, should receive a treatment similar to that provided for prisoners of war in the same Convention. It should be noted that such treatment only applies for the duration of captivity without necessarily conferring immunity for the fact of having taken up arms.[92]

Ultimately, the Diplomatic Conference declined to extend the category of legitimate combatant or POW rights to persons taking part in non-international armed conflicts under Protocol II. The prevailing opinion was that the drafts were too intrusive on States' prerogative to deal with domestic strife as the conference delegates felt necessary.[93] Non-State actors participating in a Protocol II armed conflict remain officially 'civilians who take direct part in hostilities', liable for targeting when they take direct part but regaining their civilian immunity once they cease taking direct part.[94]

between comparable individuals as to be unacceptable. Mercenaries, we think, can only be defined by reference to what they do, and not by reference to why they do it.' (Report of the Committee of Privy Counsellors Appointed to Inquire into the Recruitment of Mercenaries, Comnd 6569, para. 7, August 1976. See also debates at the Diplomatic Conferences in *Official Records XV*, CDDH/III/SR.57, at 200, para. 47 and CDDH/III/SR. 47, at 193, para. 21).

[92] Conference of Government Experts on the Reaffirmation and Development of International Humanitarian Law Applicable in Armed Conflicts (Geneva, 3 May–3 June 1972) (Second Session), *Vol I: Basic Texts*, at 40–42; see also Conference of Government Experts on the Reaffirmation and Development of International Humanitarian Law Applicable in Armed Conflicts (Geneva, 3 May–3 June 1972) (Second Session), *Vol II: Commentaries*, Part II, at 48–62; and *AP Commentary*, at 1329, para. 4386.

[93] See *AP Commentary*, at 1334–36, paras 4405–18.

[94] Under Art. 13(3) of Additional Protocol II, civilians are immune from direct attack 'unless and for such time as they take a direct part in hostilities'. Indeed, this concept was included in Protocol I as well, in Part IV, Section I, on 'General Protection Against the Effects of Hostilities'. Specifically, Art. 51(3) stated that: '[c]ivilians shall enjoy the protection afforded by this Section, unless and for such time as they take a direct part in hostilities'. The Diplomatic Conferences did not explain in any great detail what was meant by the phrase 'direct part in hostilities'. See the *Official Records XV*, CDDH/III/224, at 330; see also *AP Commentary*, at 618–19, paras 1942–5; and *New Rules*, at 301–4. The concept of direct participation in hostilities (DPH) is discussed in more detail in Ch. 3.

The Situation since 1977

The Additional Protocols remain the most recent endeavour in officially incorporating irregular participants into the treaty law of armed conflict. Since then, any steps towards regulating irregular participants in armed conflicts have been left to States and non-State groups to undertake for themselves on an ad hoc basis. These have taken the form of codes of conduct and other instruments, adopted by parties to a conflict, or else, as with the *Tallinn Manual on Cyber Warfare*, drafted by panels of experts. The efficacy of these instruments will be discussed in more detail in Chapter 8. The situation in the customary law of armed conflicts has not helped clarify the situation on the irregulars and direct participation in hostilities (DPH) either (as will be examined in the next chapter).

Conclusion

Recognizing when people are and are not permitted to take direct part in hostilities is a fundamental part of the law of armed conflict. As seen in this chapter, throughout the history of the modern laws of armed conflict certain irregulars have been granted such permission while others continue to be denied equivalent permission and immunity. By choosing to deem irregular participants to be in fact 'regulars' in armed conflict, whether meaning to or not, States have failed to examine the question of direct participation: what it is, what is direct versus indirect participation, and when a civilian will regain their civilian immunity from targeting upon ceasing to take direct part. However, determining what amounts to 'direct participation' is quite complex and is worthy of investigation. Therefore, the next chapter will look at the issue of DPH.

3

Direct Participation in Hostilities

Introduction

As noted in Chapter 1, one of the fundamental guarantees attached to civilian status is that of civilian immunity. However, this immunity can be lost if a civilian is deemed to have taken direct part in hostilities. This is uncontroversial. Indeed, as far back as 1924, Spaight wrote that 'if a certain measure of immunity is to be granted to that portion of the population which does not engage actively in hostilities, it is obviously important that the line between that portion and the active, fighting portion should be sharply drawn and loyally maintained.'[1]

International law does not prohibit civilian participation in hostilities but it does not come with any guarantees of immunity. Civilians taking direct part in hostilities do so without any attendant rights that attach to combatants. They have neither combatant immunity nor prisoner-of-war (POW) rights. If captured they will be liable for prosecution under the domestic law of the detaining State if their war-time activities amount to domestic crimes.[2] Civilian direct participation also results in the loss of civilian immunity. Thus, direct participation acts as an exemption to the principle of distinction and civilian immunity.

The idea of direct participation in hostilities (DPH) and loss of civilian immunity seems relatively straightforward: you take an active part in the armed conflict, you lose your civilian immunity and are liable to be attacked in response to your hostile acts. However, once one begins to examine the concept a number of complex questions arise. What kinds of activities amount to direct participation? At what stage in the belligerent act is immunity lost, when the decision to directly participate is made or when the hostile act is committed? Is the loss of immunity permanent or can civilian immunity be

[1] JM Spaight, *Air Power and War Rights* (Longmans Green, 1924), at 59.

[2] See Third Expert Meeting on the Notion of Direct Participation in Hostilities, 23–25 October 2005, Summary Report, at 9 (hereinafter DPH Summary Report 2005).

regained if one ceases to take direct part? How does one indicate their cessation of direct participation?

Determining the scope of direct participation is a complex task and one that has been subject to increasing attention over the past ten years. While the idea of 'direct participation' has long been a part of the law of armed conflict, renewed attempts to define the parameters of DPH has been driven by a number of factors, including the International Committee of the Red Cross's (ICRC) investigation into the question of direct participation as well as the jurisprudence of international and domestic courts and tribunals as to the scope of direct participation.

This chapter examines the emergence and development of the notion of DPH, its eventual codification in Additional Protocol I, and the debates over attempts to delineate the parameters of the concept. It will analyse and contrast the various attempts at defining DPH that have come from a number of different sources, assessing the degree to which these approaches have been accepted and embraced by the international community. This chapter also establishes an important framework for the remainder of the book, namely, how can we accurately assess when civilians such as security contractors, hackers, and criminals cross the line from committing private acts to the commission of public acts of belligerency warranting the implementation of international humanitarian law (IHL).

The Emergence of DPH as an Exception to Civilian Immunity

In the law of armed conflict, the idea of DPH as an exception to civilian immunity is almost as old as the idea of civilian immunity itself.[3] In one of the earliest international legal texts, *The Law of War and Peace*, Grotius stated that 'by the law of war armed men and those who offer resistance are killed... it is right that in war those who have taken up arms should pay the penalty, but... the guiltless should not be injured.'[4] As the thinking about the law and conduct of armed conflict developed, so too did the idea that civilians not actively engaged in hostilities should be spared from attack. Logically, the corollary of this belief was that civilians actively engaged in hostilities were subject to attack. This concept was included in some of the

[3] See further Emily Camins, 'The Past as Prologue: The Development of the "Direct Participation" Exception to Civilian Immunity', 90 IRRC 853 (2008), at 856–60.

[4] Hugo Grotius, *The Law of War and Peace*, in Friedman (ed.), *The Law of War: A Documentary History*, Book III, Chapter III, §§ VIII–X.

earliest documents on the law of armed conflict, such as the Lieber Code which stated in Article 15 that 'military necessity admits of all direct destruction of life or limb of armed enemies', defining enemies as including 'the citizen or native of a hostile country'.[5]

However, the Lieber Code illustrates some of the early problems regarding how to define a civilian taking direct part in hostilities. While it included a provision on civilian immunity,[6] there was no definition of what constituted an 'inoffensive citizen of the hostile country'.[7] Instead, the Code outlines examples of hostile unarmed civilians[8] including any citizen who 'gives information of any kind to the enemy, or hold intercourse with him',[9] and provides that such persons should be 'severely punished',[10] and should face the possibility of the death penalty.[11] In addition, General Order 30 states that any persons who harbour or give aid or food to the enemy will 'suffer death' or other punishment as ruled by a court martial.[12]

In the years that followed, more documents on the law of war were debated and adopted, but the question of how to define the parameters of direct participation remained essentially unanswered. The Brussels Declaration of 1874 defined combatants and belligerents but did not elaborate on either civilian immunity or loss of immunity due to direct participation.[13] The 1880 *Oxford Manual of the Laws of War* included reference to civilian immunity, albeit obliquely, by affirming in Article 1 that 'the state of war does not admit of acts of violence, save between the armed forces of belligerent States. Persons not forming part of a belligerent armed force should abstain from such acts.'[14]

The next major iteration of the laws of war—this time in binding treaty form as the Hague Regulations[15]—also failed to include explicit reference to the idea of non-combatant immunity, or to the idea of DPH.[16] This is in contrast with the contemporary literature which

[5] Art. 21, Lieber Code. See also Camins, 'The Past as Prologue', at 863.
[6] In Art. 22, Lieber Code. [7] Art. 25, Lieber Code.
[8] Camins, 'The Past as Prologue', at 863. [9] Art. 90, Lieber Code.
[10] Art. 91, Lieber Code.
[11] This was distinct from the category of spies in Art. 88, which provided that 'a person who secretly, in disguise or under false pretence, seeks information with the intention of communicating it to the enemy' would be considered a spy and executed by hanging.
[12] Reprinted in Richard Shelley Hartigan, *Lieber's Code and the Law of War* (Precedent, 1983), at 91–96.
[13] See further Ch. 2 of this book on the Brussels Declaration.
[14] Art. 1, *Oxford Manual on the Laws of War* (hereinafter *Oxford Manual*), although see further Art. 7 of the *Oxford Manual*, which states that 'the contest being carried on by "armed forces" only', it is thus 'forbidden to maltreat inoffensive populations.' Again, there is no explanation as to what acts would qualify as transforming the 'inoffensive' civilian to an 'offensive' one.
[15] Hague Convention IV Respecting the Laws and Customs of War on Land 1907.
[16] See Judith Gardam, *Non-Combatant Immunity as a Norm of International Humanitarian Law* (Martinus Nijhoff, 1993), at 19.

continued to affirm the principle. For example, Wheaton, writing in 1866 had stated that in time of war:

> [t]he custom of civilized nations, founded upon this principle, has therefore exempted the persons of the sovereign and his family, the members of the civil government, women and children, cultivators of the earth, artisans, laborers, merchants, men of science and letters, and, generally, all other public or private individuals engaged in the ordinary civil pursuits of life, from the direct effect of military operations, unless actually taken in arms, or guilty of some misconduct in violation of the usages of war, by which they forfeit their immunity.[17]

Thirty years later, Risley affirmed that non-belligerent subjects of a party to the conflict:

> are not liable to be killed or taken as prisoners of war as long as they do not actively engage in hostilities... combatants must be open enemies, known and knowable, and non-combatants must be harmless. As soon as an individual ceases to be harmless, he ceases to be a non-combatant, and must be reckoned a combatant; and unless he bears the distinguishing marks of an open combatant, he puts himself outside the laws of war.[18]

The next major restatement and development of the laws of armed conflict, the 1949 Geneva Conventions, likewise neglected to make explicit reference to the idea of DPH, though Common Article 3 did invoke the concept of DPH in stating its applicability to 'persons *taking no active part* in the hostilities, including members of armed forces who had laid down their arms and those placed hors de combat'.[19] As we saw in Chapter 2, the international community at Geneva in 1949 chose to define certain kinds of civilian participation in armed conflict as legally permissible, the upshot being that little to no attention was paid to attempting to acknowledge either DPH itself or the what the loss of civilian immunity from attack due to DPH might mean.

Indeed, in the years following the adoption of the Geneva Conventions (prior to the adoption of the Additional Protocols), the concept of DPH was apparently only discussed a few times in international fora, mainly by the

[17] Henry Wheaton, *Elements of International Law*, Richard Dana (ed.) (Clarendon Press: Oxford, 1936), at 362, § 345.

[18] John Risley, *The Law of War* (Innes and Co, 1897), at 107–08. See also Gardam, *Non-Combatant*, at 15, who notes that Risley's approach was supported by the military manuals of both the US and UK of the time.

[19] Emphasis added. That 'active' and 'direct' should be considered as one and the same has been affirmed by the ICTR where the Court stated 'these phrases are so similar that, for the Chamber's purposes, they may be treated as synonymous' (*Prosecutor v Akayesu*, Case No. ICTR 96-4-T, Judgment, 2 September 1998, at § 629).

ICRC. The first of these instances was in 1956 with the adoption of the Draft Rules for the Limitation of the Dangers Incurred by the Civilian Population in Time of War. The draft rules noted that civilians should be 'outside the sphere of armed attacks',[20] and defined the civilian population in Article 4 as:

all persons not belonging to one of other of the following categories:
(a) members of the armed forces, or of their auxiliary or complementary organisations;
(b) persons who do not belong to the forces referred to above, but nevertheless take part in the fighting.[21]

The second ICRC reference to DPH came in a resolution adopted by the XX International Red Cross Conference in 1965,[22] which stated that 'distinction must be made at all times between persons taking direct part in hostilities and members of the civilian population to the effect that the latter be spared as much as possible.'[23]

It was only with the adoption of the Additional Protocols in 1977 that the concept of DPH was finally expressly codified. In Protocol I, DPH is outlined in Article 51(3) providing that 'civilians shall enjoy the protection afforded by this Section, unless and for such time as they take a direct part in hostilities.'[24] Article 51(3) has, to date, had no reservations;[25] indeed, during the drafting of the Protocols, the importance of the provision was affirmed by a number of States,[26] including the UK, which declared the exception to the civilian immunity from attack contained in Article 51(3) a 'valuable reaffirmation' of an existing rule of customary international law.[27]

[20] Art. 1, Draft Rules for the Limitation of the Dangers Incurred by the Civilian Population in Time of War.

[21] This was echoed in Resolution XXVIII, from the 1965 International Conference of the Red Cross, which reaffirmed need for all parties to the conflict to distinguish between persons taking part in hostilities, and the civilian population.

[22] Protection of Civilian Populations Against the Dangers of Indiscriminate Warfare, Resolution XXVIII, adopted by the XXth International Conference of the Red Cross, Vienna (1965).

[23] Protection of Civilian Populations Against the Dangers of Indiscriminate Warfare, Resolution XXVIII.

[24] The 'protection afforded by this Section' refers to the prohibition contained in Arts 51(1), (2), and (4)–(8), which provide that civilians are not to be made the subject of attack, and that civilians are to be protected from the dangers arising from military operations, imposing prohibitions on parties to the conflict on conducting indiscriminate attacks, and from using civilians to immunise military installations or sites.

[25] Art. 51(3), API (adopted by seventy-seven votes in favour, one against, and sixteen abstentions).

[26] See *Official Records VI*, CDDH/SR.41, at 164–204, paras 119–81.

[27] *Official Records VI*, CDDH/SR.41, at 164, para. 119. The importance of this provision was affirmed in the Rome Statute of the International Criminal Court, which criminalizes attacks on civilians 'not taking direct part in hostilities' under Arts 8(2)(b)(i) and 8(2)(e)(i).

DPH is also outlined in Article 13(3) of Protocol II, and is worded similarly to Article 51(3) of Protocol I.[28]

Defining DPH in Treaties and State Practice

When debating Article 51 of Protocol I, States did not settle on a precise definition of what was meant by the phrase 'direct part in hostilities.'[29] The Report of Committee III stated that in considering the scope and definition of DPH:

> the term 'hostilities' was not defined, but a number of delegations expressed the view that the term included preparations for combat and return from combat. 'Hostilities' and 'military operations' are among the terms which should engage the close attention of the Drafting Committee in order to ensure consistency of usage and clarity of meaning.[30]

However, as the Bothe Commentary to the Protocols notes, the Drafting Committee 'regrettably'[31] did not end up engaging in a close analysis or detailed explication of what was meant by 'hostilities' or 'military operations'. The ICRC Commentary of 1973 on what was then draft Article 46 stated that, in the Committee's view, DPH 'covers acts of war intended by their nature or purpose to strike at the personnel and materiel of enemy armed forces'.[32] The Draft Commentary goes on to distinguish 'the direct part which civilians might take in hostilities... from the part in the *war effort* which they are called upon to carry out at highly different levels',[33] stating that to equate DPH with participation in the general war effort:

> would be tantamount to the nullification of all the efforts undertaken to reaffirm and develop international humanitarian law, for, in modern warfare, all the nation's

[28] The idea of DPH is expressed in a number of ways throughout Protocol I, including Art. 81(1)–(2) ('refrains from any act of hostility'); Art. 41(2) ('abstains from any hostile act'); Art. 42(2) ('engaging in a hostile act'); and Arts 13(1) and 65(1) ('used to commit... acts harmful to the enemy').

[29] See *Official Records XV*, CDDH/III/224, at 330; see also *AP Commentary*, at 618–19, paras 1942–5; and *New Rules*, at 301–04.

[30] *Official Records XV*, CDDH/215/Rev. 1, at 274, para. 53.

[31] *New Rules*, at 302.

[32] ICRC, *Commentary on the Draft Additional Protocols to the Geneva Conventions of August 12, 1949* (ICRC, 1973, hereinafter *AP Draft Commentary*), at 58.

[33] *AP Draft Commentary*, at 58, emphasis in original.

activities contribute in some way or other, to the pursuit of hostilities, and even the people's morale plays its part in this context.[34]

The ICRC Draft Commentary does not elaborate further on DPH, leaving such questions as to duration of the loss of civilian immunity unanswered. The ICRC Commentary to the Additional Protocols does not provide any more insight, stating that, regarding Article 51(3):

> [t]he immunity afforded individual civilians is subject to an overriding condition, namely, on their abstaining from all hostile acts. Hostile acts should be understood to be acts which by their nature and purpose are intended to cause actual harm to the personnel and equipment of the armed forces.[35]

The Bothe Commentary to the Additional Protocols is a little more helpful, undertaking some analysis of the scope of DPH:

> it is clear that civilians who personally try to kill, injure or capture enemy persons or to damage material are directly participating in hostilities. This is also the case of a person acting as a member of a weapons crew, or one providing target information for weapons systems intended for immediate use against the enemy such as artillery spotters or members of ground observer teams.[36]

Bothe and colleagues also include 'preparation for combat… [for example] direct logistic support for units engaged directly in battle such as the delivery of ammunition to a firing position'[37] within the scope of DPH. However, the Bothe Commentary excludes from DPH 'civilians providing only indirect support to the armed forces, such as workers in defence plants or those engaged in distribution or storage of military supplies in rear areas',[38] as such persons 'do not pose an immediate threat to the adversary.'[39]

The Bothe Commentary also notes that some additional examples of conduct not amounting to DPH can be inferred from a joint reading of Article 50 of Protocol I and Article 4A(4)–(5) of Geneva Convention III. Article 50 defines civilians as any persons who are not combatants under Article 4A(1), (2), (3), and (6) of GCIII; Article 4A(4)–(5) outlines certain civilians entitled to POW rights and treatment:

[34] *AP Draft Commentary*, at 58.

[35] *AP Commentary*, at 618, para. 1942. The commentary on the DPH provision in Art. 13(3) of APII is essentially identical to that of Art. 51(3) in API, based on the notion of 'acts of war that by their nature or purpose struck at the personnel and *matériel* of enemy armed forces', and would most likely include preparation for and return from combat activities. See *AP Commentary*, at 1453, para. 4788; and *New Rules*, at 678.

[36] *New Rules*, at 303.

[37] *New Rules*, at 303.

[38] *New Rules*, at 303.

[39] *New Rules*, at 303.

(4) Persons who accompany the armed forces without actually being members thereof, such as civilian members of military aircraft crews, war correspondents, supply contractors, members of labour units or of services responsible for the welfare of the armed forces, provided that they have received authorization from the armed forces which they accompany, who shall provide them for that purpose with an identity card similar to the annexed model.
(5) Members of crews, including masters, pilots and apprentices, of the merchant marine and the crews of civil aircraft of the Parties to the conflict, who do not benefit by more favourable treatment under any other provisions of international law.[40]

The 'threat' component is, for Bothe and colleagues, seemingly the key element in the understanding of DPH: to what degree is the act in question constitutive of a direct, immediate, or imminent threat to the adverse party? However, a 'threat-based' approach to DPH could possibly exclude what Bothe and his peers suggest might be included in a DPH paradigm: the idea of return from combat. If the hostile act amounted only to the placement of an explosive device, and the civilian taking direct part was not otherwise armed, would the individual still remain a threat when he or she returns home, unarmed? Given such definitional vagaries it is hard to get a precise fix on the scope of the concept of DPH from a textual analysis of the Protocol.

The situation has not been made any easier due to the increasing involvement of civilians in armed conflict during the twentieth century, both in the increased targeting of civilians, and the increased involvement of civilians in military and quasi-military endeavours.[41] As Camins notes, 'the twentieth century saw a blurring of the distinction between combatants and civilians in armed conflict. With no positive law protecting (or, indeed, defining) civilians, their immunity from attack was precarious and vulnerable to arguments that military necessity permitted them to be targeted.'[42]

Indeed, the idea that certain categories of non-participating civilians could and should be considered legitimate targets had been asserted throughout the

[40] However, Bothe *et al.* note that while the persons outlined in Art. 4A(4)–(5) are *prima facie* not entitled to take direct part in hostilities, there may be instances when their conduct does amount to DPH, citing, for example, the practice of having civilian technical advisers assist and advise in the installation and/or maintenance of targeting and weapons systems, acknowledging that such actions, if undertaken during an engagement would 'probably' be regarded as amounting to DPH (*New Rules*, at 304); Bothe *et al.* go on to note that the immunity from attack afforded to Art. 4A(4)–(5) civilians is somewhat 'academic' anyway due to their proximity to lawful military objectives and combatants (*New Rules*, at 303).

[41] This phenomenon is discussed in more detail in later chapters.

[42] Camins, 'The Past as Prologue' at 868.

early twentieth century. For example, during the First World War, one publicist argued that armament workers:

> occupy a position intermediate between the combatants proper and the non-combatants who are still employed on their peacetime trades and professions. The reasons for sparing them are losing force. Fundamentally they are almost in exactly the same position as the men of the auxiliary services of the armies, and the latter are certainly legitimate objects of attack.[43]

Another, writing at the end of the Second World War, observed that State practice relating to the distinction between combatants and the civilian population had 'both in point of fact and in theory... been so whittled down by the demands of military necessity that it has become more apparent than real... the trend in war is to treat combatant and noncombatant [*sic*] alike.'[44] According to such reasoning, attempts to argue for non-combatant immunity in the immediate post-Second World War era would deem this to have been contrary to State practice.[45]

However, this approach was not accepted when the Geneva Conventions were adopted in 1949, with the instruments rejecting the trend illustrated by the total warfare of the Second World War. Notwithstanding this reaffirmation of restraint in warfare, there was still no explicit provision in the Conventions that prohibited targeting civilians, nor was there any clarification on when civilians could be legitimately targeted, that is, if they were taking direct part in hostilities. Thus, also absent from the Conventions was any mention of how and why civilians lost their immunity from targeting.[46]

State practice and the practice of intergovernmental organizations

In the years following the adoption of the Conventions, State practice did little to clarify the position on DPH; there were few references in international

[43] Louis Rolland, 'Les Pratiques de la guerre aérienne dans le conflit de 1914 et le droit des gens', in Revue de Droit International (1916), cited in JM Spaight, 'Legitimate Objectives in Air Warfare', 21 BYBIL 158 (1944), at 162. Spaight concurred with Rolland's assessment, arguing that 'by no logical process can [armaments workers] be classed with the non-combatants... there is no ground for making a distinction between the person who forges a weapon and the person who conveys it from the factory to the front.'

[44] Lester Nurick, 'The Distinction between Combatant and Noncombatant in the Law of War', 39 AJIL 680 (1945), at 680.

[45] See further Ch. 1 of this book regarding arguments for the diminution or outright abandonment of civilian immunity in times of armed conflict.

[46] See Camins, 'The Past as Prologue', at 871–72; Geoffrey Best, *War and Law Since 1945* (Clarendon Press, 1997), at 115–16.

and domestic sources to DPH. In the 1967 Nigerian Operational Code of Conduct, issued in relation to the Biafran Civil War, it states that 'youths and school children must not be attacked unless they are engaged in open hostilities against Federal Government Forces',[47] without going into any detail as to what acts qualified as 'engaged in open hostilities'. Nor does the 1958 *British Manual on the Law of Armed Conflict*, which states that 'participation in hostilities by civilians' is a violation of the law of war; however, it does not clarify what such participation might be.[48]

The US *Field Manual* of 1956 was slightly more helpful, stating that 'persons who are not members of the armed forces...who bear arms or engage in other conduct hostile to the enemy thereby deprive themselves of many of the privileges attaching to the members of the civilian population',[49] going on to state that persons who are not members of the armed forces, who commit hostile acts such as 'sabotage, destruction of communications facilities, intentional misleading of troops by guides [and] liberation of prisoners of war'[50] may be tried and sentenced to execution or imprisonment; such hostile acts could thus be seen as amounting to DPH.

Other State practice did not further a more coherent understanding of DPH: national legislation in Ghana,[51] India,[52] Malaysia,[53] and Pakistan,[54] for example, contained fairly broad definitions of who could be considered an 'enemy', including 'all persons engaged in armed operations against any of His Majesty's armed forces or any force co-operating therewith and also includes armed mutineers, armed rebels, armed rioters and pirates.'[55]

The adoption of the Additional Protocols and Article 51(3), while finally codifying DPH and loss of civilian immunity, did not advance a clearer

[47] Operational Code of Conduct for the Nigerian Army July 1967, Art. 3(c), reprinted in Anthony Kirk-Greene, *Crisis and Conflict in Nigeria, A Documentary Sourcebook*, vol. I (OUP, 1971), at 455.

[48] *British Manual of Military Law* (London, 1958) at 626. It is noteworthy that the *British Manual* stated that civilian DPH is a violation of the law of war, a position at odds with the extant treaty law and with the general thinking on civilian DPH at the time. The 2004 edition does not make this statement.

[49] Field Manual 27–10, *The Law of Land Warfare* (Washington DC, 18 July 1956), modified by Change No. 1, 15 July 1976, at § 60.

[50] Field Manual 27–10, *The Law of Land Warfare*, at § 81.

[51] Art. 98, Armed Forces Act (1962).

[52] §3(x), Army Act (1950).

[53] Armed Forces Act (1972).

[54] Ch. 1, §8(8), Army Act (1952).

[55] From the Malaysian Armed Forces Act (1972), Part 1, Section 2; similar language is used in the Ghanaian, Pakistani, and Indian legislation. For more information on State practice regarding DPH, see further the Rule of Law in Armed Conflicts Project at the Graduate Institute of International and Development Studies Geneva and the University of Geneva, available at: <http://www.geneva-academy.ch/project-rulac/>, accessed 4 April 2015; and Stuart Casley-Maslen (ed.), *The War Report: Armed Conflict in 2013* (OUP, 2014).

picture of the scope of either. Numerous State military manuals included the Article 51(3) on DPH;[56] however, only a few of these gave examples as to what specific acts could be considered direct participation. For instance, the military manual of the Netherlands gave examples of 'firing on hostile troops, throwing Molotov cocktails or blowing up a bridge over which enemy materiel is transported, and transporting equipment to battle positions'[57] as amounting to DPH. However, the manual makes it clear that 'actions such as manufacturing and transporting military materiel in the rear area certainly do no constitute direct participation in hostilities.'[58] In contrast to the Netherlands' relatively strict assessment of DPH, the Ecuadorian military manual takes a broader approach, stating that 'civilians serving as guards, intelligence agents or lookouts on behalf of military forces may be attacked.'[59]

Other manuals provide frustratingly oblique definitions of what might constitute DPH. For example, the Canadian law of armed conflict manual for 2001, states that 'force used during operations must be directed against opposing forces and military objectives'[60] and that civilians 'may not be attacked unless they participate directly in hostilities.'[61] However, the 2001 manual does not define 'opposing force'; the 2005 Code of Conduct for Canadian Forces does not clarify matters, unhelpfully defining 'opposing force' very broadly as 'any individual or group of individuals who pose a threat to you or your mission.'[62]

An additional perspective was offered by the Inter-American Commission on Human Rights in 1999. In a report on human rights in Colombia, the Commission stated that a distinction should be made between direct, or active,

[56] Including Australia, Belgium, Benin, Burundi, Canada, Chad, Colombia, Côte d'Ivoire, Croatia, the Dominican Republic, Ecuador, El Salvador, Ethiopia, France, Germany, India, Indonesia, Italy, Kenya, Madagascar, the Netherlands, New Zealand, Nigeria, the Russian Federation, Sierra Leone, South Africa, Spain, Sweden, Togo, the UK, and the US. See Report on Practice on Rule 6 in the *ICRC CIHL Study*, available at: <http://www.icrc.org/customary-ihl/eng/docs/v2_rul_rule6>, accessed 29 March 2015.

[57] Humanitair Oorlogsrecht: Handleiding, Voorschrift No. 27-412, (Koninklijke Landmacht, 2005), at § 0520.

[58] Humanitair Oorlogsrecht: Handleiding, Voorschrift No. 27-412, at § 0520. See also the 2004 UK *Military Manual* (Swindon, 2004) which also excludes 'making a contribution to the war effort' from DPH (at 24, para. 2.5.2). As such, 'working in a munitions factory of otherwise supplying or supporting the war effort does not justify the targeting of civilians doing so'.

[59] Aspectos Importantes del Derecho Internacional Maritimo que Deben Tener Presente los Comandantes de los Buques, Academia de Guerra Naval (Quito, 1989), at § 11.3.

[60] The Law of Armed Conflict at the Operational and Tactical Levels, B-GJ-005-104/FP-021, Office of Judge Advocate General, Ottawa, 2001, Annex B, B-1.

[61] The Law of Armed Conflict at the Operational and Tactical Levels, at § 3-4.

[62] Code of Conduct for Canadian Forces Personnel, Rule 1, at §§ 3–5, cited in Report on Practice on Rule 6 in the *ICRC CIHL Study*, available at: <http://www.icrc.org/customary-ihl/eng/docs/v2_rul_rule6>, accessed 29 March 2015.

participation in hostilities, and indirect participation. The Commission reiterated the ICRC position, as expressed in its Commentary to the Protocols, that the phrase 'direct participation in hostilities' meant acts which, by their nature or purpose, are intended to cause actual harm to enemy personnel and material. The Commission also stressed that there needed to be a direct causal relationship between the activity engaged in and harm done to the enemy at the time and place where the activity occurs. The Commission upheld the view that:

> [c]ivilians whose activities merely support the adverse party's war or military effort or otherwise only indirectly participate in hostilities cannot on these grounds alone be considered combatants. This is because indirect participation, such as selling goods to one or more of the armed parties, expressing sympathy for the cause of one of the parties or, even more clearly, failing to act to prevent an incursion by one of the armed parties, does not involve acts of violence which pose an immediate threat of actual harm to the adverse party.[63]

Given the definitional ambiguities of the phrase 'direct participation in hostilities', and the conflicting or entirely absent attempts at defining the term, it is unsurprising that in 2006, the ICRC study into the customary status of IHL stated that 'a precise definition of the term "direct participation in hostilities" does not exist.'[64] It was with this fact in mind that the ICRC instigated a study into the concept of 'direct participation in hostilities'. Conducted over a period of five years, the project included questionnaires, reports, background papers, and expert meetings. The final result of this study was the publication in 2008 of the Interpretive Guidance on Direct Participation in Hostilities, which is discussed in more detail below.

At the same time as the ICRC published its study on DPH, a number of other judicial bodies were examining the question of DPH. The first and perhaps most significant of these was the Israeli Supreme Court in the 2006 case *The Public Committee Against Torture in Israel v The Government of Israel*, known as the *Targeted Killings* case.[65] This case are discussed in this next section.[66]

[63] *Third Report on the Human Rights Situation in Colombia*, OEA/Ser.L/V/II.102, Doc. 9 rev. 1, 26 February 1999, Ch. 4, at 53, 56.

[64] *ICRC CIHL Study*, Vol I at 22.

[65] *The Public Committee against Torture in Israel v The Government of Israel* (2006) HCJ 769/02.

[66] This list of cases is not exhaustive. For example, not discussed in detail in this chapter is the Venezuelan case of *Ballestas* in 2001, where the Venezuelan Chamber of Criminal Appeals of the Supreme Tribunal of Justice stated that 'attacks on innocent people...who have given no provocation in word or deed, are not justified even in a military war.... [These are] governed by laws that prohibit attacks on...persons uninvolved in the conflict' (Judgment of 10 December 2001,

Defining DPH in Courts and Tribunals

In addition to attempts to define DPH in both treaty and custom, State and international judicial organs have also endeavoured to add to the corpus of understanding about the scope of DPH. The first significant attempt to define DPH, and one of the most influential, was the Israeli Supreme Court in the so-called *Targeted Killings* case in 2006.

The Israel Supreme Court

The Public Committee Against Torture in Israel v The Government of Israel, also known as the *Targeted Killings* case, was brought by two Israeli human rights organizations, the Public Committee Against Torture in Israel (PCATI) and the Palestinian Society for the Protection of Human Rights and the Environment (PSPHRE), via petition in 2002. The petitioners were challenging the legality of the Israeli government practice of 'targeted killing', described as the 'policy of preventative strikes which cause the death of terrorists in Judea, Samaria, or the Gaza Strip. It fatally strikes these terrorists, who plan, launch, or commit terrorist attacks in Israel and in the area of Judea, Samaria, and the Gaza Strip.'[67] This policy began in February 2000, the start of the second *intifada*.[68] By 2008, a reported 384 Palestinians had been killed.[69] Of those, 232 were the specific targets of attack, with the remaining 152 killed designated as collateral casualties.[70]

The petitioners sought to challenge this policy in order to compel the government of Israel to explain how it was using and interpreting international law to justify the targeted killings policy. Along with arguments based on the law on the use of force and international human rights law, the petitioners sought to clarify the position of targeted killings under IHL. They argued that 'the policy of assassinations harms these civilians when they are not taking part directly in combat or hostilities, and

reported in *ICRC CIHL Study*, Practice Related to Rule 6). This chapter instead selects a few key domestic and international court decisions that have looked at the concept of DPH in some detail.

[67] *Targeted Killings*, at § 1.

[68] *Targeted Killings*, at § 1. The Israeli practice of targeted killings will be discussed in more detail in Ch. 4.

[69] See statistics compiled by B'Tselem, The Israeli Information Centre for Human Rights in the Occupied Territories, available at: <http://www.btselem.org/statistics/fatalities/before-cast-lead/by-date-of-event>, accessed 29 March 2015.

[70] <http://www.btselem.org/statistics/fatalities/before-cast-lead/by-date-of-event>, accessed 4 April 2015.

as such, it is not legal and constitutes a prohibited strike against civilian targets that constitutes a war crime'.[71] Furthermore, it was argued that the policy was in violation of the principle of proportionality, due to the high rate of civilian casualties.[72]

The petitioners' position on DPH was that Article 51(3) is customary international law, this being a necessary step to establish as Israel is not party to Protocol I. Furthermore, according to the petitioners, the concept of DPH should be interpreted narrowly:

> a civilian participating in hostilities loses the protections granted to civilians only for such time that he is actually taking a direct part in the combat activities, such as when he shoots or positions a bomb. A civilian preparing to commit hostilities might be considered a person who is taking a direct part in hostilities, if he is openly bearing arms. When he lays down his weapon or when he is not committing hostilities, he ceases to be a legitimate target for attack. Thus, a person who merely aids the planning of hostilities, or who sends others to commit hostilities might expose the civilian to arrest and trial, but it cannot turn him into a legitimate target for attack.[73]

In response, Israel's argument was that it was involved in an armed conflict with terrorist organizations.[74] The law of armed conflict states that persons taking a direct part in hostilities are lawfully targetable; therefore, it was argued, Israel's actions were lawful. Israel also argued, *inter alia*, that the restrictions outlined in Article 51(3) of Protocol I—specifically, that civilians may be targeted 'for such time'—were not applicable to Israel because it is not a party to Protocol I, and that Article 51(3) had not, in 2003, attained the status of customary international law.[75] The State of Israel argued that a broad interpretation of the phrase 'direct participation in hostilities' should be favoured and should include persons who plan, launch, and commit attacks, even if such persons never actually use or carry the weapons utilized in the attack themselves.[76]

The Court was thus faced with the question of investigating whether, if an armed conflict indeed existed between Israel and various terrorist organizations, the concept of DPH should be defined narrowly or broadly. The first step was to assess whether the law of armed conflict was the relevant body of law to apply. The Court affirmed this to be the case, citing a number of previous decisions of the Supreme Court where the existence of an armed conflict in Israel was acknowledged.[77] The Court

[71] Reply Brief on Behalf of the Appellants (8 July 2003), at 32.

[72] Reply Brief on Behalf of the Appellants, at 206.

[73] *Targeted Killings*, at § 7.

[74] Supplemental Response on Behalf of the State Attorney's Office, at 127–37.

[75] *Targeted Killings*, at § 12.

[76] *Targeted Killings*, at § 12.

[77] Including *El Saka v The State of Israel*, HCJ 9255/00; *Kna'an v The Commander of IDF Forces in the Judea and Samaria Area*, HCJ 2461/01; *Barake v The Minister of Defence*, 56(2) PD 509, HCJ

also stated that the relevant law to be applied was the law of international armed conflicts, which included the law relating to belligerent occupation.[78] The Court also affirmed the customary status of all parts of Article 51(3), stating that the contention put forward by the Israeli government—that there is no time restriction on targeting civilians taking direct part—was essentially incorrect; thus, the 'for such time' element of Article 51(3) is customary international law.[79]

Having established this groundwork, the Court then set about examining the scope of the term 'direct part in hostilities'. From the outset, the Court attempted to strike the balance between the petitioners' narrow reading of direct participation and the respondent's broader interpretation.[80] The Court noted the ICRC's Commentary on the Additional Protocols which stated that, in determining the scope of direct participation, 'undoubtedly there is room here for some margin of judgment: to restrict this concept to combat and active military operations would be too narrow, while extending it to the entire war effort would be too broad, as in modern warfare the whole population participates in the war effort, albeit indirectly.'[81]

The Court identified certain categories of persons who could be considered as taking direct part in hostilities. These included persons collecting intelligence on the armed forces, persons transporting unlawful combatants[82] to or from the place where hostilities are occurring, and persons who operate weapons that unlawful combatants use, or supervise their operation, or provide service to them.[83] The Court also considered whether civilians involved in transporting ammunition to places for use in hostilities, as well as persons acting as voluntary human shields, should be considered as taking direct part in hostilities.[84] The Court explained:

> [the] direct character of the part taken should not be narrowed merely to the person committing the physical act of attack, those who have sent him, as well, take 'a direct part'. The same goes for the person who decided upon the act, and the person

9293/01; *Almandi v The Minister of Defense*, 56(3) PD 30, HCJ 3451/02; *Ibrahim v The Commander of IDF Forces in the West Bank*, HCJ 8172/02; and *Mara'abe v The Prime Minister of Israel*, HCJ 7957/04.

78 *Targeted Killings*, at §§ 18, 20–1.

79 *Targeted Killings*, at §§ 23, 29–30.

80 *Targeted Killings*, at § 31.

81 *AP Commentary*, at 516, para. 1679.

82 The term 'unlawful combatants' was used by the Court in an essentially descriptive manner; at § 27 in the judgment, the Court noted that the respondents had requested the Court to recognize a 'third category' of persons under IHL, in line with Israel's own law regarding unlawful combatants (Detention of Unlawful Combatants Law, 2002, 1834 Sefer Hahukim [Laws of the State of Israel, Hebrew]). However, the Court declined to take a 'stance regarding the question whether it is desirable to recognise this third category. The question before us is not one of desirable law, rather one of existing law. In our opinion, as far as existing law goes, the data before us are not sufficient to recognise this third category' (at § 28).

83 *Targeted Killings*, at § 35.

84 *Targeted Killings*, at §§ 35, 36.

who planned it. It is not to be said about them that they are taking an indirect part in hostilities.[85]

Excluded, however, from the scope of DPH were certain persons and acts, including selling food and medicine to unlawful combatants, providing general strategic analysis, logistical, and other general support, including monetary aid, and distributing propaganda.[86]

Also examined was the question of duration of DPH: when civilian immunity could be lost and when (and if) it was regained. The Court stated that there was no accepted or agreed interpretation,[87] but it conceded that a person who has ceased taking a direct part in hostilities regains his or her protection from targeting.[88] The Court noted that it was necessary to draw the distinction between a person who may take sporadic part, even if such participation was only a single instance, and those persons who have actively joined a 'terrorist organisation' and, while within that organization, commit a chain of hostile acts, even if there are short 'rest' periods between such acts.[89] The Court noted that for a member of an organization such rest intervals did not constitute a cessation of active participation, but rather a brief interlude preparatory to the commission of and/or participation in the next hostile act.[90] The Court did not go into detail regarding what the criteria were for membership of a terrorist group or the assumption of combat function. The Court determined that decisions regarding whether a civilian could be targeted for taking direct part in hostilities needed to be undertaken on a case-by-case basis.[91]

The United States of America

The US has had two notable examples of judicial examination of the concept of DPH, in the case of *Al-Marri*[92] in 2007, and in the December 2007 military commission case of *Hamdan*.[93] The case of *Al-Marri* related to a Qatari citizen, legally resident in the US, who had been arrested in December 2001 on terrorism-related charges, on the grounds that he was closely associated with al-Qaeda, having engaged in preparation for acts of terrorism.[94]

[85] *Targeted Killings*, at § 37.

[86] *Targeted Killings*, at § 35.

[87] *Targeted Killings*, at § 39.

[88] *Targeted Killings*, at § 39.

[89] *Targeted Killings*, at §§ 39–40.

[90] *Targeted Killings*, at §§ 39–40.

[91] *Targeted Killings*, at §§ 34, 39.

[92] *Ali Saleh Kahlah Al-Marri v Commander John Pucciarelli, U.S.N., Consolidated Naval Brig*, US State Court of Appeals for the Fourth Circuit Court, No. 06-7427.

[93] *United States of America v Salim Ahmed Hamdan*, On Reconsideration Ruling on Motion to Dismiss for Lack of Jurisdiction, 19 December 2007, at 6; available at: <http://www.defense.gov/news/Dec2007/Hamdan-urisdiction%20After%20Reconsideration%20Ruling.pdf>, accessed 4 April 2015; hereinafter *US v Hamdan*.

[94] See further: <http://www.scotusblog.com/2008/11/act-now-on-us-detention-al-marri-argues/>, accessed 4 April 2015.

Al-Marri petitioned for a writ of *habeas corpus*, which was denied; Al-Marri then challenged this decision and won the right to have his military detention terminated.[95] The Government petitioned for the decision to be vacated and in a re-hearing *en banc*, the US Court of Appeals for the Fourth Circuit examined, *inter alia*, the question of DPH in non-international armed conflicts, stating:

> we recognize that some commentators have suggested that 'for such time as they take a direct part in hostilities', participants in non-international armed conflicts may, as a matter of customary international law, be placed in the formal legal category of 'enemy combatant.'... No precedent from the Supreme Court or this court endorses this view, and the Government itself has not advanced such an argument. This may be because even were a court to follow this approach in some cases, it would not assist the Government here. For the Government has proffered no evidence that al-Marri has taken a 'direct part in hostilities.' Moreover, the United States has elsewhere adopted a formal treaty understanding of the meaning of the term 'direct part in hostilities,' which plainly excludes al-Marri.[96]

In this respect, the 'formal treaty' relating to DPH to which the Court was referring was the US message of transmittal regarding the Convention on the Rights of the Child.[97] In that document it was made clear that, at least in the context of the participation of children in armed conflict, the US:

> understands the phrase 'direct part in hostilities' to mean immediate and actual action on the battlefield likely to cause harm to the enemy because there is a direct causal relationship between the activity engaged in and the harm done to the enemy. The phrase 'direct participation in hostilities' does not mean indirect participation in hostilities, such as gathering and transmitting military information, transporting weapons, munitions and other supplies, or forward deployment.[98]

The US position on DPH was also examined in the US Military Commission ruling *United States of America v Salim Ahmed Hamdan*. In this instance, the Military Commission found that delivery of munitions did amount to DPH, stating that:

> the accused directly participated in those hostilities by driving a vehicle containing two surface-to-air missiles in both temporal and spatial proximity to both ongoing

[95] See *Al-Marri v Wright*, 487 F.3d 160 (4th Cir. 2007).

[96] *Ali Saleh Kahlah Al-Marri v Commander John Pucciarelli, U.S.N.*, at 31, n 16.

[97] Message from the President of the United States Transmitting Two Optional Protocols to the Convention on the Rights of the Child, S. Treaty Doc. No. 106-37 (2000); available at: <http://www.gpo.gov/fdsys/pkg/CDOC-106tdoc37/pdf/CDOC-106tdoc37.pdf>, accessed 29 March 2015.

[98] Message from the President of the United States Transmitting Two Optional Protocols to the Convention on the Rights of the Child, at VII.

combat operations...Although Kandahar was a short distance away, the accused's past history of delivering munitions to Taliban and al-Qaeda fighters, his possession of a vehicle containing surface to air missiles, and his capture while driving in the direction of a battle already underway, satisfies the requirement of 'direct participation'[99]

Germany

The question of DPH was also examined by the German Federal Prosecutor General in 2010. The Prosecutor General was tasked with investigating the bombing of two fuel tankers that had been stolen by the Taliban in 2009 in Kunduz Province in northern Afghanistan. The tankers had become stuck in a sandbank trying to cross the Kunduz River, near the German-administered International Security Assistance Force (ISAF) Provincial Reconstruction Team (PRT) camp at Kunduz. The German Commander of the PRT Kunduz, Colonel Klein, was concerned that the fuel tankers and their cargo would ultimately be used in an attack on the PRT or against Afghan police stations, and thus ordered an airstrike on the tankers.[100] At the time of the strike, numerous civilians were attempting to siphon fuel from the tankers; as a result, a considerable number of people were killed.[101] The German Federal

[99] *US v Hamdan*. See also the US case *Hamlily v Obama*, 616 F. Supp. 2d 63 (D.D.C. 2009), where the Court affirmed that the scope of DPH includes the hostile act, as well as preparation for and return from the hostile act (at 20–21); and the case of *Gherebi v Obama*, 609 F. Supp. 2d 43 (D.D.C. 2009), which also looked at the concept of DPH, but did not go into detail regarding specific examples of DPH.

[100] See Report of the German Parliamentary Investigation Committee, Deutscher Bundestag, 17 Wahlperiode, Drucksache 17/7400, available at: <http://dip21.bundestag.de/dip21/btd/17/074/1707400.pdf>, accessed 4 April 2015.

[101] Reports place the casualties at between 90 to 140 people killed. See further Susanne Koelbl, 'The Dilemma of the Kunduz Bombing: How Much Is a Human Life Worth?', *Der Spiegel*, 15 December 2009, available at: <http://www.spiegel.de/international/world/the-dilemma-of-the-kunduz-bombing-how-much-is-a-human-life-worth-a-667123.html>, accessed 29 March 2015; and Matthias Gebauer, 'Aftermath of an Afghanistan Tragedy: Germany to Pay $500,000 for Civilian Bombing Victims', *Der Spiegel*, 6 August 2010, available at: <http://www.spiegel.de/international/germany/aftermath-of-an-afghanistan-tragedy-germany-to-pay-500-000-for-civilian-bombing-victims-a-710439.html>, accessed 29 March 2015. See also the United Nations Assistance Mission in Afghanistan (UNAMA), *Annual Report on Protection of Civilians in Armed Conflict, 2009* (UNAMA, 2010), available at: <http://unama.unmissions.org/Portals/UNAMA/human%20rights/Protection%20of%20Civilian%202009%20report%20English.pdf>, at 18, accessed 29 March 2015; the European Centre for Constitutional and Human Rights, *German Air Strike near Kunduz—A Year After: Evaluation of Judicial Reactions and Further Information* (ECCHR, 2010), available at: <http://www.geneva-academy.ch/RULAC/pdf_state/ECCHR-Kunduz-A-Year-After.pdf>, accessed 4 April 2015; and Constantin von der Groeben, 'Criminal Responsibility of German Soldiers in Afghanistan: The Case of Colonel Klein', 11 German L J 469 (2010).

Prosecutor investigated whether charges should be laid against the German Commander.[102] While the Prosecutor ultimately dismissed the case, he did comment on the scope of DPH:

> The notion of hostilities is not defined in the international conventions, but taken as a given. International State practice, jurisprudence and literature have, however, largely clarified its meaning... Hostilities are thus not only understood in the narrow sense as armed acts of destroying personnel and equipment of the adverse forces... Rather, the term also comprises all acts which negatively affect the military capacities and operations of a party to the conflict, with a direct causal link between the act and the disadvantage caused and an objective link (belligerent nexus) between the damage caused to the adversary and the advantage for the opposing party being required... Consequently, acts of sabotage, the disruption of the enemy's logistics and communications are covered... whereas the general disruption of the civilian infrastructure of the country in which the armed conflict is taking place, even if negatively affecting the enemy forces, is not.... The direct participation in hostilities as understood under the international law of armed conflict is independent of the individual will of the person concerned because the temporary loss of protection as a civilian is the consequence of the person objectively constituting a military threat.[103]

In this instance, the Prosecutor stated that the act of taking the fuel tankers, which had been intended for ISAF forces, was a sufficient belligerent act as it caused damage to the military capability of ISAF. As such, the requirement of the belligerent nexus between the damage caused to one party and the advantage gained by the other party was fulfilled. However, in this instance, the requisite element of proximity and causation was absent:

> Regarding the civilians who were supporting the Taliban, it must be taken into account that the abduction of the two fuel tankers which had been designated for ISAF forces in principle constitutes causing damage to the military capacities as comprised in the notion of hostilities. The requirement of a nexus... between the damage and the advantage for the other party to the conflict was also fulfilled. However, the requirement of direct causality between the act and the damage was not fulfilled... regarding the loss of fuel, the proximity to the party to the conflict and the use in armed conflict is decisive. In the present case, the fuel was intended for the ISAF forces, but was still in the possession of a private logistics company and

[102] Carla Christina Bleiker, 'German Court to Rule on Kunduz Airstrike', *Deutsche Welle*, 20 March 2013, available at: <http://www.dw.de/german-court-to-rule-on-kunduz-airstrike/a-16680014>, accessed 4 April 2015.

[103] General Prosecutor's decision of 16 April 2010, available at: <http://www.geneva-academy.ch/RULAC/pdf_state/ECCHR-Kunduz-A-Year-After.pdf>, at 59–63, accessed 4 April 2015.

was located far away from the point of destination. The necessary relationship of proximity is therefore not fulfilled.

The requirement of strengthening a party to the conflict with the consequence of directly harming the adverse party is not fulfilled in the present case either. The situation corresponds to a general strengthening of the resources of one party without direct relation to the hostilities, as is the case with supporting the Taliban by financial donations... or by smuggling weapons and ammunition across the border... If the strengthening of military capacities directly resulted in concrete military operations, for example by transporting weapons directly to an area where they will be used... the assessment would be different.[104]

The ICTY and ICTR

The issue of DPH came up frequently in the case law of the International Criminal Tribunals for the former Yugoslavia (ICTY) and for Rwanda (ICTR) as both tribunals examined how to define DPH in non-international armed conflicts.[105] The ICTY dealt with the bulk of these cases. The first of these, the case of *Simić*, looked at the lower threshold for determining DPH. In its judgment, the Court stated that mere possession of weapons does not in itself create 'a reasonable doubt as to... civilian status'.[106] Other cases gave more generalized statements on DPH, affirming the link between DPH and the causing of harm to the opposing forces. Thus, in the *Galić* case in 2003, the ICTY Trial Chamber noted that '[t]o take a 'direct' part in the hostilities means acts of war which by their nature or purpose are likely to cause actual harm to the personnel or matériel of the enemy armed forces.'[107] This position was reaffirmed in the cases of *Dragomir Milošević*[108] and *Kordić and Čerkez*.[109]

[104] General Prosecutor's decision of 16 April 2010.

[105] Although the conflict in the former Yugoslavia had elements of both international and non-international armed conflicts; see further *Tadić*, Interlocutory Appeal, at para. 70.

[106] *Prosecutor v Simić et al.*, Case No. IT-95-9-T, Judgment, 17 October 2003, at 659.

[107] *Galić*, Judgment, at 48.

[108] In its judgment in 2007, the Trial Chamber stated: 'The protection afforded to individual civilians by Article 51 of Additional Protocol I continues until such time as civilians take a direct part in hostilities. There is a need to distinguish between direct participation in hostilities and participation in the war effort. To take direct part in hostilities means to engage in acts of war which, by their nature or purpose, are likely to cause actual harm to the personnel or matériel of the enemy armed forces. A civilian who takes part in armed combat loses his or her immunity and becomes a legitimate target' (*Prosecutor v Milošević*, Case No. IT-98-29/1-T, Judgment, 12 December 2007, at 947).

[109] Stating that a civilian will be deemed as taking direct part in hostilities 'when they participate in acts of war which by nature or purpose are likely to cause actual harm to the personnel and equipment of the enemy's armed forces' (*Kordić and Čerkez*, Appeals Judgment, at 51).

Perhaps the most comprehensive assessment of DPH came in the case of *Strugar*.[110] In that case, the Appeals Chamber reaffirmed the position, outlined in the ICRC Commentary,[111] that DPH must be understood as the commission of 'acts of war which by their nature or purpose are intended to cause actual harm to the personnel or equipment of the enemy's armed forces',[112] and that in order to make a determination as to whether a civilian is taking or has taken a direct part in hostilities:

> such an enquiry must be undertaken on a case-by-case basis, having regard to the individual circumstances of the victim at the time of the alleged offence. As the temporal scope of an individual's participation in hostilities can be intermittent and discontinuous, whether a victim was actively participating in the hostilities at the time of the offence depends on the nexus between the victim's activities at the time of the offence and any acts of war which by their nature or purpose are intended to cause actual harm to the personnel or equipment of the adverse party.[113]

The ICTY reasoning echoes that of the Israeli Supreme Court and the idea of the case-by-case analysis of civilian DPH.[114] In coming to this position, the ICTY in *Strugar* examined a significant number of international and domestic cases, legislation, and other instruments, giving a comprehensive listing of acts which could amount to DPH, in contrast to acts which could only be considered indirect participation in hostilities. The Appeals Chamber stated that:

> examples of active or direct participation in hostilities include: bearing, using or taking up arms, taking part in military or hostile acts, activities, conduct or operations, armed fighting or combat, participating in attacks against enemy personnel, property or equipment, transmitting military information for the immediate use of a belligerent, transporting weapons in proximity to combat operations.[115]

These acts are to be distinguished from indirect participation in hostilities, which the Appeals Chamber identified as:

> participating in activities in support of the war or military effort of one of the parties to the conflict, selling goods to one of the parties to the conflict, expressing sympathy for the cause of one of the parties to the conflict, accompanying and supplying food to one of the parties to the conflict, gathering and transmitting military information, transporting arms and munitions, and providing supplies, and providing specialist advice regarding the selection of military personnel, their training or the correct maintenance of weapons.[116]

[110] *Prosecutor v Strugar*, Case No. IT-01-42-A, Appeals Judgment, 17 July 2008.
[111] *AP Commentary*, at 618, para. 1942.
[112] *Strugar*, at 63, para. 167.
[113] *Strugar*, at 68, para. 178.
[114] *Targeted Killings*, at §§ 34, 39.
[115] *Strugar*, at 67–68, para. 177.
[116] *Strugar*, at 68, para. 177.

In relation to one of the cited examples of indirect participation—that of transporting weapons—the ICTY distinguished this example from the case of *Hamdan*,[117] where the military commission found that the transporting of weapons amounted to direct participation. In this respect, the ICTY noted that whether a person was actively participating in hostilities depends on the nexus between his or her activities and 'any acts of war which by their nature or purpose are intended to cause actual harm to the personnel or equipment of the adverse party.'[118] In the *Hamdan* case, Hamdan was considered as having taken a direct part in hostilities due to a number of converging elements, such as his previous activities as a munitions driver, his possession of a vehicle containing missiles, and that his capture occurred while he was driving towards active hostilities.[119] Hamdan's transportation of munitions was thus considered active, rather than indirect, participation in hostilities. Mere transportation of munitions or supplies, without additional elements such as proximity to active hostilities and known association with armed groups, would thus not amount to DPH according to the *Strugar* test.[120]

Finally, DPH was examined, if only briefly, in the ICTR in the case of *Bagilishema*. In that case in 2001, the ICTR affirmed the ICRC/ICTY position on DPH, stating that 'to take a direct or active part in the hostilities covers acts which by their very nature or purpose are likely to cause harm to personnel and equipment of the armed forces.'[121]

The Special Court for Sierra Leone

The question of determining DPH came up also in the case law of the Special Court for Sierra Leone in the cases *Fofana and Kondewa*,[122] and *Sesay*.[123] In both *Fofana* and *Sesay*, the Court took the same position as the ICTY and the Israeli Supreme Court before it: that DPH needed to be assessed on a case-by-case basis, and that 'there must be a sufficient causal relationship between the act of participation and its immediate consequences. The Chamber takes the view that the direct participation should be understood to mean "acts

[117] See Ch. 3, re *US v Hamdan* (2007).

[118] *Strugar*, at 68, para. 178.

[119] *US v Hamdan*, at 6.

[120] It is interesting to note that though the Tribunal, in a number of cases, gave examples of both DPH and indirect participation, the Tribunal had itself stated in the *Tadić* decision in 1997 that it found it 'unnecessary to define exactly the line dividing those taking anactive part in hostilities and those who are not so involved' (*Tadić*, Judgment, at para. 616).

[121] *Prosecutor v Bagilishema*, Case No. ICTR-95-1A-T, Judgment, 7 June 2001, at 104.

[122] *Prosecutor v Fofana and Kondewa*, Case No. SCSL-04-14-T, Judgment, 2 August 2007; hereinafter *Fonfana and Kondewa*.

[123] *Prosecutor v Sesay et al.*, Case No. SCSL-04-15-T, Judgment, 2 March 2009; hereinafter *Sesay*.

which by their nature and purpose, are intended to cause actual harm to the enemy personnel and material." '[124] The Court also identified acts that could only be considered indirect participation in hostilities, such as accusations of collaboration with an armed force (in the absence of any additional evidence supporting a charge of DPH). As the Court noted, 'indirectly supporting or failing to resist an attacking force is insufficient to constitute such participation. In addition, even if such civilians could be considered to have taken a direct part in hostilities, they would only have qualified as legitimate military targets during the period of their direct participation.'[125]

The Court examined the question of DPH in more detail in *Sesay*. The Court reiterated its comments in *Fofana and Kondewa*[126] and noted:

> the accepted view in international humanitarian law that hostilities are acts which by their nature or purpose are intended to cause damage or actual harm to the adversary party. We have endorsed the proposition that the concept of hostilities encompasses not only combat operations but also military activities linked to combat such as the use of children at military checkpoints or as spies... [however] The Chamber is mindful that an overly expansive definition of active participation in hostilities would be inappropriate as its consequence would be that children associated with armed groups lose their protected status as persons hors de combat under the law of armed conflict.[127]

Thus, the Special Court attempted to take a moderate position, acknowledging that acts that might cause harm, such as acting as a lookout, can amount to DPH but that care should be taken (especially when dealing with children directly engaged in hostilities) to ensure that civilians are protected.

The International Criminal Court

The International Criminal Court (ICC), in the cases of *Lubanga*[128] and *Abu Garda*,[129] also examined DPH and took a very similar position to that outlined by the Special Court for Sierra Leone. In *Abu Garda*, in the decision on the confirmation of charges[130] the Pre-Trial Chamber examined the question of DPH, stating that while 'neither treaty law nor customary law expressly define what constitutes direct participation in hostilities',[131] the

[124] *Fofana and Kondewa*, at para. 134.

[125] *Fofana and Kondewa*, at para. 135.

[126] *Sesay*, at para. 86, reiterating the Court in *Fofana and Kondewa*, at para. 135.

[127] *Sesay*, at para. 1723.

[128] *Prosecutor v Thomas Lubanga Dyilo*, Case No. ICC-01/04-01/06.

[129] *Prosecutor v Bahar Idriss Abu Garda*, Case No. ICC-02/05-02/09.

[130] ICC-02/05-02/09-243-Red, 8 February 2010.

[131] ICC-02/05-02/09-243-Red, 8 February 2010, at para. 80.

definition of the phrase had been clarified by a number of sources such as the ICTY in *Strugar*, as well as by State military manuals, soft law, decisions of international bodies, and the commentaries to the Geneva Conventions and the Additional Protocols.[132] The Court noted that examples of DPH would include 'bearing, using or taking up arms, taking part in military or hostile acts, activities, conduct or operations, armed fighting or combat, participating in attacks against enemy personnel, property or equipment, transmitting military information for the immediate use of a belligerent, and transporting weapons in proximity to combat operations.'[133]

In *Lubanga*, in the decision on the confirmation of charges,[134] the Court stated that active participation in hostilities 'means not only direct participation in hostilities, combat in other words, but also covers active participation in combat-related activities.'[135] The Court stated that DPH, as carried out by children,[136] would include activities such as 'scouting, spying, sabotage and the use of children as decoys, courtiers or at military check-points'.[137] Specifically, the Court stated that DPH would be found where:

> children are used to guard military objectives, such as the military quarters of the various units of the parties to the conflict, or to safeguard the physical safety of military commanders... these activities are indeed related to hostilities in so far as i) the military commanders are in a position to take all the necessary decisions regarding the conduct of hostilities, ii) they have a direct impact on the level of logistic resources and on the organisation of operations required by the other party to the conflict whose aim is to attack such military objectives.[138]

The Court stated that DPH be excluded in situations where 'the activity in question is clearly unrelated to hostilities [such as] food deliveries to an airbase or the use of domestic staff in married officers' quarters.'[139] The ICC, in using the terms 'active' as well as 'direct' seemed to be suggesting two kinds of participation: 'direct', meaning front-line combat activities, and 'active', meaning combat-related activities connected to the conflict. *Lubanga* thus takes both a broad and a narrow approach to DPH, with direct participation only equating to active combat participation (ie the actual firing of a weapon

132 ICC-02/05-02/09-243-Red, 8 February 2010, at para. 81.

133 ICC-02/05-02/09-243-Red, 8 February 2010, at para. 81.

134 ICC-01/04-01/06-803, 29 February 2007.

135 ICC-01/04-01/06-803, 29 February 2007, at para. 261.

136 Under Art. 8(2)(b)(xxvi) and 8(2)(e)(vii) of the Rome Statute, relating to the war crime of 'conscripting or enlisting children under the age of fifteen years into the national armed forces or using them to participate actively in hostilities'.

137 ICC-01/04-01/06-803, 29 February 2007.

138 ICC-01/04-01/06-803, 29 February 2007, at para. 263.

139 ICC-01/04-01/06-803, 29 February 2007, at para. 262.

or weapons system), while active participation would encompass combat related activities such as guarding or scouting.[140]

Defining DPH in Non-Binding Instruments

In addition to the attempts to define DPH in the law and in the courts that apply that law, other instruments and documents have been produced that have attempted to offer a perspective on the law. The first significant example of this was the ICRC's Interpretive Guidance on Direct Participation in Hostilities.

The ICRC's Interpretive Guidance on DPH

While a number of courts and tribunals were considering the scope of DPH, another attempt to define DPH was taking place—under the auspices of the ICRC and the TMC Asser Institute. Over the course of five years, five informal expert meetings were held in Geneva involving around fifty legal experts from the military, government, and academia as well as experts from international and non-governmental organizations. All experts attended in their personal capacity.[141]

The aim of the expert process was the production of a non-binding document that outlined the current understanding about the scope of the term 'direct participation in hostilities.' To that end, the key legal questions the expert process discussed were (1) who is a civilian for the purposes of the principle of distinction? (2) what conduct amounts to DPH? and (3) what modalities govern the loss of protection against direct attack?[142] The result of this expert process was the publication of the ICRC Interpretive Guidance. Due to controversies during the expert process,[143] the resulting document reflects the position of the ICRC alone, and it is not a consensus document from the expert meetings.[144]

[140] For a critique of *Lubanga* and the DPH assessment, see further Natalie Wagner, 'A Critical Assessment of Using Children to Participate Actively in Hostilities in Lubanga Child Soldiers and Direct Participation', 24 Criminal Law Forum 145 (2003).

[141] ICRC, 'Overview of the ICRC's Expert Process (2003–2008)', available at: <http://www.icrc.org/eng/assets/files/other/overview-of-the-icrcs-expert-process-icrc.pdf> at 3, accessed 4 April 2015.

[142] Interpretive Guidance on the Notion of Direct Participation in Hostilities under International Humanitarian Law, Adopted by the Assembly of the International Committee of the Red Cross on 26 February 2009, published in 90 IRRC 991 (2008) (hereinafter DPHIG), at 994.

[143] Discussed further below.

[144] DPHIG, at 992.

Who is a civilian for the purposes of the principle of distinction?

The Guidance defines civilians as 'all persons who are neither members of the armed forces of a party to the conflict nor participants in a *levée en masse*'.[145] Such persons are 'entitled to protection against direct attack unless and for such time as they take a direct part in hostilities.'[146] Thus, in order to determine who is a civilian, the Guidance thus defines 'armed forces', as 'all armed actors showing a sufficient degree of military organisation and belonging to a party to the conflict.'[147] The Guidance goes on to clarify the meaning and significance of 'belonging to' a party to the conflict. In this respect, the Guidance states that 'the concept of "belonging to" requires at least a *de facto* relationship between an organised armed group and a party to the conflict'.[148] The Guidance also makes reference to the Draft Articles on State Responsibility, stating that 'an organised group can be said to belong to a State if its conduct is attributable to that State under the international law of State responsibility';[149] the Guidance concludes on this issue by stating that in order for an organized group to belong to a party to the conflict, 'it appears essential that it conduct hostilities on behalf and with the agreement of that party.'[150]

In order to determine membership in the armed forces, the Guidance notes that for regular armed forces there is generally domestic law that regulates the membership of the armed forces and requires formal steps to be completed such as 'formal integration into permanent units distinguishable by uniforms, insignia, and equipment.'[151] For irregular armed forces, functional criteria—such as combat function—are used to determine membership.[152] Finally, participants in a *levée en masse* are excluded from the definition of civilian. Thus, in an international armed conflict, civilians are all persons who are not members of the regular or irregular armed forces, or participants in a *levée en masse*.

It becomes more complicated when one looks at how to define a civilian in a non-international armed conflict. The instruments that deal with non-international armed conflict—Common Article 3 and Protocol II—acknowledge but do not authorize participation in armed conflict. Thus, there is no clear combatant/civilian divide amongst non-State persons engaged in a non-international armed conflict. The Interpretive Guidance on

[145] DPHIG, at 995. [146] DPHIG, at 997. [147] DPHIG, at 999.
[148] DPHIG, at 999. [149] DPHIG, at 999. [150] DPHIG, at 999.
[151] DPHIG, at 1001. [152] DPHIG, at 1001.

participation in non-international armed conflict is accordingly more complex than that for international armed conflict:

All persons who are not members of State armed forces or organised armed groups of a party to the conflict are civilians and, therefore, entitled to protection against direct attack unless and for such time as they take a direct part in hostilities. In non-international armed conflict, armed groups constitute the armed forces of a non-State party to the conflict and consist only of individuals whose continuous function is to take a direct part in hostilities ('continuous combat function').[153]

The idea of 'continuous combat function' was adopted to exclude certain types of participation in a non-international armed conflict from falling within the scope of DPH. The concern raised by the ICRC—and a number of the experts—was the possibility of equating membership in an organized armed group with direct participation, that is to say, membership in an organized armed group, in and of itself, should not *per se* constitute DPH.[154] The result of such an approach might be that an overly broad definition of membership in an armed group could result in vast portions of the population being considered as taking direct part in hostilities. Concerns were also raised that such an extension of the concept of DPH beyond the commission of hostile acts would blur the traditional distinction in IHL made between 'loss of protection based on conduct (civilians) and on status or function (members of armed forces of organised armed groups).'[155]

In a non-international armed conflict, armed forces are thus to include State armed forces, comparable to the Guidance definition of armed forces in international armed conflicts, and organized armed groups. 'Organised armed groups' is interpreted to include the Additional Protocol II categories of 'dissident armed forces' and 'other organised armed groups.'[156] The term 'dissident armed forces' is interpreted as members of State armed forces who have turned against the government; the term 'organised armed groups' is taken as civilians who have joined an armed group of sufficient military organization to conduct hostilities against another party to the conflict.

[153] DPHIG, at 1002.

[154] Second Informal Expert Meeting, 25–26 October 2004, Background Document on Direct Participation in Hostilities under International Humanitarian Law (hereinafter DPH Background Document 2004), at 36.

[155] DPHIG, at 1003. See also DPH Background Document 2004, at 36; and Background Document on Direct Participation in Hostilities under International Humanitarian Law, Working Sessions IV–V, 'Direct Participation in Hostilities' and Membership in Organised Armed Groups, Third Informal Expert Meeting, 23–25 October 2005 (hereinafter DPH Background Document 2005), at 10.

[156] Art. 1(1), APII.

Generally speaking, 'organised armed group' is meant to refer to the armed or military wing of a non-State party, 'its armed forces in a functional sense',[157] and not to the political, social, or humanitarian segments of a rebel or insurgent organization.

Determining membership of an armed opposition group in a non-international armed conflict is complicated and it is here that the idea of 'continuous combat function' enters the discussion. Under the Interpretive Guidance, membership in a 'dissident' armed group seems comparatively easy to determine; that is, former members of a State's armed force who have turned against their government, 'at least to the extent, and for as long as, they remain organised under the structures of the State armed forces to which they formerly belonged, these structures should continue to determine individual membership in dissident armed forces as well.'[158]

For 'other organised armed groups', determining membership is more complex but it revolves around a functional approach: 'membership must depend on whether the continuous function assumed by an individual corresponds to that collectively exercised by the group as a whole, namely the conduct of hostilities on behalf of a non-State party to the conflict.'[159] Furthermore, it is not enough for a civilian merely to be a member of an armed group for the purposes of determining DPH; there must be some evidence of ongoing high-level involvement in the planning and execution of such hostilities. This is the concept of 'continuous combat function': 'it distinguishes members of the organised fighting forces of a non-State party from civilians who directly participate in hostilities on a merely spontaneous, sporadic, or unorganised basis, or who assume exclusively political, administrative or other non-combat functions.'[160] Thus, in the context of non-international armed conflicts, a person must have some continuous combat function in the armed group to be targetable in the same manner as a regular combatant in the armed forces in an armed conflict.

The idea of 'continuous combat function' ensures that certain persons are excluded from the definition of DPH, such as civilians assuming support functions. Thus, 'recruiters, trainers, financiers and propagandists may continuously contribute to the general war effort of a non-State party, but they are not members of an organised armed group belonging to that party unless their function additionally includes activities amounting to direct participation in hostilities.'[161] The Interpretive Guidance also excludes persons whose sole function is the acquisition, manufacture, and maintenance of weapons

[157] DPHIG, at 1006.
[158] DPHIG, at 1006.
[159] DPHIG, at 1007.
[160] DPHIG, at 1007.
[161] DPHIG, at 1008.

and other equipment outside active military operations, and persons engaged in intelligence collection of a general, rather than tactical, nature.[162]

The Guidance states that determining 'continuous combat function' may be achieved in a number of ways either through visual indicia, such as the open carriage of arms or the wearing of a uniform or other distinctive sign or emblem associated with parties to the armed conflict, or else on the basis of conclusive behaviour, 'for example, where a person has repeatedly directly participated in hostilities in support of an organised armed group in circumstances indicating that such conduct constitutes a continuous function rather than a spontaneous, sporadic, or temporary role assumed for the duration of a particular operation.'[163]

What conduct amounts to DPH?

The next stage in the Guidance process is defining what conduct amounts to DPH. The basic notion behind DPH revolves around defining each of the words in the phrase 'direct participation in hostilities.' The treaty law does not have a uniform interpretation or usage of the words, often using 'hostilities' interchangeably with 'warfare',[164] 'military operations',[165] and 'operations.'[166] The Guidance defines hostilities as the '(collective) resort by the parties to the conflict to means and methods of injuring the enemy.'[167] From this basis, one needs to ascertain whether the conduct in question amounts to direct (as opposed to indirect) participation in those hostilities. The Interpretive Guidance states that, in order to qualify as direct participation:

> [a] specific act must meet the following cumulative criteria: (1) the act must be likely to adversely affect the military operations of military capacity of a party to an armed conflict or alternatively to inflict death, injury, or destruction on persons or objects protected against direct attack (threshold of harm); (2) there must be a direct causal link between the act and the harm likely to result from that act, or from a coordinated military operation of which that act constitutes an integral part (direct causation); and (3) the act must be specifically designed to directly cause the required threshold of harm in support of a party to the conflict and to the detriment of another (belligerent nexus).[168]

[162] DPHIG, at 1008.

[163] DPHIG, at 1008. The Guidance rules on DPH by private contractors and civilian employees are discussed in more detail in Ch. 6.

[164] Art. 35, API; see also Art. 22 of the Hague Regulations.

[165] Art. 53, GCIV, Art. 51(1) API, Art. 13(1), APII.

[166] Art. 48, API.

[167] DPHIG, at 1013.

[168] DPHIG, at 1016.

Again, these constitutive elements are designed to ensure that persons who might supply subsidiary or tangential support—such as essentially administrative or support function—are excluded from being targeted, reserving targeting for the more serious levels of involvement. Under the Guidance, this tripartite test comprises the following elements: threshold of harm, direct causation, and belligerent nexus.

Threshold of harm

For an act to qualify as DPH, it 'must be likely to adversely affect the military operations or military capacity of a party to an armed conflict or, alternatively, to inflict death, injury or destruction on persons or objects protected against direct attack.'[169] The Guidance defines this first element as the need for the specific harmful act to reach a certain threshold of harm of a 'specifically military nature'.[170] Encompassed in this definition is the 'killing and wounding of military personnel and the causation of physical or functional damage to military objects'[171] as well as both armed and unarmed activities against the military operations or military capacity of a party to the conflict which result in the capture or control of such objects, territory, or personnel, to the 'detriment of the adversary.'[172] Also included in the 'threshold of harm' element is the causing of death, injury, or destruction of persons or objects protected against direct attacks, such as civilians, civilian objects, and other protected installations such as hospitals.[173]

Direct causation

In order for the next limb of the DPH test to be fulfilled, 'there must be a direct causal link between the specific act and the harm likely to result either from that act, or from a coordinated military operation of which that act constitutes an integral part.'[174] The element of causation is connected to making the distinction between 'direct' and 'indirect' participation in hostilities: there must be 'a sufficiently close causal relation between the act and the resulting harm.'[175] The Guidance defines direct causation as 'meaning that the harm in question must be brought about in one causal step.'[176] This formulation was devised to exclude an activity that 'merely builds up

[169] DPHIG, at 1016. [170] DPHIG, at 1017. [171] DPHIG, at 1017, 1018–19.

[172] DPHIG, at 1017, 1018–19. Included as examples of acts amounting to DPH are purely cyber-based interference with military objectives, either through computer network attack (CNA) or computer network exploitation (CNE); this will be discussed further in Ch. 5 on cyber warfare.

[173] DPHIG, at 1018. [174] DPHIG, at 1019.

[175] DPHIG, at 1021; see also *AP Commentary*, at 1453, para. 4787.

[176] DPHIG, at 1021.

or maintains the capacity of a party to harm its adversary, or which otherwise only indirectly causes harm'.[177] Such examples of indirect participation are listed as including scientific research and design, the recruitment and training of personnel, and provision of finances, electricity, fuel, food, or construction material to the party to the conflict.[178] Thus, according to the Guidance, the mere act of manufacturing an improvised explosive device (IED) would not amount to DPH in and of itself but the act of planting or detonating the device would be DPH, due to its more direct causal link to the harm that eventuates.[179]

For direct causation in collective operations where more than one person is involved in the commission of the hostile harmful act, consideration must be taken into account to ensure that the definition of DPH and causation is not too narrowly construed. Under the Guidance, 'where a specific act does not on its own directly cause the required threshold of harm, the requirement of direct causation would still be fulfilled where the act constitutes an integral part of a concrete and coordinated tactical operation that directly causes such harm.'[180] Such acts would include the analysis and transmission of tactical data to attacking forces, and the identification and marking of targets.[181]

Finally, direct causation is dependent on the degree of causal proximity to the hostile act, as distinguished from the temporal or geographical proximity to the hostile act. That is to say, even if the hostile act is committed through remote-controlled means (such as a drone or through a computer where the person committing the act is geographically removed from the harm caused), or through a delayed mechanism (eg, a timer-controlled explosive device, as well as where the person involved is temporally removed from the harm caused), the causal proximity remains constant.[182] This is to help parties to the conflict to distinguish between persons committing DPH and persons who might be temporally or geographically proximate to the hostilities, but who are not necessarily directly participating: for example, persons who provide food to the armed forces are both temporally and geographically proximate to the hostilities but who otherwise play no direct part in the hostilities.[183]

Belligerent nexus

The rationale behind 'belligerent nexus' is that not all acts of violence against the adverse party should necessarily be considered as amounting to DPH. The idea being that in order to amount to DPH, the act of violence must, in addition to fulfilling the requirements of direct causation and threshold of

[177] DPHIG, at 1021. [178] DPHIG, at 1021–22. [179] DPHIG, at 1022.
[180] DPHIG, at 1022–23. [181] DPHIG, at 1023. [182] DPHIG, at 1023.
[183] DPHIG, at 1023.

harm, be specifically undertaken 'in support of a party to an armed conflict and to the detriment of another'.[184] This has the effect of excluding certain acts from the scope of DPH, such as acts of violence that may incidentally impact on a party to the conflict but that are done for reasons not connected to the armed conflict, nor intentionally directed at a party to the conflict. The Guidance gives the example of the exchange of gun fire between police and hostage-takers during an 'ordinary bank robbery'[185] as one such example.

The Guidance makes it clear that belligerent nexus must be assessed separately from the question of the subjective intent of the person carrying out the hostile act; that is to say, whether the hostile act was meant to harm the party to the conflict. Participants in the Expert Process commented on the unfeasibility of basing '"split-second" decisions on the subjective intent of the civilians in question.'[186] As such, a determination of belligerent nexus is to be based on an objective assessment of 'whether the conduct of a civilian, in conjunction with the circumstances prevailing at the relevant time and place, can reasonably be perceived as an act designed to support one party to the conflict by directly causing the required threshold of harm to another party.'[187]

Belligerent nexus is also to be distinguished from the broader concept of 'general nexus' as outlined by the ICTY and ICTR. In the cases of *Kunarac*[188] and *Rutaganda*,[189] both judicial bodies put forward the requirement of a 'general nexus' between a specific act and the armed conflict as a whole, in order for the specific act to be classified as a war crime.[190] The Guidance states that, 'while the general nexus requirement refers to the relation between an act and a situation of armed conflict as a whole, the requirement of belligerent nexus refers to the relation between an act and the conduct of hostilities between the parties to an armed conflict.'[191] Belligerent nexus is thus a narrower formulation, with the act in question more closely tied to the conduct of hostilities of a party to the conflict, rather than merely having taken place in a time of armed conflict. This formulation excludes individual acts of self-defence[192] and any acts involved in the exercise of power over persons or territory, for instance, the suppression of riots by an occupying power, or the prevention of escape from POW camps or other detention facilities.[193] Also excluded are acts of violence in the context of civil unrest such as the use of military forces to quell political demonstrations and riots, and 'inter-civilian'[194] violence,

184 DPHIG, at 1026. 185 DPHIG, at 1027.
186 DPH Summary Report 2005, at 26. 187 DPHIG, at 1030.
188 *Prosecutor v Kunarac et al.*, Case No. IT-96-23, Appeals Chamber, 12 June 2002.
189 *Prosecutor v Rutaganda*, Case No. ICTR-96-3, Appeals Chamber, 26 May 2003.
190 *Kunarac*, at § 58, *Rutaganda*, at § 570. 191 DPHIG, at 1026, n 147.
192 DPHIG, at 1028. 193 DPHIG, at 1028–29. 194 DPHIG, at 1029.

where civilians 'merely take advantage of a breakdown of law and order to commit violent crimes'[195] that are in no way connected to the armed conflict or the participants in that conflict.

By combining these three elements—threshold of harm, direct causation, and belligerent nexus—the Guidance aims to 'permit a reliable distinction between activities amounting to direct participation in hostilities and activities which, although occurring in the context of an armed conflict, are not part of the conduct of hostilities and, therefore, do not entail loss of protection against direct attack.'[196]

When does DPH start and finish?

Article 51(3) of Protocol I states that loss of immunity from attack occurs 'for such time' as an act of direct participation is carried out. The Guidance interprets 'for such time' to start with measures preparatory to the execution of the specific act of participation, and covers both the deployment to and return from the location of the execution of the act of DPH.[197] Preparatory measures as outlined in the Guidance are to be understood as comparable to the provision in Article 44(3) regarding military operations preparatory to an attack, that is to say, acts which are 'of a specifically military nature and so closely linked to the subsequent execution of a specific hostile act that they already constitute an integral part of that act.'[198] The Guidance makes it clear that it is not necessary for the preparatory part of DPH to be carried out immediately before the hostile act. Thus, the loading of munitions onto a delivery system, such as loading bombs on an aircraft in anticipation of an impending bombing attack, amounts to DPH even if the bombing attack does not occur for some days.[199] However, the purchase of munitions, done for general stockpiling purposes rather than in anticipation of a planned attack, would most likely fall outside the scope of direct participation.[200] The key element is that the preparatory act must be carried out 'with a view to the execution of a specific hostile act'.[201]

In terms of deployment and return, if geographical deployment forms an integral part of the hostile act—eg, one needs to relocate physically in order to carry out the hostile act—then such deployment is considered part of DPH. Return from the hostile act is also included in DPH and ends only when the person committing the hostile act lays down, stores, or hides weapons used in the act and returns to activities that can be considered distinct

[195] DPHIG, at 1030.
[196] DPHIG, at 1031.
[197] DPHIG, at 1031.
[198] DPHIG, at 1031–32.
[199] DPHIG, at 1032.
[200] DPHIG, at 1032.
[201] DPHIG, at 1032.

from the act of DPH.[202] This correlates with the debate that took place during the Diplomatic Conferences for the Additional Protocols, where a number of delegations stated that the definition of hostilities should include both preparation for and return from the hostile act itself.[203] This formulation only applies for acts that require geographic displacement. For attacks that can be carried out remotely, without relocation (eg, CNAs), then DPH is deemed to have taken place only for the 'immediate execution of the act and preparatory measures forming an integral part of that act.'[204]

What modalities govern the loss of protection against direct attack?

The remaining part of the overall test for DPH is that of 'modalities governing loss of protection'. The Guidance states that civilians directly participating will lose their protected status for the duration of each act of direct participation. This has come to be known as the 'revolving door'[205] of civilian protection; that civilians do not lose their status as civilians while engaging in DPH but that their protection against direct attack is suspended for the time that they take direct part in hostilities. Once they cease taking direct part, they regain their civilian immunity from attack. As noted by the Guidance, 'civilians lose and regain protection against direct attack in parallel with the intervals of their engagement in direct participation in hostilities'.[206] The 'revolving-door' concept is, according to the Guidance, an integral part and not a 'malfunction'[207] of IHL; it is a means by which civilians who do not or no longer pose a military threat are no longer in danger of being targeted. The Guidance indicates that this formulation ensures that civilians who only sporadically take direct part in hostilities can be distinguished from members of organized armed groups.

For members of organized groups, this 'revolving door' of protection/loss of protection does not exist. As long as such persons are deemed to be assuming a continuous combat function, they will remain targets.[208] This correlates with the position in Article 13(3) of Additional Protocol II relating to DPH where the Commentary makes it clear that persons who belong to the armed forces or to armed groups 'may be attacked at any time'.[209]

202 DPHIG, at 1033.
203 See *Official Records XV*, CDDH/III/224, at 330; see also *AP Commentary*, at 516, para. 1679.
204 DPHIG, at 1033. 205 DPHIG, at 1035. 206 DPHIG, at 1035.
207 DPHIG, at 1035. 208 DPHIG, at 1035.
209 *AP Commentary*, at 1453, para. 4789.

The Guidance states that in situations of doubt, 'all feasible precautions must be taken in determining whether a person is a civilian and, if so, whether that civilian is directly participating in hostilities. In case of doubt, the person must be presumed to be protected against direct attack.'[210] This element corresponds to Article 57(2)(a)(i) of Protocol I, which provides that persons involved in planning and executing attacks must take all feasible precautions to ensure that 'objectives to be attacked are neither civilians nor civilian objects and are not subject to special protection'.[211]

Criticisms of the ICRC Interpretive Guidance

The elements outlined by the ICRC—determination of civilian status, belligerent nexus, threshold of harm, causation, and so on—form the essential core of any formulation of DPH that is seen in the decisions of the ICTY and ICTR, in domestic courts, and in military manuals. All of these documents and institutions have grappled with how, where, and when a civilian becomes targetable as a result of taking direct part in hostilities. However, the ICRC, controversially as it turned out, went further with its Guidance, including a section on 'Restraints on the Use of Force in Direct Attack.' Recommendation IX of the Guidance states:

> in addition to the restraints imposed by international humanitarian law on specific means and methods of warfare, and without any prejudice to further restrictions that may arise under other applicable branches of international law, the kind and degree of force which is permissible against persons not entitled to protection against direct attack must not exceed what is actually necessary to accomplish a legitimate military purpose in the prevailing circumstances.[212]

Prima facie, this provision is not controversial. It reiterates several well-established and codified principles of IHL—such as the prohibition on causing unnecessary suffering and superfluous injury,[213] the rules on military necessity and precautions in attack,[214] and the rules regarding permissible choice of means and methods—that 'in any armed conflict, the right of the Parties to the conflict to choose methods and means of warfare is not unlimited.'[215]

However, the inclusion of Section IX (as it was then termed) in the final draft of the interpretive guidance in 2007, was a cause for immediate criticism by some of the experts involved in the process. As noted by W Hays Parks,

[210] DPHIG, at 996. [211] Art. 57(2)(a)(i), API. [212] DPHIG, at 1040.
[213] Art. 35(2), API. [214] Arts 51–58, API; Arts 13–16, APII.
[215] Art. 35, API; see also Art. 22 of the Hague Regulations on the Laws of War on Land.

one of the experts involved, Section IX had been inserted into the draft by the ICRC 'without consultation with participating experts or its co-sponsor, the TMC Asser Institute'[216] (though this is disputed by Nils Melzer[217]). Most of the criticism regarding the inclusion of this section was focused on the underlying approach that Section IX seemed to espouse, that 'if a combatant can be put out of action by taking him prisoner, he should not be injured; if he can be put out of action by injury, he should not be killed; and if he can be put out of action by light injury, grave injury should be avoided.'[218] For the critics of Section IX (at least fifteen of the experts), it seemed to be making 'a novel argument unknown under contemporary IHL'[219] that in combat, one must be guided by the principle of humanity above all else, including even military necessity.[220] Critics of this section felt it was unfeasible to expect combatants to 'capture rather than kill'[221] in combat situations, and that Section IX essentially implied that there was a legal obligation for combatants to use less than lethal force in a combat zone, contrary to State practice. As one expert put it, 'not even domestic law enforcement agencies trained their officers, let alone members of the armed forces, to shoot to wound.'[222]

The ICRC attempted to assuage concerns regarding Section IX, stating that it was not intended to be used in large-scale confrontations, but rather it was:

> primarily designed for situations where armed forces were confronted with individuals within their territorial control who did not benefit from civilian protection against direct attack although they did not pose an immediate threat at the time and could be captured without additional risk. For example, where unarmed members of armed groups were surprised while sleeping in the woods or sitting in a restaurant,

[216] W Hays Parks, 'Part IX of the ICRC "Direct Participation in Hostilities" Study: No Mandate, No Expertise, and Legally Incorrect', 42 NYU J Int'l L & Pol 769 (2010), at 783.

[217] Nils Melzer, 'Keeping the Balance between Military Necessity and Humanity: A Response to Four Critiques of the ICRC's Interpretive Guidance on the Notion of Direct Participation in Hostilities', 42 NYU J Int'l L & Pol 831 (2010), at 894.

[218] ICRC, Report on the Work of Experts, 'Weapons That May Cause Unnecessary Suffering or Have Indiscriminate Effects' (ICRC, 1973), at 13, para. 23.

[219] Summary Report, Fourth Expert Meeting on the Notion of Direct Participation in Hostilities, 27–28 November 2006 (hereinafter DPH Summary Report 2006), at 75.

[220] See Hays Parks, "Part IX of the ICRC "Direct Participation in Hostilities" Study", at 785. This theory of humanity over military necessity has been called 'Pictet's use-of-force continuum', as Pictet had argued that 'humanity demands capture rather than wounds, and wounds rather than death (Jean Pictet, *Humanitarian Law and the Protection of War Victims* (Henry Dunant Institute, 1975), at 32).

[221] Revised Draft, Interpretive Guidance on the Notion of Direct Participation in Hostilities (2008), at 63.

[222] DPH Summary Report 2006, at 75.

it would be unacceptable for the operating forces to simply kill them without even attempting an arrest.[223]

For the ICRC, Section IX was intended to operate as a 'counter-balance' to the concept of continuous combat function and the functional membership test. The idea being that if certain group of civilians were to be denied civilian protections on a continuous basis, due to the application of the functional membership test, then Section IX would act as an 'indispensable safeguard against arbitrary interpretation of the functional membership approach'.[224] This approach did little to salve the concerns of the experts; ultimately, the ICRC stated that anyone who wished to remove his or her name from the final document could do so. Indeed, nearly a third of the experts involved in the discussions requested that their names be removed from the final document 'lest inclusion be misinterpreted as support for the Interpretive Guidance's propositions.'[225]

Section IX was perhaps the biggest source of contention for the experts; however, concerns were also raised regarding other elements of the final Interpretive Guidance. The first of these was raised by a member of the expert process, William Boothby, who argued that the interpretation of the scope of DPH, specifically the way in which preparation, deployment, and return were characterized in the Guidance, was too narrow.[226] Furthermore, Boothby took exception to the temporal dimension to direct participation, arguing that limiting continuous loss of participation to only certain members of organized armed groups meant that regularly participating civilians who did not meet the threshold of 'continuous combat function' would be afforded a 'privileged, unbalanced, and unjustified status of protection in comparison to members of the opposing armed forces, who are continuously targetable'.[227] Boothby argued that the ICRC Guidance's formulation of the 'revolving door' was not found in customary international law, and thus the ICRC interpretation excessively narrowed the notion of DPH.[228]

Another expert, Kenneth Watkin, was critical of the ICRC formulation of membership in armed groups.[229] He criticized the definition of 'organised armed groups' and the criteria for membership as not being grounded in

[223] DPH Summary Report 2006, at 76.

[224] DPH Summary Report 2006, at 76.

[225] Michael Schmitt, 'The Interpretive Guidance on the Notion of Direct Participation in Hostilities: A Critical Analysis', 1 Harvard Nat Sec J 5 (2010), at 6.

[226] William Boothby, "'And for Such Time As": The Time Dimension to Direct Participation in Hostilities', 42 NYU J Int'l L & Pol 741 (2010), at 746–50.

[227] Boothby, '"And for Such Time As"', at 743.

[228] Boothby, '"And for Such Time As"', at 743.

[229] Kenneth Watkin, 'Opportunity Lost: Organised Armed Groups and the ICRC 'Direct Participation in Hostilities Interpretive Guidance', 42 NYU J Int'l L and Pol 641 (2010).

'existing treaty or customary law'.[230] Furthermore, in excluding support personnel from the scope of DPH, the Guidance ensured such persons enjoyed 'a form of impunity from attack not provided to similarly situated persons serving on behalf of regular state armed forces'.[231] In all, Watkin felt that the Guidance failed adequately to reflect 'the realities of how warfare is conducted... [and] fails to fully recognise how armed groups are organised or how they fight.'[232]

Finally, concerns were raised regarding how the Guidance dealt with the complex issues of voluntary human shields and hostage taking. Discussion notes from the Fifth Informal Expert Meeting indicate that some experts were vehemently opposed to the ICRC position that voluntary human shields, while in danger of injury or death due to their proximity to lawful military objectives, do not lose their status as civilians immune from direct attack. The ICRC felt that voluntary human shielding most likely fell below the requisite threshold of harm in order to qualify as DPH.[233] However, four of the experts expressed 'unequivocal disagreement with the analysis of the draft Interpretive Guidance',[234] arguing that 'voluntary human shielding—contrary to involuntary human shielding—constitutes an attempt to impede enemy military operations and, therefore, must qualify as direct participation in hostilities.'[235]

With regards to hostage taking, some experts felt that hostage taking should be expressly included in the DPH Guidance, and that 'not qualifying hostage taking as direct participation would diminish the universal condemnation of hostage taking and suggest acceptance of the increasing use of hostages as human shields despite the prohibition expressed in Article 51(7) API'.[236]

Given such widespread opposition to the final document, the ICRC eventually 'took back' the Interpretive Guidance and issued it under its own auspices. The Interpretive Guidance is thus not an expert guidance but rather the ICRC's own position on what constitutes direct participation in

230 Watkin, 'Opportunity Lost', at 643.
231 Watkin, 'Opportunity Lost', at 644.
232 Watkin, 'Opportunity Lost', at 644.
233 DPHIG, at 1024–25.
234 Discussion Notes, Working Sessions I–VII, Fifth Informal Meeting on the Notion of Direct Participation in Hostilities Under IHL, Geneva 5–6 February 2008, at 23 (hereinafter DPH Discussion Notes 2008). For more background as to the debates over human shield during the expert process, see Summary Report, Second Expert Meeting on the Notion of Direct Participation in Hostilities, 25–26 October 2004 (hereinafter DPH Summary Report 2004), at 6–7; DPH Summary Report 2006, at 44–46.
235 DPH Discussion Notes 2008, at 23.
236 DPH Discussion Notes 2008, at 25. For more of the ongoing discussions regarding hostage taking, see further DPH Summary Report 2006, at 43–44.

hostilities and it is not reflective of a 'unanimous view of majority opinion of the participating experts.'[237]

Assessing the ICRC DPH Guidance

Determining the scope of DPH, in line with existing law, was potentially always a contentious exercise, especially given the paucity of customary international law. Indeed, any formulation of DPH, even if that formulation had been reached by consensus, would most likely have been criticized for being either too narrow or too broad. However, in the case of the ICRC Guidance, the withdrawal of one-third of the experts involved in the expert process only made the final document even more controversial.

The ICRC Guidance is not, by any means, an ideal document. Indeed, examining the cumulative criteria and definitions in the Guidance, what is striking is the incongruity of the aims of the study into DPH and the outcomes; that is to say, the intention behind the study into direct participation was to clarify when a civilian could be considered as taking direct part in hostilities *for the purposes of whether they could be targeted*.[238] To clarify: a party to a conflict, or an individual participant, in making targeting decisions, has to assess whether the person or persons in question are legitimate targets due to their direct participation. However, the long, detailed, and quite complex cumulative test in the ICRC Guidance presents as a series of questions that would, in many if not most cases, be something that could only be successfully answered *ex post facto* the execution of a targeting decision. It may well be that such a complex test would prove useful when a targeting decision is being made prior to any active engagement, and against a target that is offering no immediate threat—the ICRC's own example of coming across sleeping unarmed fighters would be the obvious example.[239] However, one must question the utility of this Guidance in active hostilities. It seems exceptionally unlikely that an individual soldier could make such an assessment in a combat situation, under fire, with little time to weigh up whether the person or persons he or she is confronted with in battle meet the requisite threshold of the harm, causation, and belligerent nexus criteria.

Additionally, concerns raised by some of the experts regarding the inclusion of Section IX are understandable. The Interpretive Guidance was designed to give instruction regarding when a civilian may be targeted for his or her direct participation. It was not meant to be a document that then described the rules one needed to follow after making a DPH determination.

[237] Melzer, 'Keeping the Balance Between Military Necessity and Humanity', at 835.

[238] As noted in the DPHIG 'the Interpretive Guidance examines the concept of direct participation in hostilities... for the purposes of the conduct of hostilities' (at 993).

[239] DPH Summary Report 2006, at 76.

While it is understandable that the ICRC wanted to remind stakeholders of their additional obligations under IHL once an initial DPH assessment is made, one can see how the inclusion of a section to that effect in the Guidance might have appeared to some critics as diluting the force of the Guidance, and going beyond what some might have felt was the objective of the process.

Furthermore, while the ICRC was entitled to encourage all persons involved in both the DPH process, and in armed conflicts more generally, to adopt the Pictet philosophy on the use of force,[240] the Guidance had the unfortunate effect of presenting this as if it were law rather that a statement of policy. Indeed, as Fenrick argues:

> [a]s a statement of policy, the words of Jean Pictet as the related DPH Guidance recommendation and commentary are humane and unobjectionable. Indeed, if these words had simply been put forth as a statement of ICRC policy which the ICRC encouraged other to adopt, those involved in the expert process would probably have regarded them as a matter of little concern. Unfortunately, they were presented as an interpretation of the law.[241]

As such, one can see why some of the experts may have taken issue with the inclusion of Section IX.

That being said, the harshness of some of the criticisms regarding the inclusion of Section IX, such as the claim by Parks that it amounted to a 'breach of trust',[242] seem to have dominated the subsequent debate around and analysis of the Guidance. It is true that nearly one-third of the experts removed their names from the final document; however, this would suggest that two-thirds of the remaining experts found no overwhelming or significant problem with the Section, at least to the point that they were willing to continue their affiliation with the document. Indeed, as Melzer points out:

> [w]hile Parks rightly points out that, during the expert discussions, several participating experts were extremely critical of Section IX, he fails to note that just as many experts strongly supported its inclusion in the Interpretive Guidance, and several others even argued that Section IX was not sufficiently restrictive, but should be complemented by human rights standards on the use of force.[243]

[240] 'If we can put a soldier out of action by capturing him, we should not wound him; if we can obtain the same result by wounding him, we must not kill him. If there are two means to achieve the same military advantage, we must choose the one which causes the lesser evil.' Jean Pictet, *Development and Principles of International Humanitarian Law* (Martinus Nijhoff, 1985), at 75.

[241] William Fenrick, 'ICRC Guidance on Direct Participation in Hostilities', 12 YBIHL 287 (2009), at 298.

[242] Parks, 'Part IX of the ICRC "Direct Participation in Hostilities" Study', at 793.

[243] Melzer, 'Keeping the Balance', at 895–96. See also DPH Summary Report 2006, at 74–79; Expert Comments and Elements of Response Concerning the Revised Draft of the Interpretive Guidance in the Notion of Direct Participation in Hostilities, Fifth Informal Expert Meeting on

As such, the criticisms of Section IX should be considered within the broader context of the expert process. The section, while controversial, should not be dismissed outright, but rather should be taken as indicative of the ICRC's position on the law.

Much the same approach should inform responses to the other criticisms levelled at the Interpretive Guidance. While the concerns surrounding the 'revolving-door' conceptualization of DPH, the approach to voluntary and involuntary human shields and hostage-taking, as well as the purported introduction of a 'third category' of persons under IHL are valid, they remain essentially a minority approach coming from a group of participants who advocated for a 'more permissive targeting regime'[244] than that eventually adopted. This should be compared and contrasted with the 'many'[245] experts who 'argued that the Guidance was too permissive and insisted on a more protective interpretation of the law.'[246]

In assessing the Interpretive Guidance it can be said that, despite the controversial elements of the DPH formulation, it remains a valuable and useful tool, and is perhaps the 'outer marker' of a more narrow and restrictive approach to targeting persons directly participating in hostilities.

The Harvard Manual

Finally, one last non-binding instrument looked at the issue of DPH. In 2009, the Program on Humanitarian Policy and Conflict Research at Harvard University published its *Manual on International Law Applicable to Air and Missile Warfare*.[247] The *Harvard Manual* was the result of six years of research and debate by an international group of experts who undertook the project to produce an 'authoritative restatement'[248] on the applicable law relating to air and missile warfare. The *Harvard Manual* specifically addresses the question of DPH in Article 28, where it restates that 'civilians lose their protection from attack if and for such time as they take a

the Notion of Direct Participation in Hostilities, 5–6 February 2008 (hereinafter DPH Expert Comments 2008), at 39–44; DPH Discussion Notes 2008, at 8–12; Summary Report, Fifth Informal Expert Meeting on the Notion of Direct Participation in Hostilities, 5–6 February 2008 (hereinafter DPH Summary Report 2008), at 7–32.

244 Melzer, 'Keeping the Balance', at 835.

245 Melzer, 'Keeping the Balance', at 835.

246 Melzer, 'Keeping the Balance', at 835.

247 *Manual on International Law Applicable to Air and Missile Warfare* (Harvard, 2009), available at: <http://ihlresearch.org/amw/HPCR%20Manual.pdf> (hereinafter the *Harvard Manual*), accessed 29 March 2015.

248 Claude Bruderlein, 'Foreword', *Harvard Manual*, at iii.

direct part in hostilities.'[249] Article 29 then illustrates what kinds of conduct amount to DPH, including:

i. Defending of military objectives against enemy attacks.
ii. Issuing orders and directives to forces engaged in hostilities; making decisions on operational/tactical deployments; and participating in targeting decision-making.
iii. Engaging in electronic warfare or computer network attacks targeting military objectives, combatants or civilians directly participating in hostilities, or which is intended to cause death or injury to civilians or damage to or destruction of civilian objects.
iv. Participation in target acquisition.
v. Engaging in mission planning of an air or missile attack.
vi. Operating or controlling weapon systems or weapons in air or missile combat operations, including remote control of UAVs and UCAVs.
vii. Employing military communications networks and facilities to support specific air or missile combat operations.
viii. Refuelling, be it on the ground or in the air, of a military aircraft which is about to engage in, or which is engaged in, air or missile combat operations.
ix. Loading ordnance or mission-essential equipment onto a military aircraft which is about to combat operations.
x. Servicing or repairing of a military aircraft which is about to engage in, or which is engaged in, air or missile combat operations.
xi. Loading mission control data to military aircraft/missile soft ware systems.
xii. Combat training of aircrews, air technicians and others for specific requirements of a particular air or missile combat operation.[250]

This list of examples seems to cast the ambit of DPH notably wide, certainly wider that the ICRC Guidance would suggest. However, the *Commentary to the Harvard Manual* repeatedly draws on the terminology and definitions used by the ICRC Interpretive Guidance, such as 'threshold of harm',[251] 'direct causation',[252] and 'belligerent nexus',[253] even though it makes clear that the 'three criteria established by the ICRC Interpretive Guidance... were not unanimously accepted by the Group of Experts.'[254] That the *Manual* was produced using the ICRC terminology seems indicative of a general if cautious acceptance of at least the theoretical approach of the ICRC in this regard.

[249] Art. 28, *Harvard Manual.* [250] Art. 29, *Harvard Manual.*

[251] *Commentary on the Humanitarian Policy and Conflict Research Manual on International Law Applicable to Air and Missile Warfare* (Harvard, 2010), available at: <http://ihlresearch.org/amw/Commentary%20on%20the%20HPCR%20Manual.pdf>, at 120 (hereinafter *Commentary on the Harvard Manual*), accessed 29 March 2015.

[252] *Commentary on the Harvard Manual*, at 120.

[253] *Commentary on the Harvard Manual*, at 120.

[254] *Commentary on the Harvard Manual*, at 121.

DPH: is there a consensus approach?

Given the differing perspectives on the ICRC Interpretive Guidance, and mindful of the State practice and jurisprudence that has emerged concurrent to and following on from its issuance, is there a consensus on DPH, at least in some parts? The ICTY in *Strugar* seems to take the most reasonable overview of DPH of the threshold for direct and indirect participation, excluding basic support activities such as the supply of food and provisions, and providing advice regarding choosing and training personnel, but including activities such as transmitting military information for the immediate use of a belligerent, and transporting weapons in proximity to combat operations, in addition to more obvious acts of DPH, such as bearing, using or taking up arms, as well as actual armed fighting or combat.[255]

As with all things, it is difficult to set definitive rules applicable to the 'grey area' between these two obvious markers of direct and indirect; it is here that the 'case-by-case' approach so often evidenced in the case law and military manuals is most effective. While it was admirable for the ICRC to attempt to outline such a definitive set of rules for all kinds of DPH, such an all-encompassing approach was, arguably, unfeasible. Given the manifold ways in which persons may directly and indirectly participate in hostilities, and given the degree of subjective intent that would need to be inferred in a number of these situations, it seems unlikely that a definitive outline of DPH could ever be achieved.

For example, in relation to the controversy over human shields, determining whether such human shields are voluntary and involuntary could only be determined on a case-by-case basis according to the circumstances present at the time. Persons chained to the fence of a military base with T-shirts reading 'human shield'[256] may be voluntarily engaging in this activity for political reasons, and they may be fully prepared to die for their beliefs. By the same token, a person chained to the fence of a military base acting as a human shield may be doing so because he or she was forced there at gunpoint.[257] Even though the outcome in both situations is the same—a person is chained to a fence of a military base—the motivation behind such acts

[255] *Strugar*, at 67–68, para. 177.

[256] As was the case during the invasion of Iraq in 2003. See further: <http://www.humanshields.org/>, accessed 4 April 2015.

[257] As was frequently the case in conflicts involving Iraq; the Hussein regime often used civilians and POWs to protect sites, during the Iran–Iraq War and the two Gulf Wars. See further Human Rights Watch, *Off Target: The Conduct of War and Civilian Casualties in Iraq* (2003), at 67, available at: <http://www.hrw.org/node/12207/section/1>, accessed 29 March 2015. See also Michael Schmitt, 'Human Shields in International Humanitarian Law', 38 Israel Yearbook on Human Rights 17 (2008), at 18–19.

is diametrically opposite. The motivation behind such acts is going to be difficult, if not impossible, to determine in advance. As such, it is unwise to state without any doubt whatsoever that either all persons who are human shields are immune from targeting, or that all persons acting as human shields are DPH and therefore may be targeted.

By the same token, in relation to the 'revolving-door' approach to DPH that has been subject to criticism by practitioners such as Boothby[258] and Watkin,[259] a case-by-case approach seems the most reasonable to take. To state that all persons who take direct part in hostilities—even if only once—remain targetable until the cessation of hostilities is too extreme an approach; to limit DPH only to the specific hostile act, failing to take into account those who plan such attacks but do not execute them themselves, is too narrow. Again, whether someone's sporadic involvement in hostilities is sufficient to warrant ongoing loss of immunity from targeting is something that requires ad hoc assessment. Just as IHL must 'remain sensitive to the interests of states in conducting warfare efficiently, for no state likely to find itself on the battlefield would accept norms that place its military success, or its survival, at serious risk',[260] so too must the law be sensitive to the humanitarian interests of States seeking to protect their citizens, and members of the armed forces, who bear the brunt of the violence and devastation brought by armed conflict. A case-by-case approach would seem to be the most sensible approach and one supported by existing treaty law in other areas of IHL, the notion of decisions being made in light of circumstances ruling at the time.

Thus, operating on the presumption of civilian immunity, if in light of circumstances ruling at the time, a person appears to be taking a direct part in hostilities, and that their actions are more than indirect (ie, political support, provision of basic sustenance such as food or water) but are likely to cause actual harm to an enemy, one could feasibly maintain a charge of DPH.

Conclusion

Increased civilian involvement in the mechanics of warfare has put civilians in the line of fire in more and more situations. It is this increased civilian involvement in warfare that forms the basis of the next section of this book.

[258] Boothby, *The Law of Targeting*, at 160.

[259] Kenneth Watkin, 'Controlling the Use of Force: A Role for Human Rights Norms in Contemporary Armed Conflict', 98 AJIL 1 (2004), at 17.

[260] Schmitt, 'The Interpretive Guidance on the Notion of Direct Participation in Hostilities', at 6.

This examines a number of key areas that create problems in the light of continued unsettled understanding of DPH. The first of these chapters looks at the practice of targeted killing and the contentious criteria that informs this practice, and examines whether the current practice of targeted killings can be reconciled as lawful under IHL.

PART II

CURRENT CHALLENGES TO THE LAW ON CIVILIANS AND ARMED CONFLICT

Introduction

As seen in the first two chapters of this book, one of the fundamental principles of the law of armed conflict and the principle that has shaped the law over the last 150 years is the principle of distinction: only combatants may lawfully take part in hostilities, and parties to the conflict may only target military objectives. Civilians and civilian objects may not be made the subject of direct attack. Civilians lose their immunity from direct attack if they take direct part in hostilities. Civilian participation is not an internationally wrongful act but direct participation in hostilities (DPH) renders them liable for targeting by an adverse party.

However, as we have seen in Chapter 3, the concept of DPH is complex and its definitional scope is uncertain, with opinions divided over whether to define the concept broadly or narrowly. This lack of clarity is problematic because in the last twenty-five years, civilians have been increasingly participating in armed conflicts as both the targeted and 'targeters'. If the parameters of direct participation are uncertain, how can parties to a conflict know whether they are lawfully targeting a civilian they believe is taking a direct part in hostilities? How can civilians know whether their activities may be perceived as being DPH by a hostile party?

These questions drive the analysis in the following chapters, which look at some of the recent developments in State practice that highlight this grey area of the law. What formula of DPH is being used in targeted killings? Is the recourse to DPH under IHL appropriate? Are drone pilots and cyber warriors considered civilians taking a direct part in hostilities, and what does this mean for parties who employ such civilians? Is the use of private military and security contractors in conflict zones a violation of the principle of distinction, and are such contractors civilians taking DPH? When criminal activities reach thresholds of intensity and duration that meet the criteria for armed conflict, does that mean that these criminals are directly participating in hostilities and that IHL supplants domestic criminal law as the relevant legal regime? The next four chapters of this book look at these different developments in the conduct of armed conflict, and examine the problems raised for the current law of armed conflict generally and the principle of distinction and the development of the concept of DPH specifically.

4

Targeted Killing

Introduction

Fifty years ago, the statement that there was something troubling about carrying out a targeted killing in an armed conflict would most have likely been met with bewilderment; surely, the counter-argument would go, in armed conflicts, all lawful killing is targeted;[1] that is to say, when a soldier on the battlefield identifies a member of the enemy armed forces through his or her rifle scope, fires the shot, and the enemy solider falls dead, then that enemy soldier has been killed as a result of being targeted. Hence, in the most basic and fundamental way, a 'targeted killing' has taken place.[2]

However, when one speaks of targeted killing, this scenario of two combatants on a battlefield is not the scenario envisaged. Rather, the contemporary understanding of the term 'targeted killing' is understood as the deliberate and premeditated killing of specific persons. The targeted killing is usually, but not always, carried out in connection to ongoing military operations, and the killing frequently takes place in areas beyond the territorial control of the entity conducting the targeting.[3] Such targeted killings are also usually deployed against so-called 'terrorists'.[4]

The last fifteen years has seen the emergence of the State practice of targeted killing, with a number of States including the US, Israel, and Russia acknowledging that they have engaged, and continue to engage, in the practice of targeted killing.[5] From an international law perspective, targeted killings raise a number of interesting and complex issues, touching on questions on the law on the use of force, State sovereignty, the geographical boundaries

[1] Gabriella Blum and Philip Heymann, 'Law and Policy of Targeted Killing', 1 Harvard Nat'l Sec J 145 (2010), at 147.

[2] Gary Solis, *The Law of Armed Conflict* (CUP, 2010), at 538.

[3] Michael Schmitt, 'Drone Attacks under the Jus ad Bellum and Jus in Bello: Clearing the 'Fog of Law'', 13 YBIHL 311 (2010), at 312.

[4] Schmitt, 'Drone Attacks under the Jus ad Bellum and Jus in Bello', at 311.

[5] Examples of such practice are explored in more detail below.

of hostilities, and the spectrum of applicable laws, from domestic law enforcement to international human rights law (IHRL) and international humanitarian law (IHL).

A number of bodies, such as the Supreme Court of Israel[6] and the UN,[7] have over the last decade attempted to address the question of the legality of targeted killings. These bodies have investigated the question of whether targeted killings are legal under international law, IHL, and IHRL. One of the arguments forwarded by those undertaking the attacks is that the targeted persons are directly participating in hostilities, and as such they lose their civilian immunity and are targetable.[8] What those undertaking the targeting have been less than forthcoming about is the determinative criteria being used to target such individuals. Is the targeting in line with current thinking on direct participation in hostilities (DPH) or does it take too broad an approach, and in doing so, does it move beyond the parameters of IHL and into the law relating to human rights?[9] Indeed, one needs to query whether IHL is the appropriate legal framework to apply. These issues will be explored in this chapter.

Note on Sources of Information for Targeted Killings

It is helpful at this stage of the book to note the difficulty in ascertaining the facts regarding targeted killings (and, indeed, this is relevant for the next chapter on drones and cyber warfare). Much of the information on the operational capabilities, targeting practices, and internal policy intentions of States engaged in these activities is classified; in making determinations as to the existence of the events examined in the following chapters, much depends on media reportage, general statements of policy from leaders and governments, as well as information that has been leaked from government sources. The already difficult task of ascertaining why States act in certain ways in times of armed conflict is further compounded by the additional element 'that

[6] In the *Targeted Killings* case. See further Ch. 3.

[7] Philip Alston, *Study on Targeted Killings*, Report of the Special Rapporteur on Extrajudicial, Summary or Arbitrary Executions, UN Doc A/HRC/14/24/Add.6, 28 May 2010; Christof Heyns, Report of the Special Rapporteur on Extrajudicial, Summary or Arbitrary Executions. UN Doc. A/68/382, 13 September 2013; Ben Emmerson, Report of the Special Rapporteur on the Promotion and Protection of Human Rights and Fundamental Freedoms While Countering Terrorism, UN Doc. A/HRC/25/59, 28 February 2014.

[8] See below for a discussion of the targeting criteria.

[9] Targeted killings have often been carried out through the use of unmanned aerial vehicles (UAVs) or drones, the civilian DPH implications of which are dealt with in Ch. 5.

when one is dealing with the activities of intelligence agencies, the essential currency is deception.'[10] Indeed, this point is explained in more detail by Murphy and Radsan, who note:

> a government stamp of secrecy stands in the way of an open discussion of the formal process, if any, for approving [targeted killings]...if the President has delegated trigger authority to another person within the executive branch, that fact as well as the standards of delegation are also classified. Therefore, as with some many topics about the intelligence community, the most we are able to do is speculate on the basis of common sense and the public record.[11]

As such, this chapter and the next examine both the stated and observable practice of States and non-State actors, and both examine whether such practice is or is not in compliance with IHL.

Defining Targeted Killing under International Law

It has become commonplace in the literature to state that the term 'targeted killing' does not have a fixed definition under international law.[12] A useful working definition has been proposed by Philip Alston who, during his time as UN Special Rapporteur on Extrajudicial, Summary or Arbitrary Executions, defined targeted killing as 'the intentional, premeditated and deliberate use of lethal force, by States or their agents acting under colour of law, or by an organized armed group in armed conflict, against a specific individual who is not in the physical custody of the perpetrator.'[13] Some publicists, such as Solis, add an additional element, arguing that key to the definition of targeted killing is that the person subject to a targeted killing 'cannot be reasonably apprehended'.[14] Solis also argues that a targeted killing can only be carried out by the State, and that any targeted killing carried out

[10] Philip Alston, 'The CIA and Targeted Killings Beyond Borders', 2 Harvard Nat Sec J 283 (2011), at 299.

[11] Richard Murphy and Afsheen John Radsan, 'Due Process and Targeted Killing of Terrorists', 31 Cardozo L Rev 405 (2009), at 412.

[12] Solis, *The Law of Armed Conflict*, at 538; Alston, 'The CIA and Targeted Killings', at 295, Mary Ellen O'Connell, 'The Right to Life in War and Peace: A Legal and Moral Critique of Targeted Killing', Remarks for the Institute of Theology and Peace, 15 August 2012, available at: <https://www.law.upenn.edu/live/files/1634-oconnell-the-right-to-life-in-war-and-peace>, at 5, accessed 29 March 2015.

[13] Alston, *Study on Targeted Killings*, at 3.

[14] Gary Solis, 'Targeted Killing and the Law of Armed Conflict', 60 Naval War College Rev 127 (2007), at 127.

by 'rebellious citizens... [or] groupings of unlawful combatants'[15] would be assassination and prosecutable domestically as murder.

These additional criteria raise issues regarding the context in which the targeted killings take place which will be discussed in more detail in the latter part of this chapter. Prior to that analysis, it is useful to get an overview of the practice of targeted killings over the last fifteen years—who has carried out such attacks and where—in order to understand the legality (or otherwise) of such targeted killings, and issues such targeted killings raise in terms of DPH and the applicable law.

State Practice of Targeted Killing

Targeted killing has become part of the conventional counter-terrorism strategy of a number of States, with Israel and the US among its chief proponents, although Russia has also acknowledged the practice.

Israel

Israel was the first State to acknowledge openly that it was carrying out targeted killings,[16] after having denied such a policy for years.[17] In November 2000, the Israeli government confirmed that it had targeted and killed Fatah activist Hussein 'Abayat,[18] later stating that such acts were carried out as part of the ongoing State 'policy of liquidating those who plan or carry out attacks'[19] against Israel. Statistics collected by the human rights organization B'Tselem, the Israeli Information Centre for Human Rights in the

[15] Solis, *The Law of Armed Conflict*, at 538–39.

[16] See comments made by Colonel Daniel Reisner, Israeli Defence Force (IDF) Legal Division, Statement of 15 November 2000, available at: <http://mfa.gov.il/MFA/PressRoom/2000/Pages/Press%20Briefing%20by%20Colonel%20Daniel%20Reisner-%20Head%20of.aspx>, at 1, accessed 4 April, 2015; see also Nils Melzer, *Targeted Killings in International Law* (OUP, 2008), at xi.

[17] In 1992, when asked if the IDF carried out targeted killings of suspected terrorists, a spokesperson stated that the IDF 'wholeheartedly rejects this accusation. There is no policy and there never will be a policy of a reality of wilful killing of suspects.' (Na'ama Yashuvi, *Activity of the Undercover Units in the Occupied Territories*, B'Tselem—The Israeli Information Centre for Human Rights in the Occupied Territories, 15 May 1992, available at: <http://www.btselem.org/download/199205_undercover_units_eng.doc>, accessed 29 March 2015).

[18] See Colonel Daniel Reisner, Comments.

[19] Comments by Israeli Deputy Minister of Defense Ephraim Sneh, 14 February 2001, cited in Amnesty International, *Israel and the Occupied Territories: State Assassinations and Other Unlawful Killings* (2001), at 1, available at: <https://www.amnesty.org/en/library/info/MDE15/005/2001/en>, accessed 29 March 2015.

Occupied Territories indicate that between September 2000 and December 2008, 384 Palestinian in the West Bank and Gaza Strip were killed as the result of a targeted killing. However, only 232 of those Palestinians were the intended object of the targeting, with the remainder classified as collateral casualties.[20] Between December 2008 and January 2009, when Israel launched Operation Cast Lead,[21] the number of Palestinians killed in connection to a targeted killing operation was twenty-two.[22] From January 2009 until January of 2014, thirty-six Palestinians have been killed as the objects of a targeted killing, with a further fifty-one killed in connection to a targeted killing.[23]

Israel has justified the attacks on the grounds that the targeted killings are lawful acts of self-defence:

> The select assassination policy must be viewed as killing to preempt terror attacks. If you know the person has four times in the past sent his people to shoot at Israelis traveling on the roads, and if you have information about his intention to sponsor more activities of this sort tomorrow or the day after tomorrow, then the suspect meets the assassination criteria.[24]

Israel has also justified the targeted killing policy as legal under IHL, claiming that it is involved in a 'new kind of conflict'[25] with terrorist organizations, and that the members of such terrorist organizations are taking an active part in the hostilities[26] which, under the law of armed conflict, renders such active participants as legitimate targets.

[20] See further <http://www.btselem.org/statistics/fatalities/before-cast-lead/by-date-of-event>, accessed 29 March 2015.

[21] Operation Cast Lead was a twenty-two-day operation by the IDF to suppress rocket fire into Israel from the Occupied Territories starting on 27 December 2008 and concluding on 18 January 2009; see further Report of the United Nations Fact-Finding Mission on the Gaza Conflict (hereinafter the Goldstone Report), A/HRC/12/48, 25 September 2009, at 327–64, for an overview of the military operations conducted by Israel in Gaza during Operation Cast Lead.

[22] Two of those casualties were the object of the targeted killing; the remaining twenty were collateral casualties. See further: <http://www.btselem.org/statistics/fatalities/during-cast-lead/by-date-of-event>, accessed 4 April 2015.

[23] See <http://www.btselem.org/statistics/fatalities/after-cast-lead/by-date-of-event>, accessed 4 April 2015.

[24] Gideon Alon and Amos Harel, 'IDF Lawyers Set "Conditions" for Assassination Policy', *Haaretz*, 2 February 2002, available at: <http://www.haaretz.com/misc/article-print-page/idf-lawyers-set-conditions-for-assassination-policy-1.53911?trailingPath=2.169%2C2.225%2C2.226%2C>, accessed 29 March 2015.

[25] *Targeted Killings*, Supplemental Response on Behalf of the State's Attorney's Office, at paras 127–37.

[26] *Targeted Killings*, Supplemental Response on Behalf of the State's Attorney's Office, at para. 138.

Russia

In its conflict with Chechnya, which has been called a counter-terrorism operation,[27] Russia reportedly orchestrated the targeted killings of Chechen rebel leaders including Zelimkhan Yandarbiyev[28] and Shamil Basayev,[29] justifying their targeting as a necessary part of Russia's counter-terrorism activities.[30] At the time of these targeted killings, Russia refused to acknowledge that it had a policy of targeted killing; it likewise refused to undertake or cooperate with any investigation or prosecution of those suspected of carrying out the targeted killings.[31]

In 2006, the Russian parliament enacted a law which permitted Russian security services, on the authority of the President, to target and kill suspected terrorists, even if such persons were located outside Russia.[32] Under Article 6(4) of the law, the Armed Forces of the Russian Federation may be used for 'suppressing international terrorist activities outside the Russian Federation'.[33] At the time, Russian legislators reportedly stated that they were

[27] David Holley, 'Rebel Leader Dies in Russia', *Los Angeles Times*, 11 July 2006, available at: <http://articles.latimes.com/2006/jul/11/world/fg-basayev11>, accessed 29 March 2015; see also Luke Harding, 'Russia Ends Anti-Terrorism Operations in Chechnya', *Guardian*, 16 April 2009, available at: <http://www.theguardian.com/world/2009/apr/16/russia-chechnya-anti-terrorism>, accessed 29 March 2015.

[28] See 'Obituary: Zelimkhan Yandarbiyev', *Independent*, 14 February 2004, at <http://www.independent.co.uk/news/obituaries/zelimkhan-yandarbiyev-37996.html>, accessed 29 March 2015.

[29] See 'Obituary: Shamil Basayev', *BBC News*, 10 July 2006, available at: <http://news.bbc.co.uk/2/hi/europe/4727935.stm>, accessed 29 March 2015.

[30] See 'Chechen Rebel Chief Basayev Dies', *BBC News*, 10 July 2006, which quotes Russian FSB Security Service chief Nikolai Patrushev as saying that Basayev was killed in a 'special operation' and that he was among a group of militants killed as they prepared to carry out a 'terrorist act' in Ingushetia; available at: <http://news.bbc.co.uk/2/hi/5165456.stm>, accessed 29 March 2015. See also the ruling in a case in the Qatari courts, which resulted in two Russian secret agents being convicted of Yandarbiyev's murder, where the judge stated that the Russian leadership had issued the order to assassinate Yandarbiyev (as reported by Steven Lee Myers, 'Qatar Court Convicts 2 Russians in Top Chechen's Death', *New York Times*, 1 July 2004, available at: <http://www.nytimes.com/2004/07/01/world/qatar-court-convicts-2-russians-in-top-chechen-s-death.html>, accessed 29 March 2015).

[31] See Andrew McGregor, 'The Assassination of Zelimkhan Yandarbiyev: Implications for the War on Terrorism', *Terrorism Monitor*, 14 July 2004, available at: <http://www.jamestown.org/programs/tm/single/?tx_ttnews%5Btt_news%5D=30107&tx_ttnews%5BbackPid%5D=179&no_cache=1#.UyI8vU3xvxM>, accessed 29 March 2015.

[32] Federal Law No. 35-FZ of 6 March 2006 on Counteraction Against Terrorism, available at: <http://www.coe.int/t/dlapil/codexter/Source/country_profiles/legislation/CT%20legislation%20-%20Russian%20Federation.pdf>, accessed 29 March 2015.

[33] Art. 6(4), Federal Law No. 35-FZ. See also the European Court of Human Rights (ECtHR) in *Isayeva v Russia*, Application No 57950/00, Judgment, 24 February 2005, at § 180–1 (2005), where the Court acknowledged that Russia is entitled to use lethal force against armed insurgents actively resisting law-enforcement agents (see also ECtHR, *Isayeva v Russia*, Application No. 6846/02, 15 November 2007).

'emulating Israeli and US actions in adoption a law allowing the use of military and special forces outside the country's borders against external threats.'[34]

The US

The US has become perhaps the best-known proponent of targeted killing since the conflict with al-Qaeda began in September 2001,[35] although, as Melzer notes, prior to the September 2001 attacks, the 'United States was no stranger to the use of targeted killing',[36] with the Central Intelligence Agency (CIA) having orchestrated or attempted the assassinations of world leaders including Fidel Castro, Patrice Lumumba, Rafael Trujillo, and Ngo Dinh Diem.[37] Indeed, in response to US Senate investigations into CIA, National Security Agency (NSA), and Federal Bureau of Investigation (FBI) involvement in assassinations, President Gerald Ford issued an executive order providing that 'no persons employed by or acting on behalf of the United States Government shall engage in, or conspire to engage in, assassination.'[38]

When the US was attacked by al-Qaeda on 11 September 2001, the Bush administration declared a 'war on terrorism'.[39] Under a joint resolution passed by the US Congress on 18 September 2001,[40] it was resolved that the:

> President is authorized to use all necessary and appropriate force against those nations, organizations, or persons he determines planned, authorized, committed,

[34] Steven Eke, 'Russia Law on Killing 'Extremists' Abroad', *BBC News*, 27 November 2006, available at: <http://news.bbc.co.uk/2/hi/europe/6188658.stm>, accessed 29 March 2015.

[35] The US Congress sanctioned the 'war on terror' in Authorization for Use of Military Force Against Terrorists (Pub. L. 107–40, 115 Stat. 224), enacted 18 September 2001, hereinafter AUMF.

[36] Melzer, *Targeted Killing in International Law*, at 37.

[37] See further the 1975 investigation undertaken by the United States Senate Select Committee to Study Governmental Operations with Respect to Intelligence Activities, known as the Church Committee after its chairman, Senator Frank Church (Democrat, Idaho), and its eventual report *Alleged Assassination Plots Involving Foreign Leaders: An Interim Report of the Senate Select Committee to Study Governmental Operations with Respect to Intelligence Operations*, Senate Report No. 465, 94th Congress, 1st Session, Vols 1–7 (1975), available at: <http://www.maryferrell.org/mffweb/archive/docset/getList.do?docSetId=1014>, accessed 29 March 2015.

[38] § 2.11, Executive Order 12333 (issued by President Ronald Reagan, 4 December 1981) which superseded both Executive Order 11905 (issued by President Gerald Ford on 18 February 1976) and EO 12036 (issued by President Jimmy Carter, 24 January 1978). For more on the US practice of assassination, both pre- and post- the Church Committee, see Michael Schmitt, 'State-Sponsored Assassination in International and Domestic Law', 17 Yale J Int'l L 609 (1992), at 652–75.

[39] US President George W Bush used the term in an address to a Joint Session of Congress on 20 September 2001. In the televised address, President Bush stated that the US 'war on terror begins with al-Qaeda, but it does not end there. It will not end until every terrorist group of global reach has been found, stopped and defeated.' 'President Bush Addresses the Nation', *Washington Post*, 20 September 2001, available at <http://www.washingtonpost.com/wp-srv/nation/specials/attacked/transcripts/bushaddress_092001.html>, accessed 4 April 2015.

[40] AUMF.

or aided the terrorist attacks that occurred on September 11, 2001, or harbored such organizations or persons, in order to prevent any future acts of international terrorism against the United States by such nations, organizations or persons.[41]

Three days after this legislation was enacted, President George W Bush reportedly authorized the CIA to undertake lethal covert operations—in essence, targeted killings—of suspected al-Qaeda operatives including Osama bin Laden.[42] US authorities sought to distinguish these actions as different from assassinations, which are illegal under Executive Order 12333, arguing that the targeted killings were lawful acts of self-defence and therefore not assassinations.[43]

The first reported targeted killing by the US in the post-9/11 era took place in October 2001, when a US air strike killed suspected al-Qaeda chief Mohammed Atef in Afghanistan.[44] This was followed by strikes in Pakistan,[45] Yemen,[46] and Somalia[47] over the next twelve years. US government statements on targeted killings have always cited low civilian casualties (civilians

[41] § 2(a), AUMF.

[42] The existence, if not the contents, of the classified Presidential Finding (essentially, an executive order) to the CIA was acknowledged by the Bush White House in 2006, in response to a Freedom of Information Act litigation brought by the American Civil Liberties Union (ACLU); see the ACLU press release, 'CIA Finally Acknowledges Existence of Presidential Order on Detention Facilities Abroad', 14 November 2006, available at: <https://www.aclu.org/national-security/cia-finally-acknowledges-existence-presidential-order-detention-facilities-abroad>, accessed 29 March 2015. Former CIA Chief of Clandestine Operations in Europe, Tyler Drumheller, stated that the 17 September 2001 meeting, at which the Finding was revealed 'broadened our options for dealing with terrorist targets—one of the few times such a thing had happened since the CIA was officially banned from carrying out assassinations in 1976. It was clear the Administration saw this as a war that would largely be fought by intelligence assets' (Tyler Drumheller, *On The Brink: An Insider's Account of How the White House Compromised American Intelligence* (Carroll and Graf, 2006), at 35). See also Bob Woodward, *Bush At War* (Simon and Schuster, 2002), at 101; and Dana Priest, 'Covert CIA Program Withstands New Furor', *Washington Post*, 30 December 2005, available at: <http://www.washingtonpost.com/wp-dyn/content/article/2005/12/29/AR2005122901585.html>, accessed 29 March 2015.

[43] Priest, 'Covert CIA Program Withstands New Furor'.

[44] Khaled Dawoud, 'Mohammed Atef', *Guardian*, 19 November 2001, available at: <http://www.theguardian.com/news/2001/nov/19/guardianobituaries.afghanistan>, accessed 29 March 2015. See also Mary Ellen O'Connell, 'The Right to Life in War and Peace: A Legal and Moral Critique of Targeted Killing', available at: <https://www.law.upenn.edu/live/files/1634-oconnell-the-right-to-life-in-war-and-peace>, at 5–6, accessed 4 April 2015.

[45] New America Foundation, 'Drone Wars Pakistan: Analysis', available at: <http://securitydata.newamerica.net/drones/pakistan/analysis.html>, accessed 4 April 2015.

[46] 'CIA "killed al-Qaeda suspects" in Yemen', *BBC News*, 5 November 2002, available at: <http://securitydata.newamerica.net/drones/yemen/analysis.html>, accessed 4 April 2015. See also New America Foundation, 'Drone Wars Yemen: Analysis', available at: <http://natsec.newamerica.net/drones/yemen/analysis>, accessed 4 April 2015.

[47] David Smith, 'US Drone Strike in Somalia Kills Top al-Shabaab Explosives Expert', *Guardian*, 29 October 2013, available at: <http://www.theguardian.com/world/2013/oct/29/

being defined as persons not specifically targeted by the strike),[48] with claims that civilian casualties from drone strikes were 'exceedingly rare',[49] and possibly only in 'single digits'[50] since the start of the Obama administration. However, independent investigations have placed civilian casualty numbers much higher than those claimed by the US.[51] Indeed, current estimates place the number of targeted killings conducted by the US, through drones, missiles, or any other method at over 650, with casualties between 3000 and 5000 in total between 2002 and March 2014.[52] Even though active hostilities in Afghanistan were

us-drone-strike-somalia-al-shabaab-expert>, accessed 29 March 2015; Mark Mazzetti and Eric Schmitt, 'US Expands Its Drone War Into Somalia', *New York Times*, 1 July 2011, available at: <http://www.nytimes.com/2011/07/02/world/africa/02somalia.html?pagewanted=all&_r=0>, accessed 29 March 2015.

[48] The Obama administration's Assistant to the President for Homeland Security and Counterterrorism, John O Brennan, claimed in June 2011 that the US had not killed a single civilian since 23 August 2010; see Chris Woods, 'US Claims of "No Civilian Deaths" are Untrue', The Bureau of Investigative Journalism, 18 July 2011, available at: <http://www.thebureauinvestigates.com/2011/07/18/washingtons-untrue-claims-no-civilian-deaths-in-pakistan-drone-strikes/>, accessed 29 March 2015.

[49] John O Brennan, Assistant to the President for Homeland Security and Counterterrorism, 'The Ethics and Efficacy of the President's Counter-Terrorism Strategy', Speech to the Woodrow Wilson International Centre for Scholars, 30 April 2012, available at: <http://www.wilsoncenter.org/event/the-efficacy-and-ethics-us-counterterrorism-strategy>, accessed 29 March 2015.

[50] Jo Becker and Scott Shane, 'Secret "Kill List" Proves a Test of Obama's Principles and Will', *New York Times*, 29 May 2012, available at: <http://www.nytimes.com/2012/05/29/world/obamas-leadership-in-war-on-al-qaeda.html?pagewanted=all>, accessed 29 March 2015.

[51] See, eg, work undertaken by the Bureau of Investigative Journalism: <http://www.thebureauinvestigates.com/category/projects/drones/drones-graphs/>, accessed 4 April 2015; *The Long War Journal*, a project of the Foundation for Defence of Democracies, Bill Roggio and Alexander Mayer, 'Charting the Data for US Airstrikes in Pakistan, 2004–2012', *The Long War Journal*, available at: <http://www.longwarjournal.org/pakistan-strikes>, accessed 4 April 2015; and the Jamestown Foundation, Bryan Glyn Williams, Matthew Fricker, and Avery Plaw, 'New Light on the Accuracy of the CIA's Predator Drone Campaign in Pakistan', *Terrorism Monitor*, 11 November 2010, available at: <http://www.jamestown.org/programs/tm/single/?tx_ttnews%5Btt_news%5D=37165&tx_ttnews%5BbackPid%5D=457&no_cache=1#.UyZRxE3xvxM>, accessed 29 March 2015. See also Scott Shane, 'CIA is Disputed on Civilian Toll in Drone Strikes', *New York Times*, 11 August 2011, available at: <http://www.nytimes.com/2011/08/12/world/asia/12drones.html?pagewanted=all>, accessed 29 March 2015.

[52] These statistics have been collected by the Bureau of Investigative Journalism, which has calculated this total as including both drone strikes against targets and other covert operations. The high end of the statistics puts the number of targeted killings (using all methods) at over 650, with the low end at 560. Casualties from the strikes are estimated at between 3214 and 5172 killed, with injuries between 1312 and 2044, including both those persons targeted and collateral deaths. The statistics can be found at <http://www.thebureauinvestigates.com/category/projects/drones/>, with more on the Bureau's methodology available at: <http://www.thebureauinvestigates.com/2011/08/10/pakistan-drone-strikes-the-methodology2/>, both sites accessed 29 March 2015. The New America Foundation has focused on charting drone and other air strikes only (excluding targeted killings through non-aerial means), and has put figures at 473 strikes in Pakistan and Yemen (no statistics have been collected on strikes in Somalia) with casualties of 2802–4360 deaths (both targeted and collateral civilian deaths). These statistics can be found at:

officially brought to an end in December 2014,[53] reports indicate that drone strikes against al-Qaeda and Taliban forces are continuing in the region.[54]

State Justification for the Practice of Targeted Killing

The common argument forwarded by States to justify targeted killing of terrorist suspects has been twofold. Targeted killings are first justified by recourse to the law on self-defence and the use of force. In the *Targeted Killings* case, Israel justified its policy of targeted killings by employing the terminology of the law on the use of force:

> It is no longer controversial that a state is permitted to respond with military force to a terrorist attack against it. That is pursuant to the right to self defense determined in article 51 of the Charter of the United Nations, which permits a state to defend itself against an 'armed attack'. Even if there is disagreement among experts regarding the question what constitutes an 'armed attack', there can be no doubt that the assault of terrorism against Israel fits the definition of an armed attack. Thus, Israel is permitted to use military force against the terrorist organizations.[55]

The US has similarly claimed the right of self-defence against terrorist attacks. As outlined by Harold Koh, US State Department Legal Adviser, the US justifies its right to engage in targeted killings because the US is 'in an armed conflict with al-Qaeda, as well as the Taliban and associated forces, in response to the horrific 9/11 attacks, and may use force consistent with its inherent right to self-defence under international law.'[56] Indeed, in a 2014 speech at the National Defence University, President Obama employed much the same terminology to justify the US targeted killings program:

<http://securitydata.newamerica.net/about.html>, with more information on their methodology found at: <http://securitydata.newamerica.net/drones/methodology.html>, both sites accessed 4 April 2015. An additional perspective (and dataset) can be found from research undertaken in a joint project by Stanford University and New York University, entitled *Living Under Drones*, which examined drone strikes in Pakistan. See also the statistics collected by Roggio and Mayer for *The Long War Journal*.

[53] See Mark Thompson, 'US Ends its War in Afghanistan', *Time*, 28 December 2014, available at: <http://time.com/3648055/united-states-afghanistan-war-end/>, accessed 29 March 2015.

[54] Jack Serle, 'Obama 2015 Pakistan Drone Strikes', the Bureau of Investigative Journalism, 5 January 2015, available at: <http://www.thebureauinvestigates.com/2015/01/05/obama-2015-pakistan-drone-strikes/>, accessed 29 March 2015.

[55] *Targeted Killings*, at §10.

[56] Harold Koh, 'The Obama Administration and International Law', Keynote Address, 104th Annual Meeting of the American Society of International Law, 'International Law in a Time of Change', 24–27 March 2010, Washington DC, 104 ASIL Proceedings 207 (2010), at 218.

America's actions are legal. We were attacked on 9/11. Within a week, Congress overwhelmingly authorized the use of force. Under domestic law, and international law, the United States is at war with al Qaeda, the Taliban, and their associated forces. We are at war with an organization that right now would kill as many Americans as they could if we did not stop them first. So this is a just war—a war waged proportionally, in last resort, and in self-defense.[57]

The second argument forwarded by States to justify targeted killings has been that the State in question is engaged in a conflict with the non-State group,[58] and that members of that group are taking direct part in hostilities against the targeting state. Therefore, under IHL they are subject to targeting for such participation.[59] In the *Targeted Killings* case, Israel claimed:

since late September 2000, acts of combat and terrorism are being committed against Israel. As a result of those acts, more than one thousand Israeli citizens have been killed during the period from 2000–2005. Thousands more have been wounded. The security forces take various steps in order to confront these acts of combat and terrorism. In light of the armed conflict, the laws applicable to these acts are the laws of war, or the laws of armed conflict, which are part of international law.[60]

Given the existence of an armed conflict, Israel further stated that:

the targeted killings policy is legal... because the laws of armed conflict allow harming civilians taking a direct part in hostilities... a 'civilian' who takes a direct part in hostilities loses his immunity, and can be harmed. Thus, it is permissible to harm civilians in order to frustrate the intent to commit planned or future hostilities. Every person who takes a direct part in committing, planning, or launching hostilities directed against civilian or military targets is a legitimate target for attack. This exception reflects a customary rule of international law.[61]

[57] Remarks by the President at the National Defense University, 23 May 2013, available at: <http://www.whitehouse.gov/the-press-office/2013/05/23/remarks-president-national-defense-university>, accessed 29 March 2015.

[58] See also comments made by the Israel Ministry of Foreign Affairs, stating that Israel is engaged in 'an all-out war against Hamas and other terrorist elements' (Cabinet Communiqué, 1 September 2003, available at: <http://www.mfa.gov.il/mfa/pressroom/2003/pages/cabinet%20communique%20-%201-sep-2003.aspx>, accessed 29 March 2015); see also *Targeted Killings*, at § 2, where the Court observed that 'in its war against terrorism, the State of Israel employs... what it calls "the policy of targeted frustration" of terrorism. Under this policy, the security forces act in order to kill members of terrorist organisations involved in the planning, launching or execution of terrorist attacks against Israel' (the State position is found also at § 10). Similar comments have been made by the US, stating that they consider themselves in an armed conflict against al-Qaeda (see, eg, comments made by President Barack Obama at the National Defense University, where Obama stated that following the 9/11 attacks, the US 'went to war. We have now been at war for well over a decade' (Remarks by the President at the National Defense University)).

[59] Colonel Daniel Reisner, Comments.

[60] *Targeted Killings*, at § 10.

[61] *Targeted Killings*, at §12.

Again, this is echoed in US justifications for its own targeted killings policy, with Harold Koh stating that the US is 'in an armed conflict with al-Qaeda, as well as the Taliban and associated forces'.[62] The White House fact sheet on US Policy Standards and Procedures for the Use of Force in Counterterrorism Operations Outside the United States and Areas of Active Hostilities also states that 'whenever the United States uses force in foreign territories, international legal principles, including respect for sovereignty and the law of armed conflict, impose important constraints on the ability of the United States to act unilaterally—and in the way in which the United States can use force.'[63]

From the perspective of a law of armed conflict, two troubling issues are raised by these justifications. The first is that the terminology of the law on the use of force and of the law of armed conflict seems to be employed in one overarching continuum of justification; that is to say, the terminology is being used interchangeably.[64] This is problematic, from a theoretical perspective at least, in that such conflation of the two bodies of law is contrary to current doctrine which holds that there is fundamental distinction between *jus ad bellum* and *jus in bello*: that a violation of *jus ad bellum* has no bearing on the application of *jus in bello* and that the legal regimes of both must remain distinct. As argued by Giladi, 'a sharp divide between rules on the legality of the use of force and the application of rules limiting the manner in force is used ensures that the former are not used to justify departure from the latter'.[65] As such, it is troubling to see both *jus ad bellum* and *jus in bello* used almost interchangeably to justify the US targeted killings program, as Harold Koh has done.[66]

Indeed, some publicists, such as Laurie Blank, have cautioned against the conflation of the two areas of international law, arguing that the ramifications could be dire:

[62] Koh, 'The Obama Administration and International Law', at 218.

[63] <http://www.whitehouse.gov/the-press-office/2013/05/23/fact-sheet-us-policy-standards-and-procedures-use-force-counterterrorism>, accessed 29 March 2015.

[64] See for instance, Harold Koh's statement that the US is 'in an armed conflict with al-Qaeda, as well as the Taliban and associated forces, in response to the horrific 9/11 attacks, and may use force consistent with its inherent right to self-defence under international law' (Koh, 'The Obama Administration and International Law', at 218). See also comments by John Brennan, who stated that 'as a matter of international law, the United States is in an armed conflict with al-Qaida [*sic*], the Taliban, and associated forces, in response to the 9/11 attacks, and we may also use force consistent with our inherent right of national self-defense.' ('The Ethics and Efficacy of the President's Counter-Terrorism Strategy').

[65] Rotem Giladi, 'The Jus Ad Bellum/Jus In Bello Distinction and the Law of Occupation', 41 Israel L Rev 246 (2008), at 247.

[66] Koh, 'The Obama Administration and International Law', at 218.

the basic principle that the rights and obligations of *jus in bello* apply regardless of the justness or unjustness of the overall military operation…remains firmly entrenched. Indeed, if the cause at arms influences a state's obligation to abide by the laws regulating the means and methods of warfare and requiring protection of civilian persons *hors de combat*, states would justify all departures from *jus in bello* with reference to the purported justness of their cause. The result: an invitation to unregulated warfare.[67]

This mutable spectrum of justifications for the use of force, incorporating both the language of *jus ad bellum* and *jus in bello*, could indeed lead to a devaluing of the regimes or the importation of the principles of one body of law into the other, resulting in the application of the laws in problematic, if not outright incorrect, ways. As Blank notes, the blurring of the laws of armed conflict, use of force, and human rights in targeted killings threatens to undermine the intent and effect of all three bodies of law, arguing that 'the potential spillover between status-based targeting and direct participation in the armed conflict framework and imminence and necessity (but without belligerent nexus) in the self-defence framework provoke…consternation with regard to the protection and discriminating purposes of both bodies of law.'[68]

The *jus ad bellum/jus in bello* conflation is, for the most part, a theoretical concern. Neither the US nor Israel has asserted outright that 'a legitimate act of self-defence *within* armed conflict does not have to comply with the requirements of IHL.'[69] Thus, concerns about the blurring of the lines between *jus ad bellum* and *jus in bello* leading to the outright elimination of the protections of IHL have, perhaps, been premature.

However, what is genuinely troubling is the apparent criteria being used to determine who may be targeted and whether IHL is the relevant legal framework at all. Are these persons targetable due to DPH, or are they civilians

[67] Laurie Blank, 'Targeted Strikes: The Consequences of Blurring the Armed Conflict and Self-Defence Justifications', 38 William Mitchell L Rev 1655 (2011), at 1659. See also Geoffrey Corn, 'Self Defense Targeting: Conflict Classification or Wilful Blindness?', 88 International Law Studies (2012), at 12, who also notes the dangers in conflating *jus ad bellum* and *jus in bello* in counter-terror operations.

[68] Blank, 'Targeted Strikes', at 1697–98.

[69] Kevin Jon Heller, '"One Hell of a Killing Machine": Signature Strikes and International Law', 11 JICJ 89 (2013), at 91. However, see Kenneth Anderson, who argues that a targeted killing in an armed conflict situation does not need to comply with IHL, as the 'proper international legal rationale for targeted killing is self-defence, not that the target is a combatant under IHL.' (Kenneth Anderson, 'Targeted Killing in US Counterterrorism Strategy and Law, Working Paper of the Series on Counterterrorism and American Statutory Law', a joint project of the Brookings Institution, the Georgetown University Law Center, and the Hoover Institution, 11 May 2009, at 18, available at: <http://www.brookings.edu/~/media/research/files/papers/2009/5/11%20counterterrorism%20anderson/0511_counterterrorism_anderson.pdf>, accessed 29 March 2015.

immune from targeting? Is the targeting a lawful act covered by IHL, or is this a case where IHL does not apply, and these are extra-judicial executions covered by IHRL? While the killing of individuals 'not in the physical custody' of the targeting state or entity is a foreseen and integral part of the conduct of armed conflicts and permissible under IHL, if the campaign against terrorist organizations does *not* fall under the IHL framework, such targeted killings would seem to violate the IHRL principles on the right to life and fair trial, and would amount to an 'extra-judicial execution'.[70] Furthermore, if the prevailing law is indeed IHL, what are the targeting criteria being employed? It is these issues that will be explored in the rest of this chapter.

Is IHL the Appropriate Law?

The practice of targeted killings of al-Qaeda, Taliban, and associated forces by the US has raised questions as to whether such targeting is to be considered part of an 'armed conflict' with al-Qaeda, or whether the targeting of such persons is actually an extra-territorial, extra-judicial assassination, which would mean that IHL is not the prevailing standard to apply but rather IHRL. If this is correct, then the persons being targeted are not civilians targeted due to their DPH but rather civilians who are lawfully entitled to protection under IHRL. Resolving this question depends, in part, on how one conceptualizes armed conflict and, specifically, whether there are geographical limits to an armed conflict. Is the conflict with al-Qaeda an armed conflict? If it is, just how far, geographically, does that conflict extend?

The US has argued that it is in an armed conflict with al-Qaeda, and that it conducts its activities in compliance with the law of armed conflict.[71] However, this position seems to run counter to a number of expert opinions which state categorically that the struggle against terrorism should not be regulated under the law of armed conflict. As noted by Christopher Greenwood:

> In the language of international law there is no basis for speaking of a war on Al-Qaeda or any other terrorist group, for such a group cannot be a belligerent, it is merely a band of criminals, and to treat it as anything else risks distorting the law while giving that group a status which to some implies a degree of legitimacy.[72]

[70] See Blum and Heymann, 'Law and Policy of Targeted Killings', at 147.

[71] Koh, 'The Obama Administration and International Law', at 218.

[72] Christopher Greenwood, 'War, Terrorism and International Law', 56 Current Legal Problems 505 (2004), at 529.

This position is supported by Mary Ellen O'Connell, who asserts that 'terrorism is crime. Members of al Qaeda or other terrorist groups are active in Canada, France, Germany, Indonesia, Morocco, Saudi Arabia, Spain, the United Kingdom, Yemen and elsewhere. Still, these countries do not consider themselves in a war with al Qaeda.'[73] Indeed, the UK has stated as such: 'It is the understanding of the United Kingdom that the term "armed conflict" of itself and in its context denotes a situation of a kind which is not constituted by the commission of ordinary crimes including acts of terrorism whether concerted or in isolation.'[74]

The generally accepted[75] definition of armed conflict was stated by the International Criminal Tribunal for the former Yugoslavia (ICTY) in the *Tadić* case as 'whenever there is resort to armed force between States or protracted armed violence between governmental authorities and organised armed groups or between such groups within a State'.[76] The *Tadić* position refutes the possibility of terrorist activities being regulated under IHL.[77] This position is supported by the Venice Commission, which stated that:

> 'Armed conflict' in the sense of International Humanitarian Law refers to protracted armed violence between States or between governmental authorities and/or organised armed groups within a State... sporadic bombings and other violent acts which terrorist networks perpetrate in different places around the globe and the ensuing counter-terrorism measures, even if they are occasionally undertaken by military

[73] Mary Ellen O'Connell, 'Lawful Use of Combat Drones', Testimony to the US House of Representatives Subcommittee on National Security and Foreign Affairs, Hearing 'Rise of the Drones II: Examining the Legality of Unmanned Targeting', 28 April 2010, available at: <https://www.fas.org/irp/congress/2010_hr/042810oconnell.pdf>, at 4, accessed 29 March 2015.

[74] Reservation by the United Kingdom to Art. 1(4) and Art. 96, API; see also Marco Sassòli, 'Use and Abuse of the Laws of War in the "War on Terrorism"', 22 Law & Ineq 195 (2004).

[75] See the International Law Association (ILA) Committee on the Use of Force, *Final Report on the Meaning of Armed Conflict in International Law*, delivered at The Hague Conference (2010), available at: <http://www.ila-hq.org/download.cfm/docid/2176DC63-D268-4133-8989A664754F9F87>, at 14, accessed 4 April 2015; Art. 8 of the Rome Statute of the International Criminal Court; the European Commission for Democracy through Law (Venice Commission), Opinion on the International Legal Obligations of Council of Europe Member States in Respect of Secret Detention Facilities and Inter-State Transport of Prisoners, 17 March 2006, Op. No. 363/2005, CDL-AD (2006)009 (hereinafter the Venice Commission), available at: <http://www.venice.coe.int/webforms/documents/CDL-AD(2006)009.aspx>, accessed 29 March 2015.

[76] *Tadić*, Interlocutory Appeal, at para. 70.

[77] *Tadić*, Interlocutory Appeal, at para. 562; for other cases in the ICTY that affirmed this reasoning, see also *Prosecutor v Blagojević and Jokić*, Case No. IT-02-60-T, Judgment, 17 January 2005, at para. 536; *Prosecutor v Halilović*, Case No. IT-01-48-T, Judgment, 16 November 2005, at para. 24; *Prosecutor v Limaj et al.*, Case No IT-03-66-T, Trial Judgment, 30 November 2005, at para. 84; *Galić*, at para. 9; *Prosecutor v Stakić*, Case No. IT-97-24-T, Judgment, 31 July 2003, at paras 566–68.

units, cannot be said to amount to an 'armed conflict' in the sense that they trigger the applicability of IHL. The Venice Commission considers that counter-terrorist measures which are part of what has sometimes been called 'war on terror' are not part of an 'armed conflict' in the sense of making the regime of IHL applicable to them.[78]

As such, under such reasoning a terrorist attack, 'regardless of how serious the consequences, is not an armed conflict',[79] although such attacks may trigger a right to resort to armed force in self-defence.[80] Therefore, if a targeted killing occurs outside the context of an armed conflict, IHRL is the applicable[81] framework in which to analyse its legality, as '[t]errorist attacks generally have the hallmarks of crime; not armed attacks that give rise to the right of self-defence... terrorist attacks are usually sporadic, and they are rarely the responsibility of the state where the perpetrators are located.'[82]

[78] Venice Commission, at paras 78–79, citing the *British Manual of the Law of Armed Conflict*, at 31, para. 3.5.1.

[79] Mary Ellen O'Connell, 'The Constitutional and Human Right to Life in War and Peace', Testimony to the House Judiciary Committee, Hearing on Protecting US Citizens' Constitutional Rights During the War on Terrorism, 22 May 2013, available at: <http://docs.house.gov/meetings/JU/JU00/20130522/100888/HHRG-113-JU00-Wstate-OConnellM-20130522.pdf>, accessed 29 March 2015. See also JJ Paust, who argues that the US 'under traditional international law...cannot be at war or involved in any form of armed conflict with al Qaeda' ('Propriety of Self-Defense Targetings of Members of al-Qaeda and Applicable Principles of Distinction and Proportionality', 18 ILSA J Int'l & Comp L 565 (2012), at 566.

[80] For more on the legality of targeted killings in the context of *jus ad bellum*, see JJ Paust, 'Permissible Self-Defence Targeting and the Death of bin Laden', 39 Denv J Int'l L & Pol'y 569 (2011); Michael Schmitt, 'Extraterritorial Lethal Targeting: Deconstructing the Logic of International Law', 52 Colum J Transnat'l L 79 (2013); Gabriella Blum and Philip Heymann, 'Law and Policy of Targeted Killing'; David Kretzmer, 'Targeted Killing of Suspected Terrorists: Extra-Judicial Executions or Legitimate Means of Defence?', 16 EJIL 171 (2005).

[81] Michael Lewis, 'Drones and the Boundaries of the Battlefield', 47 Texas Int'l L J 293 (2011–12), at 299; Jeff Bovarnick, *et al.*, *The Law of War Deskbook*, International and Operational Law Department, The United States Army Judge Advocate General's Legal Center and School, available at: <http://www.loc.gov/rr/frd/Military_Law/pdf/LOW-Deskbook-2011.pdf>, at 207, accessed 29 March 2015.

[82] Mary Ellen O'Connell, 'Remarks: The Resort to Drones under International Law', 39 Denv J Int'l L & Pol'y 585 (2010–11), at 593; see also Susan Breau, Marie Aronsson, and Rachel Joyce, 'Drone Attacks, International Law and the Recording of Civilian Casualties of Armed Conflict', Oxford Research Group Discussion Paper 2, 1 June 2011, available at: <http://www.oxfordresearchgroup.org.uk/publications/briefing_papers_and_reports/discussion_paper_2>, accessed 29 March 2015. The authors state that 'those attacks that take place outside of the geographical area of armed conflict are extra-judicial killings contrary to international Human Rights Law and domestic criminal law unless the persons involved were killed while trying to evade lawful capture' (at 2). It should be noted that the existence of an armed conflict does not preclude the applicability of human rights norms; this was affirmed by the ICJ in *Legal Consequences of the Construction of a Wall in the Occupied Palestinian Territory* (Advisory Opinion) [2004] ICJ Rep, 136, at para. 139 (hereinafter *The Wall*), at paras 102–06 and *Nuclear Weapons*, at para. 25.

Indeed, even if IHL is the applicable *lex specialis*, IHRL will still be significant because, as was stated by the International Court of Justice (ICJ) in the advisory opinions of *The Wall* and *Nuclear Weapons*, it can apply concurrently to complement IHL in situations of armed conflict.[83] As such, whether the targeting of persons is permissible under IHL needs also to be considered in relation to the relevant IHRL principles, which will be discussed in this next section.

IHRL and targeted killing

Under IHRL all persons have an 'inherent' non-derogable right to life.[84] This right is not absolute: some of the IHRL treaties, such as the International Covenant on Civil and Political Rights (ICCPR),[85] the American Convention on Human Rights,[86] and the African Charter of Human and People's Rights[87] qualify the right by prohibiting the 'arbitrary' deprivation of life.[88] The European Convention for the Protection of Human Rights and Fundamental Freedoms (European Convention)[89] refers to the right not to be 'intentionally'[90] deprived of life, but states that such deprivation of life will not be unlawful if it results from the proportional use of force which is no more than absolutely necessary in certain cases, including 'defence of any persons from unlawful violence.'[91] As such, under IHRL, the deprivation of life will not be *prima facie* illegal if it is required to protect life from an imminent threat, which thus makes the deprivation of life proportional. There also must be no other means to protect against the imminent threat, such as capture or non-lethal incapacitation, which thus makes the deprivation of life necessary.[92] Any law enforcement activities, including

[83] See *Nuclear Weapons*, at para. 25; and *The Wall*, at paras 102–06; see also related comments to this effect by the UN Human Rights Committee, General Comment 29, States of Emergency (Art. 4), UN Doc. CCPR/C/21/Rev.1/Add.11 (2001), at para. 3; Concluding Observations of ECOSOC: Israel, 31/8/2001, at E/C.12/1/Add.69.

[84] Art. 6, International Covenant on Civil and Political Rights, 999 UNTS 171 (hereinafter ICCPR).

[85] Art. 6, ICCPR.

[86] 1144 UNTS 1239.

[87] OAU Doc. CAB/LEG/67/3 rev. 5, 21 ILM 58.

[88] Art. 6(1), ICCPR; Art. 4, American Convention on Human Rights; Art. 4, African Charter of Human and Peoples' Rights.

[89] 213 UNTS 231 (hereinafter European Convention).

[90] European Convention, Art. 2(1).

[91] European Convention, Art. 2(2).

[92] See Phillip Alston, *Interim Report on the Worldwide Situation in Regard to Extrajudicial, Summary or Arbitrary Executions* (2006) UN Doc. A/61/311, at paras 33–45; UN Human Rights Committee, General Comment No. 6 on the Right to Life, HRI/GEN/1/Rev.6 (1982), at para. 3; and the Inter-American Commission on Human Rights, *Report on Terrorism and Human Rights*, OEA/Ser.L/V/II.116, Doc.5, rev. 1, corr, (2002), at paras 86–92.

counter-terrorism measures, must be carried out in compliance with these basic IHRL principles.

At first glance, US justifications for targeted killings would seem to fulfil these criteria. The Obama Administration has stated that:

> lethal force will not be proposed or pursued as punishment or as a substitute for prosecuting a terrorist suspect in a civilian court or a military commission. Lethal force will be used only to prevent or stop attacks against US persons, and even then, only when capture is not feasible and no other reasonable alternatives exist to address the threat effectively.[93]

However, when one examines the pertinent IHRL rules in more detail, tensions emerge between the practice of targeted killing and IHRL. When dealing with any persons under IHRL, even those suspected of planning acts of violence, the 'fundamental assumption'[94] is that a law enforcement model prevails, as do the principles of due process. Therefore, as Kretzmer argues, the following fundamental principles must be observed at all times:

> (1) every individual benefits from the presumption of innocence; (2) persons suspected of perpetrating or planning serious criminal acts should be arrested, detained and interrogated with due process of law; and (3) if there is credible evidence that such persons were indeed involved in planning, promoting, aiding and abetting or carrying out terrorist acts they should be afforded a fair trial before a competent and independent court and, if convicted, sentenced by the court to a punishment provided by law.[95]

Given such a framework, the fundamental objective of a targeted killing—the intentional and premeditated killing of a person not in the custody of the targeting state—does not appear to be lawful under IHRL in any circumstances. This was noted by Philip Alston, who stated that under IHRL, 'unlike in armed conflict, it is never permissible for killing to be the *sole objective* of an operation.'[96]

A complication arises, however, when one looks at the question of jurisdiction under IHRL. Under the ICCPR, parties to the Covenant are obliged to respect and ensure the rights enshrined in the ICCPR 'to all individuals in its territory and subject to its jurisdiction.'[97] The very nature of targeted killings

[93] Fact Sheet, US Policy Standards and Procedures for the Use of Force in Counterterrorism Operations Outside the United States and Areas of Active Hostilities, The White House, Office of the Press Secretary, 23 May 2013, available at: <http://www.whitehouse.gov/the-press-office/2013/05/23/fact-sheet-us-policy-standards-and-procedures-use-force-counterterrorism>, accessed 29 March 2015.

[94] Kretzmer, 'Targeted Killing of Suspected Terrorists', at 178.

[95] Kretzmer, 'Targeted Killing of Suspected Terrorists', at 178.

[96] Alston, *Study on Targeted Killings*, at 11 (emphasis in original).

[97] Art. 2(1), ICCPR.

is that the targets are *not* within the territory of the targeting State, nor (usually) subject to its jurisdiction. Therefore, how can States, seeking to prevent the commission of an act of violence, respect and observe the due process norms of arrest, detention, and trial for suspected terrorists when they are beyond the territorial reach of the targeting State? As Kretzmer argues:

> the problem with the law enforcement model in the context of transnational terror is that one of its fundamental premises is invalid: that the suspected perpetrator is within the jurisdiction of the law-enforcement authorities in the victim state, so that an arrest can be effected. What is the situation when... the terrorist is in the territory of another state? The victim state may not arrest or apprehend that person without the active assistance and support of that other state. But what if that state is either unwilling to arrest the suspected terrorist or incapable of doing so?[98]

This raises the issue of the extra-territorial applicability of IHRL: can human rights obligations exist for the actions of States beyond their territorial control? Can States such as the US still be bound by IHRL norms for targeted killings carried out in Yemen or Somalia, areas far removed from the 'active hostilities'[99] in Afghanistan?

Extra-territorial applicability of IHRL was examined by the European Court of Human Rights (ECtHR) in a number of cases, the first significant case being *Banković v Belgium*.[100] In that case, the ECtHR took a narrow view on jurisdiction, stating that a party to the European Convention exercises jurisdiction only within its own territory, except in two cases: one, where the State exercises some or all of the powers of government in the territory of another State with its consent, invitation, or acquiescence; and two, where the State is an occupying power exercising effective control.[101] The question of the extraterritorial application of the European Convention was then examined in the ECtHR decisions of *Al-Skeini*[102] and *Al-Jedda*.[103] In *Al-Skeini*, the Court reaffirmed the 'exceptional' nature of instances of

[98] Kretzmer, 'Targeted Killing of Suspected Terrorists', at 179.

[99] Fact Sheet, US Policy Standards and Procedures for the Use of Force in Counterterrorism Operations.

[100] *Banković v Belgium*, 11 BHRC 435 (2000).

[101] *Banković*, at § 59–61; see also *Loizidou v Turkey*, 23 *EHRR* 513 (1996), at § 52; and *The Wall*, at para. 139. The decision in *Banković* has been subject to much criticism, with Marko Milanović criticising the result as the product of 'the Court's less than transparent weighing of competing policy considerations, and its ultimate desire to come up with a superficial, legalistic rationale that would justify making the extraterritorial application of the ECHR exceptional. Deciding the case in late 2001, in the immediate wake of 9/11, the Court was understandably torn between considerations of universality and effectiveness', Marko Milanović, 'Al-Skeini and Al-Jedda in Strasbourg', 23 EJIL 121 (2012), at 123.

[102] *Al-Skeini and others v United Kingdom*, App No. 55721/07, 7 July 2011.

[103] *Al-Jedda v United Kingdom*, App No. 27021/08, 7 July 2011.

extra-territorial application of the European Convention,[104] expanding on *Banković* by adding the idea of state jurisdiction triggered by a State's agent's personal control and authority over an individual.[105] Thus, in *Al-Skeini*, the Court held that for the purposes of the Convention, 'whenever a state through its agents exercises control and authority over an individual, and thus jurisdiction, the state is under an obligation under Article 1 to secure to that individual the rights and freedoms under [the Convention]'.[106]

However, the European Court stressed that the extra-territorial scope of the European Convention was still exceptional. The Court had to find that the UK had spatial jurisdiction and that it exercised public powers in parts of Iraq in order to find the personal control of individuals that was grounds for jurisdiction in *Al-Skeini*. Using the *Al-Skeini* reasoning, if the original spatial jurisdiction does not exist, logically personal jurisdiction cannot be found either. As Milanović puts it:

> while the ability to kill is 'authority and control' over the individual if the state has public powers, killing is not authority and control if the state is merely firing missiles from an aircraft. Under this reasoning, drone operations in Yemen or wherever would be just as excluded from the purview of human rights treaties as under *Banković*.[107]

With such a narrow scope of application, it seems questionable whether IHRL norms apply to terrorists targeted beyond the borders of the targeting State.[108]

As a final note, in regards to IHRL and targeted killing, the proportionality and necessity elements regarding a 'non-arbitrary' deprivation of life under IHRL warrant mention: how imminent must the threat of violence be before a deprivation of life will be considered 'non-arbitrary'? If 'there is strong evidence that a suspected terrorist is preparing or planning a terrorist attack against residents of the victim state, will a pre-emptive attack be regarded as an arbitrary deprivation of his life, if there was no reasonable way of apprehending or arresting him?'[109] One must query the degree to which the persons in question present an imminent threat justifying a lethal response under IHRL, specifically if such persons

[104] *Al-Skeini*, at paras 133–42.

[105] *Banković* admitted only a spatial model of jurisdiction, where a state has effective control over an area; *Banković*, at para. 71. See also Milanović, 'Al-Skeini and Al-Jedda in Strasbourg', at 122.

[106] *Al-Skeini*, at para. 137.

[107] Milanović, 'Al-Skeini and Al-Jedda in Strasbourg', at 130.

[108] See, eg, Gerald Neuman, 'Humanitarian Law and Counter-Terrorist Force', 14 EJIL 283 (2003).

[109] Kretzmer, 'Targeted Killing of Suspected Terrorists', at 180.

are outside the territorial control of the State acting in self-defence. In certain rare circumstances, such as remote detonation of an explosive located extra-territorially from the bomber, arguably lethal force could be used. The more 'conventional' examples, such as the employment of non-remote explosive devices, would most likely not allow for extra-territorial use of lethal force under human rights law.

However, the Human Rights Committee has said that while a targeted killing for the purposes of deterrence or punishment would be a violation of Article 6 of the ICCPR, the use of deadly force against a 'person suspected of being in the process of committing acts of terror'[110] would not necessarily be illegal provided that 'before resorting to the use of deadly force, all measures to arrest a person suspected of being in the process of committing acts of terror must be exhausted.'[111] As such, one would need to determine whether the subject of a targeted killing was indeed in the process of committing an act of terror, and whether 'all measures to arrest' had been exhausted.

If IHL is the Appropriate Law

However, even if one does not accept the applicability of IHRL to targeted killings, or, in the alternative, that IHRL applies but IHL is the prevailing *lex specialis*, problems still remain with the practice of targeted killing. Indeed, if one accepts the Israel and US position that they *are* involved in an armed conflict with terrorist organizations, that there is 'protracted, large-scale violence',[112] that terrorist organizations, such as al-Qaeda, comprise an 'organised insurgent group',[113] and that members of al-Qaeda are targetable due

[110] UN Human Rights Committee, Concluding Observations of the Human Rights Committee on Report of Israel, 21 August 2003, CCPR/CO/78/ISR, at [15].

[111] UN Human Rights Committee, Concluding Observations of the Human Rights Committee on Report of Israel, at [15]. The ambiguity regarding what amounts to 'exhausting all measures for arrest prior to the use of lethal force' persists, and must be resolved on a case-by-case basis. An example can be seen in the decision of the ECtHR in *McCann v UK* (Application no. 18984/91), in which the Court was divided on the issue of the legality of the use of lethal force against suspects who may be about to detonate a remote explosive device. The Court was in agreement regarding the right to use lethal force if doing so was absolutely necessary in order to defend of persons from unlawful violence (at §§ 134–35, 148, 200). However, the Court could not come to a consensus position on a number of other issues, including the question of the practicality of arresting terrorist suspects (at § 11). The minority in *McCann* noted that 'it would be wrong to conclude in retrospect that a particular course would, as things later transpired, have been better than one adopted at the time under the pressures of an on-going anti-terrorist operation' (at § 8).

[112] *Tadić*, Interlocutory Appeal, at para. 70.

[113] *Tadić*, Interlocutory Appeal, at para. 70. See also the ICTY in *Kordić and Čerkez*, at 341, regarding the meaning of 'protracted', as excluding single acts of terrorism in non-international

to their DPH, the practice of targeted killing, as carried out by the US, is still problematic for a number of reasons. First, questions have arisen as to whether the conflict with al-Qaeda allows the US to target al-Qaeda members wherever they are located in the world, regardless of whether those locations are the site of 'active hostilities'. Secondly, US targeting criteria in targeted killings raise concerns as to whether those being targeted are actually persons taking direct part in hostilities. These issues will be examined in this next section.

The geographical scope of armed conflict

One of the issues raised by commentators regarding the practice of targeted killing has been the legality of targeted killings beyond the scope of 'active' hostilities. Some have argued that IHL only applies in very specific areas; that is, where there are active, ongoing armed hostilities.[114] Thus, beyond the scope of such hostilities, IHL does not apply and the relevant law is IHRL. As Lewis notes:

> the laws of armed conflict cannot apply in a place where there is no armed conflict, and the determination of whether an armed conflict exists is based upon the intensity of the violence occurring there and the organisation of the forces involved, as laid out in the *Tadić* opinion... if the *Tadić* threshold is not met, the laws of armed conflict do not apply there. In IHL's absence IHRL would apply, as would the law enforcement restrictions on lethal force... if the strict geographic approach to defining IHL's scope... is accepted, then [targeted killing]... would be considered illegal everywhere outside Afghanistan.[115]

Indeed, this approach would seem to correlate with the outcomes of the International Law Association (ILA) expert study designed to clarify the definition of armed conflict and its geographical scope, which stated that armed conflict exists where the fighting or hostilities actually take place, and that States

armed conflicts; and the ICRC Direct Participation in Hostilities Interpretive Guidance (DPHIG), which refers to organized armed groups as those that 'develop a sufficient degree of military organisation to conduct hostilities on behalf of a party to the conflict, albeit not always the same means, intensity and level of sophistication of State armed forces' (DPHIG, at 1006).

[114] See, eg, the arguments put forward by the plaintiff in *Al-Aulaqi v Obama*, 727 F. Supp 2d 1, 9 (DDC 2010), specifically that because Anwar al-Aulaqi was located in Yemen he was 'outside the context of armed conflict' and thus not targetable. This argument has also been forwarded by Mary Ellen O'Connell (in 'Combatants and the Combat Zone', 43 U Rich L Rev 845 (2009), at 860–64), and by ACLU lawyer Hina Shamsi following the April 2014 dismissal of *Al-Aulaqi v Obama*, who noted the oddity of a government that 'claims to be at war, even far from any battlefield' (quoted in Will Dunham, 'Lawsuit over American drone strikes dismissed by U.S. judge', Reuters, 4 April 2014, available at: <http://www.reuters.com/article/2014/04/05/us-usa-courts-drones-idUSBREA331YF20140405>, accessed 4 April 2015).

[115] Lewis, 'Drones and the Boundaries of the Battlefield', at 301.

'rarely recognise armed conflict beyond the zone of intense fighting, whether the fighting is in an international or non-international armed conflict'.[116] In coming to this conclusion, the ILA examined State practice regarding the geographical extent of hostilities, decisions from the ICTY,[117] and the writings of publicists such as Christopher Greenwood, who has stated that 'military operations will not normally be conducted throughout the area of war. The area in which operations are actually taking place at any given time is known as the "area of operations" or "theatre of war" ... it cannot be assumed ... that a state engaged in armed conflict is free to attack its adversary anywhere in the area of war.'[118]

If one takes the position that extra-territorial targeting beyond the 'so-called hot battlefield'[119] is *not* permitted under the law of armed conflict, US targeted killings could be justifiable only as necessary and proportionate measures of self-defence in territory where the State in question has been unwilling or unable to prevent serious infringements of its neutrality,[120] or where such use of force has been 'permitted',[121] rather than as acts conducted as part of the active hostilities in Afghanistan. Indeed, one can see how the US has increasingly moved

[116] ILA, *Final Report on the Meaning of Armed Conflict in International Law*, at 32.

[117] See *Tadić*, Interlocutory Appeal, at para. 70.

[118] Christopher Greenwood, 'Scope of Application of International Humanitarian Law', in Dieter Fleck (ed.), *The Handbook of International Humanitarian Law* (2nd edn, OUP, 2008), at 61–62. (Note: Greenwood's chapter was included in the second edition of the *Handbook*, but was replaced in the third edition by a chapter on the scope of IHL by Jann Kleffner. This is the only reference to the second edition of Fleck in this book.)

[119] Jens David Ohlin, 'The Duty to Capture', 97 Minn L Rev 1268 (2013), at 1287.

[120] The ICJ has said that a State may exercise self-defence against non-State actors operating within the territory of another State only where the actions of the non-State actor can be imputed to the host State. *The Wall*, at 136; see also *Armed Activities on the Territory of the Congo (Democratic Republic of the Congo v Uganda)*, Judgment, [2005] ICJ Rep 168, at 223, where the Court failed to address the issue, after finding that cross-border attacks by non-State actors in the Democratic Republic of the Congo (DRC) against Uganda could not be attributed to the DRC. As such, the Court felt there was no need to consider whether this gave rise to a right of self-defence against such non-State actors; however, see the minority decisions by Judge Kooijmans (at 311–15) and Judge Simma (at 335–37) which criticized the failure of the majority to address the issue). However, the US has claimed that there needs to be no link between the non-State actor and the host State, only that the State in question is either unwilling or unable to prevent its territory being used to launch attacks against another State (see the Fact Sheet: *US Policy Standards and Procedures for the Use of Force*). See further Ashley Deeks, 'Unwilling or Unable: Toward a Normative Framework for Extra-Territorial Self-Defence', 5 Va J Int'l L 483 (2012).

[121] As noted by the Special Rapporteur on the Promotion and Protection of Human Rights and Fundamental Freedoms While Countering Terrorism, Ben Emmerson, 'a State's valid consent to the use of force by another State on its territory precludes any claim that its territorial sovereignty has been violated' (Promotion and Protection of Human Rights and Fundamental Freedoms While Countering Terrorism, 18 September 2013, UN Doc A/68/389), at 14, para. 51; see also Philip Alston, Report of the Special Rapporteur on Extrajudicial, Summary or Arbitrary Executions, UN Doc A/HRC/14/24/Add.6, at paras 37–38. Emmerson notes that in the case of Yemen, the 'United States routinely seeks prior consent, on a case-by-case basis, for lethal remote piloted aircraft operations on its territory ... where consent is withheld, a strike will not go ahead'

to justify its targeted killings as legitimate under the law relating to the use of force, with the law of armed conflict being used to assure compliance with its norms, where relevant and applicable.[122] That active hostilities have been formally terminated in Afghanistan as of December 2014 makes this move from IHL terminology to *jus ad bellum* terminology more understandable.[123]

However, to argue that *Tadić*, and IHL more generally, can only apply in the geographic regions of active hostilities and nowhere else would seem to ignore significant portions of the law of armed conflict intended to apply beyond the 'hot battlefield'. As publicists such as Ohlin have argued:

> it would be absurd if a state party could circumvent the Geneva restrictions on POW treatment if it moved the prisoner to an outlying district away from the battlefield... [*Tadić* affirms that] the notion of armed conflict should be applied broadly in both time and space, beyond the zone of intense fighting, to events that are causally connected to that intense fighting, until such time as a lasting peace is accomplished and the conflict is completed.[124]

Indeed, a narrow approach to the geographical applicability of IHL would seem to misconceive or ignore one of the fundamental points of the *Tadić* decision, where the Chamber stated that:

> international humanitarian law applies from the initiation of such armed conflicts and extends beyond the cessation of hostilities until a general conclusion of peace is reached; or, in the case of internal conflicts, a peaceful settlement is achieved. Until that moment, international humanitarian law continued to apply in the whole territory of the warring States or, in the case of internal conflicts, the whole territory under the control of a party, whether or not actual combat takes place there.[125]

Under such reasoning, US targeted killings of al-Qaeda operatives in Yemen and Somalia were causally connected to the conflict with al-Qaeda in Afghanistan and as such were legal under IHL. What would be necessary to prove, however, is whether al-Qaeda and its affiliates were parties 'in control' of territory. This could be possible in some regions: with al-Qaeda affiliate al-Shabaab in control of territory in southern Somalia,[126] and al-Qaeda in the

(at 15, para. 52). Emmerson also notes that there is strong evidence to suggest that such consent to strike existed regarding strikes in Pakistan (at 15, para. 53).

[122] Fact Sheet, US Policy Standards and Procedures for the Use of Force.

[123] 'U.S. and NATO Formally End War in Afghanistan', *New York Times*, 28 December 2014, available at: <http://www.nytimes.com/aponline/2014/12/28/world/asia/ap-as-afghanistan.html?_r=0>, accessed 29 March 2015.

[124] Ohlin, 'Duty to Capture', at 1290.

[125] *Tadić*, Interlocutory Appeal, at para. 70.

[126] 'The State of Al-Qaeda: The Unquenchable Fire', *The Economist*, 28 September 2013, available at: <http://www.economist.com/news/briefing/21586834-adaptable-and-resilient-al-qaeda-and-its-allies-keep-bouncing-back-unquenchable-fire>, accessed 29 March 2015; David Smith, 'Al-Shabaab

Arabian Peninsula (AQAP) holding territory in Yemen.[127] Former al-Qaeda affiliate ISIS has control of territory in Syria and Iraq,[128] and the Taliban also controls portions of Pakistan, which could justify strikes in those areas.[129] It seems probable that al-Qaeda and its associated forces would be likely to meet the organizational requirement necessary for meeting the *Tadić* test of 'protracted armed violence between governmental authorities and organised armed groups or between such groups within a State'.[130] It also seems that al-Qaeda does maintain a degree of organization and command structure, and it clearly engages in violence against the US.[131] The question would remain whether the violence could be classified as 'protracted'.[132] However, given the official 'end' of active hostilities in Afghanistan, such

Rebuilds Forces in Somalia as African Union Campaign Stalls', *Guardian*, 29 October 2013, available at: <http://www.theguardian.com/world/2013/oct/28/al-shabaab-somalia-african-union>, accessed 4 April 2015; Johnathan Masters, 'Backgrounder: Al-Shabab', The Council on Foreign Relations, available at: <http://www.cfr.org/somalia/al-shabab/p18650#p7>, accessed 29 March 2015.

[127] 'The State of Al-Qaeda'; Daniel Green, 'Al-Qaeda's Shadow Government in Yemen', Policy Watch 2181, The Washington Institute, available at: <http://www.washingtoninstitute.org/policy-analysis/view/al-qaedas-shadow-government-in-yemen>, accessed 29 March 2015; Yoram Schweitzer and Yoel Guzansky, 'Al-Qaeda and (In)Stability in Yemen', INSS Insight 501, 24 December 2013, available at: <http://www.inss.org.il/index.aspx?id=4538&articleid=6283>, accessed 29 March 2015.

[128] Now known as the Islamic State (previously the Islamic State of Iraq and Syria or the Islamic State of Iraq and the Levant); see further Peter Bergen and Jennifer Rowland, 'Al Qaeda Controls More Territory than Ever in Middle East', *CNN*, 8 January 2014, available at: <http://edition.cnn.com/2014/01/07/opinion/bergen-al-qaeda-terrority-gains/>, accessed 29 March 2015; Brett McGurk, Deputy Assistant Secretary for Iran and Iraq, Bureau of Near Eastern Affairs, Testimony to the US House of Representatives Foreign Affairs Committee, 'Al-Qaeda's Resurgence in Iraq: A Threat to U.S. Interests', available at: <http://www.state.gov/p/nea/rls/rm/221274.htm>, accessed 29 March 2015. However, the Islamic State was disavowed by al-Qaeda; see further Mark Tran, 'Who Are Isis? A Terror Group Too Extreme Even for Al-Qaida', *Guardian*, 11 June 2014, available at: <http://www.theguardian.com/world/2014/jun/11/isis-too-extreme-al-qaida-terror-jihadi>, accessed 29 March 2015; and Charles Lister, 'Al Qaeda Disavows ISIS', The Brookings Institute, 3 February 2014, available at: <http://www.brookings.edu/research/opinions/2014/02/03-al-qaeda-rejects-isis-lister>, accessed 29 March 2015.

[129] See Saeed Shah and Syed Shoaib Hasan, 'Taliban Take Toll on Pakistan's Biggest City', *Wall Street Journal*, 13 February 2014, available at: <http://online.wsj.com/news/articles/SB100014240527023 04558804579374901672957772>, accessed 29 March 2015; Carlotta Gall and Declan Walsh, 'How the Pakistani Taliban Became a Deadly Force', *New York Times*, 2 November 2013, available at: <http://www.nytimes.com/2013/11/02/world/asia/how-the-pakistani-taliban-became-a-deadly-force.html?_r=0>, accessed 29 March 2015.

[130] *Tadić*, Interlocutory Appeal, at para. 70.

[131] See Allen Weiner, 'Law, Just War, and the International Fight against Terrorism: Is It War?', in Steven Lee (ed.), *Intervention, Terrorism and Torture: Contemporary Challenges to Just War Theory* (Springer, 2007), at 141, where he notes that 'al-Qaeda seems to possess… clear albeit decentralised, organisational and command structures.'

[132] For a more detailed analysis of the scope of 'protracted hostilities' as set out in *Tadić*, see further Ch. 7 of this book.

justifications for striking against al-Qaeda and Taliban members, regardless of how organized the group or how protracted the violence, would seem to be tenuous as there is no longer a 'war' in Afghanistan for the US to be party to, nor for al-Qaeda and the Taliban to be causally connected.

Targeted killings under IHL: 'signature strikes' and problems with the targeting criteria

However, even if the targeted strikes are lawful under IHL, an additional problem regarding the practice of targeted killings by the US has been the criteria employed to make the determinations on targets. In commenting on the US practice of singling out individuals for targeting, Harold Koh stated:

> some have suggested that the *very act of targeting* a particular leader of an enemy force in an armed conflict must violate the laws of war. But individuals who are part of such an armed group are belligerents and, therefore, lawful targets under international law. During World War II, for example, American aviators tracked and shot down the airplane carrying the architect of the Japanese attack on Pearl Harbor, who was also the leader of enemy forces in the Battle of Midway. This was a lawful operation then, and would be if conducted today. Indeed, targeting particular individuals serves to narrow the focus when force is employed and to avoid broader harm to civilians and civilian objects.[133]

This is not a controversial position: members of an adverse party taking direct part in hostilities may be targeted. However, evidence has emerged that suggests that the US determination of the parameters of direct participation and any 'individuals who are part of such an armed group'[134] is remarkably broad. A report in the *New York Times* in May 2012 revealed some of the details regarding the Obama Administration's policy on the selection of targets, illustrating the broad scope of targeting criteria as including 'all military-age males in a strike zone'.[135] Indeed, one administration source stated that 'people in an area of known terrorist activity, or found with a top al-Qaeda operative'[136] are considered lawful targets, explaining that 'Al Qaeda is an insular, paranoid organization—innocent neighbours don't hitchhike rides in the back of trucks headed for the border with guns and bombs'.[137]

[133] Koh, 'The Obama Administration and International Law', at 219 (emphasis in original, as posted on the State Department website at: <http://www.state.gov/s/l/releases/remarks/139119.htm>, accessed 29 March 2015).

[134] Koh, 'The Obama Administration and International Law', at 219.

[135] Jo Becker and Scott Shane, 'Secret "Kill List" Proves a Test of Obama's Principles and Will'.

[136] Becker and Shane, 'Secret "Kill List" Proves a Test of Obama's Principles and Will'.

[137] Becker and Shane, 'Secret "Kill List" Proves a Test of Obama's Principles and Will'. The targeting criteria used by the US also seems to change depending on who is carrying out the strikes—the military or the CIA—with one US Congressional aide stating that, for the CIA, 'their standards of who is a combatant are different' to the standards of the Department of Defence and

This rationale can be seen in practice in the February 2002 attack on three men in Khost in Afghanistan's Paktia province. These men were spotted by Predator drone operators, who noticed that two of the men were 'acting with reverence'[138] towards a third 'tall man'.[139] Osama bin Laden was a tall man; FBI reports calculated his height to be between 6ft 4in and 6ft 6in (193–198 cm).[140] Furthermore, the three men were found at a former *mujahedeen* base known as Zhawar Kili. Zhawar Kili was known to US authorities: in 1998, President Bill Clinton had authorized missile attacks against Zhawar Kili and another suspected al-Qaeda camp in Al Badr (near Jalalabad).[141]

Authorization was given to target these men with the Hellfire missiles attached to the Predator. US government officials stated in the aftermath of the attack that at the time of the attack, they could not be sure who they killed, but they were 'convinced it was an appropriate target'[142] and that 'the initial indications afterwards would seem to say that these are not peasant people up there farming.'[143] However, it was later discovered that the 'tall man' and his associates were local villagers who had gone to the long-abandoned[144] camp site to forage for scrap metal; while one of the men, Daraz Khan, was tall (at 5ft 11in, or 180 cm), he was at least five to seven inches (approximately 12–17 cm) shorter than bin Laden. No connection between Daraz Khan and his companions and al-Qaeda could be made out post mortem.[145]

These kinds of strikes have become known as 'signature strikes',[146] ttacks against a person or persons 'who bear certain signatures or defining

the US military (see Ken Dilanian, 'Debate Grows Over Proposal for CIA to Turn Over Drones to Pentagon', *Los Angeles Times*, 11 May 2014, available at: <http://www.latimes.com/world/middleeast/la-fg-yemen-drones-20140511-story.html>, accessed 29 March 2015).

[138] Quoted in John Sifton, 'A Brief History of Drones', *The Nation*, 27 February 2012, available at: <http://www.thenation.com/article/166124/brief-history-drones>, accessed 29 March 2015.

[139] Sifton, 'A Brief History of Drones'.

[140] Federal Bureau of Investigation, 'Most Wanted Terrorists: Usama bin Laden', available at: <http://www.fbi.gov/wanted/wanted_terrorists/usama-bin-laden>, accessed 29 March 2015.

[141] Brian Glyn Williams, *Afghanistan Declassified: A Guide to America's Longest War* (University of Pennsylvania Press, 2012), at 182.

[142] Quoted in John Burns, 'A Nation Challenged: The Manhunt; US Leapt Before Looking, Angry Villagers Say', *New York Times*, 17 February 2002, available at: <http://www.nytimes.com/2002/02/17/world/a-nation-challenged-the-manhunt-us-leapt-before-looking-angry-villagers-say.html>, accessed 29 March 2015.

[143] Burns, 'A Nation Challenged: The Manhunt'.

[144] Burns, 'A Nation Challenged: The Manhunt'.

[145] Burns, 'A Nation Challenged: The Manhunt'.

[146] Columbia Law School Human Rights Clinic and the Centre for Civilians in Conflict, *The Civilian Impact of Drones: Unexamined Costs, Unanswered Questions* (2012), at 8, available at: <http://web.law.columbia.edu/sites/default/files/microsites/human-rights-institute/files/The%20Civilian%20Impact%20of%20Drones.pdf>, accessed 29 March 2015.

characteristics associated with terrorist activity, but whose identities aren't known'.[147] Signature strikes are different from 'personality strikes', attacks where there is a 'high degree of confidence'[148] that the identity of the target is known in advance. Signature strikes have been the most common form targeted killing employed by the US: as reported by the Stanford/New York University study into drone attacks, of the 500 militants killed by drones between 2008 and 2010, only 8 per cent could have been specifically targeted due to their identity, with the remaining 92 per cent killed in signature strikes.[149]

The employment of signature strikes illustrates one of the problems that has arisen from the practice of targeted killing; that of attacking persons on the basis of possible association, either due to location or appearance, rather than on any solid evidence of *actual* DPH. More recent information about the US programme has not clarified the situation. Media accounts have revealed the existence of the so-called disposition matrix[150] on suspected terrorists, a series of complex steps for whether the suspected terrorists can be arrested abroad and potentially transferred to US jurisdiction, but the 'matrix' contains no details regarding what criteria are used to determine whether this person can be targeted due to his or her DPH, and whether any IHL considerations are taken into account in targeting decisions, or if the decision to target is made solely on the basis of whether such a person 'poses an imminent threat to the United States.'[151]

Eric Holder who, while serving as US Attorney-General, has stated that the US is entitled 'to target specific senior operational leaders of al Qaeda and associated forces',[152] has also claimed that in undertaking such targeting,

[147] Daniel Klaidman, *Kill or Capture: The War on Terror and the Soul of the Obama Presidency* (Houghton Mifflin Harcourt, 2012), at 41. See also *The Civilian Impact of Drones*, at 8.

[148] *The Civilian Impact of Drones*, at 8.

[149] Stanford Law School International Human Rights and Conflict Resolution Clinic and New York University School of Law Global Justice Clinic, *Living Under Drones: Death, Injury and Trauma to Civilians from US Drone Practices in Pakistan* (2012), available at: <http://www.livingunderdrones.org/report/>, at 31, accessed 29 March 2015. In 2011, a US official confirmed that the US has killed 'twice as many 'wanted terrorists' in signature strikes than personality strikes' (*Civilian Impact of Drones*, at 9).

[150] Ian Cobain, 'Obama's Secret Kill List—The Disposition Matrix', *Guardian*, 15 July 2013, available at: <http://www.theguardian.com/world/2013/jul/14/obama-secret-kill-list-disposition-matrix>, accessed 29 March 2015; Daniel Byman and Benjamin Wittes, 'How Obama Decides Your Fate If He Thinks You're A Terrorist', *The Atlantic*, 3 January 2013, available at: <http://www.theatlantic.com/international/archive/2013/01/how-obama-decides-your-fate-if-he-thinks-youre-a-terrorist/266419/>, accessed 29 March 2015.

[151] US Attorney-General Eric Holder, Speech Delivered at Northwestern University School of Law, 5 March 2012, available at: <http://www.justice.gov/iso/opa/ag/speeches/2012/ag-speech-1203051.html>, accessed 29 March 2015.

[152] Holder, Speech Delivered at Northwestern University School of Law.

the US respects 'the principle of distinction [which] requires that only lawful targets—such as combatants, civilians directly participating in hostilities, and military objectives—may be targeted intentionally'.[153] However, no information has been forthcoming on how the US defines 'civilians directly participating in hostilities.' The high number of signature strikes as conducted by the US would seem to suggest a very liberal interpretation of DPH, and one that does not seem in accordance with existing interpretations of the concept. As Heller notes:

> status-based targeting is permissible in NIAC [non-international armed conflict], but only if the individual qualifies as a member of an organised armed group. That status, however, cannot be simply inferred from the fact that an individual is of military age and is present in an area where terrorists have previously operated. As the ICRC has pointed out, membership in an organised armed group requires actual and continuous participation in hostilities: it 'cannot depend on abstract affiliation, family ties, or other criteria prone to error, arbitrariness or abuse'.[154]

There is evidence to indicate that the US continues to rely on signature strikes. For example, in April 2012, a drone strike was ordered against a group of men travelling in a truck near Karma, in the Azzan district of Shabwa province.[155] Although the men in the car were apparently armed, there was little else to suggest that the passengers in the car were directly participating in hostilities. Later reports stated that the five men killed were al-Qaeda members but that none held senior operational roles.[156] There was no evidence to suggest that the persons in the car were on their way to commit a belligerent act (or returning from such an act), or that they were firing their weapons from the car. Thus, they would seem to fail the basic elements of a cautious but expansive DPH test: that of 'threshold of harm', 'direct causation', and 'belligerent nexus'.

The mere fact that they were carrying arms is not enough to support the contention that they were DPH. The ICTY in *Simić* did not support the contention that 'the possession of weapons, in itself, creates a reasonable doubt as to the civilian status'[157] of an individual. Indeed, this very

[153] Holder, Speech Delivered at Northwestern University School of Law.

[154] Heller, 'One Hell of a Killing Machine', at 97 (quoting the ICRC DPHIG, at 1002).

[155] 'US Drone Strikes al-Qaeda Convoy in Shabwa', *The Yemen Post*, 16 April 2012, available at: <http://www.yemenpost.net/Detail123456789.aspx?ID=3&SubID=5135&MainCat=3>, accessed 29 March 2015.

[156] Bill Roggio, 'US Predators Strike Again in Southern Yemen', *The Long War Journal*, 16 April 2012, available at: <http://www.longwarjournal.org/archives/2012/04/us_predators_strike_35.php>, accessed 29 March 2015.

[157] *Simić*, at § 659.

point was made by a Yemeni intelligence official who noted that carrying weapons was commonplace in Yemen: 'Every Yemeni is armed . . . how can they differentiate between suspected militants and armed Yemenis?'[158] If the open carrying of weapons in an al-Qaeda area was the sole determinative factor in the April 2012 strike, such a strike would seem to be in violation of IHL.

Consorting with known terrorists, or living in areas controlled by terrorist organisations of other armed groups, is not enough to support a conclusion of DPH. As noted by the UN Sub-Commission on Human Rights (in relation to civilians living in the areas controlled by the Farabundo Martí National Liberation Front (FMLN)):

> as long as the so-called 'masses' do not participate directly in combat, although they may sympathise, accompany, supply food and live in zones under the control of the insurgents, they preserve their civilian character, and therefore they must not be subjected to military attacks.[159]

This was affirmed by the Special Court for Sierra Leone in the *Fofana and Kondewa* case where the Court stated that 'persons accused of "collaborating" with the government or armed forces would only become legitimate military targets if they were taking direct part in the hostilities . . . if there is any doubt as to whether an individual is a civilian he should be presumed to be a civilian and cannot be attacked merely because he appears dubious.'[160] US practice of targeting persons due to signifiers other than their direct participation would thus be unlawful.

Conclusion

This chapter has examined the phenomenon of targeted killings, and how States have employed the tactic in their armed conflicts and other security operations. The next chapter examines a phenomenon that has become inextricably linked with targeted killings: the use of drones in warfare. What the

[158] Adam Entous, Siobhan Gorman, and Julian E Barnes, 'US Relaxes Drone Rules', *Wall Street Journal*, 26 April 2012, available at: <http://online.wsj.com/news/articles/SB10001424052702304723304577366251852418174>, accessed 29 March 2015.

[159] UN Sub-Commission on the Promotion and Protection of Human Rights, Resolution 1985/18, 29 August 1985, reaffirmed by the UN Sub-Commission on Human Rights in Resolution 1987/18, 2 September 1987, § 3; Resolution 1988/13, 1 September 1988, § 3; and Resolution 1989/9, 31 August 1989, § 3.

[160] *Fofana and Kondewa*, at § 135.

next chapter will explore is the complex issues raised by 'remote controlled warfare': when belligerent acts are carried out via remote means, and how DPH by remote means, whether by drone or through other forms of remote computer-based means, has complicated the laws of armed conflict and their application.

5

Remote Warfare

Drones and Cyber Warfare

Introduction

Technology has shaped and changed the ways in which armed conflicts have been fought for decades, if not centuries.[1] One of the most discussed and debated technological developments of recent years has been the increasing digitization of combat, how computers have radically transformed modern combat, allowing hostilities to be conducted remotely from nearly anywhere in the world. Two of the most controversial methods of computer-based, remote warfare have been the use of unmanned aerial vehicles (UAVs, also known as drones) and the deployment of cyber-based attacks against, and infiltration of, enemy computer networks. This is colloquially known as cyber warfare.

At first glance, addressing these two areas of technology in one chapter would seem incongruous: drones have caused extensive property damage and have killed thousands,[2] whereas cyber warfare has, at best, caused

[1] There have been numerous works which look at the interaction of military strategy and technological advancements, and how technology and warfare have served as driving forces on one another's development and evolution. For some insight into this area of study see generally Geoffrey Jensen, 'The Meaning of War in a Technological Age', in Geoffrey Jensen and Andrew Wiest (eds), *War in the Age of Technology: Myriad Faces of Modern Armed Conflict* (New York University Press, 2001); Martin van Creveld, *Technology and War from 2000 B.C. to the Present* (Brassey's Defence Publishers, 1991); Michael O'Hanlon, *The Science of War: Defense Budgeting, Military Technology, Logistics, and Combat Outcomes* (Princeton University Press, 2009); Thomas Mahken, *Technology and the American Way of War Since 1945* (Columbia University Press, 2008); and Michael White, *The Fruits of War: How Military Conflict Accelerates Technology* (Pocket Books, 2007).

[2] See statistics as reported in *Living Under Drones: Death, Injury and Trauma to Civilians from US Drone Practices in Pakistan* (2012), Stanford Law School International Human Rights and Conflict Resolution Clinic and New York University School of Law Global Justice Clinic, available at: <http://www.livingunderdrones.org/report/>, at 29–54, accessed 29 March 2015.

only inconvenience and disruption[3] (despite claims to the contrary).[4] The possibility for cyber warfare to cause the kinds of kinetic damage already caused by drones remains just that: a possibility. However, these two methods of combat, though very different in effect, share some fundamental similarities. One of those similarities is the role that civilians have played (and will be able to play) in the execution of the kinetic and potential damage and disruption created by these methods of conflict. In the case of drones, the US civilian intelligence agency, the Central Intelligence Agency (CIA), has long been engaged in drone strikes in foreign territories.[5] There are also reports that the US National Security Agency (NSA)[6]

[3] See reports on the cyber attacks that occurred in Estonia in 2007 and Georgia in 2008, as reported by Stephen Korns and Joshua Kastenberg, 'Georgia's Cyber Left Hook', 38 *Parameters* 60 (2008–09); John Markoff, 'Before the Gunfire, Cyberattacks', *New York Times*, 12 August 2008, available at: <http://www.nytimes.com/2008/08/13/technology/13cyber.html?_r=0>, accessed 4 April 2015; Jon Swain, 'Georgia: Russia "Conducting Cyber War" ', *Daily Telegraph*, 11 August 2008, available at: <http://www.telegraph.co.uk/news/worldnews/europe/georgia/2539157/Georgia-Russia-conducting-cyber-war.html>, accessed 29 March 2015; Ian Traynor, 'Russia Accused of Unleashing Cyberwar to Disable Estonia', *Guardian*, 17 May 2007, available at: <http://www.guardian.co.uk/world/2007/may/17/topstories3.russia>, accessed 29 March 2015; Joshua Davis, 'Hackers Take Down the Most Wired Country in Europe', *Wired*, 21 August 2007, available at: <http://www.wired.com/politics/security/magazine/15-09/ff_estonia>, accessed 29 March 2015.

[4] Claims have been made by Thomas Reed, a former official in the US National Security Council, that in 1982 a 'logic bomb' (a piece of code inserted into a programme or software system designed to execute a malicious function once certain conditions are met, eg, deletion of data or the termination of the programme (see John Daintith and Edmund Wright, *A Dictionary of Computing* (6th edn, OUP, 2008)) was inserted by the US into software used in the control system of a USSR oil pipeline. It was alleged that the logic bomb reset pump speeds and valve settings, creating a pressure build-up which directly contributed to an explosion in the pipeline in June 1982. The explosion was apparently so large as to be visible from space, and was rated at three kilotonnes, equivalent to a small nuclear device (Thomas Reed, *At the Abyss* (Random House, 2004), at 268–69). However, cyber security analysts such as Thomas Rid dispute the claim, arguing that it would have been virtually impossible to hide the malware in the technologically simple software of the time, that declassified KGB reports from the time make no mention of such an incident, and that Reed was most likely confusing the Siberia explosion with a pipeline which exploded in April of 1982, due to thawing tundra in the region. Rid generally disputes claims that cyberwar has caused any human casualties, or indeed any damage to persons or property, and that oft-proclaimed cyber wars cannot be truly considered wars, as they lack the requisite threshold of violence (Thomas Rid, *Cyber War Will Not Take Place* (Hurst and Company, 2013), at 4–7, 10).

[5] See Greg Miller, 'CIA Remains Behind Most Drone Strikes, Despite Effort to Shift Campaign to Defense', *Washington Post*, 26 November 2013, available at: <http://www.washingtonpost.com/world/national-security/cia-remains-behind-most-drone-strikes-despite-effort-to-shift-campaign-to-defense/2013/11/25/c0c07a86-5386-11e3-a7f0-b790929232e1_story.html>, accessed 29 March 2015.

[6] Although headed by General Keith Alexander, following appointment by the Secretary of Defense, the NSA is not part of the armed forces proper; it provides services to the armed forces but it is, *prima facie*, a civilian agency. See: <http://www.nsa.gov/about/faqs/about_nsa.shtml>, accessed 29 March 2015.

has been involved in drone strikes.[7] In the case of cyber warfare, civilians have been involved (and have the potential to be involved) in conducting cyber attacks against States and non-State actors.[8]

As such, the implications raised by civilian involvement in remote-controlled warfare apply equally to both civilian-run drone programmes and to civilians engaging in cyber hostilities. This chapter therefore examines the potential repercussions in civilian participation in remote-controlled warfare, and how the current thinking on direct participation in hostilities (DPH) can be applied to these new methods of armed conflict, methods which already complicate our understanding of what it means to directly participate in hostilities.

Drones

The previous chapter, on targeted killing, touched on the issue of drones, if tangentially; drones have been the method of choice for carrying out most of the targeted killings that the US has undertaken in most recent years.[9] Indeed, the first known US targeted killing, against suspected al-Qaeda leader Qaed Salim al-Harethi in Yemen in November 2002,[10] employed a Predator drone. Since then, the US has engaged in numerous drone strikes in Afghanistan, Iraq, Pakistan, Yemen, and Somalia.[11]

[7] See Greg Miller, Julie Tate, and Barton Gellman, 'Documents Reveal NSA's Extensive Involvement in Targeted Killing Program', *Washington Post*, 17 October 2013, available at: <http://www.washingtonpost.com/world/national-security/documents-reveal-nsas-extensive-involvement-in-targeted-killing-program/2013/10/16/29775278-3674-11e3-8a0e-4e2cf80831fc_print.html>, accessed 29 March 2015.

[8] See Jason Andress and Steve Winterfeld, *Cyber Warfare: Techniques, Tactics and Tools for Security Practitioners* (Elsevier, 2011), specifically Ch. 11, 'Non-State Actors in Computer Network Operations'; and Jeffrey Carr, *Inside Cyber Warfare* (2nd edn, O'Reilly, 2012), specifically Ch. 2, 'The Rise of the Non-State Hacker'.

[9] The Bureau of Investigative Journalism has stated that of the estimated total of 668 covert strikes against targets in Yemen, Somalia, and Pakistan between 2002 and 2014, 578 of those have been executed by drones. See further 'Casualty Estimates', the Bureau of Investigative Journalism, available at: <http://www.thebureauinvestigates.com/category/projects/drones/drones-graphs/>, accessed 29 March 2015.

[10] Alston, *Study on Targeted Killings*, at 7; Tony Karon, 'Yemen Strike Opens New Chapter in War on Terror', *Time*, 5 November 2002, available at: <http://content.time.com/time/world/article/0,8599,387571,00.html>, accessed 4 April 2015; Chris Woods, "'OK, Fine. Shoot Him." Four Words That Heralded a Decade of Secret US Drone Killings', the Bureau of Investigative Journalism, 23 November 2012, available at: <http://www.thebureauinvestigates.com/2012/11/03/ok-fine-shoot-him-four-words-that-heralded-a-decade-of-secret-us-drone-killings/>, accessed 29 March 2015.

[11] See Scott Shane, 'CIA Drone Use is Set to Expand Inside Pakistan', *New York Times*, 4 December 2009, available at: <http://www.nytimes.com/2009/12/04/world/asia/04drones.html?pagewanted=all&_r=0>, accessed 29 March 2015; Christopher Drew, 'For US, Drones Are Weapons

Reports have stated that drone strikes in Iraq and Afghanistan were controlled by the US Air Force (USAF),[12] but that the attacks in Pakistan, Somalia, and Yemen were under the control of the CIA. A *New York Times* report recounted one incident where CIA 'sharpshooters killed eight people suspected of being militants of the Taliban and Al Qaeda...the job in North Waziristan done, the CIA officers could head home from the agency's Langley, Va., headquarters, facing only the hazards of the area's famously snarled suburban traffic.'[13]

However, more recent reports indicate that the CIA has been integral in the oversight and orchestration of the military drone programme involving the USAF, contrary to statements that the USAF drone programme was a separate entity to that conducted by the CIA.[14] Following her interviews with the former commander at Nellis Air Force Base, Mary Ellen O'Connell reported that all drone operations carried out by the USAF from Nevada are actually joint operations in conjunction with the CIA.[15] This was confirmed for O'Connell in discussions with former Assistant General Counsel at the CIA, John Radsan, who indicated that 'all decisions to actually fire a missile are made by the CIA at their headquarters in Langley, Virginia'.[16] Further confirmation came in 2014, when a report in the *Guardian* newspaper stated that 'a regular US air force unit based in the Nevada desert is responsible for flying the CIA's drone strike programme in Pakistan...the unit conducting CIA strikes in Pakistan's tribal areas [is] the 17th Reconnaissance Squadron, which operates from a secure compound in a corner of Creech air force base.'[17]

of Choice in Fighting Qaeda', *New York Times*, 17 March 2009, available at: <http://www.nytimes.com/2009/03/17/business/17uav.html?pagewanted=all>, accessed 4 April 2015; Jane Mayer, 'The Predator War: What Are the Risks of the CIA's Covert Drone Program?', *New Yorker*, 26 October 2009, available at: <http://www.newyorker.com/reporting/2009/10/26/091026fa_fact_mayer?printable=true&currentPage=all>, accessed 29 March 2015; 'US Speeds Up Drone and Missile Deliveries to Iraq', *Daily Telegraph*, 7 January 2004, available at: <http://www.telegraph.co.uk/news/worldnews/middleeast/iraq/10555034/US-speeds-up-drone-and-missile-deliveries-to-Iraq.html>, accessed 29 March 2015.

[12] Afsheen John Radsan and Richard Murphy, 'Measure Twice, Shoot Once: Higher Care for CIA-Targeted Killing', U Illinois L Rev 1201 (2011), at 1202.

[13] Shane, 'CIA Drone Use is Set to Expand Inside Pakistan'. See also Mayer, 'The Predator War'.

[14] Mayer, 'The Predator War'.

[15] See 'Unlawful Killing with Combat Drones: A Case Study of Pakistan, 2004–2009', in Simon Bronitt, Miriama Gani, and Saskia Hufnagel (eds), *Shooting to Kill: Socio-Legal Perspectives on the Use of Lethal Force* (Hart, 2012), at 268.

[16] 'Unlawful Killing with Combat Drones', at 268.

[17] Chris Woods, 'CIA's Pakistan Drone Strikes Carried Out by Regular US Air Force Personnel', *Guardian*, 14 April 2014, available at: <http://www.theguardian.com/world/2014/apr/14/cia-drones-pakistan-us-air-force-documentary/print>, accessed 29 March 2015.

The CIA's involvement in drone strikes

The CIA is a civilian 'independent agency'[18] and not part of the armed forces of the US.[19] *Prima facie* its employees are civilians.[20] Does this mean that civilian CIA employees authorizing or otherwise conducting drone strikes are thus to be considered civilians taking a direct part in hostilities? If one looks at nearly any possible definition of DPH, the CIA operatives would seem to fit these criteria. The International Criminal Tribunal for the former Yugoslavia (ICTY) *Strugar* test[21]—whose DPH spectrum includes a lower-end threshold of transmittal of military information for the immediate use of a belligerent, to the higher end of bearing, using, or taking up arms—would seem to apply to CIA participation in drone strikes, as CIA drone operators are both gathering the information on targets and launching the strikes.[22] Even the more restrictive International Committee of the Red Cross (ICRC) DPH formulation would seem to capture CIA operatives within its ambit, as the CIA drone operators could be defined as civilians with a continuous combat function[23] whose acts meet the cumulative criteria of threshold of harm,[24] direct causation,[25] and belligerent nexus.[26]

Indeed, there seems to be ample evidence to suggest that the CIA is involved in all levels of the targeting process, from those who operate the drones to those who give the order to attack. For example, John Rizzo, the CIA's former Acting Legal Counsel, gave an interview in February 2011 during which he indicated that it was he, and not the President or the Director of the CIA, who gave the final authorization to attack a particular target.[27] Rizzo also stated that targets were suggested and selected by CIA staffers who make the case for 'neutralisation',[28] rather that the organization acting on any putative list put forward by military legal advisers or commanders. Additionally, reports suggest that private contractors hired by the CIA, along with CIA operatives themselves, are also involved in carrying out drone strikes, including firing the missiles from the drones.[29]

[18] 'Today's CIA', available at: <https://www.cia.gov/about-cia/todays-cia>, accessed 29 March 2015.
[19] 'Today's CIA'. [20] O'Connell, 'Unlawful Killing with Combat Drones', at 270.
[21] *Strugar*, at 67–68, para. 177.
[22] Alston, 'The CIA and Targeted Killings Beyond Borders', at 347–50.
[23] DPHIG, at 1006. [24] DPHIG, at 1016. [25] DPHIG, at 1019.
[26] DPHIG, at 1026. See Ch. 3 of this book for a more detailed analysis of the ICRC DPH test.
[27] Tara McKelvey, 'Inside the Killing Machine', *Newsweek*, 13 February 2011, available at: <http://www.newsweek.com/inside-killing-machine-68771>, accessed 29 March 2015.
[28] McKelvey, 'Inside the Killing Machine'.
[29] Peter Singer, 'Double-Hatting Around the Law: The Problem with Morphing Warrior, Spy and Civilian Roles', The Brookings Institute, 1 June 2010, available at: <http://www.brookings.edu/research/opinions/2010/06/01-military-roles-singer>, accessed 29 March 2015.

The status of CIA operatives involved in drone strikes

While the CIA asserts that counter-terrorism operations are conducted in 'strict accordance with American law and are governed by legal guidance provided by the Department of Justice',[30] the fact that civilian operatives are conducting and authorizing lethal strikes against other persons—even if the targets can be considered as taking DPH—is problematic. Put another way, the targets may be directly participating in hostilities but then so are the CIA operatives. As such, the US would seem to be acting in a way they themselves have condemned, by sanctioning civilians undertaking war-like acts and directly participating in hostilities.

This has knock-on effects. First, CIA operatives, as civilians, have no combatant privilege and are not immune for their war-like acts under the Conventions and Protocols. This was noted by Philip Alston:

> intelligence personnel do not have immunity from prosecution under domestic law for their conduct. They are thus unlike state armed forces which would generally be immune from prosecution for the same conduct... thus, CIA personnel could be prosecuted for murder under the domestic law of any country in which they conduct targeted drone killings, and could also be prosecuted for violations of applicable US law.[31]

Furthermore, as Alston has pointed out, certain domestic consequences may attach to such direct participation.[32] Indeed, the US Military Commissions Act of 2009 (MCA) essentially criminalizes DPH by civilians.[33] The MCA only deals with 'unprivileged enemy belligerents'[34] engaged in hostilities against the US,[35] which would thus exclude CIA operatives. Nonetheless, the US is taking the position that any person, other than a privileged belligerent as recognized under the Geneva Conventions, who takes direct part in hostilities has committed a crime that may be tried by a military commission: a 'murder in violation of the law of war'.[36] Indeed, commentary on the

[30] Singer, 'Double-Hatting Around the Law'.

[31] Alston, *Study on Targeted Killings*, at 22.

[32] See also Michael Schmitt, 'Humanitarian Law and Direct Participation in Hostilities by Private Contractors or Civilian Employees', 5 Chicago J Int'l L 511 (2005), at 520.

[33] 10 USC §§ 948a–950w (2006) and Supp. II (2009).

[34] 10 USC § 948a.

[35] See charging documents in the case of Omar Khadr at: <http://www.defense.gov/news/Apr2007/Khadrreferral.pdf>, accessed 29 March 2015; Australian David Hicks, the first person sentenced by the revised military commissions, was initially charged with 'attempted murder in violation of the laws of war'; see his charge sheet at: <http://www.defense.gov/news/d20070301hicks.pdf>, accessed 29 March 2015.

[36] Military Commissions Act of 2006, 10 USC § 950v(b)(15). See further Vogel, who notes of CIA operatives 'the CIA is a civilian agency and not a branch of the US Armed Forces. Even under a liberal reading of Art. 4 from GCIII, the CIA would not meet the requirements of lawful belligerency as a militia or volunteer corps because, while they do report to a responsible chain of

US Manual for Military Commissions, the implementing regulations for the Military Commissions Act of 2006, states that 'for the accused to have been acting in violation of the law of war, the accused must have taken acts as a combatant without having met the requirements for lawful combatancy.'[37] This, in effect, means that the US considers DPH by civilians to be a war crime, despite the fact that no existing treaty criminalizes civilian DPH in such a manner.[38] As Lewis and Crawford note:

> [b]y prosecuting murder as an IHL violation the United States is taking the position that crimes committed by unprivileged belligerents rise to the level of war crimes. If that is the case then it is arguable that the Geneva Conventions *require* the United States to prosecute CIA drone operators that have used lethal force if those operators are civilians engaged in direct participation in hostilities. Although from a practical standpoint such a prosecution would be unlikely, the US would need to provide some legal justification for failing to prosecute individuals that it regards as violating the laws of war.[39]

Indeed, concerns about the possibility that CIA operatives are taking direct part in hostilities in violation of the US position on civilian DPH seems to be reflected in the change in terminology in the 2010 *US Manual for Military Commissions* issued for the MCA, which states that:

> an accused may be convicted in a military commission... if the commission finds that the accused... engaged in conduct traditionally triable by military commission (... while the accused did not meet the requirements of privileged belligerency) even if such conduct does not violate the international law of war.[40]

The inclusion of this last section—that civilian DPH does not violate international humanitarian law (IHL)—is key in the context of the use of the CIA in conducting drone strikes. According to a report in the *New York Times*, US State Department Legal Adviser Harold Koh was seemingly concerned that the continued assertion of DPH as a war crime could have domestic

command (albeit not always a military chain of command), as a group they do not wear uniforms or otherwise distinguish themselves, nor do they carry their arms openly. CIA personnel are therefore unprivileged belligerents in this conflict.' (Ryan Vogel, 'Drone Warfare and the Law of Armed Conflict', 39 Denv J Int'l L & Pol'y 101 (2010–2011), at 134–35).

[37] *US Manual for Military Commissions* (2007), Pt IV, § 6(13)(d), at IV-11 (2007).

[38] See Schmitt, 'Humanitarian Law and Direct Participation in Hostilities by Private Contractors or Civilians Employees', at 520. See also George Fletcher, who called the US Supreme Court decision in *Quirin* and the equation of 'the status of failing to qualify as a lawful combatant to the crime of being an unlawful combatant' as 'one of the greatest legal fallacies' ever ('The Law of War and its Pathologies', 38 Colum Human Rights L Rev 517 (2007), at 541).

[39] Michael Lewis and Emily Crawford, 'Drones and Distinction: How IHL Encouraged the Rise of Drones', 44 Georgetown J Int'l L 1127 (2012–2013), at 1158–59.

[40] *US Manual for Military Commissions* (2010), Pt IV, § 5(15)(c), at IV-13.

implications for CIA drone operatives, namely that such an approach 'could be construed as a concession by the United States that CIA drone operators were war criminals'.[41] That the US would continue to assert that Guantánamo Bay detainees could be charged with taking DPH while CIA drone strike operators were acting lawfully would seem contradictory and hypocritical.[42]

Legal consequences for CIA involvement in drone strikes

As Lewis and Crawford note,[43] the possibility that CIA operatives would ever face charges in US domestic courts for their actions seems unlikely, considering that they are acting under State orders. However, their DPH may render them liable to trial overseas. Indeed, there have been attempts to indict US service members in the courts of Italy[44] and Spain.[45] These cases have not

[41] Charlie Savage, 'UN Official Asks US To End CIA Drone Strikes', *New York Times*, 28 May 2010, available at: <http://www.nytimes.com/2010/05/28/world/asia/28drones.html?_r=0>, accessed 29 March 2015.

[42] The US Military Extraterritorial Jurisdiction Act of 2005 (70 Fed Reg 75,999 (MEJA)) and its implementing instructions, Criminal Jurisdiction Over Civilians Employed By or Accompanying the Armed Forces Outside the United States, Certain Service Members, and Former Service Members (2005) (Department of Defense Instruction 5525.11) would also seem relevant, as it was designed to provide for federal, non-court-martial jurisdiction for any crimes up to and including war crimes, committed by civilians employed by the armed forces. However, as Elsea and Serafino note, the definition of persons 'employed by the armed forces' would only cover civilian employees of the Department of Defense (DoD), DoD contractors, and civilian contractors or employees from other deferral agencies 'to the extent that their employment is related to the support of the DoD mission overseas. It does not appear to cover civilian and contract employees or agencies engaged in their operations overseas' (Jennifer Elsea and Nina Serafino, *Private Security Contractors in Iraq: Background, Legal Status, and Other Issues* (Congressional Research Service, Washington, 2007), at 19). As such, civilian employees of the CIA engaged in CIA orchestrated and operated drone strikes would not be caught under MEJA.

[43] Lewis and Crawford, 'Drones and Distinction', at 1158–59.

[44] 'Italian Bid to Indict US Soldier', *BBC News*, 19 June 2006, available at: <http://news.bbc.co.uk/1/hi/5095510.stm>, accessed 29 March 2015. The case, against US solider Mario Lozano, was eventually dismissed for lack of jurisdiction: see 'Italians "Cannot Try US Soldier"', *BBC News*, 25 October 2007, available at: <http://news.bbc.co.uk/2/hi/europe/7061731.stm>, accessed 29 March 2015. It was held that the Italian courts did not have jurisdiction over US servicemen serving in Iraq, as they fell under the jurisdiction of the sending State (ie, the US). See further the report on the case, reprinted on the website of Milanese daily newspaper, *Corriere della Sera*, available at: <http://www.corriere.it/Media/Documenti/rapporto_italiano.pdf>, accessed 29 March 2015.

[45] Sgt. Shawn Gibson, Capt. Philip Wolford, and Lt. Col. Philip DeCamp were initially indicted in the 2004 death of Spanish journalist Jose Couso in 2007, with the case being closed in 2008, after the Spanish National Court ruled that Spain had no jurisdiction to hear the case. However, the case was reopened in 2011, and at the time of writing remains open. See further Al Goodman, '3 US Soldiers Indicted in Death of Spanish Journalist', *CNN*, 5 October 2011, available at: <http://edition.cnn.com/2011/10/05/world/europe/spain-us-troops/>, accessed 29 March 2015; and María Carríon, 'Seeking Justice 10 Years After US Attack on Hotel', *The*

made it to trial but it is not unreasonable to think that further attempts may eventuate.[46] A successful indictment would effectively render the indicting States (as well any other State which has extradition treaties with the indicting State) 'off-limits' to CIA operatives for fear of arrest and trial in the courts of the indicting State. CIA operatives taking direct part in drone strikes may feel this potential consequence of their participation is unreasonable.

Geographical restrictions imposed on CIA operatives due to their DPH are not the only consequences that follow on from participation in drone strikes. Indeed, decidedly more deadly consequences could follow. As noted in Chapter 1, when a civilian takes direct part in hostilities they may be lawfully targeted due to such direct participation. Thus, if CIA personnel are considered to be taking direct part in hostilities, they may be themselves targeted and killed for such participation.[47] As noted by Solis:

> CIA agents are, unlike their military counterparts but like the fighters they target, unlawful combatants. No less than their insurgent targets, they are fighters without uniforms or insignia, directly participating in hostilities, employing armed force contrary to the laws and customs of war. Even if they are sitting in Langley, the CIA pilots are civilians violating the requirement of distinction, a core concept of armed conflict, as they directly participate in hostilities... it makes no difference that CIA civilians are employed by, or in the service of, the U.S. government or its armed forces. They are civilians; they wear no distinguishing uniform or sign, and if they input target data or pilot armed drones in the combat zone, they directly participate in hostilities—which means they may be lawfully targeted... moreover, CIA civilian personnel who repeatedly and directly participate in hostilities may have what recent guidance from the International Committee of the Red Cross terms 'a continuous combat function.' That status, the ICRC guidance says, makes them legitimate targets whenever and wherever they may be found, including Langley.[48]

The only possible grounds for finding that CIA drone operators are not unprivileged belligerents would be to demonstrate that the operators are members of a paramilitary group or an 'armed law enforcement agency' that have been 'incorporated into the armed forces' as provided for by Article 43 of Additional Protocol I.[49] Indeed, CIA Director John Brennan has called CIA

Progressive, 9 April 2013, available at: <http://www.progressive.org/10-years-after-u-s-attack-on-palestine-hotel>, accessed 29 March 2015.

46 See further Alston, 'The CIA and Targeted Killings Beyond Borders', at 439–40.

47 Alston, *Study on Targeted Killings*, at 22.

48 Gary Solis, 'CIA Drone Attacks Produce America's Own Unlawful Combatants', *Washington Post*, 12 March 2010, available at: <http://www.washingtonpost.com/wp-dyn/content/article/2010/03/11/AR2010031103653_pf.html>, accessed 29 March 2015.

49 Art. 43(3), API.

lethal targeting operations 'paramilitary' operations.[50] However, in order to fulfil these requirements, CIA operatives must be subject to an internal disciplinary system which 'inter alia, shall enforce compliance with the rules of international law applicable in armed conflict.'[51] While the US has stated that it conducts its drone operations in compliance with IHL,[52] there is little information to indicate whether CIA drone operators themselves receive IHL training, or whether there is any investigation mechanism in place for CIA violations of IHL.[53]

Moreover, the US is not party to Additional Protocol I, having signed but not ratified it.[54] As such, the Protocol would not, *prima facie*, apply to US activities. Furthermore, while Article 43 has been claimed, by the *ICRC CIHL Study*, to be accepted as customary international law in international armed conflicts,[55] one must question whether the US conflict with al-Qaeda is indeed international: the US Supreme Court decision in *Hamdan* would seem to suggest that it is non-international in character. As the Court noted in that case:

The Court of Appeals thought, and the Government asserts, that Common Article 3 does not apply to Hamdan because the conflict with al Qaeda, being 'international in scope,' does not qualify as a 'conflict not of an international character.' That reasoning is erroneous. The term 'conflict not of an international character' is used here in contradistinction to a conflict between nations.

. . .

Common Article 3 . . . affords some minimal protection, falling short of full protection under the Conventions, to individuals associated with neither a signatory nor even a non-signatory 'Power' who are involved in a conflict 'in the territory of' a signatory. The latter kind of conflict is distinguishable from the conflict described

[50] See Mark Mazetti, 'Delays in Effort to Refocus CIA from Drone War', *New York Times*, 5 April 2014, available at: <http://www.nytimes.com/2014/04/06/world/delays-in-effort-to-refocus-cia-from-drone-war.html>, accessed 29 March 2015; see also Daniel Klaidman, 'Exclusive: No More Drones for CIA', *Newsweek*, 19 March 2013, available at: <http://www.thedailybeast.com/articles/2013/03/19/exclusive-no-more-drones-for-cia.html>, accessed 29 March 2015.

[51] Art. 43(1), API.

[52] Koh, 'The Obama Administration and International Law', at 218.

[53] See Human Rights Watch, 'Q&A: US Targeted Killings and International Law', available at: <http://www.hrw.org/news/2011/12/19/q-us-targeted-killings-and-international-law#14>, accessed 29 March 2015. What concerns are raised by the CIA's involvement in targeted killings?; see also Mary Ellen O'Connell, 'Spy vs Soldier: The CIA May Lose a Power it Never Legally Had', *The New Republic*, 2 April 2013, available at: <http://www.newrepublic.com/article/112810/cia-drone-program-move-pentagon>, accessed 29 March 2015.

[54] See the ICRC website for the list of States who have signed but not ratified Additional Protocol I, available at: <http://www.icrc.org/applic/ihl/ihl.nsf/States.xsp?xp_viewStates=XPages_NORMStatesSign&xp_treatySelected=470>, accessed 29 March 2015.

[55] Rule 4, *ICRC CIHL Study*.

in Common Article 2 chiefly because it does not involve a clash between nations (whether signatories or not). In context, then, the phrase 'not of an international character' bears its literal meaning.[56]

In either case, Article 43 would not apply to the US use of the CIA in drone strikes, either because the conflict is non-international or because US non-ratification of Protocol I would result in the Protocol's inapplicability, for the US at least.

Finally on this issue, even if one accepts the position that CIA operatives are lawfully participating in hostilities as privileged belligerents, this itself raises questions about the US conducting hostilities (even with lawful combatants) from fundamentally civilian installations such as the CIA headquarters in Langley. In the first instance, use of civilians to conduct military operations would seem to put the US in breach of the provision outlined in Article 58 of Additional Protocol I, which states that:

The Parties to the conflict shall, to the maximum extent feasible:
(a) without prejudice to Article 49 of the Fourth Convention, endeavour to remove the civilian population, individual civilians and civilian objects under their control from the vicinity of military objectives;
(b) avoid locating military objectives within or near densely populated areas;
(c) take the other necessary precautions to protect the civilian population, individual civilians and civilian objects under their control against the dangers resulting from military operations.

While the US is not party to Protocol I, Rules 22–24 of the *ICRC CIHL Study* state that Article 58 is declaratory of customary international law.[57] By using civilians to conduct military operations, the US would appear to be violating these principles.

More significant concerns arise when one looks at the underlying rationale of the targeted killing program. Supporters of the drone programme have forwarded an argument that seems to suggest that while the US practice of targeted killing is permissible in foreign countries, the employment of a similar strategy against the US would somehow not be permissible; thus Heymann and Kayyem point out that even when a targeted killing overseas (ie, extraterritorial to the US) was justifiable, 'there shall be no targeted killing of: a US person [or] any person found in the United States.'[58]

[56] *Hamdan v Rumsfeld*, 548 US 557 (2006), at 67–68.

[57] Rules 22–24, *ICRC CIHL Study*.

[58] Philip Heymann and Juliette Kayyem, *Protecting Liberty in an Age of Terror* (MIT Press, 2005), at 21.

This seems an untenable position. As Anne-Marie Slaughter noted following the death of Osama bin Laden, 'having a list of leaders that you are going to take out is very troubling morally, legally and in terms of precedent. If other countries decide to apply that principle to us, we're in trouble.'[59] Applying this reasoning to the use of civilian CIA operatives in targeted killings, the US continuing to justify its use of civilians in carrying out lethal strikes in foreign countries would seem to be setting bad precedent. That is to say, if the US is acting lawfully in targeting so-called 'unprivileged belligerents' in other States, what is to stop other States targeting CIA unprivileged belligerents in their cubicles in Langley, or even in their homes? Recent reports state that some forty countries are developing or have the capability to develop armed drone programs;[60] indeed, US investment in drones accounts for less than one-third of global money spent on UAVs worldwide.[61] As Alston warns, 'the rules being set today are going to govern the conduct of many States tomorrow. I'm particularly concerned that the United States seems oblivious to this fact when it asserts an ever-expanding entitlement for itself to target individuals across the globe',[62] going on to note that 'there are strong reasons to believe that a permissive policy on drone-fired targeted killings will come back to haunt the United States in a wide range of potential situations in the not too distant future.'[63]

The US government has been encouraged to surrender oversight and execution of the drone programme to the Department of Defense (DoD);[64]

[59] 'Interview with Ann-Marie Slaughter: 'The UN Should Issue Death Warrants Against Dangerous Dictators', *CNN World—Global Public Square*, 13 May 2011, available at: <http://globalpublicsquare.blogs.cnn.com/2011/05/13/the-un-should-issue-death-warrants-against-dangerous-dictators/>, accessed 29 March 2015.

[60] See Alston, 'The CIA and Targeted Killings Beyond Borders', at 441.

[61] Peter Singer, 'Defending Against Drones: How Our New Favourite Weapon in the War on Terror Could Soon Be Turned Against Us', *Newsweek*, 25 February 2010, available at: <http://www.thedailybeast.com/newsweek/2010/02/25/defending-against-drones.html>, accessed 29 March 2015.

[62] Comments by Philip Alston, 'UN Expert Criticizes 'Illegal' Targeted Killing Policies and Calls On the US to Halt CIA Drone Killings', available at: <http://www.ohchr.org/en/NewsEvents/Pages/DisplayNews.aspx?NewsID=10094&LangID=E>, accessed 29 March 2015.

[63] Alston, 'The CIA and Targeted Killings Beyond Borders', at 441. See also Singer, 'Defending Against Drones'.

[64] See Savage, 'UN Official to Ask US to End CIA Drone Strikes', in which Philip Alston states that the DoD and not the CIA should have sole responsibility for carrying out lethal targeted killings. See also Micah Zenko, 'Transferring CIA Drone Strikes to the Pentagon', Policy Innovation Memorandum No. 31, Council on Foreign Relations, April 2013, available at: <http://www.cfr.org/drones/transferring-cia-drone-strikes-pentagon/p30434>, accessed 29 March 2015.

media reports have indicated that the Obama Administration intends to do just that.[65] However, at the time of writing, attempts to relocate control of the drone programme to the DoD appear to be mired in Congressional debates and deadlock.[66] Indeed, there seems to be considerable Congressional resistance to the handover. Democratic Senator for California and Chairman of the Senate Intelligence Committee, Dianne Feinstein stated that 'she had seen the CIA "exercise patience and discretion specifically to prevent collateral damage" and that she "would really have to be convinced that the military would carry it out that well." '[67] As such, the questions and problems raised by CIA involvement in targeted killings seem likely to remain a major issue in the ongoing debate on the use of drones.

Cyber Warfare

Cyber warfare has become the focus of considerable attention in recent years, spurred in large part by highly publicized cyber attacks against Georgia,[68] Estonia,[69] and Iran.[70] These attacks raised a number of questions regarding cyber warfare and international law, including the relevance of the law on

[65] Daniel Klaidman, 'No More Drones for CIA', *Daily Beast*, 19 March 2013, available at: <http://www.thedailybeast.com/articles/2013/03/19/exclusive-no-more-drones-for-cia.html>, accessed 29 March 2015. See also comments made by President Obama at the National Defense University in May 2013.

[66] Allen McDuffee, 'Congress Blocks Plan to Transfer Drone Control from CIA to Pentagon', *Wired*, 16 January 2014, available at: <http://www.wired.com/2014/01/drone-strikes-likely-stay-cia/>, accessed 29 March 2015; Greg Miller, 'Lawmakers Seek To Stymie Plan To Shift Control Of Drone Campaign From CIA To Pentagon', *Washington Post*, 16 January 2014, available at: <http://www.washingtonpost.com/world/national-security/lawmakers-seek-to-stymie-plan-to-shift-control-of-drone-campaign-from-cia-to-pentagon/2014/01/15/c0096b18-7e0e-11e3-9556-4a4bf7bcbd84_story.html>, accessed 4 April 2015; Ken Dilanian, 'Debate Grows over Proposal for CIA to Turn Over Drones to Pentagon', *Los Angeles Times*, 11 May 2014, available at: <http://www.latimes.com/world/middleeast/la-fg-yemen-drones-20140511-story.html>, accessed 29 March 2015.

[67] Greg Miller, 'Obama's New Drone Policy Leaves Room for CIA Role', *Washington Post*, 26 May 2013, available at: <http://www.washingtonpost.com/world/national-security/obamas-new-drone-policy-has-cause-for-concern/2013/05/25/0daad8be-c480-11e2-914f-a7aba60512a7_story.html>, accessed 29 March 2015.

[68] See Korns and Kastenberg, 'Georgia's Cyber Left Hook'.

[69] Traynor, 'Russia Accused of Unleashing Cyberwar to Disable Estonia'; Davis, 'Hackers Take Down the Most Wired Country in Europe'.

[70] John Markoff, 'A Silent Attack, But Not a Subtle One', *New York Times*, 26 September 2010, <http://www.nytimes.com/2010/09/27/technology/27virus.html>, accessed 29 March 2015.

the use of force and self-defence,[71] State responsibility,[72] and the applicability of IHL norms such as distinction, proportionality, and targeting.[73] Within the conceptual framework of this book, the question of DPH and cyber warfare is of primary interest. As noted in the *Targeted Killings* case, 'it is possible to take part in hostilities without using weapons at all'.[74] Thus, the rest of this chapter will examine the question of when a person is considered to be directly participating in cyber hostilities.

Cyber attacks: a brief background

For the purposes of this chapter it is useful to have a brief overview of the concept of cyber attacks, and what cyber warfare actually involves. Academics and practitioners[75] in the field have divided cyber warfare into two broad groups: computer network attack (CNA) and computer network exploitation (CNE) A CNA is defined as 'operations to disrupt, deny, degrade, or destroy information resident in computers and computer networks, or the computer and networks themselves',[76] while CNE is defined as 'the ability to gain access to information hosted on information systems and the ability to make use of the system itself.'[77] Cyber warfare is considered a subset of what is known in the military as information operations (or information warfare (IW)): the 'integrated employment, during military operations, of information-related capabilities in concert with other lines of operation to influence, disrupt, corrupt, or usurp the decision-making of adversaries and

[71] Matthew Hoisington, 'Cyberwarfare and the Use of Force Giving Rise to the Right of Self-Defence', 32 BC Int'l & Comp L Rev 439 (2009).

[72] Scott Shackleford, 'State Responsibility For Cyber Attacks: Competing Standards For A Growing Problem', Conference on Cyber Conflict Proceedings 2010, in Christian Czosseck and Karlis Podins (eds) (CCD COE Publications, 2010).

[73] See Ruth Wedgwood, 'Proportionality, Cyberwar and the Law of War', 76 International Law Studies 219 (2000); James Terry, 'The Lawfulness of Attacking Computer Networks in Armed Conflict and in Self-Defence in Periods Short of Armed Conflict: What are the Targeting Constraints?', 169 Mil L Rev 70 (2001); JTG Kelsey, 'Hacking into International Law: The Principles of Distinction and Neutrality in the Age of Cyber Warfare', 106 Mich L Rev 1427 (2008).

[74] *Targeted Killings*, at § 33.

[75] See Heather Harrison Dinniss, *Cyber Warfare and the Laws of War* (CUP, 2012), at 4; Michael Schmitt, 'Computer Network Attack and the Use of Force in International Law: Thoughts on a Normative Framework', 37 Colum J Transnat'l L 885 (1999); Myriam Dunn Cavelty, 'Cyberwar', in George Kassimeris and John Buckley (eds), *The Ashgate Research Companion to Modern Warfare* (Ashgate, 2010).

[76] Background Document, Expert Meeting on Direct Participation in Hostilities under International Humanitarian Law, 2 June 2003 (hereinafter DPH Background Document 2003), at 15.

[77] DPH Background Document 2003, at 15.

potential adversaries while protecting our own.'[78] Information operations can include 'such diverse activities as operations security, psychological operations, military deception, electronic warfare, physical attack, and computer network attack'.[79]

CNA and CNE are distinguished from other forms of information or electronic warfare (EW) by their methodology. EW may disrupt or destroy computer networks or computer-based information, much like CNA, but EW will achieve these ends through means external to the network itself, that is, through the use of disruptive or destructive electromagnetic energy such as an electromagnetic pulse (EMP) or some form of electronic-jamming technology.[80] CNA, by contrast, will achieve disruption or destruction through the use of computer code directly transmitted to such computer networks or systems in order to effect the disruption or destruction from within the network itself. As such, CNA 'covers a broad range of hostile techniques involving computer code.'[81]

Cyber warfare involves its own unique 'weapons'. Although it is not possible to outline in any detail the mechanics of such cyber weapons (due in large part to the technological complexity of such weapons), it is useful to touch briefly on some of the more common and accessible kinds of cyber-weapons.[82] Of the more basic 'cyber weapons' are what are known as denial of service (DoS) attacks, where the aim is to 'flood the target of the attack with an abnormally large amount of legitimate traffic to the effect of rendering it inaccessible to other users'.[83] When DoS attacks are conducted by numerous computer systems, it is known as a distributed denial of service attack (DDoS). In the attacks against Estonia in 2007, pro-Russian message boards encouraged readers to download software to allow their own computers to participate in DDoS attacks against Estonian websites;[84] the DDoS attacks against Estonia rendered the Estonian parliamentary email servers inaccessible for twelve hours and reputedly disrupted banking services

[78] US Joint Chiefs of Staff, Joint Publication 1-02, *Department of Defense Dictionary of Military and Associated Terms*, 8 November 2010 (as amended to 15 January 2015), available at: <http://fas.org/irp/doddir/dod/jp1_02.pdf>, accessed 4 April 2015.

[79] Michael Schmitt, 'Computer Network Attack: The Normative Software', 4 YBIHL 53 (2001), at 54.

[80] Harrison Dinniss, *Cyber Warfare and the Laws of War*, at 4.

[81] Harrison Dinniss, *Cyber Warfare and the Laws of War*, at 5.

[82] For a more detailed description and analysis of cyber weaponry, see generally Carr, *Inside Cyber Warfare*, at 141–60; and Andress and Winterfeld, *Cyber Warfare*, at 104–68.

[83] Paulo Shakarian, Jana Shakarian, and Andrew Ruef, *Introduction to Cyber-Warfare: A Multi-Disciplinary Approach* (Elsevier/Syngress, 2013), at 12–13.

[84] Davis, 'Hackers Take Down the Most Wired Country in Europe'.

such as automated teller machines (ATMs).[85] Similar DDoS attacks were experienced in Georgia in 2008, when Georgian–Russia hostilities in South Ossetia were accompanied by 'substantial'[86] DDoS attacks against Georgian governmental websites, in which the 'Georgian government found itself cyber-locked, barely able to communicate on the internet.'[87] DDoS attacks are frequently inconvenient and disruptive but have not, to date, caused any notable or serious physical damage to persons or property.[88]

Other, more complex, kinds of cyber weapons include so-called logical weapons, 'used to conduct reconnaissance, scout out the networks and systems of our opponents, and attack the various targets we might find.'[89] Such weapons scan for vulnerabilities in networks and systems of adversaries, access such systems, and either retrieve information from them or otherwise disrupt such systems in order to render them inoperative or defective.[90] The Stuxnet worm that was inserted into the closed network of the Iranian nuclear facility at Natanz is an example of a logical weapon designed to disrupt a network through malware.[91] Logical weapons can also cause damage to physical systems and hardware that are dependent on the software being attacked by the logic weapons. For example, the Stuxnet attack in Iran contained malware that caused the IR-1 centrifuges used for enriching uranium to spin at higher or lower frequencies than was within optimal operations limits; the result was reported mechanical damage to some centrifuges and sub-optimal performance of other centrifuges (which prevented the enrichment of uranium).[92]

[85] Davis, 'Hackers Take Down the Most Wired Country in Europe'; see also Dunn Cavelty, 'Cyberwar', at 135–36; Jason Richards, 'Denial-of-Service: The Estonian Cyberwar and Its Implications for U.S. National Security', International Affairs Review, available at: <http://www.iar-gwu.org/node/65>, accessed 29 March 2015.

[86] Korns and Kastenberg, 'Georgia's Cyber Left Hook', at 60.

[87] Korns and Kastenberg, 'Georgia's Cyber Left Hook', at 60.

[88] See further: 'Cyber-Attacks: Computer Says No', *The Economist*, 22 June 2013, available at: <http://www.economist.com/news/international/21579816-denial-service-attacks-over-internet-are-growing-easier-and-more-powerful-their>, accessed 29 March 2015.

[89] Andress and Winterfeld, *Cyber Warfare: Techniques, Tactics and Tools*, at 83.

[90] Andress and Winterfeld, *Cyber Warfare: Techniques, Tactics and Tools*, at 83, Ch. 5 of Andress and Winterfeld's text examines logical weapons in detail.

[91] See further Shakarian *et al.*, *Introduction to Cyber Warfare*, specifically Ch. 13, which examines the Stuxnet attack in detail. Stuxnet is the name that was given to the worm by hackers who had discovered the worm once it infected computers and networks outside of Natanz; the code-name given to the worm by its purported creators—the US and Israel—was 'Olympic Games'. A detailed analysis of the Olympic Games programme can be found in David Sanger, *Confront and Conceal: Obama's Secret Wars and Surprising Use of American Power* (Crown, 2012), at 188–225.

[92] See Shakarian *et al.*, at 224–35 for an overview of the Stuxnet attack; see also Paulo Shakarian, 'Stuxnet: Cyberwar Revolution in Military Affairs', Small Wars Journal, 14 April 2011, available at: <http://smallwarsjournal.com/jrnl/art/stuxnet-cyberwar-revolution-in-military-affairs>, accessed 29 March 2015.

Thus, a software-based weapon was able to create physical or kinetic effects.[93] However, these kinds of weapons are considerably more complex than the basic DDoS weapons and require commensurately more complex levels of knowledge and skill to develop and deploy. While the software for a DDoS attack can be easily downloaded from the internet, logical weapons require considerably more time to develop and require detailed analysis of the target system. As such, these kinds of weapons have tended to be used by powerful States rather than by intrepid individuals or groups of individuals.[94] That said, the possibility of purchasing the components of a logical weapon or hiring groups of experts to design such a weapon remain distinct possibilities for interested individuals or groups.[95]

Cyber attacks, the *Tallinn Manual*, and DPH

Recent years have seen increased attention focused on cyber hostilities and the question of whether cyber attacks can and should be dealt with by the law of armed conflict.[96] Academic, governmental, and practitioner attention on this question, spurred in part by the cyber attacks on Estonia in 2007 and Georgia in 2008, culminated in the 2013 publication of the *Tallinn Manual on the International Law Applicable to Cyber Warfare*.[97] The result of three years of discussion by independent experts in the field, the *Tallinn Manual* is a non-binding instrument that examines the applicable extant international law relevant to cyber hostilities. The *Manual* acknowledges that cyber

[93] For an additional overview of the tools of cyber warfare, see further Sean Watts, 'Combatant Status and Computer Network Attack', 50 Va J Int'l L 391 (2010), at 397–410; and Arie Schaap, 'Cyber Warfare Operations: Development and Use under International Law', 64 Air Force L Rev 121 (2009), at 134–39.

[94] For general discussion, see further Martin Libicki, 'Don't Buy the Cyberhype: How to Prevent Cyberwars from Becoming Real Ones', Foreign Affairs, 14 August 2013, available at: <http://www.foreignaffairs.com/articles/139819/martin-c-libicki/dont-buy-the-cyberhype>, accessed 29 March 2015; and Thomas Rid, 'Think Again: Cyberwar', Foreign Policy, 27 February 2012, available at: <http://foreignpolicy.com/2012/02/27/think-again-cyberwar/>, accessed 29 March 2015.

[95] See further Aditya Sood and Richard Enbody, *Targeted Cyber Attacks: Multi-staged Attacks Driven by Exploits and Malware* (Syngress, 2014), specifically Ch. 7, where the authors examine the ease with which the components for conducting a targeted cyber attack can be purchased on the global black market.

[96] The first major investigation into the field arguably came in 1999, with the convening of a legal conference on 'Computer Network Attack and International Law' at the United States Naval War College (proceedings published as *Computer Network Attack and International Law*, Michael Schmitt and Brian O'Donnell (eds), 76 International Law Studies (2002).

[97] Michael Schmitt (ed.), *The Tallinn Manual on the International Law Applicable to Cyber Warfare* (CUP, 2013).

operations bring unique challenges for international law, in terms of adopting old laws to fit new technologies.[98] However, the *Manual* fundamentally affirms the position stated by the US in 2011 that 'the development of norms for State conduct in cyberspace does not require a reinvention of customary international law, nor does it render existing international norms obsolete. Long-standing international norms guiding State behaviour—in times of peace and conflict—also apply in cyberspace.'[99] The *Tallinn Manual* states, in Rule 20, that 'cyber operations executed in the context of an armed conflict are subject to the law of armed conflict.'[100]

Given the applicability of the law of armed conflict to cyber operations conducted in times of armed conflict, the *Tallinn Manual* also looked at the question of direct participation in cyber hostilities. It affirms combatant status for members of the armed forces, in line with Articles 4A(1)–(3) of Geneva Convention III, as well as civilians engaged in cyber hostilities as part of a *levée en masse*, in line with Article 4A(6) of Convention III.[101] In regards to direct participation in cyber hostilities by civilians, in Rule 29 the *Manual* states that 'civilians are not prohibited from directly participating in cyber operations amounting to hostilities, but forfeit their protection from attacks for such time as they so participate.'[102]

The *Manual* does not outline any particular test for the threshold for direct participation; it defines civilians in accordance with Article 50(1) of Additional Protocol I as all persons who are neither members of the armed forces not of a *levée en masse*, and states that the majority of the International Group of Experts were of the opinion that civilians retain civilian status even if they directly participate in cyber hostilities, but that they will lose their immunity from attack due to such participation, whether in international or non-international armed conflicts.[103] More generally, for the purposes of DPH, a cyber attack is defined by the *Manual* as a 'cyber operation, whether offensive or defensive, that is reasonably expected to cause injury or death to persons or damage or destruction to objects.'[104]

With this definition of 'attack' in mind, and keeping in mind the potential scope of DPH as outlined in Chapter 2, what are the issues that arise

[98] *Tallinn Manual*, at 3.

[99] The White House, International Strategy For Cyberspace: Prosperity, Security, and Openness in a Networked World, May 2011, available at: <http://www.whitehouse.gov/sites/default/files/rss_viewer/international_strategy_for_cyberspace.pdf>, at 9, accessed 29 March 2015.

[100] Rule 20, *Tallinn Manual*, at 75.

[101] Rule 26 (armed forces) and Rule 27 (*levée en masse*), *Tallinn Manual*.

[102] Rule 29, *Tallinn Manual*, at 104.

[103] Commentary on Rule 29, *Tallinn Manual*, at 104–5.

[104] Rule 30, *Tallinn Manual*.

regarding DPH in cyber operations? The DDoS attacks against Estonia were a very basic form of CNAs, executable by anyone with a computer, Internet access, and basic computer literacy.[105] In contrast, Stuxnet was notably more complex and was most likely the result of large-scale, State-funded, and State-orchestrated endeavours.[106] Both attacks caused varying degrees of damage to their target systems and would, in theory, meet the criteria outlined in Rule 30 of the *Tallinn Manual*: that of causing damage or destruction to objects.

However, neither Stuxnet nor the Estonia attacks occurred within the context of an ongoing armed conflict and, as such, they fall outside the scope of the *Tallinn Manual* and, indeed, the scope of IHL altogether. Indeed, some theorists, such as Thomas Rid, argue that 'cyber war has never happened in the past, it does not occur in the present, and it is highly unlikely that it will disturb our future.'[107] That said, the statement that cyber war is 'highly unlikely to happen' is not an absolute repudiation; it suggests that cyber operations that may cause death or injury to persons or damage or destruction to property may yet happen; indeed, the Independent Group of Experts who drafted the Tallinn Manual are certainly of the opinion that such an attack is, at the very least, foreseeable, if not on the almost apocalyptic scale predicted by former US White House counter-terrorism and cyber-security staff member, Richard Clarke.[108]

A military communications system is rendered equally inoperative if it is disabled by a computer virus of in a bombing raid. Indeed, both were discussed by the ICRC during the DPH process, leading to the assessment that 'electronic interference with military computer networks could... suffice [as DPH], whether through computer network attacks (CNA) or computer network exploitation (CNE), as well as wiretapping the adversary's high command or transmitting tactical targeting information for attack'.[109]

[105] See 'Marching Off to Cyber War', *The Economist*, 4 December 2008, available at: <http://www.economist.com/node/12673385>, accessed 29 March 2015.

[106] See Sanger, *Confront and Conceal*, at ix.

[107] Rid, *Cyber War Will Not Take Place*, at xiv.

[108] Clarke, speaking of his book (co-authored with Robert Knake) *Cyber War: The Next Threat to National Security and What to Do About It* (Harper Collins, 2010), prophesized a cyber attack on the US that could bring about 'a catastrophic breakdown within 15 minutes. Computer bugs bring down military e-mail systems; oil refineries and pipelines explode; air-traffic control systems collapse; freight and metro trains derail; financial data are scramble; the electrical grid goes down in the eastern United States; orbiting satellites spin out of control. Society soon breaks down as food becomes scarce and money runs out' (quoted in 'Cyberwar: War in the Fifth Domain—Are the Mouse and Keyboard the New Weapons of Conflict?', *The Economist*, 1 July 2010, available at: <http://www.economist.com/node/16478792>, accessed 29 March 2015.

[109] DPHIG, at 1017–18.

However, as we have seen in Chapter 2 of this book, determining direct participation in 'conventional' hostilities is complex, determining direct participation in cyber hostilities especially so; for example, is the person who inputs the malicious software code taking direct part? What of the person who writes but does not execute the code? And the person who gives the order for the code to be written in the first place? As already noted, the *Tallinn Manual* does not explain in detail any criteria for DPH in cyber hostilities. However, some guidance can be ascertained from Rule 30 on the definition of a cyber attack.

For a cyber attack to amount to an attack for the purpose of triggering the application of IHL, it must be an act of violence against the adversary, whether in offence or defence.[110] This draws on the definition in Article 49(1) of Protocol I and excludes 'non-violent operations, such as psychological cyber operations or cyber espionage'.[111] The *Manual* goes on to clarify that:

> 'acts of violence' should not be understood as limited to activities that release kinetic force... the crux of the notion lies in the effects that are caused... the consequences of an operation, not its nature, are what generally determine the scope of the term 'attack'; 'violence' must be considered in the sense of violent consequences and is not limited to violent acts... [if] the consequences are destructive, the operation is an attack.[112]

The notion that the operation must have 'destructive consequences' hearkens back to the first limb of the ICRC DPH Guidance: that of 'threshold of harm'. Indeed, this interpretation is confirmed when one looks at the Commentary to Rule 30 of the *Tallinn Manual*, where it is stated that the scope of the Rule 30 requirement of causing injury or death to persons or damage or destruction to objects 'is not limited to effects on the targeted cyber systems. Rather, it encompasses any reasonably foreseeable consequential damage, destruction, injury, or death.'[113] The ICRC DPH standard of an act reaching a particular threshold of harm seems to be congruent with the Rule 30 standard. Furthermore, the ICRC DPH standard of 'belligerent nexus', though not explicitly referred to in the *Tallinn Manual*, also seems to have been contemplated in Rule 30: where the Commentary states that:

> care is required when identifying the originator of an attack. To illustrate, an individual may receive an email with an attachment containing malware. Execution

[110] Commentary to Rule 30, *Tallinn Manual*, at 106.
[111] Commentary to Rule 30, *Tallinn Manual*, at 106.
[112] Commentary to Rule 30, *Tallinn Manual*, at 106–07.
[113] Commentary to Rule 30, *Tallinn Manual*, at 107.

of the malware, which occurs automatically upon opening, will cause the requisite level of harm. If that individual unwittingly forwards the email and it does cause such harm, he or she will not have conducted an attack; the email's originator will have done so. By contrast, if the intermediary forwards the email knowing it contains the malware, both individuals will have conducted an attack.

Thus, the *Manual* seems to acknowledge that, absent the intent to cause harm, a cyber attack that causes damage through an inadvertent act would probably not amount to DPH. Indeed, an example of this can be seen in the Stuxnet attack. The Natanz facility was, at the time of the attack, self-contained in that it was not connected to the Internet and thus could not be remotely accessed.[114] As such, the worm had to be introduced into the Natanz Intranet by a person within the facility; an analysis of the worm by the technology company Symantec surmised that infection of the Natanz system 'may have occurred [through] a willing or unknowing third party, such as a contractor who perhaps had access to the facility, or an insider. The original infection may have been introduced by removable drive.'[115] Thus, under Rule 30, the willing participant in the infection has committed a direct act of cyber attack.[116] However, if it was an unwilling third party who inserted a removable drive into his or her computer and unknowingly released Stuxnet into the Natanz system,[117] then such a person was not committing a cyber attack.

There are a number of examples where DPH seems clear: for example, a civilian contracted by the armed forces or other party to the conflict to write malicious code or otherwise engage in CNA/CNE, a scenario similar to the CIA practice of using civilians to pilot drones in targeted killing strikes,[118] or the employment of private military and security contractors (PMSCs) in places such as Afghanistan and Iraq,[119] all would clearly be instances of DPH.

[114] Sanger, *Confront and Conceal*, at 194.

[115] See Nicolas Falliere, Liam O'Murchu, and Eric Chien, *W32.Stuxnet Dossier* (Version 1.4), February 2011, available at: <http://www.symantec.com/content/en/us/enterprise/media/security_response/whitepapers/w32_stuxnet_dossier.pdf>, at 3, accessed 29 March 2015.

[116] Some reports claim that Natanz was infiltrated by Iranian double agents working for Mossad—see further Daniel Terdiman, 'Stuxnet Delivered to Iranian Nuclear Plant on Thumb Drive', *CNET*, 13 April 2012, available at: <http://www.cnet.com/au/news/stuxnet-delivered-to-iranian-nuclear-plant-on-thumb-drive/>, accessed 29 March 2015.

[117] Sanger, in *Confront and Conceal*, reports on conversations had with the architects of Stuxnet, who attribute the release of the worm into Natanz to Iranian engineers at the facility who may have picked up an infected USB drive planted at the site by an Israeli operative, and then inserted the drive into their own laptops. Aas one of the architects said to Sanger, 'it turns out there is always an idiot around who doesn't think much about the thumb drive in their hand' (at 196).

[118] See David Cloud, 'Civilian Contractors Playing Key Roles in US Drone Operations', *Los Angeles Times*, 29 December 2011, available at: <http://articles.latimes.com/2011/dec/29/world/la-fg-drones-civilians-20111230>, accessed 29 March 2015.

[119] See Ch. 6 on PMSCs and DPH.

Thus, while civilians employed to maintain computer networks for an armed force (in the capacity of general IT services such as email, websites, etc.) would most likely not be considered as taking direct part in cyber hostilities, any employee or contractor who was specifically employed to conduct hostile CNA/CNE *would*, in theory, be considered as taking direct part in hostilities.

Where DPH in the context of cyber warfare becomes problematic is when one examines the remaining limb of the DPH test: direct causation. The ICRC DPH guidance excludes indirect effects;[120] the harm that results from a person taking direct part in hostilities must objectively be likely.[121] However, cyber attacks are, more so than regular attacks, dependent on 'chains of causality...with many...intervening effects between initial cause and ultimate effect'.[122] As such, there are a number of other situations which would *seem* to amount to DPH but that, due to the lack of a direct causal link, would fall beyond the DPH spectrum as currently envisaged. For example, a civilian unilaterally engaging in CNA/CNE for the purposes of disrupting networks and gathering information might, *prima facie*, seem to be a hostile act that may well cause damage to enemy personnel or objects, but the nature of producing the hostile act through cyber means would make the causal link too remote.

For example, during the cyber attacks against Georgia in 2008, Russian websites and blogs posted instructions on how to set up computers to run DDoS attacks automatically,[123] with some even offering downloadable DDoS programs.[124] Even if, in some future war, DDoS attacks were able to cause damage to meet the 'threshold of harm' and 'belligerent nexus' tests, the nature of such attacks would not meet the 'direct causation' test. As Heather Harrison Dinniss has argued, 'the requirement that the act forms an integral part of a concrete and coordinated tactical operation will exclude those who download script to join in unspecified

[120] DPHIG, at 1017. [121] DPHIG, at 1017.

[122] William Owens, Kenneth Dam, and Herbert Lin (eds), *Technology, Policy, Law, and Ethics Regarding US Acquisition and Use of Cyberattack Capabilities* (National Academies Press, 2009), available at: <http://www.nap.edu/catalog/12651/technology-policy-law-and-ethics-regarding-us-acquisition-and-use-of-cyberattack-capabilities>, at 127, accessed 4 April 2015.

[123] See Evgeny Morozov, 'How I Became a Soldier in the Georgia–Russia Cyber War', *Slate*, 14 August 2008, available at: <http://www.slate.com/articles/technology/technology/2008/08/an_army_of_ones_and_zeroes.html>, accessed 29 March 2015.

[124] Morozov, 'How I Became a Soldier in the Georgia-Russia Cyber War'; see also Asher Moses, 'Georgian Websites Forced Offline in Cyber War', *Sydney Morning Herald*, 12 August 2008, available at: <http://www.smh.com.au/news/technology/georgian-websites-forced-offline-in-cyber-war/2008/08/12/1218306848654.html>, accessed 29 March 2015.

DDoS attacks, where control of the computer is merely handed over to a command and control server which selects the targets.'[125]

Another example is that of a civilian who writes a malware programme and gives it to the armed forces or other party to the conflict, but does not execute the malware him or herself; again, the threshold of harm and the belligerent nexus threshold would seem to be met, but the lack of 'causal proximity'[126] would likewise exclude such a person. Indeed, this scenario is roughly equivalent to the 'bomb maker': someone who creates the mechanism through which the destructive act is executed but is not him or herself involved beyond the construction phase; all subsequent actions—such as the deployment of the destructive mechanism—are the responsibility of other persons. The ICRC Guidance seems to suggest that such acts would *not* amount to direct participation, in that the 'causation' test would not be met. The Guidance states:

> individual conduct that merely builds up or maintains the capacity of a party to harm its adversary...is excluded from the concept of direct participation in hostilities...[examples of non-DPH] include scientific research and design, as well as production and transport of weapons and equipment.[127]

The problem for IHL is that, given the strictness of the criteria for DPH, there is a genuine possibility that most cyber attacks undertaken by civilians would fall outside the scope of most of the criteria for DPH which could lead to, as David Turns puts it, civilians engaging in cyber warfare 'with impunity'.[128]

In this legal grey zone, it is not hard to foresee States (and non-State groups alike) enlisting civilians to conduct cyber warfare on their behalf, without running the risk of having such civilians be considered as taking direct part in hostilities. Indeed, such activities undertaken by civilians could be dismissed as simply common criminal acts and the activities disavowed as the acts of individuals having no real connection to the armed conflict.[129]

[125] Heather Harrison Dinniss, 'Cyber Warriors, Patriotic Hackers and the Laws of War', in Dan Saxon (ed.), *International Humanitarian Law and the Changing Technology of War* (Martinus Nijhoff, 2013), at 271. See also Harrison Dinniss, *Cyber Warfare and the Laws of War*, at 159–72 on civilian DPH in cyber war.

[126] Harrison Dinniss, 'Cyber Warriors', at 272.

[127] DPHIG, at 1021. However, the experts involved in the DPH process were divided as to whether civilian scientists and weapons experts could always be considered as not taking direct part. For instance, some were of the opinion that constructing improvised explosive devices could be considered as exceeding mere capacity-building and amount to a measure 'preparatory to a concrete military operation'. See further DPH Summary Report 2006, at 48–60.

[128] David Turns, 'Cyber Warfare and the Notion of Direct Participation in Hostilities', 17 J Conflict & Sec L (2012), at 288.

[129] The vernacular term is 'black hat hacker': see 'Timeline: A Forty Year History of Hacking', *CNN Tech*, 19 November 2001, available at: <http://articles.cnn.com/2001-11-19/tech/hack.

In such a case, the appropriate response would lie with domestic law enforcement rather than under the law of armed conflict.[130] However, as with the use of civilians to pilot drones, a State or non-State group using civilians to conduct cyber attacks could put such persons in line for targeting by an adverse party, and put such persons at risk if they were captured by an adverse party.

Furthermore, the tacit use of civilians to conduct cyber warfare on behalf of the State could lead to additional problems for those States. As Sean Watts has pointed out:

> civilian participation in hostilities raises concerns of state responsibility. Classically understood, law-of-war treaties operate as contracts between states. When confronted with breaches of these treaties, states may resort to a number of remedies including diplomatic negotiations, mediation, litigation, sanction by international bodies, and, in extreme cases, treaty suspension or even war. Existing treaty-based definitions of the combatant class thus could be interpreted to restrain individual conduct as well as states' composition of their fighting forces . . . states that employ civilians to take direct part in hostilities would be in breach of such limits.[131]

As noted, in using civilians to conduct military operations, a State could run foul of the provisions outlined in Article 58 of Additional Protocol I, which oblige parties to the conflict to take all feasible precautions to protect the civilian population and civilian objects under its control against the effects of attacks, including avoiding locating military objectives within or near densely populated areas, taking any other necessary precautions to protect the civilian population, individual civilians, and civilian objects under their control against the dangers resulting from military operations. As Schmitt notes: 'the use of civilians, whether contractors or government employees, is fraught with legal pitfalls. Clearly, a prudent approach would be to employ military personnel for information warfare purposes.'[132]

history.idg_1_phone-phreaks-chaos-computer-club-emmanuel-goldstein?_s=PM:TECH>, accessed 29 March 2015.

130 For example, the UK banned DDoS attacks under § 36 of the Police and Justice Act 2006, available at: <http://www.legislation.gov.uk/ukpga/2006/48/section/36>, accessed 29 March 2015; see also Tom Espiner, 'U.K. Outlaws Denial-Of-Service Attacks', CNET, 10 November 2006, available at: <http://news.cnet.com/U.K.-outlaws-denial-of-service-attacks/2100-7348_3-6134472.html>, accessed 29 March 2015.

131 Watts, 'Combatant Status and CNA', at 423.

132 Schmitt, 'Wired Warfare: Computer Network Attack and the Jus in Bello', in Schmitt and O'Donnell (eds), *Computer Network Attack and International Law*, at 198.

Conclusion

Advancements in technology have made it possible for civilians to participate directly in hostilities without having to be present, corporeally, in the battlefield itself. Whether through piloting drones or launching cyber attacks, civilians are able to have an immediate and direct impact on hostilities while remaining geographically distant from those hostilities as they happen. These technological advances have had a profound impact on the manner in which modern wars are fought, removing entire categories of direct participant from the geographical zone of active hostilities.

However, the ability to fight wars remotely has not been the only development in the conduct of armed conflicts in the last quarter of a century. Economic considerations have driven additional changes in the conduct of armed conflict and these have resulted in a new category of civilian participant in hostilities: the PMSC. As with targeted killings and remote warriors, the use of PMSCs has contributed to a blurring of the distinction between the civilian and the military , a distinction on which rests the entire modern law of armed conflict. This creates its own problems for both those parties to a conflict who employ PMSCs as well as those who find themselves confronting PMSCs and the States (or non-State groups) who employ them. The next chapter of this book thus explores the problems that arise regarding the use of PMSCs in war zones.

6

Private Military and Security Contractors

Introduction

In the last decade, civilian involvement in battlefield affairs has become particularly pronounced in one respect: through the increasing use of private military and security contractors (PMSCs). In the conflicts in Iraq and Afghanistan, PMSCs have been widely used and have, unfortunately, been involved in a number of high-profile incidents, including the March 2004 ambushing, mutilation, and eventual deaths of four Blackwater[1] contractors,[2] the abuse of detainees at the Abu Ghraib Detention Facility,[3] and the 2006 Nisour Square attacks that resulted in the deaths of seventeen Iraqi civilians at the hands of Blackwater security contractors.[4] It has been reported that between 2005 and 2007, Blackwater employees were allegedly involved in 195 shooting incidents; 163 of those cases involved Blackwater personnel firing first.[5]

[1] Blackwater International rebranded themselves as Xe Services in 2009: 'Blackwater Changes its Name to Xe', *New York Times*, 14 February 2009, available at: <http://www.nytimes.com/2009/02/14/us/14blackwater.html>, accessed 29 March 2015. They rebranded as Academi in 2011: Jason Ukman, 'Ex-Blackwater Firm Gets a Name Change, Again', *Washington Post*, 12 December 2011, available at: <http://www.washingtonpost.com/blogs/checkpoint-washington/post/ex-blackwater-firm-gets-a-name-change-again/2011/12/12/gIQAXf4YpO_blog.html>, accessed 29 March 2015.

[2] The contractors, Scott Helvenston, Jerko Zovko, Wesley Batalona, and Mike Teague were all former armed services members. See Jeffrey Gettleman, 'Enraged Mob in Fallujah Kills 4 American Contractors', *New York Times*, 31 March 2004, available at: <http://www.nytimes.com/2004/03/31/international/worldspecial/31CND-IRAQ.html>, accessed 29 March 2015.

[3] See further Anthony Jones and George Fay, 'Investigation of Intelligence Activities at Abu Ghraib/Investigation of the Abu Ghraib Prison and the 205th Military Intelligence Brigade, August 2004', reprinted in Karen Greenberg and Joshua Dratel (eds), *The Torture Papers: The Road to Abu Ghraib* (CUP, 2005).

[4] David Johnston and John Broder, 'F.B.I. Says Guards Killed 14 Iraqis without Cause', *New York Times*, 14 November 2007, available at: <http://www.nytimes.com/2007/11/14/world/middleeast/14blackwater.html>, accessed 29 March 2015.

[5] House of Representatives, Hearing before the Committee on Oversight and Government Reform on Blackwater USA, No. 110-89, 2 October 2007, available at: <https://house.resource.org/110/org.c-span.201290-1.1.pdf>, at 3, accessed 29 March 2015.

The increasing use of PMSCs in combat zones raises questions with regards to their status, which has knock-on effects for State (and non-State) compliance with the principle of distinction. This chapter will examine the issues raised with regards to the principle of distinction and civilian participation in armed conflicts specific to the use of PMSCs. After a brief examination of the origins and development of the PMSC and some of the roles filled by PMSCs in current conflicts, this chapter will explore the legal problems that arise when PMSCs are employed in war zones.

A Brief History of the PMSC

Many commentaries on PMSCs position the rise of the private military firm as a comparatively new phenomenon.[6] Most locate the origins of the current rise in private military firms at the end of the Cold War,[7] sometimes with passing reference to the historical use of mercenaries and soldiers of fortune in ancient conflicts. However, the use of the private warrior and the outsourcing of military functions are actually 'as old as war itself.'[8] The modern international legal system, based on the Westphalian notion of the centralized authority of the sovereign State,[9] holds that armed force may only be legitimately wielded by the sovereign State.[10] However, prior to this development, wars were fought by whoever had the money to mount the campaign. Furthermore, when States did go to war, they often called on hired soldiers to compensate for their lack of regular standing armies. Mercenaries and

[6] Louise Doswald-Beck, 'Private Military Companies under IHL', in Simon Chesterman and Chia Lehnardt (eds), *From Mercenaries to Market: The Rise and Regulation of Private Military Companies* (OUP, 2007), at 115; Lindsay Cameron, 'Private Military Companies—Their Status under International Humanitarian Law and its Impact on their Regulation', 88 IRRC 573 (2006), at 573.

[7] Daniel Ridlon, 'Contractors or Illegal Combatants? The Status of Armed Contractors in Iraq', 62 Air Force L Rev 199 (2008), at 201.

[8] Peter Singer, *Corporate Warriors: The Rise of the Privatized Military Industry*, at 19. See also Juan Carlos Zarate, 'The Emergence of a New Dog of War: Private International Security Companies, International Law, and the New World Disorder', 35 Stanford J Int'l L 75 (1998).

[9] Leo Gross, 'The Peace of Westphalia 1648–1948', 42 AJIL 20 (1948).

[10] The classic statement to this effect is Max Weber's definition of the modern state as an entity which is defined by its 'monopoly of legitimate physical violence within a certain territory' (Max Weber, *Political Writings* (Peter Lassman and Ronald Speirs (eds), CUP, 1994), at 310–11); see also Kyle Ballard, 'The Privatization of Military Affairs: A Historical Look into the Evolution of the Private Military Industry', in Thomas Jäger and Gerhard Kümmel (eds), *Private Military and Security Companies: Chances, Problems, Pitfalls and Prospects* (VS Verlag für Sozialwissenschaften, 2007), at 37–40.

hired soldiers were used in numerous armed conflicts over the centuries, with records on their use from the Peloponnesian War to the Crimean War.[11]

By the mid-1800s, national defence forces were primarily composed of citizens, a norm that continued until the Second World War.[12] However, it was that conflict that began to change the ways in which the defence forces met their requirements. Due to the scale and scope of the Second World War, it was necessary for corporations to be contracted to provide goods to the defence forces. This occurred on both sides of the conflict: among the Allies, corporations such as Chrysler, de Havilland, Rolls-Royce, Ford, and Hughes Aircraft were some of the major defence contractors supplying the war efforts in Europe and the Pacific; on the Axis side, BMW, Krupp, Bayer, and Siemens were recipients of numerous military and defence contracts.[13]

The end of the Second World War did not end the civil–military relationship.[14] However, until the Vietnam War, private military contracts remained primarily domestic; that is, companies were contracted to provide matériel, munitions, supplies, equipment, and so on, but the task of soldiering remained public, undertaken by either enlisted or conscripted citizens. The task of fighting in the field remained a citizen's role.[15] That began to change somewhat during the Vietnam War as significant numbers of private contractors were deployed to combat zones. While still remaining in support roles, these private contractors nonetheless found themselves in proximity to active hostilities, far removed from the assembly workers in factories 'back home' that typified military contracting previously. In 1969, at the peak of US deployment in Vietnam, 550,000 members of US armed forces were

[11] See Matthew Trundle, *Greek Mercenaries: From the Late Archaic Period to Alexander* (Routledge, 2004), and CC Bayley, *Mercenaries for the Crimea: The German, Swiss and Italian Legions in British Service 1854–56* (McGill, 1977).

[12] Ballard, 'The Privatization of Military Affairs', at 38–40; Elke Krahmann, *States, Citizens and the Privatization of Security* (CUP, 2010), at 52–65.

[13] See generally Mark Harrison, 'Resource Mobilisation for World War II: the USA, UK, USSR and Germany, 1938–1945', 41 Economic History Rev 171 (1988).

[14] Indeed, the increasingly close relationship between government and military industry was of such concern, that US President Dwight D Eisenhower, himself former Supreme Allied Commander of European forces during the Second World War, made specific reference to the dangers of the allegiance between government, military, and corporations in his farewell speech in 1961, where he used the now-famed term 'the military-industrial complex'. President Dwight D Eisenhower's Farewell Address to the Nation, 17 January 1961; a full transcript can be found at: <http://avalon.law.yale.edu/20th_century/eisenhower001.asp>, accessed 6 April 2015.

[15] The use of mercenary armies in Africa was, however, widespread during the post-Second World War era; see further Ch. 2 of this book. Mercenaries should, however, be distinguished from PMSCs, as will be seen later in this chapter. For more on the use of mercenaries in decolonisation wars, see generally Abdel-Fatau Musah and J 'Kayode Fayemi (eds), *Mercenaries: An African Security Dilemma* (Pluto, 2000), and Sarah Percy, *Mercenaries: The History of a Norm in International Relations* (OUP, 2007), specifically Ch. 5.

joined by 9000 civilian contractors, putting the ratio of civilian contractor to serviceman at one to sixty.[16] However, the US armed forces did not contract any service that might involve active participation in hostilities, such as security and body-guarding duties, the administration of military detention facilities, or the operation of any weapons system.[17]

A significant change in military policy came about in the twenty years following the end of the Vietnam War, one which set the scene for the evolution and rise of the 'modern' PMSC. Accepted wisdom at the time maintained that it was no longer necessary to keep large standing national armies; technological advances were such that large-scale ground forces would no longer be cost effective.[18] The end of the Cold War in the late 1980s and early 1990s contributed further to this rethinking of domestic military policy. Most of the major powers began a process of downsizing and outsourcing military functions. Under Presidents George HW Bush and Bill Clinton, the US active duty force was reduced by 30 per cent.[19] This was in line with a general global trend towards the privatization and outsourcing of governmental functions. One study reported that armed services personnel employed worldwide dropped from a high of nearly 9 million in 1990 to just over 3 million by 1997;[20] US armed services personnel were reduced by nearly 1 million active-duty troops in the five-year period following the end of the Cold War.[21]

It was under these circumstances that the modern private military industry emerged. The outsourcing and downsizing that arose following the Cold War left vacancies in defence force roles that companies now stepped in to fill. Where mess halls were once run by enlisted personnel, private corporations now purchased franchise rights from Pizza Hut,[22] and employed

[16] According to official US government records; see George Prugh, *Law at War: Vietnam 1964–1973* (Vietnam Studies Series, Department of the Army, Washington DC, 1975), available at: <http://www.history.army.mil/books/Vietnam/Law-War/law-fm.htm>, at 88, accessed 29 March 2015.

[17] See Joseph Heiser, *Logistics Support* (Vietnam Studies Series, Department of the Army, Washington, 1974), available at: <http://www.history.army.mil/books/Vietnam/logistic/index.htm>, at 88–89, accessed 29 March 2015.

[18] See the DPH Background Document 2003, at 4: 'the dependence of modern armies on technology combined with decreasing military budgets and the relative cost-efficiency of private companies... has led some countries to outsource some of their military activities.'

[19] Peter Singer, 'Outsourcing War', 84 Foreign Affairs 119 (2005), at 120.

[20] Kevin O'Brien, 'PMCs, Myths, and Mercenaries: The Debate on Private Military Companies', 145 RUSI Journal (2000), at 59–64.

[21] Ballard, 'The Privatization of Military Affairs', at 44.

[22] Peter Singer, 'Outsourcing the Fight', Brookings Institute Commentary (2008), available at: <http://www.brookings.edu/opinions/2008/0605_military_contractors_singer.aspx>, accessed 29 March 2015.

subcontractors to operate concessions at US military bases across the world. However, the PMSC as we understand it now would not truly reach its apotheosis until the 2003 US invasion of Iraq when PMSCs—including nearly 30,000 armed contractors—would at one point outnumber 'regular' military personnel 180,000 to 165,000.[23]

The Current Roles of PMSCs

Often PMSCs are talked about as though they comprise one homogenous entity when in fact, PMSCs serve multiple functions.[24] Singer has identified three different categories of private military firm: military support firms, military consulting firms, and military provider firms.[25] Military consulting firms provide advisory and training services integral to the operation and restructuring of a client's armed forces. Military Professional Resources Incorporated (MPRI), a training firm, is one such example, providing instruction to the US military, including running training exercises and simulations for the US armed forces, as well as administering the Reserve Officer Training Corps (ROTC) and Staff College programmes.[26]

Military support firms are, generally, engaged in the field; they are often on the ground providing logistical support for armed forces, such as the acquisition, maintenance, and transportation of military matériel, facilities, and personnel.[27] DynCorp is a prime example. In 2012, it was awarded a contract by the US Navy to 'provide facility support services for personnel from the Naval Mobile Construction Battalion unit in Dili, Timor-Leste.'[28]

[23] Accurate figures regarding the numbers of contractors deployed in Iraq are hard to find; the US Government Accountability Office's 2005 Report to Congress on PMSCs cited Department of Defense (DoD) figures which put the number of PMSCs at least sixty companies, with nearly 25,000 employees (2005 United States Government Accountability Office Report, July 2005, GAO-05-7370). The 2006 report cites the Director of the Private Security Company Association of Iraq's estimate of 181 PMSCs and around 48,000 employees (Rebuilding Iraq: Actions Still Needed to Improve Use of Private Security Providers, United States Government Accountability Office, Testimony before the Subcommittee on National Security, *Emerging Threats, and International Relations*, Committee on Government Reform, 13 June 2006, GAO-06-865T). However, a census undertaken of all PMSC employees, including US, Iraqi, and third State nationals came to a figure of 100,000 (Renae Merle, 'Census Counts 100,000 Contractors in Iraq', *Washington Post*, 5 December 2006, available at: <http://www.washingtonpost.com/wp-dyn/content/article/2006/12/04/AR2006120401311.html>, accessed 29 March 2015.

[24] Singer, *Corporate Warriors*, at 88.

[25] Singer, *Corporate Warriors*, at 91.

[26] Singer, *Corporate Warriors*, at 123.

[27] Singer, *Corporate Warriors*, at 137.

[28] 'DynCorp International Awarded Contract Valued at up to $15.5 Million to Provide Facility Support Services for Naval Facilities Engineering Command Pacific', *Business Wire*, 2 April 2012, available at: <http://www.businesswire.com/news/home/20120402006330/en/DynCorp-International-Awarded-Contract-Valued-15.5-Million#.U-1cdk2KAdU>, accessed 29 March 2015.

Among those support services were the construction and maintenance of living quarters, communications supply including Internet access and telephone, as well as bathroom facilities, laundry services, and kitchen facilities.

Finally, military provider firms are 'defined by their focus on the tactical environment.'[29] These companies, such as Academi, provide on-site security services such as intelligence gathering and support, as well as armed security details for both fixed and mobile objectives. For example, Academi has been reportedly involved in the US drone programme, including assisting in 'planning the assassinations of suspected Taliban and al Qaeda operatives',[30] as well as assembling and loading 'Hellfire missiles and 500-pound laser-guided bombs on remotely piloted Predator aircraft'[31] used in targeted killings in Pakistan and Afghanistan.[32]

In practice, these categories—military provider, military consulting, military support—are not distinct from each other, in that firms may provide several or all of these services. For example, Academi provides training and consulting services, along with security services, which would qualify it as a military support, consulting, and provider firm, according to Singer's categories.[33] Regardless of this, it is the actual services provided and functions fulfilled that will have a determinative effect on how PMSCs are dealt with under international humanitarian law (IHL). Indeed, as Cameron and Chetail note, 'whether the company officially sees itself as providing combat services is not decisive for how their activities may be gauged and regulated under IHL.'[34] It is the services that these companies are contracted to supply, and how they carry them out, that is of significance when it comes to the next issue that must be addressed when dealing with PMSCs: what status do PMSCs have under IHL? Are they combatants, mercenaries, or civilians?

The Status of PMSCs under International Law

Identifying what kind of status PMSCs have under international law is vital for the correct application of the relevant law by all parties concerned.

[29] Singer, *Corporate Warriors*, at 92–97.

[30] Jeremy Scahill, *Dirty Wars: The World is a Battlefield* (Serpent's Tail, 2013), at 251.

[31] Scahill, *Dirty Wars*, at 251.

[32] See further Jennifer Elsea, Moshe Schwartz, and Kennon Nakamura, *Private Security Contractors in Iraq: Background, Legal Status, and Other Issues*, Congressional Research Service Report for Congress, August 2008, available at: <http://fas.org/sgp/crs/natsec/RL32419.pdf>, accessed 29 March 2015.

[33] Singer, *Corporate Warriors*, at 91.

[34] Lindsey Cameron and Vincent Chetail, *Privatizing War: Private Military and Security Companies under Public International Law* (CUP, 2013), at 5.

Therefore, an elaboration of the possible applicable law is helpful at this stage to help determine whether PMSCs are combatants, civilians, or mercenaries. In order to answer this question, it is necessary to look to a number of key IHL treaties, namely the 1949 Geneva Conventions and its 1977 Additional Protocols.

Are PMSCs combatants?

PMSCs are not combatants under the law of armed conflict. In the first instance, PMSCs are not members of the armed forces, as outlined in the ambit of Article 4A(1) of Geneva Convention III. Indeed, the very essence of the PMSC is that they are contractors external to the hierarchy of the armed forces. Incorporating such persons within the armed forces would seem to be contrary to the reasons why they were employed in the first instance. Aas noted by Cameron and Chetail, 'the whole point of privatization is . . . to devolve on the private sector what was previously the preserve of government authorities and state actors . . . the doctrine and practice of states that rely heavily on PMSCs confirm that, as a general rule, PMSCs are not incorporated into their armed forces, and certainly not as combatants.'[35]

Indeed, as Bosch notes, 'the majority of states making use of PSCs [private security contractors] are at pains to emphasize that they are merely civilian contractors'.[36] This is demonstrated by the US Department of Defense (DoD) Instruction 3020.41 on contractor personnel authorized to accompany the US Armed Forces, which, in its 2005 iteration, stated that 'contractors may support military operations as civilians accompanying the force, so long as such personnel have been designated as such by the force they accompany'.[37] The most recent version of this document, issued in 2011,[38] does not explicitly mention contractors as being civilians, but states that contractors may be used 'for all functions not inherently governmental and . . . in support of such operations in a non-combat role as long as contractor personnel residing with the force in foreign contingencies have been designated as CAAF [contractors authorized to accompany the force] by the force they

[35] Cameron and Chetail, *Privatizing War*, at 391.

[36] Shannon Bosch, 'Private Security Contractors and International Humanitarian Law', 16 African Sec Rev 34 (2007), at 38.

[37] US Department of Defense, Instruction 3020.41 on Contractor Personnel Authorised to Accompany the US Armed Forces (2005), available at: <http://fas.org/irp/doddir/dod/i3020_41.pdf>, at 6.1.1, accessed 29 March 2015.

[38] US Department of Defense, Instruction 3020.41 on Contractor Personnel Authorised to Accompany the US Armed Forces (2011), available at: <http://www.dtic.mil/whs/directives/corres/pdf/302041p.pdf>, accessed 29 March 2015 (DoDI 3020.41).

accompany'.[39] As noted by Bosch,[40] and confirmed by Ipsen,[41] Cameron,[42] and Gillard,[43] 'state practice suggests that commercial contracts, on their own, are not considered by states to be sufficient to incorporate PSCs into the armed forces.'[44]

It also seems unlikely that PMSCs would fall under Article 4A(2) of Convention III, which would grant combatant status to:

> [m]embers of other militias and members of other volunteer corps, including those of organized resistance movements, belonging to a Party to the conflict and operating in or outside their own territory, even if this territory is occupied, provided that such militias or volunteer corps, including such organized resistance movements, fulfil the following conditions:
> (a) that of being commanded by a person responsible for his subordinates;
> (b) that of having a fixed distinctive sign recognizable at a distance;
> (c) that of carrying arms openly;
> (d) that of conducting their operations in accordance with the laws and customs of war.

First, for a militia or volunteer corps to be considered as 'belonging' to a party to the conflict, the State 'must accept that a group fights on its behalf'.[45] As noted, the US has been steadfast in maintaining that private contractors are civilians who accompany the armed forces in non-combat roles.[46] As such, it seems perverse to attempt to designate such persons as combatants when the very authority that has employed them is doing its utmost to prevent such a classification.

Indeed, even though the 'belonging' element will have implications under the law of State responsibility,[47] for the purposes of applying IHL, 'using the state responsibility test to determine whether a group 'belongs' to a party to the conflict'[48] is problematic because the intention of the 'belonging' element

[39] DoDI 3020.41, Enclosure 2, at 1(a)(1).

[40] Bosch, 'Private Security Contractors and International Humanitarian Law', at 38.

[41] Knut Ipsen, 'Combatants and Non-Combatants', in Dieter Fleck (ed.), *The Handbook of International Humanitarian Law* (3rd edn, Oxford, 2013), at 105.

[42] Cameron, 'Private Military Companies', at 584.

[43] Emanuela-Chiara Gillard, 'Business Goes to War: Private Military/Security Companies and International Humanitarian Law', 88 IRRC 525 (2006), at 533.

[44] Bosch, 'Private Security Contractors and International Humanitarian Law', at 38.

[45] Cameron and Chetail, *Privatizing War*, at 395.

[46] DoDI 3020.41, Enclosure 2, at 1(a)(1).

[47] See Cameron and Chetail, *Privatizing War*, specifically Ch. 2 on the international responsibility of States and PMSCs; see also generally Hannah Tonkin, *State Control over Private Military and Security Companies in Armed Conflict* (CUP, 2013).

[48] Cameron and Chetail, *Privatizing War*, at 394.

in Article 4A(2) is not, *prima facie*, to prove that a State is responsible for the acts of the militia or volunteer group, but rather to determine whether such persons are to be considered combatants, entitled to prisoner-of-war (POW) rights and combatant immunity.

Furthermore, while some PMSCs may well fulfil the additional criteria of 'being commanded by a person responsible for his subordinates',[49] openly carrying arms,[50] and conducting themselves in accordance with the laws of armed conflict,[51] there is less chance of compliance with the wearing of a 'fixed distinction sign recognisable at a distance'. As noted by Swisspeace, in its study on the use of PMSCs in Angola and Afghanistan:

> PSC staff does [*sic*] often not wear clearly identifiable uniforms or IDs badges, making it difficult to identify and monitor them. While some do wear visible company logos on hats, T-shirts or even uniforms, others wear civilian clothing and do not display company identification at all (or show IDs upon request). Marked cars are rare . . . and many cars do not even feature license plates.[52]

Indeed, the US DoD makes it clear that as a general rule, 'commanders shall not issue military clothing to contractor personnel or allow the wearing of military or military look-alike uniforms'.[53] Thus, while they may accompany the armed forces, PMSCs are not integrated into the armed forces as combatants. As noted by Schmitt:

> it is difficult to imagine a situation in which individual government civilian or contractor employees might qualify as formal members of the armed forces,

[49] Largely due to the fact that many modern private military and security companies are 'founded and run by ex-military and thus have a natural tendency toward military hierarchy and structure that would meet the test of command responsibility' (Cameron and Chetail, *Privatizing War*, at 402); see also Schmitt, 'Direct Participation in Hostilities by Private Contractors', at 530.

[50] A perfunctory Google Images search of private military and security contractors brings up numerous images of companies such as Blackwater/Academi, Dyncorp, and CACI openly carrying arms while guarding convoys or personnel. See, eg, the image taken by Saurabh Das for the Associated Press (accompanying Karen DeYoung's story 'State Department Struggles To Oversee Private Army', *Washington Post*, 21 October 2007, available at: <http://www.washingtonpost.com/wp-dyn/content/article/2007/10/20/AR2007102001325.html>, accessed 29 March 2015) which depicts Paul Bremer, the civilian administrator of Iraq, arriving at a soccer stadium in Baghdad in 2004 surrounded by openly armed Blackwater security guards.

[51] See Cameron and Chetail, *Privatizing War*, at 405–06.

[52] Ulrike Joras and Adrian Schuster (eds), *Private Security Companies and Local Populations: An Exploratory Study of Afghanistan and Angola*, Swisspeace Working Paper 1/2008, available at: <http://www.swisspeace.ch/fileadmin/user_upload/Media/Publications/WP1_2008.pdf>, at 13–14, accessed 29 March 2015.

[53] DoDI 3020.41, Enclosure 2, at 3(j).

regardless of the duties they perform. In the first place, most armed forces have set procedures for enlistment or conscription. An individual failing to comply with them cannot individually become a member thereof... the fact that no formal recruitment has occurred is dispositive evidence of a state's understanding that the civilian in question does not enjoy Article 4(A)(1) status... since civilian employees and private contractors do not wear uniforms denoting combatant status, seldom fall under the formal command of military personnel, and generally lie beyond the reach of military discipline that the armed forces use to enforce adherence to the 'laws and customs of war', it would be a stretch to style them members of the armed forces.[54]

To argue that PMSCs could be considered combatants under Article 4A(2) is also not supported by a:

teleological interpretation of Article 4A(2)... as such a use of the provision runs counter to its historical purpose, which was to allow for groups such as the partisans in the Second World War to have POW status... while there is no obligation to restrict the interpretation of Article 4A(2) to its historical purpose, advertence to that purpose provides some indication of the inadequacy and inappropriateness of using that provision in the context of modern private military and security companies.[55]

Finally, PMSCs are likely not to be deemed combatants under Article 43 of Protocol I. Article 43 outlines provisions similar to those in Article 4A(2) of Convention III: the necessity for any 'organised armed forces, groups and units'[56] to be 'under a command responsible for the conduct of its subordinates... subject to an internal disciplinary system which, inter alia, shall enforce compliance with the rules of international law applicable in armed conflict.'[57] Article 43 would not grant combatant status to PMSCs, according to the same reasoning outlined for Article 4A(1)–(2).[58] It would thus seem that PMSCs would not be considered combatants under any current IHL, unless such PMSCs were clearly and unequivocally incorporated into the armed forces by their State of origin.

[54] Schmitt, 'Direct Participation in Hostilities by Private Contractors or Civilian Employees', at 524, 526.

[55] Cameron and Chetail, *Privatizing War*, at 407.

[56] Art. 43, API.

[57] Art. 43, API.

[58] See Gillard, 'Business Goes to War', at 536. Cameron and Chetail, in *Privatizing War*, at 408, concur, noting that PMSCs would fail any currently accepted test for 'de facto incorporation' into the armed forces and that, even if such de facto incorporation was shown to have taken place, the additional element of notification of incorporation to other parties to the conflict would defeat any claims to combatant status. See also Dale Stephens and Angeline Lewis, 'The Targeting of Civilian Contractors in Armed Conflict', 9 YBIHL 25 (2006), at 36.

Are PMSCs mercenaries?

A common refrain in a number of commentaries is that PMSCs are 'mercenaries',[59] with some of the literature either using the terms 'PMSC' and 'mercenary' interchangeably, conflating the two categories, or discussing the historical use of mercenaries in armed conflict, without drawing the distinction between mercenaries who are hired to take active part in hostilities and PMSCs who have been hired for non-combat duty.[60] Also common is reference to PMSCs as mercenaries in a colloquial sense; that is, they are called contractors mercenaries due to the high salaries such contractors are frequently paid.[61] As Abdel-Fatau Musah and J 'Kayode Fayemi have argued, 'private military companies are nothing but the old poison of vagabond mercenaries in new designer bottles'.[62] Indeed, a 2007 report to the UN General Assembly from the Working Group on the use of mercenaries warned that, in many instances, the use of PMSCs amounted to 'new modalities of mercenary-related activities.'[63]

As such, it is necessary to determine whether PMSCs are mercenaries, as if they are they would not be entitled to either combatant rights or privileges,[64] would be committing an offence under the UN Convention on Mercenaries,[65] and would lose their civilian immunity from targeting during the armed conflict for the duration of their direct participation as

[59] See David Usborne, 'Blackwater Mercenaries Face Justice for Bloodbath in Baghdad That Caused 14 Civilian Deaths', *Independent*, 31 August 2014, available at: <http://www.independent.co.uk/news/world/americas/blackwater-mercenaries-face-justice-for-bloodbath-in-baghdad-that-caused-14-civilian-deaths-9701810.html>, accessed 29 March 2015.

[60] See for example Anna Leander, *Global Ungovernance: Mercenaries, States and the Control over Violence*, COPRI Working Paper 4/2002, Copenhagen Peace Research Institute; Zoe Salzman, 'Private Military Contractors and the Taint of a Mercenary Reputation', 40 NYU J Int'l & Pol 853 (2007–2008). See also Imke-Ilse Drews, 'Private Military Companies: The New Mercenaries?—An International Law Analysis', in Jäger and Kümmel (eds), *Private Military and Security Companies*, at 339, where she argues that Blackwater could fulfil the criteria for mercenary status under API and the UN Convention.

[61] In 2004, a corporal with three-years' experience in the US military could expect to earn around US$20,000 (this is a base pay rate—see generally: <http://www.military.com/Resources/ResourcesContent/0,13964,62603-mil_status_active-1,00.html>, accessed 29 March 2015). At the time of his leadership of US forces in Iraq, General Tommy Franks was reportedly earning around US$150,000. A contractor in Iraq could expect to earn up to US$200,000 per annum (source: <http://www.redrat.net/BUSH_WAR/mercenaries/index.htm>, accessed 29 March 2015); contractors do not have the same range of benefits that soldiers often have—bonuses and benefits covering relocation and deployment to active combat, subsidized groceries and housing, and veterans benefits—however, the pay differential is striking.

[62] Abdel-Fatau Musah and J 'Kayode Fayemi, 'Conclusion', in Musah and Fayemi (eds), *Mercenaries: An African Security Dilemma*, at 258.

[63] UN Doc A/62/301, Report of the Working Group on the Use of Mercenaries as Means of Violating Human Rights and Impeding the Exercise of the Right of Peoples to Self-Determination, 24 August 2007, at 20.

[64] Under Art. 47, API.

[65] Under Art. 4, UN Convention against the Recruitment, Use, Financing and Training of Mercenaries.

mercenaries. However, as outlined in Chapter 2, the threshold for classification as a mercenary is notably high.[66] Under Article 47 of Protocol I, the cumulative criteria for designation as a mercenary is any person who:

(a) is specially recruited locally or abroad in order to fight in an armed conflict;
(b) does, in fact, take direct part in the hostilities;
(c) is motivated to take part in the hostilities essentially by the desire for private gain and, in fact, is promised, by or on behalf of a Party to the conflict, material compensation substantially in excess of that promised or paid to combatants of similar ranks and functions in the armed forces of that party;
(d) is neither a national of a Party to the conflict nor a resident of territory controlled by a Party to the conflict;
(e) is not a member of the armed forces of a Party to the conflict; and
(f) has not been sent by a State which is not a Party to the conflict on official duty as a member of the armed forces.

The other relevant international instrument, the UN Convention Against the Recruitment, Use, Financing and Training of Mercenaries, adopted in 1989, also has a similarly high threshold.[67] Under Article 1 of the Convention, a mercenary is defined as any person who:

(a) is specially recruited locally or abroad in order to fight in an armed conflict;
(b) is motivated to take part in the hostilities essentially by the desire for private gain and, in fact, is promised, by or on behalf of a party to that conflict, material compensation substantially in excess of that promised or paid to combatants of similar rank and function in the armed forces of that party;
(c) is neither a national or a party to the conflict nor a resident of territory controlled by a party to the conflict;
(d) is not a member of the armed forces of a party to the conflict;
(e) has not been sent by a State which is not a party to the conflict on official duty as a member of its armed forces.

So far, the Convention simply replicates the main elements of Article 47 of Protocol I. However, in subsection 2 of Article 1, additional elements are required, which state that a mercenary is any person who, in any situation not amounting to an armed conflict:

(a) is specially recruited locally or abroad for the purpose of participating in a concerted act of violence aimed at:
    (i) overthrowing a Government or otherwise undermining the constitutional order of a State; or
    (ii) Undermining the territorial integrity of a State;

[66] See further Ch. 2 on mercenaries, and the debate during the Diplomatic Conferences at Geneva in 1974–1977.

[67] GA Res 44/34, UN Doc A/44/766 (1989).

(b) is motivated to take part therein essentially by the desire for significant private gain and is prompted by the promise or payment of material compensation;
(c) is neither a national nor a resident of the State against which such an act is directed.

The multi-stage, cumulative test for mercenary status in these instruments means that the vast majority of PMSCs will not fall within the definition of mercenary, at the minimum because most PMSCs 'are not de jure or de facto incorporated into the armed forces of a party and are therefore not combatants but civilians'.[68]

Furthermore, additional elements are missing: the definition of mercenary precludes nationals of a party to the conflict,[69] as well as national of other states on 'official duty',[70] which would most likely rule out many of the PMSCs operating on behalf of States, such as the US, which frequently employ former US armed forces members.[71] Additionally, the requirement of 'being specially recruited... in order to fight in an armed conflict' may also fail to apply, as PMSCs are often existing employees of the contracting company and may well have been employed by the company prior to any deployment to a combat zone. As such, they have not been specially recruited.[72]

Finally, it is debatable whether the 'motivated for private gain'[73] element of Article 47 could be met. As noted by Kinsey:

> For many countries, compensation by way of private gain distinguishes mercenaries from non-resident non-nationals who volunteer to fight for political, religious and ideological reasons. However, while motivation for those working for PSCs is, in part, private gain, it is different to the private gain that motivates mercenaries. Those who work for PSCs receive a salary from the security company for whom they work. Consequently, they are not profit driven. In this respect, they are no different from professional soldiers.[74]

As such, given the number of high thresholds that need to be met, and the failure of PMSCs to meet such thresholds, it seems unlikely that most, if not all, PMSCs could not be considered mercenaries under current international law.

[68] Sassòli, Bouvier, and Quintin, *How Does Law Protect in War*, at 172. This was the case with the use of Executive Outcomes in Sierra Leone. See further Zarate, 'The Emergence of a New Dog of War', at 124.

[69] Art. 47(d), API. [70] Art. 47(f), API.

[71] Alexandre Faite, 'Involvement of Private Contractors in Armed Conflict: Implications under International Humanitarian Law', 4 Defence Studies 166 (2004), at 169–70.

[72] Faite, 'Involvement of Private Contractors in Armed Conflict', at 170.

[73] Art. 47(c), API.

[74] Christopher Kinsey, 'Challenging International Law: A Dilemma of Private Security Companies', 5 Conflict, Security and Development 269 (2005), at 282.

PMSCs as civilians accompanying the armed forces

If PMSCs are neither combatants nor mercenaries, the only remaining option is that PMSCs are civilians,[75] most likely within the definition outlined in Article 4A(4) of GCIII, which provides that 'persons who accompany the armed forces without actually being members thereof, such as...supply contractors' are entitled to POW treatment if captured (but not combatant status or rights, and thus they may not take direct part in the hostilities).[76] Such persons are civilians and are entitled to civilian immunity. Indeed, the International Committee of the Red Cross (ICRC) Interpretive Guidance affirms this assessment, stating that:

> as long as they are not incorporated into the armed forces, private contractors and civilian employees do not cease to be civilians simply because they accompany the armed forces and or assume functions other that the conduct of hostilities that would traditionally have been performed by military personnel...a different conclusion must be reached for contractors and employees who, to all intent and purposes, have been incorporated into the armed forces of a party to the conflict, whether through a formal procedure under national law or de facto by being given a continuous combat function....such personnel would be members of an organised armed force, group or unit under a command responsible to a party to the conflict and...would no longer qualify as civilians.[77]

This assessment is supported by documents from the US government, which refer to PMSCs as CAAFs,[78] specifically mentioning that captured CAAFs are entitled to treatment as POWs;[79] this is in keeping with an assessment of PMSCs as civilians accompanying the armed forces under Article 4A of GCIII.

Classifying PMSCs as civilians is also the approach generally taken by the Montreux Document on Pertinent International Legal Obligations

[75] See the commentary to Art. 4(4), GCIV, which makes it clear that under IHL one is either entitled to combatant status or civilian status but that 'there is no intermediate status; nobody in enemy hands can be outside the law' (Jean Pictet (ed.), *Commentary to Geneva Convention IV Relative to the Protection of Civilian Persons in Time of War* (ICRC, 1958); hereinafter *GCIV Commentary*), at 51).

[76] Cameron and Chetail, *Privatizing War*, at 418–20. See also generally Giulio Bartolini, 'PMS Contractors as "Persons who Accompany the Armed Forces"', in Francesco Francioni and Natalino Ronzitti, *War by Contract: Human Rights, Humanitarian Law, and Private Contractors* (OUP, 2011).

[77] DPHIG, at 1010–11; the Guidance goes on to note that the statements regarding PMSCs and civilian employees in international armed conflicts 'also apply, *mutatis mutandis*, in non-international armed conflicts.'

[78] DoDI 3020.41, Glossary.

[79] DoDI 3020.41, Enclosure 2, 1(a)(1), at 9.

and Good Practices for States related to Operations of Private Military and Security Companies during Armed Conflict, the instrument adopted in 2008 to outline the relevant international law obligations for States employing PMSCs.[80] Article 24 states that the status of the personnel of PMSCs is to be determined by IHL on a case-by-case basis according to the nature and circumstances of the functions in which they are involved. Article 25 outlines that if they are civilians under IHL, the personnel of PMSCs may not be the object of attack, unless and for such time as they directly participate in hostilities. Finally Article 26 provides that the personnel of PMSCs:

> are protected as civilians under international humanitarian law, unless they are incorporated into the regular armed forces of a State or are members of organised armed forces, groups or units under a command responsible to the State; or otherwise lose their protection as determined by international humanitarian law... [and] are entitled to prisoner of war status in international armed conflict if they are persons accompanying the armed forces meeting the requirements of article 4A(4) of the Third Geneva Convention[81]

If PMSCs are civilians however, this raises a number of complex issues for parties to conflicts where PMSCs are used. These issues serve as the focus for the remainder of this chapter.

Are PMSCs Taking Direct Part in Hostilities?

In using PMSCs in times of armed conflict, problems arise for both those who employ the PMSCs and those who fight an adversary who has employed PMSCs. When PMSCs are hired to provide security and quasi-military functions, such as providing protection to legitimate military targets including high-level officials and military matériel transports, this creates fertile ground for complications in the application of the principle of distinction.

[80] The Montreux Document on Pertinent International Legal Obligations and Good Practices for States related to Operations of Private Military and Security Companies during Armed Conflict, UN Doc A/63/467, S/2008/636, 17 September 2008. The Montreux Document was developed on the basis of four inter-governmental meetings between 2006 and 2008, involving experts from government, industry, and civil society. The document was finalized in 2008 and adopted by consensus by seventeen States: Afghanistan, Angola, Australia, Austria, Canada, China, France, Germany, Iraq, Poland, Sierra Leone, South Africa, Sweden, Switzerland, the UK, Ukraine, and the US. The details of the Montreux Document are discussed further in Ch. 8 of this book.

[81] Art. 26, the Montreux Document.

Complications for those parties employing PMSCs

For parties to a conflict who use PMSCs, problems arise when PMSCs are tasked with quasi-military responsibilities such as guarding high-profile military or governmental officials or installations, escorting military convoys, or transporting military matériel to locations close to active hostilities. If those objects, transports, or personnel constitute legitimate targets, then any person involved in guarding them will be considered as taking direct part in hostilities. This assessment is in keeping with Article 49(1) of Protocol I, which refers to attacks as being 'acts of violence against the adversary, whether in offence or in defence.'[82] It also correlates to some approaches to DPH; for example, the HPCR (Humanitarian Policy and Conflict Research) Manual on Air and Missile Warfare specifically states that 'the defence of military objectives against enemy attacks is a clear case of direct participation in hostilities.'[83] Indeed, Michael Schmitt definitively states that 'a civilian government employee or private contractor defending military personnel or military objectives from enemy attack directly participates in hostilities. His or her actions are indistinguishable from the quintessential duties of combat personnel.'[84]

States that employ PMSCs, and the PMSCs themselves, are thus in uniquely difficult positions. The general rules on contracting emphasize, in the US context at least, that contractors are civilians and that they may not take direct part in hostilities.[85] However, by their very presence guarding their objectives, they are deemed as taking a direct part in hostilities. Furthermore, even if a restrictive approach to DPH is taken, PMSCs are still vulnerable, in that their proximity to military objectives renders them more susceptible to acts of violence: this is noted in the US DoD Instruction on contractors, where it states that although contractors are civilians who are entitled to take no part in hostilities, they are nonetheless 'at risk of injury or death incidental to enemy actions while supporting military operations'.[86]

[82] Art. 49(1), API; see also *AP Commentary*, at 603, para. 1880: "'attack" means "combat action"... the restrictions imposed by humanitarian law on the use of force should be observed both by troops defending themselves and by those who are engaged in an assault or taking the offensive.'

[83] *Commentary on the Harvard Manual*, at 121. See also *Targeted Killings*, where the Court stated that transporting weapons would amount to DPH (at §§ 35–36); the Court in *Hamdan* likewise considered transportation to be indicative of DPH (at 6).

[84] Schmitt, 'Humanitarian Law and Direct Participation by Private Contractors or Civilian Employees', at 538.

[85] DoDI 3020.41, Enclosure 2, 1(a)(1), at 9.

[86] DoDI 3020.41, Enclosure 2, 1(a)(1), at 9.

Additional problems arise regarding the use of PMSCs to guard military objects. One of the tasks routinely entrusted to PMSCs in the conflict in Iraq was the guarding of personnel and installations. For these tasks, these PMSCs were, by necessity, armed, as outlined in the US National Defense Authorization Act for Fiscal Year 2008,[87] private security functions as defined as those involving 'the guarding of personnel, facilities, or properties, and any other activity for which personnel are required to be armed.'[88]

The ability of PMSCs to use force in self-defence is integral to the process of contracting the PMSC in the first place. As Cameron and Chetail note:

> domestic and international private security industries rely on the ability of an individual to use force in self-defence as a means of fulfilling the terms of contracts requiring the use of violence without having the benefit of state-conferred powers of arrest and detention and the capacity to use force.[89]

However, the law on whether PMSCs may use force in self-defence of others or of property is less than straightforward. The international law relating to the legal framework relating to use of force under both domestic and international law is complex, and it draws on a number of different fields, including domestic criminal law, international human rights law, and, furthermore, this is complicated by whether the use of force in self-defence is carried out in international versus non-international armed conflicts. It is not the aim of this chapter to explore these issues in detail, but rather to sketch a few of the problems that arise when PMSCs are deployed in situations where they may face uncertainty regarding the permissible use of force in self-defence.

Most domestic legal systems include the right of individuals to defend themselves against attack;[90] under international law, self-defence, if not a 'right' *per se* under international law[91] is, as some have argued, at least a necessary corollary to the right to life.[92] This 'right' of self-defence has been

[87] P.L. 110-181 Sec. 864. [88] P.L. 110-181 Sec. 864.

[89] Cameron and Chetail, *Privatizing War*, at 455.

[90] Eg, §§ 418–23 of the Crimes Act 1900 (NSW) outlines the provisions regarding lawful self-defence; similar provisions can be found in the domestic laws of many States; see further P Haggenmacher, 'Self Defence as a General Principle of Law and its Relevance to War', in Arthur Eyffinger, Alan Stephens, and Sam Muller (eds), *Self-Defence as a Fundamental Principle* (TMC Asser, 2009) and generally Fiona Leverick, *Killing in Self-Defence* (OUP, 2006).

[91] For arguments that the 'right of self-defence' is not a right *per se* but rather a justification for taking the life of another person in certain permissible circumstances, see the Final Report submitted by Barbra Frey, Special Rapporteur on the Prevention of Human Rights Violations Committed with Small Arms and Light Weapons, where she states that there is no 'international human right of self-defence…expressly set forth in the primary sources of international law' (UN Doc. A/HRC/Sub.1/58/27, 27 July 2006).

[92] Guido den Dekker and Eric PJ Myjer, 'The Right to Life and Self-Defence of Private Military and Security Contractors in Armed Conflict', in Francioni and Ronzitti (eds), *War by Contract*,

enshrined in the Rome Statute of the International Criminal Court which provides, in Article 31(1)(c), that there is no criminal responsibility when:

> [t]he person acts reasonably to defend himself or herself or another person or, in the case of war crimes, property which is essential for the survival of the person or another person or property which is essential for accomplishing a military mission, against an imminent attack and unlawful use of force in a manner proportionate to the degree of danger to the person or the other person or property protected.[93]

However, a number of issues are raised by this provision which makes the use of self-defence by PMSCs problematic. The concept of 'unlawful use of force' raises concerns: how can PMSCs make the determination that an attack against them is unlawful? An attack against PMSCs, who are *prima facie* civilians, may not be unlawful if they are guarding a military objective. The comingling of civilian and military objectives makes it notably difficult for PMSCs to determine accurately whether they are permitted to use force to defend themselves: as Cameron and Chetail note: 'in a situation of armed conflict, due to the complexity of IHL and the factual situations often prevailing on the ground, it may often be very difficult to make a determination about the lawfulness of imminent violence, such that security personnel ostensibly using force only in self-defence may (inadvertently) cross the line into direct participation in hostilities.'[94]

Indeed, it is the guarding of property that is particularly problematic when it comes to the use of force in self-defence by PMSCs. Article 31(1)(c) of the ICC Statute states that lawful self-defence of property is permissible only for property 'which is essential for the survival of the person or another person or property which is essential for accomplishing a military mission'.[95] However, the right to use lethal force to defend property in the name of accomplishing a military mission was a controversial inclusion in the Rome Statute,[96] with Eric David calling it a 'Pandora's Box that is rigorously incompatible with the law of armed conflict.'[97]

Furthermore, there seems to be a logical problem with endowing PMSCs with a limited scope to use lethal force to defend military property. As defined

at 179; see also Andrew Ashworth, 'Self-Defence and the Right to Life', 34 Cambridge L J 282 (1975): 'if a legal system is to uphold the right to life, there must be a liberty to use force for the purpose of self-defence' (at 283).

[93] Art. 31(1)(c) of the Rome Statute of the International Criminal Court; see also *Prosecutor v Kordić*, Case No. IT-95-14/2/T, Judgment, 26 February 2001 at paras 449–51, where the ICTY notes the customary status of the justification of self-defence.

[94] Cameron and Chetail, *Privatising War*, at 465.

[95] Art. 31(1)(c), Rome Statute.

[96] See further William Schabas, *An Introduction to the International Criminal Court* (4th edn, CUP, 2011), at 241–42.

[97] Eric David, *Principes de droit des conflits armés* (2nd edn, Bruylant, 1999), at 693.

under the US DoD Instruction, contractors accompanying the armed forces may be 'utilised in support of…operations in a non-combat role';[98] That is, they are not to take direct part in hostilities. This designation would, however, seem to put PMSCs who are tasked with defending property in an untenable position, for as den Dekker and Myjer point out, 'it is hardly conceivable that a PMS contractor can defend property essential for the accomplishment of a military mission—i.e. a military objective—without thereby being required to participate directly in the hostilities.'[99] Thus, the complexity and uncertainty in the law would seem to put PMSCs, and the States that use them, in potentially problematic situations.

Complications for those parties facing PMSCs

The use of PMSCs in combat zones creates problems for those on the other side of the equation; those who face an adversary employing such PMSCs. As noted in Chapter 1, the 'cardinal'[100] principle of the law of armed conflict is the principle of distinction and the prohibition on the direct targeting of civilians. If, as outlined in this chapter, PMSCs are civilians, then it is a war crime to target them in an armed conflict deliberately. If such PMSCs are taking a direct part in hostilities, they may be lawfully targeted for such DPH. However, an obvious complication arises for persons facing PMSCs: when confronting a person carrying or otherwise displaying weaponry, wearing fatigues or camouflage, sporting clothing and armoured vehicles bearing insignia, an adversary might reasonably assume that he or she was dealing with a combatant or a person taking direct part in the hostilities. How then is someone to make the assessment that the person he or she confronts is (or is not) lawfully targetable, especially if the potential target looks like someone taking direct part in hostilities?

Commentaries on PMSC use have noted just how difficult it is to distinguish between regular armed forces and PMSCs. For example, Ridlon remarks that PMSCs:

> operate and are equipped much like military units. PMFs [private military firms] in Iraq use sophisticated military equipment. Some even employ armoured vehicles and helicopters in support of their operations. PMFs are not only equipped like military units, but…also use sophisticated military tactics and organisational tools to

[98] DoDI 3020.41, Enclosure 2, 1(a)(1).

[99] den Dekker and Myjer, 'The Right to Life and Self-Defence of Private Military and Security Contractors', at 181–82.

[100] *Nuclear Weapons*, at 226, para. 78.

conduct their operations... [additionally] they are also staffed mainly by former members of special forces units.[101]

Thus, understandable confusion may arise for parties to a conflict regarding who may be a legitimate target: a party to the conflict may find itself mistakenly targeting essentially civilian objects, and contractors may find themselves being targeted because they 'appear' to be military.

Conversely, for the regular armed forces, the presence of PMSCs in active hostilities can be highly disruptive. Those responsible for making targeting decisions must have clear information to order to make decisions that fulfil their obligations of targeting military and not civilian objects. The presence of PMSCs, wearing fatigues and camouflage similar to regular armed forces, guarding convoys, installations, and persons who might, on closer examination, have predominantly non-military functions, clearly make such targeting decisions more complicated. As Schmitt has argued:

> The more armed civilians in an area, the more difficult it is for lawful combatants to distinguish between unlawful combatants and those who are merely armed for defensive purposes. This in turn endangers the civilian population by eroding the practical implementation of the principle of distinction. Soldiers may be more inclined to employ force against civilians who they feel pose a threat. Alternatively, soldiers may refrain from the use of force when it is appropriate, thereby assuming greater risk than necessary.[102]

Thus, the use of PMSCs complicates matters for all parties to the armed conflict, and makes the principle of distinction harder to respect.

Conclusion

It seems unlikely that States will willingly give up using PMSCs in combat situations, especially as the trend for downsizing large standing armies seems likely to continue.[103] Given the potential problems raised by the use of PMSCs, it seems

[101] Ridlon, 'Contractors or Illegal Combatants?', at 217–18.

[102] Schmitt, 'Direct Participation in Hostilities by Private Contractors', at 539.

[103] See Thom Shanker and Helene Cooper, 'Pentagon Plans to Shrink Army to Pre-World War II Level', *New York Times*, 23 February 2014, available at: <http://www.nytimes.com/2014/02/24/us/politics/pentagon-plans-to-shrink-army-to-pre-world-war-ii-level.html?_r=0>, accessed 29 March 2015. See also plans by the UK Ministry of Defence, which announced in August 2014 that it had contracted out nearly £14 billion of maintenance and supply work to US firms Bechtel and CH2M Hill; see further Mark Leftly, 'Uproar As Mod Brings In American Giants To Manage Military Procurement', *Independent*, 16 August 2014, available at: <http://www.independent.co.uk/news/business/news/uproar-as-mod-brings-in-american-giants-to-manage-military-procurement-9672666.html>, accessed 29 March 2015.

logical to query whether there should be moves to grant PMSCs some form of international status by way of an international instrument.[104] The Montreux Document has gone some way to clarifying the situation (the Document is discussed in more detail in Chapter 8); however, whether more laws would clarify the situation, and whether more laws would actually be accepted by the international community, are questions that needsto be examined. These will be considered in more detail in Chapter 8.

The next chapter of this book looks at a seemingly incongruous topic: should high-level criminal activity fall under the ambit of the law of armed conflict? However, the question fits within the overall scope of this book, and the questions this book seeks to examine, namely, how has IHL conceptualized civilians who participate in armed conflict, how have recent developments in civilian participation in armed conflict created challenges for the existing law, and how can we address those challenges? In the context of so-called criminal armed conflict,[105] Chapter 7 of this book will examine the debate as to whether participants in high-level criminal violence warrant regulation under the law of armed conflict.

[104] See Richard Morgan, 'Professional Military Firms under International Law', 9 Chicago J Int'l L 213 (2008), and Michael Scheimer, 'Separating Private Military Companies from Illegal Mercenaries in International Law: Proposing an International Convention for Legitimate Military and Security Support that Reflects Customary International Law', 24 Am U Int'l L Rev 609 (2008–09).

[105] Stephen Haines has termed high-level criminal violence 'criminal warfare'; see Steven Haines, 'The Nature of War and the Character of Contemporary Armed Conflict', in Elizabeth Wilmshurst (ed.), *International Law and the Classification of Conflicts* (OUP, 2012), at 24.

7

'Criminal' Armed Conflict

Introduction

In 2005, David Crane, former Chief Prosecutor at the Special Court for Sierra Leone, gave an address at a conference on international criminal tribunals. Among his final remarks were the following comments:

> I have been in public service my entire adult life, many of those years in harms [*sic*] way. Yet, when I arrived in West Africa, I faced a new combatant, the international criminal element…[who] led gun runners, diamond dealers, Eastern European mafias, other international thugs, and terrorists, including Hezbollah and al Qaeda, in a whirlwind of death and destruction the likes of which the world has never seen…the unrest through the West African region, particularly in Sierra Leone, the Ivory Coast, and Liberia, was started by criminals for their own personal and criminal gain. The civil war in Sierra Leone did not begin on account of the more traditional causes behind warfare, legitimate or otherwise, such as political, religious, cultural, ethnic, or social reasons. Rather, the *impetus for the civil war was pure criminal avarice and greed.* They did it because they could. Where there is no law, there is anarchy.[1]

In some respects, warfare and certain criminal acts are indistinguishable from one another. In times of war, individuals destroy public and private property, engage in acts which are disruptive to the peace, and cause bodily damage, including debilitating and sometimes permanent injury and even death, to other human beings. All of these activities are, in most if not all domestic criminal laws, considered criminal acts. Indeed, the fundamental principle underlying the 'combatants' privilege' is the acknowledgement that war-time activities would be usually considered criminal acts were it not for the nexus of the armed conflict.[2] As noted in the Commentaries to the

[1] David Crane, 'Terrorists, Warlords, and Thugs', 21 Am U Int'l L Rev 505 (2005–06), at 515 (emphasis added).

[2] Yoram Dinstein, 'The Distinction between Unlawful Combatants and War Criminals', in Yoram Dinstein and Mala Tabory (eds), *International Law at a Time of Perplexity: Essays in Honour of Shabtai Rosenne* (Martinus Nijhoff, 1989), at 104–05; Waldemar Solf, 'The Status of

Additional Protocols, 'the combatants' privilege...provides immunity from the application of municipal law prohibitions against homicides, wounding and maiming, or capturing persons and destruction of property, so long as these acts are done as acts of war and do not transgress the restraints of the rules of international law applicable in armed conflict.'[3]

This distinction in the law—that war-time activities are not criminal acts 'so long as these acts are done as acts of war'[4]—is predicated on the ability to distinguish clearly between acts of war and other hostile acts which happen coterminous with the armed conflict, but with no other direct connection to the hostilities. Such distinctions are not always easy to make. This is further complicated when one examines situations of armed conflict where the hostilities are funded or otherwise intertwined with high-level criminal activities, such as drug smuggling, illicit trade in ivory or gemstones, or other forms of organized crime.

Prima facie, the reasons why armed violence has erupted has no effect on the applicability of international humanitarian law (IHL). As noted by the International Committee of the Red Cross (ICRC) in its report to the 31st International Conference of the Red Cross and Red Crescent, 'under IHL the motivation of organised groups involved in armed violence is not a criterion for determining the existence of an armed conflict'.[5] Indeed, one of the objections to Additional Protocol I was that it 'introduced the regrettable innovation of making the motives behind a conflict a criterion for the application of humanitarian law.'[6] However, when it comes to examining the direct participation of civilians in armed conflict, motivation may be crucial when it comes to determining whether a civilian is directly participating and is thus targetable, or whether he or she is committing a criminal act that does not amount to direct participation in hostilities (DPH) (which would result in the targeting of this individual being classified as a war crime).

It is possible to discern two distinct strands in the literature on armed conflict and criminal activity; the first of these examines how certain kinds of criminal activities are intricately connected to the armed conflict, as is the case where drug trafficking or other illegal activities funds

Combatants in Non-International Armed Conflicts under Domestic Law and Transnational Practice', 33 AULR 53 (1983–84), at 57–58.

[3] *New Rules*, at 243–44. [4] *New Rules*, at 243–44.

[5] ICRC, *International Humanitarian Law and the Challenges of Contemporary Armed Conflicts*, Report to the 31st International Conference of the Red Cross and Red Crescent (October 2011), at 11.

[6] John Redvers Freeland, British Representative at the Diplomatic Conferences of 1974–77, *Official Records VI*, CDDH/SR.36, at 46, para. 83.

the ongoing hostilities.[7] A second, less explored, strand in the literature examines situations where the criminal activity is of a scope and intensity that it is indistinguishable from 'conventional' armed conflicts; the widespread, protracted, and high-intensity violence that has beset States such as Mexico has often prompted such States to respond with military force,[8] which has in turn prompted some writers to suggest that such activities should be designated as non-international armed conflicts or insurgencies.[9] In both cases, implications arise both for IHL and for those who must apply the law. This chapter will examine the question of so-called criminal warfare[10] and looks at some of the implications that arise for participants in these activities.

Where Organized Criminal Activities are Indistinguishable from Armed Conflict in Scope and Intensity

The use of the term 'war' when describing any protracted or high-level engagement against some sort of threat is commonplace in political rhetoric: for instance, various US administrations and the US media have spoken about the US being engaged in a 'war on drugs',[11] a 'war on poverty',[12] even

[7] See generally Svante Cornell, 'Narcotics and Armed Conflict: Interaction and Implications', 30 Studies in Conflict and Terrorism 207 (2007).

[8] See, eg, Mary Beth Sheridan, 'U.S. Military Helping Mexican Troops Battle Drug Cartels', *Washington Post*, 10 November 2012, available at: <http://www.washingtonpost.com/wp-dyn/content/article/2010/11/09/AR2010110907297.html>, accessed 29 March 2015.

[9] See Carina Bergal, 'The Mexican Drug War: The Case for a Non-International Armed Conflict Classification', 34 Fordham Int'l L J 1042 (2011); John Sullivan and Adam Elkus, 'Plazas for Profit: Mexico's Criminal Insurgency', Small Wars Journal (26 April 2009), available at: <http://smallwarsjournal.com/blog/journal/docs-temp/232-sullivan.pdf?q=mag/docs-temp/232-sullivan.pdf>, accessed 29 March 2015; Callin Kerr, 'Mexico's Drug War: Is it Really a War?', 54 S Tex L Rev 193 (2012); Craig Bloom, 'Square Pegs and Round Holes: Mexico, Drugs, and International Law', 34 Houston J Int'l L 345 (2012); and Gregg Etter and Erica Lehmuth, 'The Mexican Drug Wars: Organised Crime, Narco-Terrorism, Insurgency or Asymmetric Warfare?', 20 J Gang Research 1 (2013).

[10] The term has been used by David Crane, 'Terrorists, Warlords, and Thugs', at 515; and by Steven Haines, 'The Nature of War and the Character of Contemporary Armed Conflict', at 24.

[11] See for example, Gary Fields, 'White House Czar Calls for End to "War on Drugs"', *Wall Street Journal*, 14 May 2009, available at: <http://online.wsj.com/news/articles/SB124225891527617397?mg=reno64-wsj&url=http%3A%2F%2Fonline.wsj.com%2Farticle%2FSB124225891527617397.html>, accessed 29 March; and Emily Dufton, 'The War on Drugs: How President Nixon Tied Addiction to Crime', *The Atlantic*, 26 March 2012, available at: <http://www.theatlantic.com/health/archive/2012/03/the-war-on-drugs-how-president-nixon-tied-addiction-to-crime/254319/>, accessed 29 March 2015.

[12] The term was used by President Lyndon Johnson in 1964, when his administration declared an 'unconditional war on poverty', See further *The War on Poverty 50 Years*

a 'war on obesity'.[13] When dealing with situations that call on States to use armed force, deploying the 'war' metaphor can be an appealing means to galvanize public opinion and highlight the threat presented by object of the 'war', whether it be poverty or drugs.[14] Furthermore, by labelling a given situation, such as high-intensity criminal violence, as a 'war', certain practical benefits follow. In labelling such activities as armed conflicts, the State is thus able to use a war rubric in their dealings with the newly designated rebels or insurgents; IHL becomes the *lex specialis* and domestic law-enforcement rules, as well as certain human rights obligations, can be suspended. As noted by Hauck and Peterke, employing an armed conflict model to respond to criminal activities means that:

> the state concerned no longer has to strictly abide by the constitutional state's 'law enforcement model' and can target the 'criminals'—as fighters directly participating in hostilities—in accordance with IHL. Especially in urban violence, the simultaneous application of both legal regimes [IHL and IHRL] may water down the presumption of innocence, the right to a fair trial, and the states obligations to punish human rights violations committed by its security forces.[15]

Prima facie, there are superficial similarities between the organized armed groups in non-international armed conflicts and armed criminal groups operating in situations of high-intensity protracted violence. However, for IHL to be applicable, certain criteria need to be met, first with regards to the violence itself, and second with regards to those persons who participate in the violence. These criteria will be examined in this next section.

Later: A Progress Report, The Council of Economic Advisers, Executive Office of the President of the United States, January 2014, available at: <http://www.whitehouse.gov/sites/default/files/docs/50th_anniversary_cea_report_-_final_post_embargo.pdf>, accessed 29 March 2015.

[13] See for example Brian Vastag and NC Aizenman, 'New Tactic In War On Obesity: Attack Portion Size', *Washington Post*, 2 June 2012, available at: <http://www.washingtonpost.com/national/health-science/new-tactic-in-war-on-obesity-attack-portion-size/2012/06/02/gJQA4wzi9U_story.html>, accessed 6 April 2015; Jeffrey Friedman, 'A War on Obesity, Not the Obese', 299 Science 856 (2003); Morgan Korn, 'Has the 'War on Obesity' Gone Too Far?', *CNBC*, 13 November 2012, available at: <http://www.cnbc.com/id/49810996#>, accessed 29 March 2015.

[14] For a discussion of the power of 'war' rhetoric, see further Susan Stuart, 'War as Metaphor and the Rule of Law in Crisis: The Lessons We Should Have Learned from the War on Drugs', 36 Southern Illinois U L J 1 (2011); and Tawia Ansah, 'War: Rhetoric and Norm-Creation in Response to Terror', 43 Va J Int'l L 797 (2003).

[15] Pierre Hauck and Sven Peterke, 'Organised Crime and Gang Violence in National and International Law', 92 IRRC 407 (2010), at 431.

Designating violence as an armed conflict: thresholds of applicability for IHL

In order for the international law of armed conflict to apply to situations of violence, the violence must meet a particular threshold of intensity, especially in the case of non-international armed conflicts. This is so that 'common' acts of violence that might occur, such as riots or other domestic conflicts, remain within the jurisdictional purview of the State and its law enforcement agencies.[16] The currently accepted definition for the existence of an armed conflict comes from the *Tadić* Interlocutory Appeal, where the Appeals Chamber held that 'an armed conflict exists whenever there is a resort to armed force between States or protracted armed violence between governmental authorities and organised armed groups or between such groups within a State'.[17] Thus, there must be protracted armed violence.

What amounts to protracted armed violence was considered by the International Criminal Tribunal for the former Yugoslavia (ICTY) in the *Haradinaj*[18] case, where the Trial Chamber identified the following indicative factors for protracted violence including:

> the number, duration and intensity of individual confrontations; the type of weapons and other military equipment used; the number and calibre of munitions fired; the number of persons and type of forces partaking in the fighting; the number of casualties; the extent of material destruction; and the number of civilians fleeing combat zones. The involvement of the UN Security Council may also be a reflection of the intensity of a conflict.[19]

The Chamber in *Haradinaj* noted that not all factors needed to be present for a non-international conflict to exist.[20] Indeed, as Sivakumaran notes, the ICTY was 'dealing with large-scale non-international armed conflicts and, as such, many of the same indicia may not be present in smaller and shorter conflicts.'[21] Thus, the absence of one or more of the *Haradinaj* indicia would not, in itself, militate against designation as a non-international armed conflict.[22]

However, a number of additional factors need to be considered in an assessment of violence as armed conflict. First, as noted by the ICTY in

[16] See *AP Commentary*, at 1354–55, paras 4471–78; and Sivakumaran, *The Law of Non-International Armed Conflict*, at 161–62.

[17] *Tadić*, Interlocutory Appeal, at para. 70.

[18] *Prosecutor v Haradinaj et al.*, Case No. IT-04-84, Trial Judgment, 3 April 2008.

[19] *Haradinaj*, at para. 49.

[20] *Haradinaj*, at para. 49.

[21] Sivakumaran, *The Law of Non-International Armed Conflict*, at 167.

[22] Various cases in the ICTY examined similar indicia to that outlined in *Haradinaj*. See further *Tadić*, Trial Judgment, at paras 565–66; *Limaj*, Trial Judgment, at paras 135–67; *Prosecutor v Boškoski and Tarčulovski*, Case No. IT-04-82-T, Trial Judgment, 10 July 2008, at paras 216–34.

Boškoski, the deployment of armed forces on the part of the State, rather than just law enforcement agencies, should be given weight in any assessment of the hostilities.[23] Furthermore, the involvement of international organizations such as the ICRC, as well as appeals from both sides to relevant rules of international law should also be given due consideration.[24] Also significant to any assessment are the tactics employed and targets chosen by the parties to the armed conflict: are the targets and tactics fundamentally military in nature? It was this element that the Inter-American Commission on Human Rights, in the *La Tablada*[25] case, felt was also significant, perhaps more so than duration or intensity of hostilities. As the Inter-American Commission held in that case:

> what differentiates the events at the La Tablada base from [internal disturbances] are the concerted nature of the hostile acts undertaken by the attackers, the direct involvement of governmental armed forces, and the nature and level of the violence attending the events in question. More particularly, the attackers involved carefully planned, coordinated and executed an armed attack, i.e., a military operation, against a quintessential military objective—a military base.[26]

Additional threshold requirements

In addition to these indicia of the existence of an armed conflict, other factors must also be found to exist for violence to be classified as an armed conflict. These factors relate to the non-State participants in the violence. In order for the law of armed conflict to apply to situations of armed violence, the non-State participant must demonstrate a degree of organization within their group. Common Article 3 makes no mention of whether parties to the conflict must be organized. However, Additional Protocol II requires that the conflict take place in 'the territory of a High Contracting Party between its armed forces and dissident armed forces or other organized armed groups which, under responsible command, exercise such control over a part of its territory as to enable them to carry out sustained and concerted military operations and to implement this Protocol.'[27] Additional Protocol II thus requires that the armed group have a degree of organization, maintain control of territory, and must be 'in a position to implement the Protocol.'[28]

[23] *Boškoski*, Trial Judgment, at paras 243, 245–46.
[24] *Boškoski*, Trial Judgment, at paras 243, 245–46.
[25] *Abella v Argentina*, Case No, 11.137.
[26] *Abella v Argentina*, at paras 154–56.
[27] Art. 1(1), APII.
[28] *AP Commentary*, at 1353, para. 4470.

However, even in the absence of reference to organization in Common Article 3, in practice, the case law has indicated that some degree of organization within the armed opposition group is indeed necessary for a finding of a non-international armed conflict.[29] As to the relevant indicia of organization, the *Haradinaj* judgment is again useful, the Trial Chamber noting that the following elements would indicate an organizational structure in an armed group:

> the existence of a command structure and disciplinary rules and mechanisms within the group; the existence of a headquarters; the fact that the group controls a certain territory; the ability of the group to gain access to weapons, other military equipment, recruits and military training; its ability to plan, coordinate and carry out military operations, including troop movements and logistics; its ability to define a unified military strategy and use military tactics, and its ability to speak with one voice and negotiate and conclude agreements such as cease-fire or peace accords.[30]

The requirement of responsible command is connected to the concept of organization; the ICTY, International Criminal Tribunal for Rwanda (ICTR), and Special Court for Sierra Leone have all stated that 'there cannot be an organised military force save on the basis of responsible command',[31] an approach confirmed by the International Criminal Court (ICC) also.[32] As Sivakumaran notes, 'the notion of responsible command is inherent in non-state party fighting in a non-international armed conflict'.[33] Indicia of responsible command, in addition to the organization of the armed force, include any internal disciplinary system[34] or otherwise factual relationship of actual control over the actions of subordinates.[35]

The final elements in the Protocol II threshold for the existence of an armed conflict is the necessity for the armed group to 'exercise such control over a part of its territory as to enable them to carry out sustained and

[29] See *Akayesu*, Trial Judgment, at para. 620; *Limaj*, Trial Judgment, at para. 89; and *Tadić*, Interlocutory Appeal, at para. 70.

[30] *Haradinaj*, at para. 60. See also *Limaj*, Trial Judgment, at paras 97, 100–01, 125–29; and *Boškoski*, Trial Judgment, at 284–89.

[31] *Prosecutor v Hadžihasanović et al.*, Case No. IT-01-47-AR72, Decision on Interlocutory Appeal Challenging Jurisdiction in Relation to Command Responsibility, 16 July 2003, at paras 16–17. See also *Akayesu*, Trial Judgment, at para. 626; and *Fofana and Kondewa*, at para. 127.

[32] *Prosecutor v Katanga and Chui*, Case No. ICC-01/04-01/07, Decision on the Confirmation of Charges, 30 September 2008, at para. 239.

[33] Sivakumaran, *The Law of Non-International Armed Conflict*, at 175.

[34] *Katanga*, Decision on the Confirmation of Charges, at para. 239; see also *Prosecutor v Bemba Gombo*, Case No. ICC-01/05-01/08, Decision Pursuant to Art. 61(7)(a) and (b) of the Rome Statute on the Charges of the Prosecutor against Jean-Pierre Bemba-Gombo, 15 June 2009, at para. 234.

[35] *Prosecutor v Delalić et al.*, Case No. IT-96-21, Trial Judgment, 16 November 1998, at para. 736; see also *Prosecutor v Delalić et al.*, Case No. IT-96-21-A, Appeals Judgment, 20 February 2001, at paras 186–99.

concerted military operations and to implement this Protocol'. The element of territorial control is absent from Common Article 3. As such, in situations where the armed group meets the organizational threshold but does not control territory, Additional Protocol II will not apply, but Common Article 3 will.[36]

Protocol II applies to armed groups who have a degree of organization and territorial control which enables them to carry out sustained and concerted military operations, 'and to implement this Protocol'. The question thus arises: is the *ability* to apply the Protocol to be interpreted as a *requirement* to implement the Protocol, in order for Protocol II to apply? Must the armed groups apply the Protocol in order for the Protocol to apply, or is it that they must only be organizationally capable of applying the Protocol? There is only limited State practice regarding this question. In relation to the application of Protocol II to the situation in El Salvador, the Swiss Directorate for Public International Law stated that 'Article 1 of Protocol II requires that the insurgents be able to implement this Protocol. Therefore, it is necessary to establish, having regard to the actual situation, whether the dissidents are able to implement that instrument. The question of whether or not they do so effectively is of little importance.'[37]

This interpretation is supported by the ICTY in *Boškoski*, where the Trial Chamber spoke of the 'organisational *ability* to comply with the obligations of international humanitarian law'[38] as a prerequisite for the application of Additional Protocol II. Indeed, as Sivakumaran has pointed out, this approach seems to fit best with the drafting history of Article 1(1) of Additional Protocol II, where the Conference of Government Experts took the position that it was the 'material means of observing and ensuring the

[36] See further Sivakumaran, at 181, where he discusses the ICC pre-trial chamber in *Katanga*: 'when ICC pre-trial chambers note that specific armed groups "had the capacity to plan and carry out sustained and concerted military operations, insofar as they held control of parts of the territory of the Ituri District", and that "control over the territory by the relevant organised armed groups has been a key factor in determining whether they has the ability to carry out military operations for a prolonged period of time", it is submitted that they should be understood as meaning that territorial control was *evidence* of the ability of the armed group in these regards and not that territorial control is a required *condition* for such. A means of proof must not be turned into a condition precedent' (emphasis in original, footnotes omitted).

[37] Note of the Directorate for Public International Law of the Federal Department of Foreign Affairs of January 20, 1986, 43 Annuaire Suisse de Droit International 185 (1987), unofficial translation reprinted in Marco Sassòli *et al.*, *How Does Law Protect in War? Cases, Documents and Teaching Materials on Contemporary Practice in International Humanitarian Law* (3rd edn, ICRC, 2011), Vol II at 1330.

[38] *Boškoski*, at para. 205.

observance of the rules of Humanitarian Law in force'[39] that was decisive, rather than the 'circular'[40] approach which would have the Protocol 'applicable only in situations in which the armed group actually implements it.'[41]

Applying the IHL criteria to high-level criminal activities

A case study of Mexico

Given these criteria—intensity of hostilities, internal organization, responsible command, the ability (if not the actuality) of implementation of IHL—we can examine whether high-level criminal violence, such as that occurring in Mexico, could be classified as a non-international armed conflict. In regards to the intensity of the hostilities, the violence in Mexico would seem to fit the criteria in a number of respects. To that end, some background on the situation is useful. In 2006, the Mexican government launched Operation Michoacán, a campaign designed to dismantle the drug cartels that were operating with impunity in Mexico.[42] The 2006 operation, launched by then-President Felipe Calderón, mobilized over 6000 federal troops.[43] Since 2006, some 50,000 members of the Mexican military have been deployed alongside federal police.[44]

The drug-related violence encompasses conflict between the government and the cartels, as well as inter- and intra-cartel violence.[45] The weaponry used by the cartels has included assault rifles similar to US Army-issue M-16s,[46]

[39] See Conference of Government Experts on the Reaffirmation and Development of International Humanitarian Law Applicable in Armed Conflicts (Second Session, 3 May–3 June 1972), *Report on the Work of the Conference* (Geneva, July 1972), Vol II at 35–36.

[40] Sivakumaran, *The Law of Non-International Armed Conflict*, at 189.

[41] Sivakumaran, *The Law of Non-International Armed Conflict*, at 189.

[42] For a more detailed history of the drug trade in Mexico, see further Peter Watt and Roberto Zepeda, *Drug War Mexico: Politics, Neo-Liberalism and Violence in the New Narcoeconomy* (Zed Books, 2012), Chs 1 and 2; and Ioan Grillo, *El Narco: Inside Mexico's Criminal Insurgency* (Bloomsbury, 2011), Part 1.

[43] See 'Armed Conflict in Mexico in 2012', in Stuart Casey-Maslen (ed.), *The War Report 2012* (OUP, 2013), at 127.

[44] June Beittel, *Mexico's Drug Trafficking Organisations: Source and Scope of the Rising Violence*, Congressional Research Service Report for Congress, 15 April 2013, available at: <http://fas.org/sgp/crs/row/R41576.pdf>, accessed 29 March 2015.

[45] See *The War Report*, at 129–31.

[46] See Chris McGreal, 'How Mexico's Drug Cartels Profit from Flow of Guns Across the Border', *Guardian*, 9 December 2011, available at: <http://www.theguardian.com/world/2011/dec/08/us-guns-mexico-drug-cartels>, accessed 29 March 2015. The flow of US weapons into Mexico was the subject of a botched US Bureau of Alcohol, Tobacco and Firearms (ATF) operation dubbed 'Fast and Furious', the aim of which was to allow weapons from the US to be acquired by suspected gun smugglers, so the weapons could eventually be traced to the upper ranks of the Mexican cartels. However, the ATF lost track of hundreds of the weapons, with many eventually being used violent crimes, including the fatal shooting of Border Patrol Agent Brian Terry in

as well as grenades and landmines stolen from military stockpiles and armouries.[47] Estimates place the number of deaths that have occurred in relation to the violence in Mexico at between 50,000 and 125,000 people in the six years of Calderón's administration.[48] The number of civilians displaced by the violence has been estimated at 160,000.[49]

Given the scope and duration of the violence, the number of casualties, the kinds of weapons used, and the degree of civilian displacement, the violence in Mexico could, using the *Haradinaj* reasoning, be conceived of as a non-international armed conflict. However, it is not the violence alone that triggers the applicability of IHL but the degree to which the parties to the conflict meet certain organizational criteria, including responsible command. For the regular armed forces of the State, the organizational criteria are presumed;[50] it is therefore necessary to determine whether the cartels also display the relevant degree of organization.

A number of the cartels would seem to fit the requirement of organization; as per the ICTY in *Haradinaj*, cartels such as Los Zetas, Sinaloa, Cártel del Golfo, Beltrán Leyva, and Knights Templar, all control parts of Mexican territory, often to the exclusion of the other cartels and the Mexican government.[51] Some of them also have clear internal organizational structures and follow prescribed codes of conduct; for example, the Knights Templar, a cartel that is an offshoot of older cartel La Familia Michoacana, has issued

December 2010. For an analysis of the operation, see further Michael Krantz, 'Walking Firearms to Gunrunners: ATF's Flawed Operation in a Flawed System', 103 J Crim L & Criminology 585 (2013).

[47] See further Robert Beckhusen, 'The Tools of Mexico's Drug Cartels, From Landmines to Monster Trucks', *Wired*, 30 November 2012, available at: <http://www.wired.com/2012/11/cartel-weapons/?viewall=true>, accessed 29 March 2015>, accessed 29 March 2015; and Ken Ellingwood and Tracy Wilkinson, 'Drug Cartels' New Weaponry Means War', *Los Angeles Times*, 15 March 2009, available at: <http://www.latimes.com/world/la-fg-mexico-arms-race15-2009mar15-story.html#page=1>, accessed 29 March 2015.

[48] The higher statistic comes from research undertaken by Cory Molzahn, Octavio Rodriguez Ferreira, and David Shirk, published in *Drug Violence in Mexico: Data and Analysis Through 2012*, Trans-Border Institute at the University of San Diego, February 2013, available at: <http://justiceinmexico.files.wordpress.com/2013/02/130206-dvm-2013-final.pdf>, at 13, accessed 29 March 2015. The lower figure comes from the Mexican government, with statistics for the period 2007–2011 reprinted in Cory Molzahn, Octavio Rodriguez Ferreira, and David Shirk, *Drug Violence in Mexico: Data and Analysis Through 2011*, Trans-Border Institute at the University of San Diego, March 2012, available at: <https://justiceinmexico.files.wordpress.com/2010/07/2012-tbi-drugviolence.pdf>, accessed 6 April 2015.

[49] Internal Displacement Monitoring Centre (IMDC), 'Global Overview 2012', April 2013, available at: <http://www.internal-displacement.org/assets/publications/2013/2012-global-overview-corporate-en.pdf>, at 39, accessed 29 March 2015.

[50] Sivakumaran, *The Law of Non-International Armed Conflict*, at 170.

[51] See Haines, 'The Nature of War', at 25–26; and Sullivan and Elkus, 'Plazas for Profit'.

its own code of conduct in the form of a twenty-two-page booklet, outlining its internal disciplinary system.[52]

Is IHL the appropriate framework?

Given the existence of such indicia—the intensity of the violence, and the level of organization demonstrated by some of the cartels—the criteria for establishing the existence of a non-international armed conflict would, *prima facie*, seem to be met. Indeed, that the violence in Mexico is a war in everything but name has been noted by former Mexican President Vincente Fox, who remarked in 2011, 'we're undergoing a war, no doubt—35,000, maybe 40,000 people killed, either members of the cartels or members of the police force or members of the army. So yes, we're undergoing a war, no doubt. Everybody's trying to deny that we're going through a war, but that's what it is.'[53]

Mexico is not party to Additional Protocol II.[54] As such, the rules contained in Additional Protocol II would not apply to the violence in Mexico, excluding those that are considered as having achieved customary status.[55] As such, the lower threshold of Common Article 3 would be the remaining legal regime that could apply. However, there are a few qualifying factors that may well undermine attempts to designate the Mexico conflict as an armed conflict for the purposes of IHL, even under the lower threshold of Common

[52] See Jude Webber, 'Mexico's Knights Templar on Deadly Quest for Drug Trade Efficiency', *Financial Times*, 26 January 2014, available at: <http://www.ft.com/intl/cms/s/0/fe712150-84f5-11e3-8968-00144feab7de.html#axzz3DKw3YHUB>, accessed 29 March 2015.

[53] Jim Myers and Kathleen Walter, 'Vicente Fox: Mexico at 'War', Obama's Approach a Failure', *Newsmax*, 22 March 2011, available at: <http://www.newsmax.com/Headline/VicenteFox-Mexico-DrugWar-Cartels/2011/03/22/id/390385/#ixzz3DLOCso49>, accessed 29 March 2015. See also similar comments made by US politicians, who have dubbed the violence in Mexico an 'insurgency' and the drug cartels as 'terrorists': see comments made by Congressman Michael McCaul, Press Release: McCaul Seeks To Classify Mexican Drug Cartels as Terrorists, 30 March 2011, available at: <http://mccaul.house.gov/media-center/press-releases/mccaul-seeks-to-classify-mexican-drug-cartels-as-terrorists>, accessed 6 April 2015; statements made by Senator Richard Lugar, Speech to Rule of Law Training Conference for Mexican Prosecutors, 27 September 2010, available at: <https://votesmart.org/public-statement/558502/lugar-speech-to-rule-of-law-training-conference-for-mexican-prosecutors#.UdIOLz7EqKw>, accessed 29 March 2015; and comments by former Representative Connie Mack and former Chairwoman of the House Foreign Affairs Committee Ileana Ros-Lehtinen, *Emerging Threats and Security in the Western Hemisphere: Hearing Before the House Committee on Foreign Affairs* (2011), available at: <http://www.gpo.gov/fdsys/pkg/CHRG-112hhrg70665/pdf/CHRG-112hhrg70665.pdf>, accessed 29 March 2015.

[54] See the ICRC website at: <https://www.icrc.org/applic/ihl/ihl.nsf/vwTreatiesByCountrySelected.xsp?xp_countrySelected=MX>, accessed 29 March 2015.

[55] See further Sivakumaran, *The Law of Non-International Armed Conflict*, at 182–92.

Article 3. The ICTY in *Haradinaj* noted that, in making a determination as to the existence of an armed conflict, a number of factors relating to the 'intensity' of the violence would need to be examined, such as the types of weapons used as well as the numbers of persons involved in the fighting, the extent of material destruction, and the numbers of civilians fleeing the combat zones.[56] In applying these criteria to the violence in Mexico, certain shortfalls become apparent.

First, while the Mexican armed forces have indeed been deployed throughout the State in response to the drug violence, most, if not all of the forces have been used in an essentially law enforcement capacity—that is, arresting cartel members and interdicting drug shipments—rather than in a typical military capacity.[57] Indeed, the use of the military in combatting the cartels has arguably less to do with treating the violence as an armed conflict, and more to do with trying to circumvent the close ties that Mexican police and law enforcement agencies traditionally maintain with the cartels.[58]

Furthermore, the intensity of violence in Mexico might also fail to meet the threshold for a non-international armed conflict. While the casualties since 2006 have been significant, the armed engagements between the cartels, or between the cartels and the government, have not, typically, been of the kind envisaged by the ICTY in its various examinations of the 'intensity' requirement. There have not been, as the ICTY noted in *Mrkšić et al.*, 'daily combat, usually involving artillery, mortars, armoured vehicles, including tanks, weapons such as multiple rocket launchers and anti aircraft batteries, as well as infantry weapons, and at times air and naval forces',[59] nor 'artillery bombardment'[60] that destroys numerous dwellings. Indeed, as noted in a recent newspaper report, 'grenade attacks, car bombs and wild urban gun battles have also become rarer. In one especially telling shift, Mexico's military says the number of attacks on its soldiers dropped more than 50% last year, a sign that traffickers were looking to avoid—not ambush—army patrols.'[61] Indeed, evidence indicates that Mexico's 2012 homicide statistics of 21.5 per 100,000 people is significantly lower than

[56] *Haradinaj*, Trial Judgment, at para. 49.

[57] Beittel, *Mexico's Drug Trafficking Organisations*, at 3–4.

[58] Beittel, *Mexico's Drug Trafficking Organisations*, at 6–8, 34–35.

[59] *Prosecutor v Mrkšić et al.*, Case No. IT-95-13/1-T, Trial Judgment, 27 September, 2007, at para. 419.

[60] *Tadić*, Trial Judgment, at para. 565.

[61] Nick Miroff, 'Mexico's Drug War Grows Quieter', *Washington Post*, 1 February 2013, available at: <http://www.washingtonpost.com/world/the_americas/mexicos-drug-war-grows-quieter/2013/02/01/37d50cde-670d-11e2-889b-f23c246aa446_story.html>, accessed 6 April 2015.

that of other Central American States, including Belize, Guatemala, and Honduras.[62]

Additionally, the organizational requirement may be found lacking in the case of a number of the cartels. The ICTY in *Haradinaj* spoke of 'the existence of a command structure and disciplinary rules and mechanisms within the group... its ability to plan, coordinate and carry out military operations, including troop movements and logistics; its ability to define a unified military strategy and use military tactics, and its ability to speak with one voice and negotiate and conclude agreements such as cease-fire or peace accords.'[63] When the ICTY was ascertaining whether the Kosovo Liberation Army could be considered a party to the non-international armed conflict (in the *Limaj* case), the Tribunal looked at additional factors such as the issuance of political statements and communiqués informing the international community of its aims and objectives,[64] and the distribution of regulations to subordinate units.[65]

In the context of the cartels, these criteria may not be met: research into the cartels has indicated that there is little connection between the enforcement organizations that are contracted to carry out the acts of violence and the cartels themselves. These enforcers are not part of any chain of command or organizational hierarchy in the cartel, and they owe no allegiance to the cartel once their contract is complete.[66] Some have suggested that the cartels are more akin to loosely associated, horizontally structured, semi-autonomous cells,[67] rather than vertical, hierarchical organizations able to control all aspects of the violence carried out in their name.[68] Gaining membership in the cartels is, in some cases, remarkably easy: media reports have noted that while the Los Zetas cartel was 'originally a tight-knit paramilitary-style unit of deserters from the Mexican army special forces',[69] the cartel has now

[62] See statistics compiled by the UN Office on Drugs and Crime, available at: <http://www.unodc.org/gsh/en/data.html>, accessed 29 March 2015.

[63] *Haradinaj*, at para. 60. See also *Limaj*, Trial Judgment, at paras 97, 100–01, 125–29; and *Boškoski*, Trial Judgment, at 284–89.

[64] *Limaj*, Trial Judgment, at para. 101.

[65] *Limaj*, Trial Judgment, at para. 98.

[66] See Colleen Cook, *Mexico's Drug Cartels*, Congressional Research Service, Report for Congress, 16 October 2007, available at: <http://fas.org/sgp/crs/row/RL34215.pdf>, at 6, accessed 29 March 2015. See also US Department of Justice, Attorney-General's Report to Congress on the Growth of Violent Street Gangs in Suburban Areas, April 2008, available at: <http://www.justice.gov/archive/ndic/pubs27/27612/growth.htm>, accessed 29 March 2015.

[67] Beittel, *Mexico's Drug Trafficking Organisations*, at 18.

[68] See Phil Williams, 'The Terrorism Debate over Mexican Drug Trafficking Violence', 24 Terrorism & Pol Violence 259 (2012), at 270.

[69] Malcolm Beith, 'Mexico's Drug War: The Battle without Hope', *The New Statesman*, 8 August 2012, available at: <http://www.newstatesman.com/politics/politics/2012/08/mexicos-drug-war-battle-without-hope>, accessed 29 March 2015.

devolved into 'independent gangs',[70] with little coordination from a central hierarchy.

Furthermore, evidence seems to indicate that the majority of the violence in Mexico has taken place in areas where territorial control is highly contested; that is, where there are two or more parties (either among the cartels and/or the Mexican government) vying for exclusive control.[71] As such, the requirement for 'exclusive administrative power'[72] within the State appears absent, contributing to negative assessment of territorial control by the cartels.

Indeed, the notion that any of the cartels would be capable of 'speak[ing] with one voice [and being able to] negotiate and conclude agreements such as cease-fire or peace accords'[73] seems untenable. While the cartels may control some territory and may have some indicia of organization, they seem to lack any overarching or unified military objective or military strategy—one of the *Haradinaj* criteria[74]—beyond making money. They do not wish to overthrow the Mexican government nor form a new State; their only aim seems to be to achieve monetary gain through criminal activities. As noted by Hauck and Peterke, 'as their violence is not driven by an ideology or legitimate political intentions, the criminal organisations not only have no interest in confronting the government and assuming its powers and responsibility'.[75]

A note of caution should be sounded here: that the cartels have a non-political motive—that is, accruing a financial gain from drug trafficking and other criminal activities—would not necessarily militate against designating the violence in Mexico as an armed conflict under international law.[76] As Sivakumaran notes, the motive for fighting the conflict is, in theory, irrelevant:

> the motives of the armed group, as indeed the motives of the state, are irrelevant to the decision as to whether or not a non-international armed conflict exists. Armed groups may, and do, fight for different reasons. Some seek to create a new state, others to overthrow the government, still others for greater autonomy. Some fight to claim a share of natural resources; others wish to engage in ethnic cleansing, to

[70] Beith, 'Mexico's Drug War: The Battle without Hope'.

[71] See Cory Molzahn, Viridiana Ríos, and David Shirk, *Drug Violence in Mexico: Data and Analysis Through 2011* (Transborder Institute, University of San Diego, March 2012), available at: <http://justiceinmexico.files.wordpress.com/2010/07/2012-tbi-drugviolence.pdf>, at 25, accessed 29 March 2015.

[72] *Tadić*, Trial Judgment, at para. 125.

[73] *Haradinaj*, at para. 60.

[74] *Haradinaj*, at para. 60.

[75] Hauck and Peterke, 'Organised Crime and Gang Violence in National and International Law', at 433.

[76] See further Dapo Akande, 'Classification of Armed Conflicts: Relevant Legal Concepts', in Elizabeth Wilmshurst (ed.), *International Law and the Classification of Armed Conflicts*, at 52.

pillage, or to terrorize. The reasons that motivate the fighting are irrelevant insofar as the existence of a non-international armed conflict is concerned.[77]

However, it is submitted that, for policy reasons, in the case of organized crime groups, the motives of the parties should be taken into consideration if IHL is to be the *lex specialis*. As Hauck and Peterke note regarding organized armed cartels, the motivation of such cartels may be pivotal in making a determination as to whether IHL should apply. Armed criminal groups, they argue:

have no interest in imposing disciplinary rules and mechanisms to guarantee respect for IHL. This, however, is a crucial point, although compliance with IHL is not needed.[78] While the qualification as an organised armed group is based on objective criteria in order to avoid the application of subjective elements such as the group's motivation, the law is not completely 'blind' in that respect... the organisational criterion, by demanding an objectively verifiable military strategy or capacity to carry out military operations, rules out entities that rely exclusively on terrorist, guerrilla, and other perfidious methods.[79]

The cartels do not seem interested in defeating the Mexican State; instead, they 'seek to subvert, not defeat, the State through intimidation and bribes'[80] so that they may continue their operations 'undisturbed'.[81] Their only aim appears to be to 'preserve the illicit power structure set up alongside the state'.[82]

The cartels' objectives are financial, not ideological or political, which would suggest that the cartels are better addressed under the rubric of the UN Convention against Transnational Organised Crime,[83] which defines an organized criminal group as a 'structured group of three or more persons, existing for a period of time and acting in concert with the aim of committing one or more serious crimes or offences [as outlined in the Convention]... in

[77] Sivakumaran, *The Law of Non-International Armed Conflict*, at 182.

[78] Hauck and Peterke, 'Organised Crime and Gang Violence in National and International Law', at 433.

[79] Hauck and Peterke, 'Organised Crime and Gang Violence in National and International Law', at 433.

[80] Andrea Nill Sánchez, 'Mexico's Drug 'War': Drawing a Line between Rhetoric and Reality', 38 Yale J Int'l L 467 (2013), at 488.

[81] Beittel, *Mexico's Drug Trafficking Organisations*, at 11.

[82] Ami Carpenter, 'Beyond Drug War: Transforming Factional Conflict in Mexico', 27 Conflict Resolution Quarterly 401 (2010), at 407. See also Beittel, *Mexico's Drug Trafficking Organisations*, at 26, where she notes that 'Mexican traffickers do not seek to replace the government and provide services, but they are committed to manipulating it with bribery and violence to continue their illegal activities without interference.'

[83] United Nations Convention against Transnational Organised Crime, 2225 UNTS 209.

order to obtain, directly or indirectly, a financial or other material benefit.'[84] Indeed, as noted by Sanchez:

> almost every definition of insurgency employed by countries around the world requires that the insurgent force possess a political agenda [and while] ... there is no legal consensus concerning the international definition of 'terrorism', most nations contemplate the use of violence to achieve political aims. Given the drug cartel's relative political apathy, they do not easily qualify as either terrorists or insurgents.[85]

One final point can be made contributing to the weight of the argument against designating the Mexican violence as an armed conflict for the purposes of applying IHL: neither the parties to the supposed conflict nor the international community at large are treating the violence as an armed conflict *stricto sensu*. For example, since the start of Operation Michoacán in December 2006, neither the UN General Assembly nor the Security Council have specifically addressed the violence in Mexico in the form of a resolution or declaration. While the ICRC conducts operations and activities through its regional delegation in Mexico, none of its reported activities seem to indicate that it considers the violence in Mexico as amounting to an armed conflict; for example, there appear to be no references by the ICRC in Mexico to suggest that the drug violence has triggered IHL.[86]

While the ICRC does not generally publicly qualify acts of violence as amounting to armed conflict, it nonetheless tends to couch its press releases and other public statements in IHL terminology if the ICRC takes the position that IHL is the relevant law. As noted by Rogier Bartels:

> the ICRC rarely qualifies a situation as an armed conflict by means of its press releases ... hints to how the ICRC views a situation can nevertheless be found in many of its press releases ... [in such cases] ... the terminology used is that of IHL (as opposed to, eg, human rights law or national criminal law) and as such it indicates that the ICRC also then considered this body of law applicable). Since IHL is applicable only in times of armed conflict (apart from a few rules that apply in peace time or continue to apply after the armed conflict has ended) [the use of such terminology] ... indicates how the ICRC considered the situation at the time.[87]

[84] Art. 2(a), UN Convention against Transnational Organised Crime.

[85] Sánchez, 'Mexico's Drug "War" ', at 502–03.

[86] See the ICRC Regional Delegation Report on the Activities of the ICRC Delegation for Mexico, Central America, and Cuba, available at: <https://www.icrc.org/en/document/activities-icrc-delegation-mexico-central-america-and-cuba#.VCtWZ02KAdU>, accessed 29 March 2015.

[87] Comments by Rogier Bartels, 'Follow-up on the organisational requirement: ICRC statements and conflict qualification', Armed Groups and International Law blog, 10 August 2012, availableat:<http://armedgroups-internationallaw.org/2012/08/10/follow-up-on-the-organisational-requirement-icrc-statements-and-conflict-qualification/>, accessed 6 April 2015.

The ICRC has not appeared to employ IHL terminology in its publications or public statements regarding Mexico; indeed, reference tends to be to 'organised crime'[88] or 'situations of violence.'[89] Indeed, the ICRC seems reluctant to use the terminology of armed conflict and IHL in the context of armed violence, especially drug-related armed violence. As noted by an IHL adviser on negotiating with armed groups and criminal gangs, 'you don't speak about IHL'[90] to criminal gangs. Speaking in 2012, Senior Legal Adviser of the ICRC Delegation to the European Union, NATO, and Belgium, Stéphane Kolanowski, was more categorical: 'although in theory, one can imagine that urban violence related to organised crime can fulfil [the *Tadić* criteria of organisation and intensity] and consequently be considered as an armed conflict, in actual practice it is difficult to identify any occurrence of urban violence that matches these criteria.'[91]

Furthermore, none of the cartels seem to have engaged with, or been approached to engage with, international law in any way; for example, Geneva Call, the non-governmental organization that is 'dedicated to promoting respect by armed non-State actors (ANSAs) for international humanitarian norms in armed conflict and other situations of violence, in particular those related to the protection of civilians', has not engaged with any of the cartels in their endeavours.[92] None of the cartels has signed any of Geneva Call's deeds of commitment to IHL principles;[93] this could suggest that both

[88] See, eg, the ICRC Annual Report 2011, available at: <https://www.icrc.org/ara/assets/files/annual-report/current/icrc-annual-report-mexico-city.pdf>, at 355, accessed 29 March 2015.

[89] Stéphane Kolanowski, 'Applicable Legal Frameworks Pertaining to Urban Violence', in Joint Report of the European Union Institute for Security Studies and the International Committee of the Red Cross, Colloquium on Urban Violence and Humanitarian Challenges, 19 January 2012, available at: <http://www.iss.europa.eu/uploads/media/Urban_violence_and_humanitarian_challenges.pdf>, at 24, accessed 29 March 2015.

[90] Amy Serafin, 'Urban Violence: War By Any Other Name', *The Magazine of the International Red Cross and Red Crescent Movement*, Volume 1 (2010), available at: <http://www.redcross.int/EN/mag/magazine2010_1/20-23.html>, accessed 29 March 2015. In the article, Serafin also notes: 'Can regular armed confrontations between police or armed forces and gangs be considered noninternational armed conflict and should international humanitarian law be applied? The general consensus is, in principle, "no"—IHL falls short and might even be detrimental. It would legitimize the killing of rivals as "combatants", for example, and would also allow for a certain amount of collateral damage close to the fighting—a dangerous prospect in the confines of an urban environment.'

[91] Kolanowski, 'Applicable Legal Frameworks Pertaining to Urban Violence', at 26.

[92] See: <http://www.genevacall.org/how-we-work/armed-non-state-actors/> and <http://www.genevacall.org/where-we-work/> for a list of the States where Geneva Call operates, and the non-State armed groups with whom Geneva Call has engaged; both sites accessed 6 April 2015.

[93] See: <http://www.genevacall.org/how-we-work/armed-non-state-actors/> and <http://www.genevacall.org/where-we-work/>, both sites accessed 6 April 2015.

the cartels, and Geneva Call, do not consider the violence in Mexico to warrant international legal involvement.

One would also have to question whether IHL would aid the parties involved. Designating the violence in Mexico as an armed conflict would allow the Mexican authorities to employ the armed forces in response to the cartels; however, the Mexican armed forces are already being employed against the cartels, if only in a law enforcement capacity. Indeed, more generally speaking, the aims of IHL—that of balancing the requirements of military necessity with the objective of sparing the civilian population as far as possible from the effects of the hostilities—seem ill-suited to deal with the violence in Mexico. For example, one of the key 'tests' in IHL is that of proportionality: that any damage to civilians and civilian infrastructure that results from an attack against a military objective must be proportionate to the anticipated military advantage gained.[94] As such, death and injury to civilians, and destruction of civilian objects, is not *prima facie* illegal under IHL if the attack that brings about such damage or injury can be considered proportionate. It seems unlikely that the Mexican government would publicly embrace such an approach, that the loss of dozens, if not hundreds of civilian lives would be acceptable if it meant destroying a major cartel production facility.

Thus, certain situations of armed violence, though widespread and sustained, are perhaps best kept out of the framework of IHL. More specifically, given the weight of cumulative criteria needed to assess a situation as an armed conflict—intensity and duration of hostilities, as well as organization of the groups involved—it is submitted that the armed violence in Mexico does not meet these standards and thus IHL is not triggered. However, were the Mexico violence to evolve into an armed conflict, implications regarding DPH would necessarily arise and would need to be considered in detail. At what point would a cartel member change from being a criminal to a person taking direct part in hostilities? How do you make the distinction between an act done purely for criminal purposes to a criminal act that also amounts to DPH?

These questions arise when one examines situations where armed conflicts exist coterminous to widespread organized criminal activity. In such situations, IHL is already applicable. What problems are thus raised when armed conflicts are started and even sustained by such organized crime groups and endeavours? What are the problems for IHL when the boundaries between crime and war blur? The next part of this chapter examines these questions.

[94] Art. 51(5)(b), API; see also Art. 57(2)(a)(iii).

Where Organized Criminal Activities are Interconnected with the Armed Conflict

That organized criminal activities exist alongside armed conflicts and, indeed, often serve to fuel and prolong such conflicts, has been well documented in the literature in recent years.[95] In a number of instances, States and non-State actors have 'used proceeds from criminal activities as a "war resource"',[96] enabling them to continue their armed conflicts with their adversaries. Diamonds,[97] oil,[98] and narcotics[99] have all, in recent years, fuelled conflicts in Africa, South America, and the Middle East.[100] Indeed, in some cases, such as the armed conflict in Sierra Leone, criminal gangs have started conflicts over access to such resources.[101]

The intermingling of criminals and combatants, and conflict and criminal activities, raise problematic questions for parties to a conflict, with regards to targeting and DPH: can an opportunistic criminal in a combat zone be lawfully targeted for acts connected to the conflict? What level of involvement must be proved before a civilian act crosses the threshold from criminal

[95] See for example, Svante Cornell, 'Narcotics and Armed Conflict: Interaction and Implications'; Karen Ballentine and Jake Sherman (eds), *The Political Economy of Armed Conflict: Beyond Greed and Grievance* (Lynne Rienner, 2003); Ekaterina Stepanova, 'Armed Conflict, Crime and Criminal Violence', 41 SIPRI Yearbook 38 (2010); Elisabeth Gilmore, Nils Petter Gleditsch, Paivi Lujala, *et al.*, 'Conflict Diamonds: A New Dataset', 22 Conflict Management and Peace Science 257 (2005); Hal Brands, 'Crime, Irregular Warfare, and Institutional Failure in Latin America: Guatemala as a Case Study', 34 Studies in Conflict and Terrorism 228 (2011); Stéphanie Lavaux, 'Natural Resources and Conflict in Colombia: Complex Dynamics, Narrow Relationships', 62 International Journal 19 (2006).

[96] Stepanova, 'Armed Conflict, Crime and Criminal Violence', at 41.

[97] See, for background, John Hirsch, *Sierra Leone: Diamonds and the Struggle for Democracy* (Lynne Rienner, 2001); Ian Smillie, *Diamonds* (Polity Press, 2014); and J Anyu Ndumbe and Babalola Cole, 'The Illicit Diamond Trade, Civil Conflicts, and Terrorism in Africa', 16 Mediterranean Quarterly 47 (2005).

[98] For background, see Philippe Le Billon, 'Oil and Armed Conflicts in Africa', 29 African Geographical Review 63 (2010); Yu-Hsiang Lei and Guy Michaels, 'Do Giant Oilfield Discoveries Fuel Internal Armed Conflicts?', 110 Journal of Development Economics 139 (2014); and Paivi Lujala, Jan Ketil Rod, and Nadja Thieme, 'Fighting over Oil: Introducing a New Dataset', 24 Conflict Management and Peace Science 239 (2007).

[99] In the form of opium poppy crops in Afghanistan and coca crops in Colombia. For background, see further Felicity Szesnat and Annie Bird, 'Colombia', in Wilmshurst (ed.), *International Law and the Classification of Conflicts*, at 203–41; and Michael Schmitt, 'Targeting Narcoinsurgents in Afghanistan: The Limits of International Humanitarian Law', 12 YBIHL 301 (2009).

[100] See generally Michael Ross, 'Oil, Drugs, and Diamonds: The Varying Roles of Natural Resources in Civil War', in Ballentine and Sherman (eds), *The Political Economy of Armed Conflict*, at 47–68; and Phillipe Le Billon, 'The Political Ecology of War: Natural Resources and Armed Conflicts, 20 Political Geography 561 (2001), at 561–84.

[101] Crane, 'Terrorists, Warlords, and Thugs', at 515.

act occasioning a law enforcement response to an act occasioning a lawful military response? When does targeting a civilian committing a criminal act cease to be a war crime and become a response to DPH? Should high-level organized criminality that is deeply interconnected with an armed conflict be treated any differently from 'ordinary' DPH? The remainder of this chapter will examine these questions, using the situation in Colombia as a case study.

Drugs and armed conflict in Colombia

Since the 1960s, Colombia has been riven by internal armed conflict involving a number of non-State armed groups engaged in conflict against one another and the State, including the leftist Fuerzas Armadas Revolucionarias de Colombia (Revolutionary Armed Forces of Colombia, or FARC) and Ejército de Liberación National (the National Liberation Army, or ELN), the right-wing paramilitary Autodefensas Unidas de Colombia (United Self-Defense Forces of Colombia, or AUC, active 1994–2003),[102] and the newer armed groups, the Aguilas Negras (Black Eagles), Los Rastrojos, and the Organización Nueva Genaración (ONG).

This decades-long period of civil war was inaugurated in the late 1940s with '*La Violencia*', a ten-year civil conflict between supporters of the Colombian Liberal Party and the Colombian Conservative Party, which resulted in nearly 300,000 people killed.[103] In the years following the end of '*La Violencia*', the ELN and FARC emerged from the rural areas of the country, seeking to overthrow the Colombian government and end the perceived social inequality of the Colombian social and political system.[104]

As FARC and ELN grew more active and became more organized and strategic in their military campaigns and internal administrative structure, the Colombian government began to engage with the armed groups, negotiating ceasefires with FARC, which fielded candidates for the Colombian Congress in the 1986 general elections.[105] However, at the same time, right-wing death squads with links to paramilitary groups began their own

[102] For an examination of the Colombian conflict up to 1999, see generally Arturo Carrillo-Suárez, '*Hors de Logique*: Contemporary Issues in International Humanitarian Law as Applied to Internal Armed Conflict', 15 Am U Int'l L Rev 1 (1999), at 10–18.

[103] Szesnat and Bird, 'Colombia', at 204.

[104] See June Beittel, *Colombia: Background, U.S. Relations, and Congressional Interest*, Congressional Research Service Report for Congress, 28 November 2012, available at: <http://fas.org/sgp/crs/row/RL32250.pdf>, at 13–19, accessed 29 March 2015; and June Beittel, *Peace Talks in Colombia*, Congressional Research Service Report for Congress, 3 April 2014, available at: <http://fas.org/sgp/crs/row/R42982.pdf>, at 1–12, accessed 29 March 2015.

[105] Szesnat and Bird, 'Colombia', at 206.

campaigns against FARC and ELN. Initially hired by Colombian landowners and ranchers to provide security protection from kidnapping (a common FARC tactic in the 1980s), these 'self-defence' groups[106] ended up consolidating in 1997 as the AUC, and undertaking a campaign of murders of FARC and ELN members and supporters, as well as engaging both FARC and ELN in active battles.[107] The activities of the AUC and other paramilitary groups were frequently ignored, if not tacitly sanctioned, by the Colombian armed forces.[108] However, the AUC's support for drug cartels put the groups at cross-purposes with the anti-drug Colombian government.[109] The AUC eventually entered into a peace agreement with the Colombian government, which lead to the demobilization of over 32,000 AUC members.

Following the disbanding of the AUC, both FARC and ELN experienced a diminution of their control and influence. Current estimates place FARC's membership at around 9000 fighters,[110] forming 100 operational units, controlling around 20 per cent of Colombian territory.[111] ELN is reported to have only 1300 fighters,[112] and it has, according to reports, only been able to mount less than twenty military actions a year, down from a peak of nearly 200.[113]

The withdrawal of the AUC from the conflict left space for new armed groups to enter into the conflict, such as the Black Eagles and the ONG.[114] These armed groups developed complex relationships with the Colombian government and the FARC and ELN, in some cases engaging in combat against FARC and ELN,[115] while in other areas, collaborating with the insurgent groups to control drug production and trafficking.[116] Other armed groups, such as Los

[106] Szesnat and Bird, 'Colombia', at 209; see also Beittel, *Colombia: Background, U.S. Relations, and Congressional Interest*, at 19.

[107] Beittel, *Colombia: Background, U.S. Relations, and Congressional Interest*, at 19.

[108] Beittel, *Colombia: Background, U.S. Relations, and Congressional Interest*, at 19.

[109] Szesnat and Bird, 'Colombia', at 210.

[110] International Crisis Group, *Colombia: Peace at Last?*, Latin America Report No. 45, 25 September 2012, available at: <http://www.crisisgroup.org/~/media/Files/latin-america/colombia/045-colombia-peace-at-last.pdf>, at 4, accessed 29 March 2015.

[111] Szesnat and Bird, 'Colombia', at 210–11.

[112] International Crisis Group, *Left in the Cold? The ELN and Colombia's Peace Talks*, Latin America Report No. 51, 26 February 2014, available at: <http://www.crisisgroup.org/~/media/Files/latin-america/colombia/051-left-in-the-cold-the-eln-and-colombia-s-peace-talks.pdf>, at 3, accessed 29 March 2015.

[113] Szesnat and Bird, 'Colombia', at 210–11.

[114] For background on these' new armed groups', see further International Crisis Group, *Colombia's New Armed Groups*, Latin America Report No. 20, 10 May 2007, available at: <http://www.crisisgroup.org/~/media/Files/latin-america/colombia/20_colombia_s_new_armed_groups>, accessed 29 March 2015.

[115] International Crisis Group, *Colombia's New Armed Groups*, at 25, 26.

[116] International Crisis Group, *Colombia's New Armed Groups*, at 12, 25.

Rastrojos,[117] were (and are) primarily involved in drug production and trafficking, as well as running gold-mining operations;[118] however, Los Rastrojos have engaged in political and military activities, including supporting candidates for local and national elections,[119] as well as engaging in battles with ELN and FARC.[120]

Classification of the conflict

Colombia is a party to the Geneva Conventions and Additional Protocol II.[121] Classifying the conflict in Colombia is greatly assisted by the fact that the parties to the conflict—Colombia, FARC, and ELN—as well as a number of third States and inter-governmental organizations, have made statements regarding their assessment of the state of the hostilities in Colombia. Colombia has, at various stages throughout the history of the conflict, declared that it considers the hostilities to be a Common Article 3 conflict,[122] a Protocol II conflict,[123] or, according to statements made by

[117] Los Rastrojos started as an offshoot of the Norte del Valle drug cartel; see further *Insight Crime*, 'Rastrojos', available at: <http://www.insightcrime.org/colombia-organized-crime-news/rastrojos-profile>, accessed 29 March 2015.

[118] Simon Romero, 'In Colombia, New Gold Rush Fuels Old Conflict', *New York Times*, 3 March 2011, available at: <http://www.nytimes.com/2011/03/04/world/americas/04colombia.html?_r=0>, accessed 29 March 2015.

[119] Edward Fox, 'Colombian Mayor Investigated for Rastrojos Ties', *Insight Crime*, 31 August 2012, available at: <http://www.insightcrime.org/news-analysis/colombia-choco-mayor-rastrojos?highlight=WyJyYXN0cm9qb3MiLCJyYXN0cm9qb3MnIiwiJ3Jhc3Ryb2pvcyciLCIncmFzdHJvam9zJywiLCIncmFzdHJvam9zIiwicG9saXRpY2FsIiwiJ3BvbGl0aWNhbCciLCIncG-9saXRpY2FsIiwicmFzdHJvam9zIHBvbGl0aWNhbCJd>, accessed 29 March 2015.

[120] 'FARC Clash with Rastrojos in Cauca', *Insight Crime*, 14 February 2011, available at: <http://www.insightcrime.org/news-analysis/farc-clash-with-rastrojos-in-cauca?highlight=WyJyYXN0cm9qb3MiLCJyYXN0cm9qb3MnIiwiJ3Jhc3Ryb2pvcyciLCIncmFzdHJvam9zJywiLCIncmFzdHJvam9zIiwiZmFyYyIsImZhcmMncyIsIidmYXJjIiwiJ2ZhcmMnIiwicmFzdHJvam9zIGZhcmMiXQ>, accessed 29 March 2015.

[121] Colombia acceded to the Geneva Conventions in 1961, and to Additional Protocol II in 1995. See further: <https://www.icrc.org/applic/ihl/ihl.nsf/vwTreatiesByCountrySelected.xsp?xp_countrySelected=CO>, accessed 29 March 2015.

[122] See the Organisation of American States, *Third Report on the Situation of Human Rights in Colombia*, Doc No. OEA/Ser.L/V/II.102 Doc. 9 rev. 1, 26 February 1999, available at: <http://www.cidh.org/countryrep/Colom99en/table%20of%20contents.htm>, at 4 (accessed 29 March 2015), where it is stated that 'Colombia, unlike other States that all too frequently choose to deny the existence of such hostilities within their territory for political or other reasons, has openly acknowledged the factual reality of its involvement in such a conflict and the applicability of Art. 3 common to the four 1949 Geneva Conventions ("common Art. 3"), the 1977 Protocol Additional to the Geneva Conventions of August 12, 1949, Relating to the Protection of Victims of Non-International Armed Conflicts ("Protocol II"), and other customary law rules and principles governing internal armed conflicts.' Art. 214(2) of the Colombian Constitution also affirms the applicability of IHL in Colombia.

[123] See the Organisation of American States, *Third Report on the Situation of Human Rights in Colombia*, at 4; see also the Colombian Constitutional Court Decision No. C-574, October 28,

President Uribe in 2008, that there is no internal armed conflict at all,[124] only a law enforcement action against criminals (known as '*bandas criminales*' or 'BACRIM').[125]

However, comments made by President Juan Manual Santos in 2011 have reversed the stance taken by President Uribe in 2008, when Santos acknowledged the existence of an armed conflict in Colombia.[126] This position was affirmed with the adoption, in 2011, of the Victims and Land Restitution Law.[127] The law states, in Article 3, that it is intended to provide for 'those persons who individually or collectively have suffered harm... as a result of violations of International Humanitarian Law or serious and flagrant violations of international standards of human rights that occurred during the internal armed conflict.'[128] Furthermore, armed groups FARC and ELN have both acknowledged the applicability of IHL;[129] the UN Human Rights Committee and the ICRC have also acknowledged the existence of an internal armed conflict in Colombia,[130] as has the Inter-American Commission on Human Rights.[131]

1992, and Ruling on the Constitutional Conformity of Protocol II, Ruling No. C-225/95, Re: File No. LAT-040, 18 May 1995, and the Supreme Court of Colombia case *Gian Carlo Gutierrez Suarez*, Radicado No. 32.022, 21 September 2009, at 59.

[124] See comments made by President Uribe to the 38th General Assembly of the Organisation of American States in 2008, denying the existence of a non-international armed conflict: 'No dar estatus de beligerancia a las guerrillas pidió Uribe en instalación de asamblea de la OEA', *El Tiempo*, 2 June 2008, available at: <http://www.eltiempo.com/archivo/documento/CMS-4223723>, accessed 29 March 2015. The Colombian Commission of Jurists was of the contrary opinion to Uribe in 2009, stating that an Additional Protocol II armed conflict was taking place in Colombia; see further Comisión Colombiana de Juristas, *Tiempos de sequía: Situación de derechos humanos y derecho humanitario en Colombia 2002–2009*, available at: <http://www.coljuristas.org/documentos/libros_e_informes/tiempos_de_sequia.pdf>, at 56, accessed 29 March 2015.

[125] See Amnesty International, *Colombia: The Victims and Land Restitution Law—An Amnesty International Analysis* (Amnesty International, 2012), available at: <https://www.amnesty.org/en/documents/AMR23/018/2012/en/>, at 6, accessed 6 April 2015.

[126] Edmundo López Gómez, '¡Sí hay conflicto armado!', *El Universal*, 10 May 2011, available at: <http://www.eluniversal.com.co/columna/%C2%A1si-hay-conflicto-armado>, accessed 29 March 2015.

[127] Ley de Víctimas y Restitución de Tierras, Law 1448.

[128] Art. 3, Ley de Víctimas y Restitución de Tierras, Law 1448.

[129] Carrillo-Suárez, '*Hors de Logique*', at 26, 29–30.

[130] See *Report of the United Nations High Commissioner for Human Rights on the Situation of Human Rights in Colombia*, UN Doc. A/HRC/19/21/Add.3, 31 January 2012, available at: <http://www.ohchr.org/Documents/HRBodies/HRCouncil/RegularSession/Session19/A-HRC-19-21-Add3_en.pdf>, at 4, accessed 6 April 2015; and ICRC, Annual Report 2013, available at: <https://www.icrc.org/eng/assets/files/annual-report/current/icrc-annual-report-colombia.pdf>, at 418, accessed 29 March 2015.

[131] See the *Third Report on the Human Rights Situation in Colombia*, at 4.

DPH implications in cases of conflict and crime

That there is a non-international armed conflict taking place in Colombia seems uncontroversial; however, problems arise when one considers that some of the parties to the conflict are either financing their military activities through criminal endeavours (FARC, ELN), or are otherwise using the political instability to further their criminal activities, while occasionally engaging in military activities against other armed groups (Black Eagles, Los Rastrojos). Reports state that FARC currently derives the bulk of its income from the drug trade,[132] with recent reports placing its income from the drug trade at over US$1 billion per year.[133] A 2009 report states that over half of FARC's 110 operational units are involved in the drug trade, either in production, manufacturing, or exporting.[134] This involvement in criminal activity has prompted some to label FARC and ELN as 'narco-terrorists'[135] rather than fighters, or, as FARC members see themselves, 'belligerents'.[136]

Regardless of the often politically driven designations that attach to such groups,[137] the practical problems that arise regarding applying IHL

[132] Stephanie Hanson, *FARC, ELN: Colombia's Left-Wing Guerrillas*, Backgrounder for the Council on Foreign Relations, 19 August 2009, available at: <http://www.cfr.org/colombia/farc-eln-colombias-left-wing-guerrillas/p9272>, accessed 29 March 2015.

[133] Helen Murphy and Luis Jaime Acosta, 'FARC Controls 60% of Drug Trade—Colombia's Police Chief', *Reuters*, 22 April 2013, available at: <http://uk.reuters.com/article/2013/04/22/uk-colombia-rebels-police-idUKBRE93L18Y20130422>, accessed 29 March 2015; Geoffrey Ramsay, 'FARC "Earns $2.4 to $3.5 Billion" from Drugs: Govt', *Insight Crime*, 24 October 2012, available at: <http://www.insightcrime.org/news-briefs/farc-earns-24-to-35-billion-drugs>, accessed 29 March 2015.

[134] Hanson, *Colombia's Left-Wing Guerrillas*.

[135] See, eg, comments by Colombian Minister for Mines and Energy, and former Brookings Institute Fellow Mauricio Cárdenas (writing with Pablo Villar), 'Colombia: Defeating FARC's Narcoterrorism', 27 September 2010, available at: <http://www.brookings.edu/blogs/up-front/posts/2010/09/27-colombia-narcoterrorism-cardenas>, accessed 29 March 2015; FARC and ELN are both officially designated terrorist organisations under the US 'Designated Foreign Terrorist Organisations' protocol, as determined by the Secretary of State in accordance with § 219 of the US Immigration and Nationality Act; the list is available at: <http://www.state.gov/j/ct/rls/other/des/123085.htm>, accessed 29 March 2015.

[136] FARC has often used the terminology of 'belligerent' in its statements; see, eg, the communique issued after the release of Colombian politicians Clara Rojas and Consuelo González de Perdomo in 2008, available at: <http://www.noticias24.com/actualidad/noticia/11148/hablan-las-farc-somos-beligerantes-y-esperamos-el-reconocimiento/>, where it states that FARC is a belligerent 'waiting to be recognised by the world's governments' (website accessed 29 March 2015). FARC and ELN have been supported in their quests for belligerent status by other states; in 2008, the Venezuelan National Assembly voted in support of ongoing calls by President Chavez for Colombia to recognize FARC and the ELN as belligerents under international law. See 'The FARC Files', *The Economist*, 22 May 2008, available at: <http://www.economist.com/node/11412645>, accessed 29 March 2015.

[137] As the Commentary to Convention I notes, in 'a civil war, the lawful Government, or that which so styles itself, tends to regard its adversaries as common criminals' (*GCI Commentary*, at 39).

to situations of DPH in conflict and criminal activity persist: in targeting a FARC or ELN fighter, how can one be sure that he or she is engaging in a military act amounting to DPH, thus rendering targeting this individual permissible under international law? How can parties to the conflict be sure that an armed ELN or FARC fighter is not engaging in a 'purely' criminal activity and is not otherwise engaged in DPH (which would suggest that a law-enforcement model would be a preferred response to such a fighter)?

Indeed, similar concerns have arisen in the context of Afghanistan where, in 2008, the International Security Assistance Force (ISAF) was given authorization to 'act in concert with the Afghans against facilities and facilitators supporting the insurgency, in the context of counter-narcotics'.[138] The move to allow ISAF to target drug traffickers and producers who supported any insurgent forces was justified on the grounds that the drug traffickers were 'fuelling the insurgency, destabilizing Afghanistan, and killing our troops'.[139] However, a number of governments and experts voiced concern that such an order unacceptably blurred the distinction between insurgents, who should come under the international law of armed conflict, and narcotics producers, who should be dealt with by domestic law enforcement.[140] While the authorization was eventually rescinded, the issues raised by such approaches in Afghanistan and in Colombia remain: can civilians who participate in illegal activities for the purposes of funding an internal armed conflict be targeted under IHL for such activities? This question will be explored in the next section.

[138] NATO Press Release, 'NATO Steps Up Counter-Narcotics Efforts in Afghanistan', 10 October 2008, available at: <http://www.nato.int/docu/update/2008/10-october/e1010b.html>, accessed 29 March 2015.

[139] Comments made by Pentagon press secretary, Geoff Morrell, reported in Judy Dempsey, 'NATO Allows Strikes on Afghan Drug Sites', *New York Times*, 10 October 2008, available at: <http://www.nytimes.com/2008/10/10/world/asia/10iht-nato.4.16856342.html?_r=0>, accessed 29 March 2015.

[140] See comments made by Afghan Foreign Minister Rangin Dadfar Spanta, who stated that drug traffickers who were not involved in the armed conflict 'should be arrested and convicted, but not killed. That's a job for the police' ('Afghanistan Foreign Minister: "We Need Help from the West"', *Der Spiegel*, 9 February 2009, available at: <http://www.spiegel.de/international/world/afghanistan-foreign-minister-we-need-help-from-the-west-a-606481.html>, accessed 29 March 2015); and reported concerns voiced by Germany, Italy, Poland, and Spain, as noted in Thom Shankar, 'Obstacle in Bid to Curb Afghan Trade in Narcotics', *New York Times*, 23 December 2009, available at: <http://www.nytimes.com/2008/12/23/world/asia/23poppy.html>, accessed 29 March 2015. See further Dapo Akande, 'US/NATO Targeting of Afghan Drug Traffickers: An Illegal and Dangerous Precedent?', EJIL: Talk!, 13 September 2009, available at: <http://www.ejiltalk.org/usnato-targeting-of-afghan-drug-traffickers-an-illegal-and-dangerous-precedent/>, accessed 6 April 2015.

DPH and criminal armed conflict

The blurring of criminal activity and conflict in places such as Colombia and Afghanistan makes the task of distinguishing the fighter taking DPH and the criminal engaging in illicit activities a problematic situation to address. At its core, however, is the fundamental question that underpins all assessments of DPH: is the person in question a legitimate military objective, by virtue either of status or actions, because he or she is making an effective contribution to the conflict? This issue is related to a controversial topic of IHL: specifically, is the targeting of economic objects lawful under IHL? Are commercial industries that financially sustain the hostilities lawful military objectives? As such, are persons engaged in such economic activities taking direct part in hostilities?

Some States maintain that economic targets may be lawful targets under IHL. In the US Commander's *Handbook on the Law of Naval Operations*,[141] a lawful military objective is defined as, *inter alia*, any of 'those objects which, by their nature, location, purpose, or use, effectively contribute to the enemy's war-fighting or war-sustaining capability'.[142] The origins of the notion of a party's 'war-sustaining' capability being lawfully targetable can be found in the US Civil War, where the American–British Claims Commission of 1871 examined whether the destruction of cotton crops was legitimate. The Union justified the destruction of this economic asset as militarily allowable, due to the close connection between cotton production and the acquisition of munitions for the Confederate army, stating:

> that cotton in the insurrectionary States was peculiarly and eminently a legitimate subject for such destruction, from its relation to the enemy's government, as the great staple from which were derived the principle means of that government for the carrying on of the war, which was the principal basis of its credit, the source of its military and naval supplies, and on which it relied to maintain its independent existence and to carry on the war against the United States.[143]

[141] *The Commander's Handbook on the Law of Naval Operations*, NWP 1-14M/MCWP 5-12.1/COMDTPUB P5800.7A, Department of the Navy, Office of the Chief of Naval Operations and Headquarters, US Marine Corps, Department of Homeland Security and US Coast Guard (2007), available at: <https://www.usnwc.edu/getattachment/a9b8e92d-2c8d-4779-9925-0defea93325c/>, accessed 29 March 2015.

[142] *The Commander's Handbook on the Law of Naval Operations*, § 8.2. See also § 8.2.5 on the targeting of objects, which states 'economic objects of the enemy that indirectly but effectively support and sustain the enemy's war-fighting capability may also be attacked.'

[143] *Cotton Claims*, in *Papers Relating to the Treaty of Washington* (Volume VI, Government Printing Office, 1874), at 53. See also similar statements made in *Ford v Surget*, 97 US 594, 24 L.Ed. 1018 (1878), where it was argued that 'the property of the plaintiff alleged to have been destroyed at his residence in Mississippi, May 5, 1862, was cotton, an article which each belligerent regarded as possessing a special character, and treated, even in the hands of non-combatants, differently from ordinary private property. "It is well known," said this court in *Mrs. Alexander's*

Indeed, the US has continued to affirm this position, as seen in the Commander's *Handbook*,[144] as well as in section 950(p)(a)(1) of the Military Commissions Act of 2009. The US position seems to suggest that where a belligerent derives essentially all its material sustenance from a particular source, such a source becomes a legitimate military target, because without it, the belligerent would be incapable of maintaining their belligerent activities. As such, cotton plantations in the South were legitimate targets, as the Confederates would have been unable to continue their war with the Union without the economic output derived from the plantations. Likewise, in Colombia, the bulk of FARC's funding has been reported as deriving from the drug trade;[145] thus, targeting the drug crops would be considered, according to the US formulating, permissible under IHL.

However, there are a few points that render this approach problematic. In the first instance, the US position has been rejected by a number of experts,[146] such as Dapo Akande, who has noted that for the targeting of an object to be considered lawful, 'there must [be] a proximate connection between the object and the military action. The fact that an object provides the finances for military action is not sufficient.'[147] Indeed, this position is affirmed in the San Remo *Manual on International Law Applicable to Armed Conflicts at Sea*, which states that it would not be lawful to target merchant ships carrying exports from an adverse party, even if such exports 'might be vital for

Cotton (2 Wall. 420), "that cotton has constituted the main reliance of the rebels for means to purchase the munitions of war in Europe. It is a matter of history, that, rather than permit it to come into possession of the national troops, the rebel government has everywhere devoted it, however owned, to destruction." The regulations established by the Federal government, the acts of its officers,—military, naval, civil,—and the decisions of its courts, show what importance it attached during the war to that species of property, and how it would be disposed of if found in the hands of a resident of a State in rebellion. It was treated by the respective belligerents as contraband of war, and was by each the subject of special governmental control and action, whether for its preservation, seizure, confiscation, or destruction.'

[144] The Commander's *Handbook on the Law of Naval Operations*, at § 8.2.

[145] Helen Murphy and Luis Jaime Acosta, 'FARC Controls 60% of Drug Trade—Colombia's Police Chief', *Reuters*, 22 April 2013, available at: <http://uk.reuters.com/article/2013/04/22/uk-colombia-rebels-police-idUKBRE93L18Y20130422>, accessed 29 March 2015; Geoffrey Ramsay, 'FARC "Earns $2.4 to $3.5 Billion" from Drugs: Govt', *Insight Crime*, 24 October 2012, available at: <http://www.insightcrime.org/news-briefs/farc-earns-24-to-35-billion-drugs>, accessed 29 March 2015.

[146] Sivakumaran, *The Law of Non-International Armed Conflict*, at 345; Dinstein, *The Conduct of Hostilities Under the Law of International Armed Conflict*, at 95–96; Henderson, *The Contemporary Law of Targeting*, at 144; Boothby, *The Law of Targeting*, at 106.

[147] Akande, 'US/NATO Targeting of Afghan Drug Traffickers: An Illegal and Dangerous Precedent?'.

financing the war efforts because the connection between the exports and military action would be too remote.'[148]

Secondly, it is misleading for the US to rely on the *Cotton Claims* case as being an authoritative example for the lawfulness of targeting economic objects. As Sivakumaran points out, the facts of the *Cotton Claims* are exceptional:[149] cotton was essentially the only economic asset the Confederates held. As such, 'the particular nexus between the production and sale of cotton during the US civil war and the Confederate forces needs to be borne in mind—the historical specificities of the Confederate-cotton nexus makes it difficult to extrapolate to other situations.'[150] Indeed, while much has been written about the connection between the drug trade and the conflict in Afghanistan,[151] the UN has stated that only 10–15 per cent of the funding needed to finance Taliban operations is derived from drugs,[152] though ISAF officials have placed the figure at closer to 20–40 per cent.[153] Forty per cent of funding is not insignificant; indeed, as Michael Schmitt notes, 'the insurgency's dependence on the drug trade is considerable. Starving the insurgency of

[148] Commentary on Rule 68 of the *San Remo Manual on International Law Applicable to Armed Conflicts at Sea*, Louise Doswald-Beck (ed.) (CUP, 1995), at 161. However, see further the Ethiopia–Eritrea Claims Commission, Partial Award, Western Front, Aerial Bombardment and Related Claims, Eritrea's Claims, 1, 3, 4, 9–13, 14, 21, 25, and 26, 19 December 2005, available at: <legal.un.org/riaa/cases/vol_XXVI/291-349.pdf>, where the Commission upheld Ethiopia's claim that an Eritrean power station was a lawful target because, *inter alia*, 'it was of economic importance to Eritrea' (at para. 119; website accessed 6 April 2015). Nonetheless, the Commission took steps to affirm that it was the proximity of the power station to a port and naval base, and its intended use of powering the port and base, were also key in assessing the power station as a legitimate military objective (at paras 118–20).

[149] Sivakumaran, *The Law of Non-International Armed Conflict*, at 345.

[150] Sivakumaran, *The Law of Non-International Armed Conflict*, at 345.

[151] See, eg, Rachel Ehrenfeld, 'Stop the Afghan Drug Trade, Stop Terrorism', *Forbes*, 26 February 2009, available at: <http://www.forbes.com/2009/02/26/drug-trade-afghanistan-opinions-contributors_terrorism_mycoherbicides.html>, accessed 6 April 2015; Phillip Swarts, 'Terrorist Organizations Still Profit from Afghan Drug Trade', *Washington Times*, 20 September 2013, available at: <http://www.washingtontimes.com/news/2013/sep/20/terrorist-organizations-still-profit-afghan-drug-t/>, accessed 29 March 2015; Pamela Falk, 'U.N.: Afghan's $61B Drug Trade Funding Terrorism', *CBS News Online*, 23 June 2011, available at: <http://www.cbsnews.com/news/un-afghans-61b-drug-trade-funding-terrorism/>, accessed 29 March 2015; Gretchen Peters, *Seeds of Terror: How Drugs, Thugs, and Crime Are Reshaping the Afghan War* (Picador, 2010).

[152] United Nations Office on Drugs and Crime (UNODC), *Addiction, Crime and Insurgency: The Transnational Threat of Afghan Opium* (2009), available at: <http://www.unodc.org/documents/data-and-analysis/Afghanistan/Afghan_Opium_Trade_2009_web.pdf>, at 111, accessed 29 March 2015.

[153] Reported in the UK House of Commons International Development Select Committee, *Reconstructing Afghanistan*, Fourth Report of Session 2007–08, Vol I, HC 65-I (incorporating HC 1097-i, Session 2006–07), 14 February 2008, available at: <http://www.publications.parliament.uk/pa/cm200708/cmselect/cmintdev/65/65i.pdf>, at 45, accessed 29 March 2015.

drug related funding therefore makes military sense.'[154] However, 'military sense' and 'lawful military objective' are not synonymous. Indeed, even if 40 per cent of Taliban funding is derived from the opium trade, it still seems far from the *Cotton Claims* formula, which was that of an economic asset 'as the great staple from which were derived the principle means of that government for the carrying on of the war, which was the principal basis of its credit, the source of its military and naval supplies, and on which it relied to maintain its independent existence'.[155]

Finally, and perhaps most relevant in the context of the targeting of individuals, is a point raised by Dapo Akande regarding the targeting of drug traffickers.[156] Even if the situation in Colombia were to meet the *Cotton Claims* test, and that FARC, as an organization, would be completely incapable of continuing its side of the hostilities without engaging in the drug trade, one would still need to make the distinction between the drugs (and the drug crops) being a legitimate military objective, and the persons involved in the production of those drugs, who, if they are not otherwise directly participating in hostilities, are not legitimate military objectives. As Akande argues:

> For purposes of targeting, it matters little that drugs traffickers are engaging in illegal activity. The reason they are now being subject to targeting is not the illegality of their activity but the consequences of their conduct—that it funds the adverse party. From that perspective, their activity is no different to that of an executive in any industry (say, oil or manufacturing) which provides the bulk of the income of a belligerent State. Although some have argued (and still argued) that factories and objects connected with war sustaining industries are legitimate targets, I don't recall it being argued in the past that individuals connected with these industries are lawful targets.[157]

Thus, even if one were to accept the broad US perspective on the targeting of economic assets, such an approach would only permit the deliberate targeting of the object, not those persons working the coca or poppy fields, unless such workers were also found to meet DPH criteria. Their working the fields alone would seem insufficient to render their targeting lawful. Even the drug traffickers would fall outside the lawful targeting schema by this reckoning.[158]

[154] Schmitt, 'Targeting Narcoinsurgents in Afghanistan', at 307.

[155] *Cotton Claims*, at 53.

[156] Akande, 'US/NATO Targeting of Afghan Drug Traffickers'.

[157] Akande, 'US/NATO Targeting of Afghan Drug Traffickers'.

[158] See Schmitt, 'Targeting Narcoinsurgents', at 319, where he states 'even if the war-sustaining argument is accepted, the status of civilians working in war-sustaining drug-related targets would remain unchanged. General consensus exists that civilians engaged in "war-sustaining activities" are not directly participating in hostilities and may not be subjected to direct attack.'

The targeting of drug producers and traffickers would seem beyond the scope of a number of formulations of DPH, both the strict ICRC test of 'one causal step'[159] and the broader *Targeted Killings* formulation of DPH, which excludes those providing logistical or monetary support.[160] As noted in this chapter, most States (the US excluded) hold to the notion that 'war-sustaining' activities are too remote to be considered DPH. As Akande notes, 'to permit anyone who is involved in the war sustaining effort to be a direct target is to allow for unrestricted warfare—practically everyone could be a target. This would be a regressive move.'[161] Indeed, even critics of the ICRC's strict approach, such as Michael Schmitt, have acknowledged that drug production by persons who are not also members of armed groups taking a direct part in hostilities would most likely fail to meet even a broad causation threshold. As Schmitt notes regarding Afghanistan:

> no evidence exists that the insurgent groups in Afghanistan finance specific military missions... instead, the funds typically comprise part of their 'operations and maintenance' (O & M) budget... whether conducted by non-fighting Taliban or civilians, drug activities would generally fail the direct causation test as applied by both supporters and critics of the [ICRC DPH] Guidance, for such activities are not 'integral' to specific military operations.[162]

However, this does not mean that a member of an armed group who engages in the drug trade (or any other criminal activity) is immune from targeting; his or her own acts of DPH, separate from any criminal activities will render him or her targetable. Furthermore, any person, whether engaged in armed conflict or criminal activity, will run the risk of being targeted, through arrest in the context of a law-enforcement operation, or with lethal force, as part of an armed conflict. However, it would be too broad a categorization to say that all persons engaged in criminal activities that sustain warfare could be targeted, distinct from any acts amounting to DPH.

Conclusion

It is understandable why some would want to dub high-level violence committed by armed criminal gangs as 'warfare'. The kinetic effects of violence—wounding, death, property destruction—are the same, regardless of whether the violence has been committed by a drug trafficker or a member

159 DPHIG, at 1021. 160 *Targeted Killings*, at § 35.
161 Akande, 'US/NATO Targeting of Afghan Drug Traffickers'.
162 Schmitt, 'Targeting Narcoinsurgents', at 317.

of the armed forces. However, as explored in this chapter, there are compelling legal and policy reasons why high-level criminal activities either indistinguishable from warfare, or else intricately connected to existing warfare, should remain outside the sphere of regulation under IHL. This is not to say that international law more generally cannot have any impact on such criminal activities, but rather that IHL should not impose an additional set of rules to govern conduct in widespread systematic criminal activities. Indeed, in such cases, where there is clearly already a situation of refusal to observe the rule of law, it may perhaps devalue the impact of IHL to introduce its regulatory framework.

PART III

CIVILIAN PARTICIPATION IN ARMED CONFLICT AND THE LAW IN THE TWENTY-FIRST CENTURY

Introduction

As we have seen in the previous chapters, civilian participation in armed conflict, either direct or indirect, is problematic for parties to an armed conflict. The involvement of civilians in quasi-combatant roles or other roles that place them at the centre of active hostilities makes observing the principle of distinction measurably more difficult for all parties to a conflict.

Ideally, States would no longer employ civilians in roles that put them in danger of direct targeting, and civilians would not themselves take direct part. While in some instances, a ban on civilian participation would be preferred (such as in the case of the Central Intelligence Agency's use of civilian analysts in conducting targeted killings), a blanket approach seems unlikely to be adopted in all cases.

However, the law should respond in some way. Given these developments in the practice of armed conflicts, and given the definitional ambiguities that still remain regarding the concept of direct participation in hostilities, how the current law of armed conflict should respond? Is it time for a new international humanitarian law (IHL) treaty, or would a different approach be more appropriate? It is these questions that serve as the focus for the remaining chapter of these book, namely, how should IHL respond to these new categories of civilians who take direct part in hostilities?

8

The Way Forward

How Can International Law Effectively Deal with Civilians Who Take Direct Part in Hostilities?

Introduction

As the second chapter of this book has shown, when the international community has been called upon to address the question of irregular civilian participants in armed conflict in treaties, States have usually chosen to deems as regulars such irregular participants, compelling them to comply with existing norms of relating to conduct of hostilities. In return, such irregulars are granted combatant status and prisoner-of-war (POW) rights. However, certain categories of irregular combatants have continually been excluded from such rights, namely, those who participate in non-international armed conflicts. For those irregulars, legal attention was instead turned towards outlining the rules of conduct in armed conflict, starting with the limited list of prohibitions and recommendations in Common Article 3, to a longer, but still essentially limited set of rules on means and methods in Additional Protocol II. Customary international law went some way to elaborate on the substantive content and interpretation of those limited rules, but the normative gap between international and non-international armed conflict remained (and still remains).[1]

Despite this normative gap, certain principles are considered common to the rules applicable in both international and non-international armed conflicts. One of these is the principle, not codified until 1977, which states that civilians are immune from targeting unless they take direct part in the hostilities.[2] However, as noted in Chapters 2 and 3 of this book, there

[1] See further Lindsay Moir, 'Towards the Unification of International Humanitarian Law?', in Richard Burchill, Justin White, and Nigel Morris (eds), *International Conflict and Security Law: Essays in Memory of Hilaire McCoubrey* (CUP, 2005), and Emily Crawford, 'Unequal before the Law: The Case for the Elimination of the Distinction between International and Non-international Armed Conflicts', 20 Leiden J Int'l L 441 (2007).

[2] Art. 51(3), API.

has, historically, been little examination of the contours of the concept of direct participation. Only in the last fifteen years has the notion been subject to serious, sustained scrutiny from courts and tribunals, and from non-governmental, inter-governmental, and academic sources.

At the same time as the concept of direct participation in hostilities (DPH) was being explored and discussed, the international community was grappling with increasing levels of civilian involvement in armed conflicts (as outlined in Chapters 4 to 7). The changing nature and character of warfare in the twenty-first century and the proliferation of these new kinds of participants has prompted a number of articles expounding on this 'new warfare' and the need for new regulations to govern them.[3]

It is this question that serves as the focus for this final chapter of this book. In the face of increased civilian irregular participation in armed conflict is the best response to be found in the adoption of another treaty, such as a fourth Additional Protocol to the Geneva Conventions, or would the situation be better addressed by other means? This chapter will examine the merits and drawbacks of a treaty-based response to DPH and increased civilian participation in armed conflict, and it will explore the merits of alternative approaches. This chapter will argue that the most promising way forward for international humanitarian law (IHL) regarding irregulars in armed conflict is through the adoption of so-called soft law instruments, such as codes of conduct, manuals, draft conventions, or equivalent statements of best practice.

Using a number of these soft law instruments as case studies, this chapter will examine the degree to which such instruments have been pivotal in influencing and shaping State practice and thus have contributed to the formation of customary international law. This chapter will also note the (self-evident) point that in order for such instruments to have any meaningful and lasting impact, they must carefully balance the *lex lata* and the *lex ferenda*, and that any policy-based statements on the law 'as it should be' (or even attempts to declare a customary norms where State practice and *opinio juris* may be found somewhat wanting), must be weighed carefully against the law 'as it is'.

[3] See, eg, William Banks (ed.), *New Battlefields/Old Laws: Critical Debates on Asymmetric Warfare* (Columbia University Press, 2011); M. Cherif Bassiouni, 'The New Wars and the Crisis of Compliance with the Law of Armed Conflict by Non-State Actors', 98 J Crim L & Criminology 711 (2008); and Mary Kaldor, *New and Old Wars: Organized Violence in a Global Era* (Polity Press, 1999). See also arguments outlined by Andreas Paulus and Mindia Vashakmadze, 'Asymmetrical War and the Notion of Armed Conflict—A Tentative Conceptualisation', 91 IRRC 95 (2009), at 108–11; and Herfried Münkler, 'The Wars of the 21st Century', 849 IRRC 7 (2003), at 7.

New International Law for Irregulars?

In assessing how best to address increasingly complex civilian participation in armed conflicts, the first suggestion from policy makers and public commentators has often been that a revision of the Geneva Conventions is required, or that an entirely new Convention should be adopted.[4] Indeed, nearly forty years has passed since the last major treaty on the laws of armed conflict—the Additional Protocols of 1977—was adopted. Over the last 150 years, major international law treaties on the law of war were adopted every thirty years or so, starting with the 1864 Geneva Convention, the 1899 and 1907 Hague Regulations, the 1929 Geneva Conventions, followed by the 1949 Geneva Conventions, and the 1977 Additional Protocols. If this pattern were to be followed, the international community should have debated and adopted a new treaty on IHL sometime in the last ten years.

International law making does not follow a prescribed schedule. Laws are not revised or adopted simply because a certain amount of time has passed. Nonetheless, the passage of time since the adoption of the Geneva Conventions has been one of the recurring points in the public debate on the Conventions in the twenty-first century, with commentary often labelling the Conventions as 'outdated' or 'obsolete'.[5] As such, would a treaty to

[4] See, eg, Dominic Hoerauf, '10 Years After 9/11: And Still Fighting New Wars With Old Weapons: Why and How The Geneva Conventions Must Be Amended To Cover Al-Qaeda', 2 American University National Security Law Brief 107 (2012); Brad Allenby and Carolyn Mattick, 'Why We Need New "Rules of War"', *Slate*, 12 November 2012, available at: <http://www.slate.com/articles/technology/future_tense/2012/11/drones_cyberconflict_and_other_military_technologies_require_we_rewrite.html>, accessed 6 April 2015; Bela Bonita Chatterjee, 'Ready, Aim, Click: We Need New Laws To Govern Cyberwarfare', *The Conversation*, 21 August 2014, available at: <http://theconversation.com/ready-aim-click-we-need-new-laws-to-govern-cyberwarfare-30734>, accessed 29 March 2015; Eric Posner, 'The Killer Robot War Is Coming: The New Laws We Need to Govern the Use of Drones', *Slate*, 15 May 2013, available at: <http://www.slate.com/articles/news_and_politics/view_from_chicago/2013/05/drone_warfare_and_spying_we_need_new_laws.html>, accessed 29 March 2015; David Ignatius, 'Dazzling New Weapons Require New Rules For War', *Washington Post*, 11 November 2011, available at: <http://www.washingtonpost.com/wp-dyn/content/article/2010/11/10/AR2010111005500.html>, accessed 29 March 2015; and Zbigniew Brzezinski, 'The Cyber Age Demands New Rules of War', *Financial Times*, 24 February 2013, available at: <http://www.ft.com/intl/cms/s/0/170b2a62-7c5a-11e2-99f0-00144feabdc0.html#axzz3HaCMBcKv>, accessed 29 March 2015.

[5] See, eg, Scott Holcomb and Mark Ribbing, 'War Has Changed. The Laws of War Must, Too', *Christian Science Monitor*, 16 November 2006, available at: <http://www.csmonitor.com/2006/1116/p09s01-coop.html>, accessed 30 March 2015; Alan Dershowitz, 'Rules of War Enable Terror', *Baltimore Sun*, 28 May 2004, available at: <http://articles.baltimoresun.com/2004-05-28/news/0405280166_1_innocent-civilians-noncombatants-terrorism>, accessed 30 March 2015; UK House of Commons Foreign Affairs Select Committee, *Visit to Guantanamo Bay*, Second Report of Session 2006–07, available at: <http://www.publications.parliament.uk/pa/

define and regulate civilian participation in armed conflict be the solution to the problems which arise regarding defining what exactly comprises DPH?

Adopting a new treaty regarding participants in armed conflict would be likely to come up against a number of barriers, some of which seem potentially insurmountable. First, State practice over the last twenty-five years has indicated a willingness to adopt specialized *sui generis* treaties on means of armed conflict, such as chemical weapons,[6] landmines,[7] and cluster munitions.[8] However, while States have been prepared to say that the Geneva Conventions are outdated, or that they require development and expansion,[9] they have done little in practice matter to ensure that such amendments are made. Furthermore, the International Committee of the Red Cross (ICRC) has stated that it has no immediate plans for any comprehensive revision of either the Geneva Conventions or the Additional Protocols;[10] current ICRC treaty focus seems to be directed primarily towards the adoption of a treaty banning nuclear weapons.[11] As such, there does not seem to be much groundswell towards drafting and adopting any new comprehensive IHL treaties. As Yves Sandoz has remarked: 'my personal opinion is that the time for global conferences devoted to international humanitarian law might well be over'.[12]

More generally speaking, adopting a new comprehensive treaty would come up against the considerable barrier of achieving consensus. The increasing difficulty in adopting new treaties is partially due to the increasing number

cm200607/cmselect/cmfaff/44/44.pdf>, at 27, para. 85, accessed 30 March 2015; and John Reid, 'Twenty-First Century Warfare—Twentieth Century Rules' 151 RUSI Journal 14 (2006).

6 Convention on the Prohibition of the Development, Production, Stockpiling and Use of Chemical Weapons and on their Destruction, 1974 UNTS 45.

7 Convention on the Prohibition of the Use, Stockpiling, Production and Transfer of Anti-Personnel Mines and on their Destruction, 2056 UNTS 211.

8 Convention on Cluster Munitions. 2688 UNTS 39.

9 See, eg, the UK House of Commons Foreign Affairs Select Committee, *Visit to Guantanamo Bay*, where it was recommended that 'the Government should recognise that the Geneva Conventions are failing to provide necessary protection because they lack clarity and are out of date. We recommend that the Government work with other signatories to the Geneva Conventions and with the International Committee of the Red Cross to update the Conventions in a way that deals more satisfactorily with asymmetric warfare, with international terrorism, with the status of irregular combatants, and with the treatment of detainees' (at 27, para. 85).

10 François Bugnion, 'The International Committee of the Red Cross and the Development of International Humanitarian Law', 5 Chicago J Int'l L 191 (2004), at 211–12.

11 See the ICRC campaign for a treaty banning nuclear weapons, available at: <https://www.icrc.org/eng/war-and-law/weapons/nuclear-weapons/overview-nuclear-weapons.htm>, accessed 30 March 2015.

12 Yves Sandoz, 'Preface to the New Edition of 'New Rules for Victims of Armed Conflicts'', in Michael Bothe, Karl Josef Partsch, and Waldemar Solf (eds), *New Rules for Victims of Armed Conflicts: Commentary on the Two 1977 Protocols Additional to the Geneva Conventions of 1949* (2nd edn, Martinus Nijhoff, 2013), at xxiii.

of players on the international stage. For example, the Geneva Conventions of 1949 were debated and drafted by fifty-nine delegations, comprising almost 300 plenipotentiaries and delegates, mainly drawn from Europe and the Americas, with the average delegation numbering five people.[13] Over the period of four months, these States debated and adopted four conventions, comprising nearly 400 articles. Asia, Africa, and the Middle East were virtually unrepresented at the Geneva conference: only two African States were at there,[14] along with only six Middle Eastern States,[15] and four States from Asia.[16] When the international community met less than thirty years later to debate and adopt the Additional Protocols, 134 delegations met in Geneva; average delegations comprising eleven plenipotentiaries and delegates, making a total of 1400 delegates.[17] Over a period of three years, they debated and eventually adopted two conventions, comprising 130 articles. This time, Africa, Asia, and the Middle East were far better represented, frequently outnumbering the European and American delegations.

As the number of participants expanded, so too did the scope for disagreement over contentious and divisive provisions or topics. For example, the first draft of Additional Protocol II was far more comprehensive in scope and detail than the document that was eventually adopted. The threshold of application was similar to that of Common Article 3[18] and there were provisions for captured combatants to be treated in a manner similar to POWs, provided they fulfilled the requirements of Article 4(2) of Convention III.[19] However, the Diplomatic Conferences responsible for adopting the Protocols rejected both the 1971 and 1972 draft Protocols.[20] The majority opinion was that the drafts were too intrusive on States' prerogative to deal with domestic strife as they felt necessary.[21] Indeed, even a more restrictive 1973 draft was in danger of being rejected out of hand until the intervention of the Pakistani delegation at the Diplomatic Conference itself,

[13] *Final Record*, Vol. 1 at 158–78.

[14] Egypt and Ethiopia.

[15] Afghanistan, Iran, Israel, Lebanon, Pakistan, and Syria.

[16] Burma, China, India, and Thailand.

[17] *Final Record*, Vol. II at 29–408.

[18] See Conference of Government Experts (1972), *Basic Texts*, at 35–45.

[19] Conference of Government Experts (1972), *Basic Texts*, at 33. This had first been suggested by the ICRC at its XXIst International Conference of the Red Cross (1969), in Resolution XVIII, 'Status of Combatants in Non-International Armed Conflicts', which states that 'combatants and members of resistance movements who participate in non-international armed conflicts and who conform to the provisions of Article 4 of the Third Geneva Convention of 2 August 1949 should when captured be protected against any inhumanity and brutality and receive treatment similar to that which that Convention lays down for prisoners of war.'

[20] See *AP Commentary*, at 1334–36, paras 4405–18.

[21] *AP Commentary*, at 1334–36, paras 4405–18.

which worked to secure the eventual draft Protocol II, with twenty-four articles, down from the proposed forty-eight.[22]

Given that the current number of States in the world,[23] and considering the continuing and often contradictory practice of labelling some organized insurgent groups as terrorists while others are designated as legitimate opposition groups,[24] the possibility of drafting and adopting a treaty dealing with civilian participants in armed conflicts seems unlikely. Indeed, as MacLaren and Schwendimann note:

> In principle, gaps in IHL could be filled by new treaty provisions rather than custom. Obtaining the state support necessary for their adoption and ratification would, however, be tricky, time-consuming and treacherous... the divisions prevailing in the state community and a climate dominated by 11.9.2001 might, if anything, lead to a codification to the detriment of the protection of individuals through the enhancement of coercive measures available for state security.[25]

As such, it seems that customary international law provides the most obvious avenue for addressing the question of civilian participation in armed conflicts.

[22] *Official Records IV*, CDDH/427. For more on this process, see generally *AP Commentary*, at 1325–36, paras 4360–418; and Sylvie Junod, 'Additional Protocol II: History and Scope', 33 AULR 29 (1983).

[23] This figure is sometimes disputed: the number of sovereign States which are UN members is 193; two States have observer status (Vatican City and Palestine); ten other States have disputed status, having claimed statehood (or independence) without widespread acceptance, including Somaliland, South Ossetia, Taiwan, Abkhazia, Nagorno-Karabakh, Pridnestrovian Moldavian Republic, Northern Cyprus, Kosovo, Transnistria, and the Sahrawi Arab Democratic Republic. See further the UN Member State listing at: <http://www.un.org/en/members/index.shtml>, accessed 30 March 2015; and the *CIA World Factbook* at: <https://www.cia.gov/library/publications/the-world-factbook/index.html>, accessed 29 March 2015.

[24] See, eg, US practice regarding Syria, where one opposition group was officially designated as a terrorist organization, while another opposition group was formally recognized as a legitimate opposition entity. See Dana Hughes, 'U.S. Declares Syria Rebel Group Terrorists, Sending Message to Opposition', ABC News, 12 December 2012, available at: <http://abcnews.go.com/blogs/politics/2012/12/u-s-declares-syria-rebel-group-terrorists-sending-message-to-opposition/>, accessed 30 March 2015. This entire debate is encapsulated in the clichéd truism, 'your terrorist is my freedom fighter'. For a critique of this debate, see Robert Kennedy, 'Is One Person's Terrorist Another's Freedom Fighter? Western And Islamic Approaches To "Just War" Compared', 11 Terrorism and Political Violence 1 (1999); Conor Friedersdorf, 'Is One Man's Terrorist Another Man's Freedom Fighter?', *The Atlantic*, 16 May 2012, available at: <http://www.theatlantic.com/politics/archive/2012/05/is-one-mans-terrorist-another-mans-freedom-fighter/257245/>, accessed 30 March 2015; and Boaz Ganor, 'Defining Terrorism: Is One Man's Terrorist another Man's Freedom Fighter?', 3 Police Practice and Research: An International Journal 287 (2002).

[25] Malcolm MacLaren and Felix Schwendimann, 'The New ICRC Study on Customary International Humanitarian Law as an Exercise in the Development of International Law', 6 German Law Journal 1217 (2005), at 1222.

However, as the ICRC has noted, State practice in relation to DPH has been less than 'clear and uniform'.[26] As such, there is significant scope for State practice to be influenced and developed by other stakeholders such as non-State actors, inter-governmental and non-governmental international organizations, practitioners, and academics. Indeed, as Yves Sandoz has noted, the task of developing and reaffirming IHL has probably been removed from the fora of international conferences and is instead to be found in 'dialog, expert meetings and doctrinal works.'[27] The proliferation of international codes of conduct and manuals in the last twenty-five years, such as the *Tallinn Manual on Cyberwarfare*, the Montreaux Document on PMSCs, and the *Harvard Manual*, would seem to support such an assessment.

Nevertheless, the question to be asked is do these mechanisms actually work? Will States pay heed to reports of expert meetings and adjust their behaviour accordingly, thus developing customary international law? This raises the question as to whether so-called 'soft law' instruments—for example, manuals of instruction such as the *Tallinn* and *Harvard Manuals*—have any normative force or influence. It is this question that will be explored in the rest of this chapter.

Defining 'Soft Law'

Before any assessment of the value of soft law can be undertaken, it is first necessary to define the concept. Soft law is a term that has a variety of definitions and interpretations regarding its scope.[28] A comparatively narrow approach sees soft law as binding norms that lack sufficient precision, such as vaguely or generally worded treaty obligations. Such instruments, however, are meant to be taken 'seriously'[29] by States, and treated with 'some measure of respect'.[30] According to such an approach to soft law, the 'law' element is

[26] Rule 6, *ICRC CIHL Study*.

[27] Yves Sandoz, 'Preface to the New Edition', at xxiii.

[28] For an assessment of the different approaches to and definitions of soft law, see further RR Baxter, 'International Law in "Her Infinite Variety"', 29 ICLQ 549 (1980), Jaye Ellis, 'Shades of Grey: Soft Law and the Validity of Public International Law', 25 Leiden J Int'l L 313 (2012), at 315–23; and Andrew Guzman and Timothy Meyer, 'Soft Law', in Eugene Kontorovich (ed.), *The Research Handbook on the Economics of Public International Law* (Elgar, 2015, paper available on SSRN at <http://papers.ssrn.com/sol3/papers.cfm?abstract_id=2437956>, at 4–6, website accessed 30 March 2015).

[29] Joseph Gold, 'Strengthening the Soft International Law of Exchange Arrangements', 77 AJIL 443 (1983), at 443.

[30] Gold, 'Strengthening the Soft International Law of Exchange Arrangements', at 443.

paramount; these norms are adopted by States with the intention and understanding that their behaviour should be in compliance with such norms, even if the precise content of the norms is imprecise.[31] More expansive approaches define soft law as any non-binding instrument or set of instructions designed to either restate, affirm, develop, and/or clarify the binding norms that regulate conduct in a particular area.[32]

For the purposes of this book, soft law will be defined broadly, using some of the key determinants as outlined by Christine Chinkin, including that soft law instruments are those which 'have been articulated in non-binding form according to traditional modes of law-making',[33] which 'emanate from bodies lacking international law-making authority';[34] are often directed at or designed to include 'non-state actors whose practice cannot constitute customary international law';[35] and may be based on 'voluntary adherence, or rely upon non-juridical means of enforcement.'[36] This approach is taken because the soft law instruments that have been explored in this book—the ICRC DPH Guidance, the *Tallinn Manual*, the Montreux Document—all fit this broader definition.

The Benefits of Soft Law Instruments in IHL

The proliferation of soft law instruments in IHL in the last twenty-five years has been remarkable. The benefits of soft law in armed conflicts, especially non-international armed conflicts, are obvious. Where treaty consensus has been hard to achieve,[37] or where non-State actors and parties to conflicts have

[31] For an assessment of this approach, see Gold, 'Strengthening the Soft International Law of Exchange Arrangements', at 443–45; and Jonathan Carlson, 'Hunger, Agricultural Trade Liberalisation, and Soft International Law: Addressing the Legal Dimensions of a Political Problem', 70 Iowa L Rev 1187 (1984–85), at 1200–04.

[32] See Christine Chinkin, 'Normative Development in the International Legal System', in Dinah Shelton (ed.), *Commitment and Compliance: The Role of Non-Binding Norms in the International Legal System* (OUP, 2000), at 30–31. Note however, some theorists reject the notion of soft law outright, arguing that a particular rule or norm is either binding or not, and if it is not binding, it cannot be law, soft or otherwise. For this approach, see generally Jan Klabbers, 'The Redundancy of Soft Law', 65 Nordic J Int'l L 167 (1996); Jean d'Aspremont, *Formalism and the Sources of International Law: A Theory of the Ascertainment of Legal Rules* (OUP, 2011); and Oscar Schachter, 'The Twilight Existence of Nonbinding Agreements', 71 AJIL 296 (1977).

[33] Chinkin, 'Normative Development in the International Legal System', at 30.

[34] Chinkin, 'Normative Development in the International Legal System', at 30.

[35] Chinkin, 'Normative Development in the International Legal System', at 30.

[36] Chinkin, 'Normative Development in the International Legal System', at 30.

[37] See the issues that arose during the debate over Protocol II, detailed in *AP Commentary*, at 1334–36, paras 4405–18.

been excluded from participation in the politico-legal process,[38] soft law has often stepped in to fill the normative gaps, especially in non-international armed conflicts. For States and non-State actors, soft law instruments allow them to engage with international law in a number of traditional and non-traditional ways: they can use soft law to help clarify or define existing norms, but in ways which require no 'formal steps of adherence'[39] or new or additional accountability or enforcement mechanisms. An example of this can be seen with the proliferation of humanitarian agreements and declarations, drafted between, or unilaterally issued by, rebel groups and/or States, regarding conduct in internal armed conflicts. These documents, often termed 'Ground Rules', 'Memorandum of Understanding', or 'Codes of Conduct', have been adopted in a number of instances of internal conflict in countries such as the Philippines,[40] Sudan,[41] Colombia,[42] and El Salvador.[43]

[38] Eg, the Ejército de Liberación National (ELN) in Colombia has sometimes been excluded from peace talks and other negotiations, with some administrations choosing to deal solely with Fuerzas Armadas Revolucionarias de Colombia (FARC), even though the ELN has repeatedly declared its willingness to negotiate for lasting peace. See further Daniel García-Peña, 'The ELN Creates a Different Peace Process', *Colombia Journal*, 27 November 2000, available at: <http://colombiajournal.org/colombia41.htm>, accessed 30 March 2015; Vicenç Fisas Armengol, 'A Possible Peace Process with the ELN in Colombia', Norwegian Peacebuilding Resource Centre Report, August 2013, available at: <http://www.peacebuilding.no/var/ezflow_site/storage/original/application/6fbc91d2529b493119d3d26a1be9b6e6.pdf>, accessed 30 March 2015; Adam Isaacson, 'Peace in Colombia Requires Deal With ELN as Well as FARC', *World Politics Review*, 22 July 2013, available at: <http://www.worldpoliticsreview.com/articles/13106/peace-in-colombia-requires-deal-with-eln-as-well-as-farc>, accessed 30 March 2015.

[39] Chinkin, 'Normative Development in the International Legal System', at 34.

[40] Comprehensive Agreement on Respect for Human Rights and International Humanitarian Law Between the Government of the Republic of the Philippines and the National Democratic Front of the Philippines (16 March 1998), available at: <http://www.hdcentre.org/files/CARHRIHL.pdf>, accessed 30 March 2015; see also the Government of the Republic of the Philippines (GRP): Moro Islamic Liberation Front (MILF) Tripoli Agreement on Peace of 22 June 2001; and the Implementing Guidelines on the Humanitarian, Rehabilitation and Development Aspects of the GRP–MILF Tripoli Agreement on Peace of 2001, available at: <http://www.c-r.org/our-work/accord/philippines-mindanao/tripoli-agreement-peace.php>, accessed 30 March 2015, and <http://www.c-r.org/sites/default/files/06s_3Key%20texts_2003_ENG.pdf>, accessed 6 April 2015.

[41] Agreement on Ground Rules, concluded between the Sudan People's Liberation Army and Operation Lifeline Sudan (July 1995), reprinted in Humanitarian Policy Group Report 4, The Agreement on Ground Rules in South Sudan: Study 3 in the Politics of Principle: the Principles of Humanitarian Action in Practice (prepared by Mark Bradbury, Nicholas Leader and Kate Mackintosh, 2000), available at the website of the Humanitarian Policy Group at the Overseas Development Institute, available at: <http://www.odi.org.uk/resources/download/250.pdf>, accessed 30 March 2015.

[42] Declaration and Code on Humanitarian Law, by the Ejercito de Liberacion Nacional in Colombia (15 July 1995), cited in ICRC, *Increasing Respect for International Humanitarian Law in Non-International Armed Conflict*, available at: <http://www.icrc.org/web/eng/siteeng0.nsf/html/p0923>, at 20, accessed 30 March 2015.

[43] Special Agreement between the Frente Farabundo Marti Para La Liberacion Nacional (FMLN) and the Government of El Salvador (26 July 1990), cited in ICRC, *Increasing Respect for*

These agreements have given substance to the Common Article 3 recommendation that 'parties to the conflict should further endeavour to bring into force, by means of special agreements, all or part of the other provisions of the present Convention.'[44]

Some soft law instruments can go further, by essentially creating instruments that replicate existing treaty obligations and allow non-State actors to take on commitments and consent to enforcement mechanisms. The ongoing work of the non-governmental organization Geneva Call is noteworthy in this respect. Geneva Call is a neutral humanitarian organization whose aim is to foster compliance with humanitarian and human rights norms amongst non-State armed groups.[45] Its most significant work has been in the creation of humanitarian instruments to which armed non-State groups can pledge their adherence, much like States sign and ratify treaties. The first of these instruments was the 'Deed of Commitment for Adherence to a Total Ban on Anti-Personnel Mines and for Cooperation in Mine Action', adopted in 2000,[46] which allows non-State actors to make a public pledge their commitment to cease using anti-personnel mines.[47] The possible norm-generating effects of the Deed of Commitment are explicitly noted in the Preamble, where signatories to the Deed affirm they are 'resolved to play our role not only as actors in armed conflicts but also as participants in the practice and development of legal and normative standards for such conflicts, starting

International Humanitarian Law in Non-International Armed Conflicts. See also the Transitional Justice Institute/International Conflict Research Institute Peace Agreements Database, available at: <http://www.peaceagreements.ulster.ac.uk/cgi-bin/Agreements/agree.pl?list=all>, for a comprehensive listing of numerous agreements concluded between parties to internal armed conflicts regarding implementation of human rights and humanitarian law norms (website accessed 30 March 2015).

[44] Common Art. 3.

[45] See <http://www.genevacall.org/who-we-are>, accessed 30 March 2015.

[46] <http://www.genevacall.org/wp-content/uploads/dlm_uploads/2013/12/DoC-Banning-anti-personnel-mines.pdf>, accessed 6 April 2015.

[47] Two additional Deeds of Commitment have been adopted in recent years: the Deed of Commitment under Geneva Call for the Protection of Children from the Effects of Armed Conflict, adopted in November 2010, which aims to have non-State armed groups affirm the importance of protecting children under the age of 18 from the deleterious effects of armed conflict, including (but not limited to) a prohibition on conscription, whether forced or voluntary, ensuring legal protections, including prohibition of the death penalty, protection from all forms of violence, and ensuring continuing access to education, health services, food, and water. See: <http://www.genevacall.org/wp-content/uploads/dlm_uploads/2013/12/DoC-Protecting-children-in-armed-conflict.pdf>, accessed 30 March 2015. The Deed of Commitment for the Prohibition of Sexual Violence in Situations of Armed Conflict and towards the Elimination of Gender Discrimination was launched in 2012, available at: <http://www.genevacall.org/wp-content/uploads/dlm_uploads/2013/12/DoC-Prohibiting-sexual-violence-and-gender-discrimination.pdf> accessed 30 March 2015. For a listing of the signatories to both deeds, see further: <http://www.genevacall.org/how-we-work/armed-non-state-actors/>, accessed 30 March 2015.

with a contribution to the overall humanitarian effort to solve the global landmine problem for the sake of its victims'.[48] As of November 2014, forty-eight non-State groups have signed the document.[49] Its effectiveness in securing compliance with its dictates will be discussed in more detail later in this chapter.

Soft law instruments can also go further still, beyond stating the law or providing a mechanism for non-State participation. Some instruments expand and develop the law in a particular area, by setting out the applicable law in a particular area, but also including policy-based *lex ferenda*. In doing so, the authors of such documents may hope to influence future State and non-State behaviour, and potentially develop such soft norms into 'hard' rules on a particular area. As Chinkin notes, 'soft law is a device that can be deliberately used by non-state actors to influence state behaviour when there is little prospect of successfully concluding a treaty... once a prospective norm has been formulated in soft form it can become a catalyst for the development of customary international law.'[50] In some respects, the ICRC DPH Guidance arguably fits in this category; sections of the Guidance have been considered by some as *lex ferenda* rather than *lex lata*.[51]

Soft law offers the potential for both States and non-State groups to engage with international law in a cooperative and flexible manner, with the aim of ensuring 'some change in behaviour without producing the harsh and possible counter-productive consequences of breach.'[52] Soft law also offers the promise of increased normative pull for actors who have been intentionally excluded from conventional norm generation. That is to say, there is some research to suggest that non-State armed groups are more inclined to comply with rules they feel 'ownership'[53] over, that is, rules that they themselves were

[48] Deed of Commitment on Landmines.

[49] <http://www.genevacall.org/how-we-work/armed-non-state-actors>, accessed 30 March 2015.

[50] Chinkin, 'Normative Development in the International Legal System', at 31–32.

[51] See generally Hays Parks, 'Part IX of the ICRC "Direct Participation in Hostilities" Study', which offers a critique of the Study's use of Pictet's theoretical 'use of force' continuum, arguing that there is no support in State practice to suggest that Pictet's continuum is accepted as law (at 799).

[52] Chinkin, 'Normative Development in the International Legal System', at 34.

[53] The idea of 'ownership' of IHL norms is central to much of the literature on non-State groups and compliance with IHL, and is often argued as being pivotal to whether non-State groups comply with IHL norms; see further Sandesh Sivakumaran, 'The Ownership of International Humanitarian Law: Non-State Armed Groups and the Formation of Enforcement of IHL Rules', in Benjamin Perrin (ed.), *Modern Warfare: Armed Groups, Private Militaries, Humanitarian Organisations, and the Law* (UBC Press, 2012); Pascal Bongard and Jonathan Somer, 'Monitoring Armed Non-State Actor Compliance with Humanitarian Norms: A Look at International Mechanisms and the Geneva Call Deed of Commitment', 93 IRRC 673 (2011), at 681; Peter Maurer, 'Establishing A Dedicated IHL Compliance System', Opening Speech at the Third

involved in developing and codifying. Armed groups have sometimes repudiated the applicability of IHL norms, stating that due to their own exclusion from the creation and adoption of such norms, they feel no compulsion to observe them. For example, in interviews with Human Rights Watch, some Colombian non-State groups argued that Additional Protocol II did not apply to their conflict as the instrument had not been 'negotiated directly with them.'[54] However, research undertaken by the International Council on Human Rights Policy suggests that when armed groups have been involved in the development of codes of conduct, there is an increased probability of compliance.[55] Preliminary research undertaken into the effectiveness of Geneva Call's Deeds of Commitment also supports the contention that collaboration and cooperation with non-State groups in norm-generation (rather than 'top-down' imposition of rules) fosters a culture of compliance.[56] There is also evidence to suggest that State compliance with IHL norms increases when non-State actors participate in norm generation and norm adherence:[57] this will be discussed in more detail later in this next section.

Does Soft Law Work?

Given the supposed benefits of soft law—its flexibility and accessibility, the sense of ownership of rules—such instruments would seem to be an ideal panacea to the issues and problems raised by civilian participation in armed conflict. However, before such an assessment can be made, questions must

Meeting of States on Strengthening Compliance with International Humanitarian Law, Geneva, 30 June–1 July 2014, available at: <https://www.icrc.org/eng/resources/documents/statement/2014/06-30-compliance-ihl-maurer.htm>, accessed 30 March 2015; Andrew Clapham, 'The Rights and Responsibilities of Armed Non-State Actors: The Legal Landscape and Issues Surrounding Engagement' (2010, available on SSRN at <http://www.ssrn.com/abstract=1569636>, accessed 30 March 2015), at 19.

[54] Human Rights Watch, *War without Quarter: Colombia and International Humanitarian Law* (1998), available at: <http://www.hrw.org/legacy/reports98/colombia/Colom989-03.htm#P457_59724>, accessed 30 March 2015. See also Anthea Roberts and Sandesh Sivakumaran, 'Lawmaking by Nonstate Actors: Engaging Armed Groups in the Creation of International Humanitarian Law', 37 Yale J Int'l L 107 (2012), at 127.

[55] The International Council on Human Rights Policy, Ends and Means: Human Rights Approaches to Armed Groups (2000), available at: <http://www.ichrp.org/files/reports/6/105_report_en.pdf>, at 52, accessed 30 March 2015.

[56] See comments by Elisabeth Decrey Warner, 'Engaging with Non-State Armed Groups: Lessons Learned', 36th Round Table on Current Issues of International Humanitarian Law, 'Respecting IHL: Challenges and Perspectives', Institute of International Humanitarian Law, San Remo, 5–7 September 2013, available at: <http://www.iihl.org/iihl/Documents/DECREY-WARNER.pdf>, accessed 30 March 2015.

[57] See Roberts and Sivakumaran, 'Lawmaking by Nonstate Actors', at 129–30.

first be asked: do soft law instruments actually work? Do they achieve their aims of changing State (and non-State) behaviour and ensure compliance with norms, even if such norms are non-binding? In answering these, this next section examines two soft law instruments—one from civil society, directed at non-State actors; one from the UN, directed at States—to examine whether soft law can be considered a viable mechanism for ensuring compliance with norms.

Before proceeding with an assessment of specific soft law instruments and their rates of adoption and compliance, a note of caution is needed here. The reasons why States and non-State groups comply with rules (either in hard or soft law forms) can be manifold.[58] It is not the intention of this chapter to suggest that the soft law instruments under examination have been *solely* responsible for State and non-State implementation of and compliance with specific rules. Rather, what this section of the chapter aims to demonstrate is how the adoption of these two instruments—Geneva Call's Deed of Commitment on Landmines[59] and the UN's Standard Minimum Rules for the Treatment of Prisoners[60]—have been influential, perhaps even pivotal, in changing the ways in which States and non-State actors conduct their affairs with regards to landmines and prisoners respectively.

Geneva Call's Deed of Commitment on Landmines

Some background to the Deed of Commitment has been noted. The Deed was designed as essentially a 'parallel instrument' to the Ottawa Convention on Landmines, and Geneva Call set about engaging with non-State groups, encouraging them to sign the Deed of Commitment, and commit to ending their use of anti-personnel landmines, and destroying any existing stockpiles

[58] For an introduction to the increasingly complex field of soft law theory and analysis, see further Kenneth Abbott and Duncan Snidal, 'Hard and Soft Law in International Governance', 54 International Organisation 421 (2000), at 434–50; Alan Boyle and Christine Chinkin, *The Making of International Law* (OUP, 2007), specifically 211–29; Peter Haas, 'Choosing to Comply: Theorising from International Relations and Comparative Politics', in Shelton (ed.), *Commitment and Compliance*; Matthias Goldman, 'We Need to Cut Off the Head of the King: Past, Present, and Future Approaches to International Soft Law', 25 Leiden J Int'l L 335 (2012); and Mary Ellen O'Connell, 'The Role of Soft Law in a Global Order', in Shelton (ed.), *Commitment and Compliance.*

[59] Deed of Commitment for Adherence to a Total Ban on Anti-Personnel Mines and for Cooperation in Mine Action.

[60] Standard Minimum Rules for the Treatment of Prisoners, Adopted by the First United Nations Congress on the Prevention of Crime and the Treatment of Offenders, held at Geneva in 1955, and approved by the Economic and Social Council by its resolutions 663 C (XXIV) of 31 July 1957 and 2076 (LXII) of 13 May 1977.

of these weapons. Since its creation in 2000, the Deed of Commitment on Landmines has attracted forty-eight signatories from Africa, Asia, Europe, and the Middle East. The Deed of Commitment is a straightforward instrument: it contains a seven-paragraph preamble and ten articles, in which the non-State signatory to the Deed pledges to 'adhere to a total ban on anti-personnel mines',[61] and 'to cooperate in and undertake stockpile destruction, mine clearance, victim assistance, mine awareness, and various other forms of mine action'.[62]

Crucially, the Deed of Commitment contains a number of important implementation, enforcement, and accountability mechanisms. Article 3 requires that signatories 'allow and cooperate in the monitoring and verification'[63] of their commitment to the Deed, which may include 'include visits and inspections in all areas where anti-personnel mines may be present, and the provision of the necessary information and reports, as may be required for such purposes in the spirit of transparency and accountability.'[64] Article 4 requires that non-State groups undertake to train their armed forces in the rules outlined in the Deed, disseminate the Deed amongst their armed forces, and, importantly, implement 'disciplinary sanctions in case of non-compliance'.[65]

It has been nearly fifteen years since the Deed was adopted; as such, it is possible now to assess its record to see whether it has managed to achieve its stated aims. As noted, forty-eight non-State groups have signed the Deed (out of ninety-two non-State groups approached).[66] One of the first non-State groups engaged was the Sudan People's Liberation Movement/ Army (SPLM/A), who signed the Deed of Commitment in October 2001.[67] At the time, Sudan was not a party to the Ottawa Convention. However, within a year of the SPLM/A signing the Deed, the government of Sudan was negotiating and adopting a Memorandum of Understanding with the SPML/A and the United Nations, with the aim of reducing mine and unexploded ordnance injuries in Sudan, and working towards the development of

[61] Art. 1, Deed of Commitment.

[62] Art. 2, Deed of Commitment.

[63] Art. 3, Deed of Commitment.

[64] Art. 3, Deed of Commitment.

[65] Art. 4, Deed of Commitment. The remainder of the Deed of Commitment reiterates the need for all to respect IHL and international human rights law (Art. 5); that signatories should promote the Deed and encourage others to adopt it (Art. 8); that a group's compliance or non-compliance with the Deed may be publicized by Geneva Call (Art. 7); that signing the Deed does not affect a group's legal status, per Common Art. 3 (Art. 6); and that in signing the Deed, the commitment comes into effect immediately (Art. 10), and either complements or supersedes any previous unilateral declarations on anti-personnel mines made by the group (Art. 9).

[66] For a complete listing of non-State groups approached by Geneva call, see <http://www.genevacall.org/how-we-work/armed-non-state-actors/>, accessed 30 March 2015.

[67] See <http://www.genevacall.org/country-page/sudan/>, accessed 30 March 2015.

a jointly agreed Mine Action Plan.[68] By October 2003, the Sudanese government had signed and ratified the Ottawa Convention.[69]

The timing of the acts by the SPLM/A and the Sudanese government is noteworthy; despite the SPLM/A in 1996 declaring their intention to de-mine areas within their control,[70] the Sudanese government had not signed the Ottawa Treaty prior to Geneva Call engaging with the SPLM/A, and the SPLM/A signing the Deed of Commitment. Indeed, as noted by the Director of the UN Mine Action Service, Martin Barber, in 2005, 'it is clear from conversations with senior officials of the Government [in Sudan], that they would not have felt able to ratify the [Ottawa] Treaty, if the SPLM/A had not already made a formal commitment to observe its provisions in the territory under its control.'[71]

Following the adoption of the Deed, the SPLM/A set about fulfilling its obligations under the Deed, including de-mining territory under its control, and destroying stockpiles of anti-personnel mines.[72] The SPLM/A also took further steps to fulfil its obligations under the Deed, including issuing orders and directives to commanders, disseminating the contents of the Deed, and implementing disciplinary sanctions for non-compliance.[73] In addition, the SPLM/A also acted pursuant to the Article 8 obligation to promote the Deed and encourage other groups to sign the Deed, sending a letter to the Ejército de Liberación National (ELN) in Colombia outlining its reasons for prohibiting landmines in its territory and urging the Government of Colombia, and

[68] Memorandum of Understanding between The Government of Sudan, The Sudan Peoples Liberation Movement and The United Nations Regarding United Nations Mine Action Support to Sudan, 19 September 2002, available at: <http://reliefweb.int/report/sudan/memorandum-understanding-between-govt-sudan-splm-and-un-regarding-un-mine-action>, accessed 30 March 2015.

[69] A full listing of signatories and dates of signing/ratification is available at the ICRC website, at: <https://www.icrc.org/applic/ihl/ihl.nsf/States.xsp?xp_viewStates=XPages_NORMStatesParties&xp_treatySelected=580>, accessed 30 March 2015.

[70] Resolution on Problem Posed by Proliferation of Anti-Personnel Mines in Liberated Parts of New Sudan, 1 November 1996, available at Geneva Call's affiliated site 'Their Words: Directory of Armed Non-State Actor Humanitarian Commitments', at: <http://theirwords.org/media/transfer/doc/sc_sd_splm_a_1996_07-f22cfb3dee8032a783d5df4c3d1f2bae.pdf>, accessed 30 March 2015.

[71] Martin Barber, 'Preface', *Armed Non-State Actors and Landmines: Volume I—A Global Report Profiling NSAs and Their Use, Acquisition, Production, Transfer and Stockpiling of Landmines* (Geneva Call and the Program for the Study of International Organisations, Geneva, 2005), available at: <http://www.genevacall.org/wp-content/uploads/dlm_uploads/2013/12/5.pdf>, at 1, accessed 30 March 2015.

[72] See *Engaging Armed Non-State Actors in a Landmine Ban: The Geneva Call Progress Report (2000–2007)*, available at: <http://www.genevacall.org/wp-content/uploads/dlm_uploads/2013/12/raport.pdf>, at 16, accessed 30 March 2015.

[73] Under Art. 4 of the Deed of Commitment; see further *The Geneva Call Progress Report (2000–2007)*, at 18–19.

the armed groups operating within the State, to 'save Colombia... as the roof of the continent from further landmines contamination.'[74]

The SPLM/A signed a peace agreement with the Sudanese government in 2005,[75] ultimately leading to the creation of the new SPLM/A-led State of South Sudan, in 2011.[76] During the interim period between signing the agreement and the creation of South Sudan, the SPLM/A-led interim Government destroyed 6078 anti-personnel mines;[77] upon the creation of South Sudan, the government then signed the Ottawa Convention.[78] Additionally, other non-State groups in Sudan have adopted the Deed, including the Justice and Equality Movement (JEM)[79] and the Sudan People's Liberation Movement–North (SPLM–N),[80] with JEM reported to have modified its Code of Conduct to affirm compliance with and implementation of the Deed of Commitment.[81]

The example of Sudan is demonstrative of the widespread success Geneva Call has enjoyed in its near fifteen-year existence. Numerous stockpiles of anti-personnel mines have been destroyed, with reports placing anti-personnel mine destruction at over 20,000, as well as thousands of IEDs, unexploded ordnance, and other explosive remnants of war having been destroyed since

[74] Letter from Aleu Ayieny Aleu, Executive Director, New Sudan Mine Action Directorate, Sudan, to the Ejército de Liberación Nacional, June 2004, transcript available at: <http://theirwords.org/media/transfer/doc/1_sd_splm_a_2004_12-9f1d7098a9577aa3a57ff4353301fbc0.pdf>, accessed 30 March 2015. As of the time of writing, the ELN has not signed the Deed of Commitment but has publicly pledged to limit its use of anti-personnel mines, and to clear mines from civilian areas: see further <http://theirwords.org/media/transfer/doc/co_eln_2006_15-069c39f6b295b4c114f791506fe3a8b0.pdf>; <http://theirwords.org/media/transfer/doc/1_co_eln_2005_05-5a6160cf2808db7f9c0cf60066f8c085.pdf>;and<http://theirwords.org/media/transfer/doc/1_co_eln_2004_08-55d2f9fa948487d6c516d8cecad98483.pdf>, all websites accessed 30 March 2015.

[75] Comprehensive Peace Agreement between the Government of Sudan and the SPLM/SPLA, 9 January 2005, available at: <http://peacemaker.un.org/sites/peacemaker.un.org/files/SD_060000_The%20Comprehensive%20Peace%20Agreement.pdf>, accessed 30 March 2015.

[76] UN, 'Independence of South Sudan', available at: <http://www.un.org/en/peacekeeping/missions/past/unmis/referendum.shtml>, accessed 30 March 2015; see also Jeffrey Gettleman, 'After Years of Struggle, South Sudan Becomes a New Nation', *New York Times*, 9 July 2011, available at: <http://www.nytimes.com/2011/07/10/world/africa/10sudan.html>, accessed 30 March 2015.

[77] <http://www.genevacall.org/country-page/sudan/>, accessed 6 April 2015.

[78] A full listing of signatories and dates of signing/ratification is available at the ICRC website, at: <https://www.icrc.org/applic/ihl/ihl.nsf/States.xsp?xp_viewStates=XPages_NORMStatesParties&xp_treatySelected=580>, accessed 30 March 2015.

[79] Available at: <http://theirwords.org/media/transfer/doc/sc_sd_jem_2012_17-df49a41ccfcf6fde0d90562e2a0a7da8.pdf>, accessed 30 March 2015.

[80] Available at: <http://www.genevacall.org/wp-content/uploads/dlm_uploads/2013/12/http___www.genevacall.org_resources_list-of-signatories_f-list-of-signatories_2001-2010_2013-SPLMN-Landmines.pdf>, accessed 6 April 2015.

[81] As reported by Geneva Call at: <http://www.genevacall.org/country-page/sudan/>, accessed 30 March 2015.

the creation of the Deed.[82] The success of the Deed of Commitment on Landmines indicates that non-State groups can and do comply with soft law instruments, even when participation is voluntary, and the only possible sanction for non-compliance contained in the Deed is public 'shaming'.[83]

Indeed, voluntary adoption by non-State actors has been seen with regards to private military companies. The Montreux Document on Pertinent International Legal Obligations and Good Practices for States related to Operations of Private Military and Security Companies during Armed Conflict was adopted in 2008 and was intended for States only.[84] However, in 2010, the International Code of Conduct for Private Security Service Providers[85] was adopted, and was intended for PMSCs to adopt, demonstrating the willingness of some irregular participants to abide by relevant rules.

Notwithstanding the success of these soft law instruments with non-State actors, can the same be said for State actors? Non-State actors may have any number of reasons to commit to international law norms publicly—such as increased legitimacy on the national and international stage, or hopes of reciprocal application of the rules with other groups and States—especially as they are not able to participate in the traditional international law-making mechanisms of treaties and custom.[86] But why would States choose to take

[82] As reported by Geneva Call at: <http://www.genevacall.org/what-we-do/landmine-ban/>, accessed 30 March 2015. For statistics, see generally *Engaging Armed Non-State Actors in a Landmine Ban: The Geneva Call Progress Report (2000–2007)*, and *Armed Non-State Actors and Landmines: Volume I—A Global Report Profiling NSAs and Their Use, Acquisition, Production, Transfer and Stockpiling of Landmines*.

[83] Art. 7 allows Geneva Call to publicize the compliance or non-compliance of signatories.

[84] Currently 51 States have signed the document. See further: <https://www.eda.admin.ch/eda/en/fdfa/foreign-policy/international-law/international-humanitarian-law/private-military-security-companies/participating-states.html>, accessed 30 March 2015.

[85] Signed in Geneva on 9 November 2010 by fifty-eight companies; see <http://www.dcaf.ch/Project/International-Code-of-Conduct-for-Private-Security-Service-Providers>, accessed 6 April 2015; since its initial signing date, over 700 companies from have signed the Code, which outlines IHL and human rights law principles for security companies, and includes an independent external oversight mechanism to ensure compliance. See further: <http://www.icoc-psp.org/ICoCSignatoryCompanies.html>, accessed 30 March 2015.

[86] For an analysis of the reasons why non-State actors comply with soft law norms, see further Stefanie Herr, *Binding Non-State Armed Groups to International Humanitarian Law—Geneva Call and the Ban of Anti-Personnel Mines: Lessons from Sudan*, Peace Research Institute Frankfurt, Report No. 95, 2010, available at: <http://www.operationspaix.net/DATA/DOCUMENT/6858~v~Binding_Non-State_Armed_Groups_to_International_Humanitarian_Law.pdf>, accessed 30 March 2015; Sophie Rondeau, 'The Pragmatic Value of Reciprocity: Promoting Respect for International Humanitarian Law among Non-State Armed Groups', in Benjamin Perrin (ed.), *Modern Warfare*; Kristian Gleditsch, Simon Hug, Livia Schubiger, and Julian Wucherpfennig, 'International Conventions and Non-State Actors: Selection, Signalling and Reputation Effects', Households in Conflict Network (HiCN) Working Paper 108 (2011), available at: <http://www.hicn.org/wordpress/wp-content/uploads/2012/06/wp1082.pdf>, accessed 30 March 2015.

on soft law norms when the full panoply of international law participation is already available to them? And when States do engage with soft law, do they comply with the non-binding rules? As with non-State actors, the reasons why States participate in soft law creation are also varied and complex; however, there is strong evidence to suggest that States are willing to take on soft law norms and to abide by them, thereby contributing to the process of making such soft norms binding under international law. As a case study, the next section of this chapter will examine the UN Standard Minimum Rules on the Treatment of Prisoners.

The UN Standard Minimum Rules on the Treatment of Prisoners

The Standard Minimum Rules for the Treatment of Prisoners (Standard Minimum Rules or SMR) were adopted by the UN in 1955, the result of work being undertaken by the UN into the prevention of crime and the treatment of offenders.[87] The ninety-four rules contained in the SMR cover what have come to be considered the basic minimum requirements for persons in detention,[88] essentially a set of 'best practice' guidelines, including, *inter alia*, instruction on the cell occupancy and minimum space requirements for cells;[89] minimums standards for bedding, clothing, and personal hygiene facilities;[90] access to medical services and exercise facilities;[91] the prohibition on corporal punishment and cruel, inhuman, and degrading punishments;[92] the prohibition on discrimination in prisoner management,[93] and the recognition of the right to religious belief and practice.[94]

When the SMR were adopted by the Economic and Social Council (ECOSOC) in 1957, they 'became an officially endorsed set of minimum standards of the United Nations.'[95] In the resolution adopting the SMR, the Council recommended that States give the SMR 'favourable consideration'[96]

[87] See the First UN Congress on the Prevention of Crimes and the Treatment of Offences, Annex 1(a), UN Doc A/CONF.6/1 (1956). The 1955 rules were themselves a development of earlier work undertaken by the International Penal and Penitentiary Commission in 1926; on the drafting background, see further William Clifford, 'The Standard Minimum Rules for the Treatment of Prisoners', 66 AJIL 232 (1972); Daniel Skoler, 'World Implementation of the United Nations Standard Minimum Rules for Treatment of Prisoners', 10 J Int'l L & Econ 453 (1975), at 454–55; and Gary Hill, 'The Evolution of the UN Standard Minimum Rules for the Treatment of Prisoners', 37 Corrections Compendium 33 (2012).

[88] Skoler, 'World Implementation of the United Nations Standard Minimum Rules', at 455.

[89] Rule 9, SMR. [90] Rules 15–19, SMR. [91] Rules 21–22, SMR.

[92] Rule 31, SMR. [93] Rule 6, SMR. [94] Rule 41, SMR.

[95] Skoler, 'World Implementation of the United Nations Standard Minimum Rules', at 456.

[96] ECOSOC Resolution 663(c), UN Doc E/3048 (1957).

with a view to adopting and applying the rules, that the rules should be publicized widely, and that the Secretary General review State application of the rules every five years.[97] The SMR have remained non-binding guidelines, despite calls for them to be adopted as a binding convention.[98]

In the aftermath of their adoption, initial moves towards implementation of the SMR were mixed. ECOSOC had requested progress reports on implementation, with the aim of examining nation-by-nation implementation at the Fourth United Nations Crimes Congress in 1970;[99] however, only forty-three states responded to the surveys, and only fifteen claimed that the Rules had played an influential role in the drafting of national legislation. Those numbers had improved by the 1974 survey, with sixty-two member states affirming the importance of the SMR, a return replicated in the 1984 survey.[100] At the Ninth UN Crimes Congress, held in 1995, it was found that the majority of Member States had implemented or applied the Standard Minimum Rules to 'a large extent'.[101]

In 2012, the UN established an 'Open-Ended Intergovernmental Expert Group on the United Nations Standard Minimum Rules for the Treatment of Prisoners',[102] which held its first meeting in Vienna in 2012. At that meeting, the Group of Experts noted that the SMR had 'stood the test of time and were universally acknowledged as the minimum standards for the detention of prisoners'.[103] In reports submitted for the first Expert Meeting,

[97] ECOSOC Resolution 663(c).

[98] See the Working Paper on Standard Minimum Rules for the Treatment of Prisoners, Fourth UN Congress on the Prevention of Crime and the Treatment of Offenders, § IV: Legal Status of the Rules, UN Doc. A/CONF.43/3 (1970), at paras 40–53.

[99] Roger Clark, *The United Nations Crime Prevention and Criminal Justice Program: Formulation of Standards and Efforts at their Implementation* (University of Pennsylvania Press, 1994), at 234–38.

[100] Roger Clark, *The United Nations Crime Prevention and Criminal Justice Program*, at 234–38. See also Sara Rodriguez, 'The Impotence of Being Earnest: Status of the United States Standard Minimum Rules for the Treatment of Prisoners in Europe and the United States', 33 New Eng J on Crim & Civ Confinement 61 (2007), at 83–88 on the early implementation of the SMR.

[101] See UN Doc. A/51/327, Report of the Secretary-General, regarding Crime Prevention and Criminal Justice: Progress Made in the Implementation of General Assembly Resolutions 50/145 and 50/146, at para. 51. This widespread acceptance was seen also with the UN Rules and Declarations comprising the Code of Conduct for Law Enforcement Officials, together with the Basic Principles on the Use of Force and Firearms by Law Enforcement Officials, Basic Principles on the Independence of the Judiciary, Declaration of Basic Principles of Justice for Victims of Crime and Abuse of Power, and Safeguards Guaranteeing Protection of the Rights of Those Facing the Death Penalty.

[102] <https://www.unodc.org/unodc/en/justice-and-prison-reform/ieg-standards.html>, accessed 30 March 2015.

[103] Report on the meeting of the Expert Group on the Standard Minimum Rules for the Treatment of Prisoners held in Vienna from 31 January–2 February 2012, UN Doc UNODC/CCPCJ/EG.6/2012/1, 16 February 2012, available at: <https://www.unodc.org/documents/justice-and-prison-reform/AGMs/Meetings_Report-E-.pdf>, accessed 30 March 2015.

a considerable number of States, including Austria, China, Finland, Japan, Mauritius, Mexico, New Zealand, South Africa, and the United Kingdom, 'indicated that their national legislation on the treatment of prisoners was based, or had been greatly influenced by the Rules.'[104]

Noteworthy is the example of Europe, an 'early adopter' of the SMR, implementing the Rules outright in 1973,[105] revising them in 1987 (renamed the European Prison Rules),[106] and revising them again in 2006.[107] The European Court of Human Rights (ECtHR) and European Commission of Human Rights have made considerable use of both the SMR and the European Rules; as Rodley and Pollard note, the findings of the ECtHR in the Greek case 'constituted the first systematic application of the international standard to conditions of detention.'[108] The European Court has also cited the SMR, in the cases of *Dickson*,[109] *Khudoyorov*,[110] and *Mamedova*.[111] The SMR have also been affirmed by the African Commission on Human and People's Rights, in resolutions adopted in 1995[112] and 2003.[113]

A note of caution is worthwhile at this point: despite the encouraging signs of adoption of the SMR at national and inter-governmental levels, widespread adoption of the SMR is yet to be achieved. While, as noted, previous investigations into the adoption of the SMR have indicated that a considerable number of States have implemented or applied the SMR to

[104] Background Note, Open-Ended Intergovernmental Expert Group Meeting on the United Nations Standard Minimum Rules for the Treatment of Prisoners, Vienna, 31 January–2 February 2012, available at: <https://www.unodc.org/documents/justice-and-prison-reform/AGMs/Background_note.pdf>, at § 3.1, accessed 30 March 2015.

[105] Council of Europe, Resolution (73)5, Standard Minimum Rules for the Treatment of Prisoners, 19 January 1973, available at: <https://wcd.coe.int/com.instranet.InstraServlet?command=com.instranet.CmdBlobGet&InstranetImage=588982&SecMode=1&DocId=645672&Usage=2>, accessed 30 March 2015.

[106] Council of Europe, Recommendation R(87)3, of the Committee of Ministers to Member States on the European Prison Rules, 12 February 1987, available at: <https://wcd.coe.int/com.instranet.InstraServlet?command=com.instranet.CmdBlobGet&InstranetImage=2622640&SecMode=1&DocId=692778&Usage=2>, accessed 30 March 2015.

[107] Council of Europe, Recommendation Rec(2006)2 of the Committee of Ministers to Member States on the European Prison Rules, 11 January 2006, available at: <https://wcd.coe.int/ViewDoc.jsp?id=955747>, accessed 30 March 2015.

[108] Nigel Rodley and Matt Pollard, *The Treatment of Prisoners under International Law* (3rd edn, OUP, 2009), at 393. See also 'The Greek Case', 12 Yearbook of the European Convention on Human Rights 468 (1969).

[109] *Dickson v United Kingdom*, Application No. 44362/04, ECHR, 4 December 2007, at para. 30.

[110] *Khudoyorov v Russia*, Application No. 6847/02, ECHR, 8 November 2005, at para. 97.

[111] *Mamedova v Russia*, Application No. 7064/05, ECHR, 1 June 2006, at para. 51.

[112] Resolution on Prisons in Africa, ACHPR/Res.19 (XVII) 95.

[113] Resolution on the Adoption of the Ouagadougou Declaration and Plan of Action on Accelerating Prison and Penal Reform in Africa, ACHPR/Res.64 (XXXIV) 03.

a large extent, it has often been the case that such findings are based on a limited response group. For example, in the lead up to the Expert Meetings on the SMR in 2012, States were 'to provide information on best practices, as well as national legislation and existing international law'[114] regarding prison conditions and compliance with the SMR. Only thirty-four States responded to the requests.[115] As such, one needs to be cautious in assessing the SMR as having any possible customary force. However, for the purposes of this chapter, what is useful about State responses to the SMR is that States have been willing to embrace instructions given by a third party, and they have been prepared to implement those instructions domestically.

The Drawbacks of Soft Law Instruments in IHL

Soft law instruments are not a panacea to all the shortcomings of international law. Soft law instruments, much like treaties, require consensus, or at the very least, a majority of stakeholders to agree to the terms. In order to achieve such consensus, soft law instruments are vulnerable to being 'watered down', having their obligations or resolutions rendered less encompassing, less demanding, more general in their terms and recommendations. In the realm of IHL, this attenuation of applicable standards is clearly undesirable. However, the attenuation of standards and rules in IHL is not unique to soft law; the experience of the drafting of Additional Protocol II is evidence of how humanitarian rules can be downgraded in a binding document.

[114] See Note Verbale of 8 March 2011 (CU/2011/26) requesting information on the issue raised in operative para. 10 of General Assembly resolution 65/230; and Note Verbale of 11 September 2012 (CU 2012/157/DO/JS) requesting information on the issue raised in operative paras 5, 6, and 14 of ECOSOC resolution 2012/13 of 27 July 2012 entitled 'Standard Minimum Rules for the Treatment of Prisoners'.

[115] These States were: Argentina, Austria, Bahrain, Belgium, Brazil, Canada, Chile, China, Congo (Republic of), Denmark, Ecuador, El Salvador, Egypt, Estonia, Finland, Germany, Guatemala, Israel, Italy, Japan, Jordan, Lebanon, Mauritius, Mexico, New Zealand, the Philippines, Romania, South Africa, Switzerland, Thailand, Ukraine, the United Arab Emirates, the United Kingdom of Great Britain and Northern Ireland, and the United States of America. Nine replies were received in response to the Note Verbale of 11 September 2012. These were: Argentina, Algeria, Bahrain, Finland, Germany, Japan, Jordan, New Zealand, and Switzerland. The Secretariat also received a reply from the Permanent Observer Mission of Palestine to the United Nations (Vienna). See further Expert Group Meeting on the Standard Minimum Rules for the Treatment of Prisoners Buenos Aires, 11–13 December 2012, Summaries of Replies from Member States to the Notes Verbales of 8 March 2011 and 11 September 2012, UN Doc. UNODC/CCPCJ/EG.6/2012/CRP.1, 30 November 2012, available at: <https://www.unodc.org/documents/justice-and-prison-reform/EGM-Uploads/IEGM-SMR_II_CRP_prepared_by_the_Secretariat.pdf>, accessed 30 March 2015.

Furthermore, the non-binding quality of the soft law instrument may well allow for higher, rather than lower, standards to be set, thereby contributing to better compliance with the law. For example, Article 2(1) of the Ottawa Convention prohibits the use of anti-personnel mines 'designed to be exploded by the presence, proximity or contact of a person.'[116] The Geneva Call Deed of Commitment sets the bar higher, prohibiting anti-personnel mines the effect of which is to 'explode by the presence, proximity or contact of a person.'[117] The Deed of Commitment thus sets a higher standard of conduct than the Ottawa Convention by prohibiting landmines because of their effect rather than their design. Given the widespread acceptance of the Deed of Commitment, concerns about the downgrading of standards may well be misplaced.

However, there are other causes for concern or caution regarding soft law instruments and IHL, which can be categorized as concerns regarding origins and those relating to time. With regards to concerns regarding origins, this refers to the source of the instrument: who was involved in its drafting? Were they experts in the specific field? Was any particular agenda behind the adoption of the instrument that might colour the reading of the instrument? What the process that led to the adoption of the instrument one of consensus or conflict? All of these factors can contribute to a particular soft law instrument being viewed with caution as to its merits. The experience of the ICRC DPH Guidance is illustrative on this point. As noted in Chapter 3, consensus during the Expert Process was difficult to reach, as a number of experts disagreed with the ICRC position on DPH in a number of respects; furthermore, there were some experts who felt that the ICRC approach weighed too heavily against military necessity in favour of principles of humanity, and that such an approach was operationally untenable.[118]

The DPH Guidance is thus in a unique position of being a document issued by a well-respected and undoubted leader in IHL affairs,[119] but one that came out of a process which was marked by dissent and, ultimately,

[116] Art. 2, Ottawa Convention. [117] Art. 1, Deed of Commitment.

[118] As William Boothby stated of the Guidance, it risks 'producing law that will be regarded by states' armed forces as impractical or worse, and which may therefore be ignored. The notion of DPH is, however, central to the core objective of IHL to protect victims. It is therefore critical that the notion be interpreted in a way that makes sense on the modern battlefield and will be applied by all states, or at the very least by most states, when engaged in armed conflict.' ('"And for Such Time As": The Time Dimension To Direct Participation In Hostilities', at 768).

[119] See, eg, J Jeremy March and Scott Glabe, 'Time for the United States to Directly Participate', 1 Va J Int'l L Online 13 (2011), at 14, where they note the 'ICRC's unique role in shaping customary international law'.

disavowal by some of the participants.[120] The potential ramifications for the DPH Guidance's reception are well summarised by Boothby:

> clearly, there will be those . . . who will note the terms of the debate on this vital topic, who will accordingly be well aware of the absence of expert consensus and who will therefore consider the statements made in the Interpretive Guidance in the context of that wider debate. Equally, there will be hard-pressed advisers of States who, knowing the ICRC's respected position in IHL, will tend to accept without question guidance that that institution chooses to issue ignorant, perhaps, of the diversity of . . . respectable and conflicting interpretations among informed commentators.[121]

For soft law instruments to have any impact, especially in such a contentious area as armed conflict, they must originate from a reputable source but must also ensure that any part of the document that might be seen as *lex ferenda* is clearly identified as such.

Time and duration are also matters of concern regarding soft law instruments, specifically the amount of time is takes some instruments to be drafted, and the amount of time it can take before such instruments gain any measure of acceptance by the wider international community. For example, while the Montreux Document was debated and adopted within three years,[122] and the *Tallinn Manual* likewise took only three years to debate, draft, and adopt,[123] the *San Remo Manual on Naval Warfare* was debated over a notably longer period of eight years, before its publication in 1994.[124] Furthermore, it took several years before its principles were adopted by States into their own military manuals.[125] As such, the purported benefits offered by soft law instruments may be tempered if the process of drafting and adopting such an instrument is protracted.

That being said, the time it takes for treaties to be drafted, adopted, and then given domestic force can often rival, if not eclipse, that of soft law instruments; for example as noted, the *Tallinn Manual* was debated and adopted within three years. It took over twice as long (if not longer) to debate and adopt the Additional Protocols.[126] In any event, any potential

[120] See Ch. 3 for a more detailed examination of the DPH process and the controversy over the final instrument.

[121] William Boothby, *Conflict Law: The Influence of New Weapons Technology, Human Rights and Emerging Actors* (TMC Asser Press, 2014), at 79.

[122] See: <https://www.icrc.org/eng/resources/documents/publication/p0996.htm>, accessed 6 April 2015.

[123] See: <https://ccdcoe.org/research.html>, accessed 30 March 2015.

[124] See: <https://www.icrc.org/ihl/INTRO/560?OpenDocument>, accessed 30 March 2015.

[125] See generally Boothby, *Conflict Law*, at 74–76, on States which have adopted the *San Remo Manual*.

[126] While there is, arguably, no 'official' point where the process of adopting the Protocols started, the process could be reasonably considered as having started in 1962, with the convening of the ICRC conference of experts on the need to aid victims of internal conflicts (see

norm-influencing power that international law instruments may have will be limited by the degree to which the instruments are accepted by States, and incorporated into State practice.

Soft Law and Civilian Participation in Hostilities

Soft law instruments cannot be customary international instruments themselves. However, as Dinstein notes, these documents 'may at times be perceived as accurate replicas of international law, and even in their innovative parts may influence the general practice of States or pace the road for future treaties.'[127] The potential impact of soft law instruments cannot therefore be dismissed. In the absence of new treaties, and given the extant vagaries regarding civilian participation in all its forms, the most promising prospects for regulating civilian participation in armed conflicts seems to lie in the adoption of soft law instruments. As Boothby notes:

> do the International Manuals have an indirect effect on the formation of customary law? Indeed they would seem to, but only to the extent that their proposed rules are actually followed by the armed forces of states and, thus, are translated into state practice. To the extent that this occurs, a law-forming process may be initiated or inspired by provision in an International Manual, perhaps in circumstances where states were unable, or perhaps disinclined, to achieve agreement as to a treaty text... there would seem to be considerable value in such a process, where subject matter experts, operating independently of state pressures, produce a clinically objective assessment of what the law is and in which states can either implement the suggested rules in their own practice, or reject or ignore them.[128]

further 'Humanitarian Aid to the Victims of Internal Conflicts: Meeting of a Commission of Experts in Geneva', 3 IRRC 79 (1963)), perhaps even as early as 1956, with the ICRC's adoption of the 'Draft Rules for the Limitation of the Dangers Incurred by the Civilian Population in Time of War' (see *Final Record Concerning the Draft Rules for the Limitation of Dangers Incurred by the Civilian Population in Time of War* (ICRC, April 1958), available at: <https://www.icrc.org/applic/ihl/ihl.nsf/xsp/.ibmmodres/domino/OpenAttachment/applic/ihl/ihl.nsf/FEA0B928100D3135C12563CD002D6C10/FULLTEXT/Draft-ICRC-Rules-1956-EN.pdf>, accessed 30 March 2015). The process was definitely underway by 1969, with the Twenty-First International Conference of the Red Cross adopting a resolution urging greater respect for IHL principles in international and non-international armed conflicts, and suggesting that the law on non-international armed conflicts be expanded and clarified (see further Resolution XVII, 'Protection of Victims of Non-International Armed Conflicts', XXth International Red Cross Conference, Istanbul 1969, and *Reaffirmation and Development of the Law and Customs Applicable in Armed Conflicts: Report Submitted by the International Committee of the Red Cross* (May 1969)). The Conference of Government Experts which drafted a first draft of the Protocols finally met in 1971.

[127] Dinstein, *The Conduct of Hostilities*, at 17.

[128] Boothby, *Conflict Law*, at 89.

Soft law instruments thus present a unique opportunity for States and non-State groups and civil society as well, to play an active role in influencing and shaping customary international law relating to civilian participation in armed conflicts, and how States specifically define the concept and parameters of DPH. In contentious areas, such as the use of civilian military contractors in war zones, or the use of civilian agencies or contractors in conducting drone strikes, soft law offers the potential for interested parties to place issues on the international agenda, often with a rapidity that may be lacking from more formalized law-making process.

However, there is already a soft law instrument on DPH: the ICRC Interpretive Guidance. As such, it is reasonable to question why further instruments or additional documents on DPH would be needed. Surely this question has been addressed, if not to everyone's satisfaction. However, while the ICRC document has been a valuable and useful contribution to the discussion on DPH, the document itself is unfortunately, for want of a better word, tainted. Considering the backlash that accompanied the production of the document, and the fact that the instrument was published as the ICRC's assessment of DPH rather than a consensus document from a group of experts, it means that the document will remain tied to the controversy. As such, any further instrument on DPH would need to be as free from similar controversy as possible.

Furthermore, given the disparate and complex areas in which DPH assessments must be made, as have been highlighted in previous chapters, it is valid to query the utility of a single document on DPH, rather than having a number of smaller, shorter, more specific documents on specific areas, such as the Montreux Document, and the *Tallinn Manual. Sui generis* instruments seem better placed to address the specificities of DPH in different contexts, rather than having one blanket generic instrument on DPH. Individual documents could start with the basic ICRC formulation—belligerent nexus, causation, threshold of harm—but add their own context-specific examples and guidance. Indeed, there is scope in both the Montreux Document and the *Tallinn Manual* for further elucidation on the scope of DPH. For instance, the Montreux Document notes that the status of private military and security contractor (PMSC) personnel must be determined on a case-by-case basis, dependent on the nature and function of their activities[129] but that civilian PMSCs will be liable for targeting if they take a direct part in the hostilities.[130] However, the Document does not clarify what kinds of acts amount to DPH; even in Part Two of the Document, on 'good practices' relating to PMSCs,

[129] Art. 24, Montreux Document.

[130] Art. 25, Montreux Document.

the Document merely states that Contracting States should take into account 'factors such as whether a particular service could cause PMSC personnel to become involved in direct participation in hostilities'.[131] Likewise, the *Tallinn Manual* notes that 'civilians are not prohibited from directly participating in cyber operations amounting to hostilities, but forfeit their protection from attacks for such time as they so participate',[132] but it does not explain what kinds of DPH would result in loss of civilian immunity.

Individual, context-specific instruments on DPH could conceivably address some of the more contentious aspects of DPH, such as the membership requirements, and the loss/resumption of civilian immunity better. Subject-specific DPH instruments could draw on more concrete examples to illustrate these issues, such as indicating whether providing tactical advice on targets in a targeted killing would amount to DPH, or whether distributed denial of service attacks or the construction of malware would only be considered indirect participation. Such instruments would be able to take any agreed upon assessments of DPH in the abstract and apply them to context-specific situations, much like the *Harvard Manual* has done.

In the complex and often contradictory process of identifying the enemy under IHL, instruction manuals and codes of conduct can actively contribute to clarifying the contours of direct participation. In order to advance our understanding of DPH, future international soft law instruments will need to take the lead from other institutions and organizations, such as the International Criminal Tribunal for the former Yugoslavia and spell out what acts they consider as amounting to DPH. The ICRC DPH Guidance was much criticized as being too restrictive and operationally unworkable.[133] If this is true, then interested stakeholders should take up the challenge to develop a more specific DPH model that will be more widely accepted. Only by continuing to examine the question of DPH can a workable definition of the concept be developed.

Conclusion

One of the recurrent criticisms of the law of armed conflict is that it is 'one war behind reality',[134] that it can only be retrospective, responding to events after they have happened rather than pre-empting or foreseeing developments. Soft law instruments, however, offer the opportunity to both respond to problems and pre-empt or predict foreseeable issues. The *Tallinn Manual*

131 § A(I)(1), Part Two, Montreux Document.
132 Rule 29, *Tallinn Manual*.
133 See Ch. 3 on DPH, and the criticisms of the ICRC DPH Guidance.
134 As noted by Sassòli, Bouvier, and Quintin, *How Does Law Protect in War*, at 149.

has certainly been an exemplar in this respect, by setting out the existing law as relevant to cyber operations, theorizing possible developments, and examining which areas of the law require revision or development. States and non-State groups alike should take advantage of the growing influence of soft law instruments to help develop and reaffirm the law.

Conclusions

Where to from Here?

In an ideal world, civilians would not be affected by armed conflicts, and would never take direct part in the hostilities (indeed, in an ideal world, there would be no armed conflicts at all). Private military and security contractors would never be used in war zones, civilian Central Intelligence Agency employees would not pilot drones, and civilians would not participate in cyber hostilities. There would be no need to determine the parameters of direct participation in hostilities (DPH) because no civilian would ever take direct part in hostilities.

However, in reality, civilians are affected, deeply, by armed conflicts, and many civilians feel impelled to take up arms to defend their families and their cities, towns. and villages, their beliefs and ideologies; others participate for financial reasons; still others are placed in combat roles when governmental policy decisions change the nature of their employment. It is a fact of life that civilians take direct part in hostilities and they must face the consequences of such participation. Such participation is not unlawful under international law, but civilian participants do not enjoy combatant immunity for their direct participation and, furthermore, they lose their civilian immunity from targeting for as long as they take direct part.

This seemingly straightforward concept—that civilians lose their immunity from targeting for as long as they directly participate in hostilities—is actually notably complicated and contains a number of complex elements. In order to improve our understand of the concept, one must define 'civilian' as well as 'combatant', and understand why each category of persons enjoys certain privileges and immunities while the others do not. One must then inquire into the ways in which those privileges and immunities are lost and how they might be regained. At the same time, those that apply the law of armed conflict must also adhere to one of the fundamental rinciples of the law: that of the principle of distinction, which requires that parties to the conflict to distinguish between combatants and civilians at all times, and only direct their attacks against military objectives. While these two concepts—distinction and civilian immunity except in cases of

DPH—would seem to be working towards shared goals (that of the protection of the civilian population), they come into conflict when civilians are used in quasi-military roles, or when definitions of civilians are so narrow (or definitions of military objectives so wide) they render the concept of civilian immunity almost meaningless.

As the law of armed conflict developed throughout the later nineteenth century, and throughout the twentieth century, States (for the most part) repeatedly embraced and affirmed the cardinal principle of distinction in the treaty law and in practice. When confronted with widespread or systematic civilian participation in armed conflict, States responded by developing and revising the law[1] to extend combatant privileges and immunities. However, these privileges and immunities were given only to certain categories of irregular, and only if they conducted themselves as if they were combatants; that is, through the wearing of uniforms or other distinctive markers, and through the open carriage of arms. This historical focus on making irregulars behave like regulars has meant that one particular part of the civilian irregular equation has been essentially overlooked: that of the issue of what kinds of direct participation will result in the loss of civilian immunity.

This sidelining of the concept of civilian, civilian immunity, and civilian loss of immunity is evident when one considers that it was not until 1977, and the appearance of the Additional Protocols, that a definition of civilian was first enshrined in the treaty law,[2] remarkable considering that the fourth Geneva Convention was adopted to protect civilians. Furthermore, it was only in 1977 that the specific term 'direct participation in hostilities' was first used, and only then was specific reference made to the loss of civilian immunity from targeting due to such direct participation. Even then, no specific direction as to the scope and parameters of DPH were given at the time.

The last ten to twenty-five years has seen civilians directly participating in armed conflicts in manifold ways, and in a number of direct and indirect ways. The lack of a clear understanding of DPH has thus been thrown into sharp relief; the need for clarity on this question is pressing. There have been steps taken to try and address this issue: the International Committee of the Red Cross (ICRC) notably tried to formulate

[1] As Sibylle Schiepers notes, irregular civilian participations was a primary driver in the progressive development of the law of armed conflict throughout its modern incarnation and that the modern law of armed conflict is 'a peculiar field of law as it refuses to regulate a phenomenon that repeatedly provided the main impetus for its progressive codification: irregular fighters' (Sibylle Scheipers, 'Fighting Irregular Fighters: Is the Law of Armed Conflict Outdated?', 43 Parameters 45 (2013), at 56).

[2] Indeed, even then the concept of civilian was given short shrift, as civilian was defined as being 'not a combatant'.

an expansive and complete set of rules regarding DPH. However, controversy over the drafting process of the ICRC document has placed the document under something of a cloud. It is up to States, and to non-State groups, to engage on the question of DPH, to work towards a consensus opinion on the question, in order to ensure that one of the fundamental principles of international humanitarian law—that of protecting civilians from the deleterious effects of armed conflict—continues to be respected.

Bibliography

Abbott K, and Snidal D. 'Hard and Soft Law in International Governance', 54 International Organisation 421 (2000).

Academia de Guerra Naval. *Aspectos Importantes del Derecho Internacional Maritimo que Deben Tener Presente los Comandantes de los Buques* (Quito, 1989).

Akande D. 'US/NATO Targeting of Afghan Drug Traffickers: An Illegal and Dangerous Precedent?', EJIL: Talk!, 13 September 2009.

Akande D. 'Classification of Armed Conflicts: Relevant Legal Concepts', in E Wilmshurst (ed.), *International Law and the Classification of Conflicts* (OUP, 2012).

Aldrich G. 'New Life for the Laws of War', 75 AJIL 764 (1981).

Aldrich G. 'Guerrilla Combatants and Prisoner of War Status', 31 AULR 871 (1981–82).

Aldrich G. 'Progressive Development of the Laws of War: A Reply to Criticisms of the 1977 Geneva Protocol I', 26 Va J Int'l L 693 (1985–86).

Aldrich G. 'Prospects for United States Ratification of Additional Protocol I to the 1949 Geneva Conventions', 85 AJIL 1 (1991).

Aldrich G. 'The Taliban, Al Qaeda, and the Determination of Illegal Combatants', 96 AJIL 891 (2002).

Alston P. 'The CIA and Targeted Killings Beyond Borders', 2 Harvard Nat Sec J 283 (2011).

Andress J, and Winterfeld S. *Cyber Warfare: Techniques, Tactics and Tools for Security Practitioners* (Elsevier, 2011).

Ansah T. 'War: Rhetoric and Norm-Creation in Response to Terror', 43 Va J Int'l L 797 (2003).

Ashworth A. 'Self-Defence and the Right to Life', 34 Cambridge L J 282 (1975).

Ballard K. 'The Privatization of Military Affairs: A Historical Look into the Evolution of the Private Military Industry', in T Jäger and G Kümmel (eds), *Private Military and Security Companies: Chances, Problems, Pitfalls and Prospects* (VS Verlag für Sozialwissenschaften, 2007).

Ballentine K, and Sherman J (eds). *The Political Economy of Armed Conflict: Beyond Greed and Grievance* (Lynne Rienner, 2003).

Bartolini G. 'PMS Contractors as "Persons who Accompany the Armed Forces"', in F Francioni and N Ronzitti (eds), *War by Contract: Human Rights, Humanitarian Law, and Private Contractors* (OUP, 2011).

Baxter R. 'So-Called "Unprivileged Belligerency": Spies, Guerrillas, and Saboteurs', 28 BYBIL 323 (1951).

Baxter R. 'The First Modern Codification of the Law of Armed Conflict—Francis Lieber and General Order No. 100', 25 IRRC 171 (1963).

Baxter R. 'International Law in "Her Infinite Variety"', 29 ICLQ 549 (1980).

Baxter R. 'The Duties of Combatants and the Conduct of Hostilities (Law of the Hague)', in *International Dimensions of Humanitarian Law* (UNESCO/Henri Dunant Institute/Martinus Nijhoff, 1988).

Bayley CC. *Mercenaries for the Crimea: The German, Swiss and Italian Legions in British Service 1854–56* (McGill, 1977).

Bergal C. 'The Mexican Drug War: The Case for a Non-International Armed Conflict Classification', 34 Fordham Int'l L J 1042 (2011).

Best G. *Humanity in Warfare: The Modern History of the International Law of Armed Conflicts* (Weidenfeld and Nicholson, 1980).

Best G. *War and Law Since 1945* (Clarendon Press, 1997).

Blank L. 'Targeted Strikes: The Consequences of Blurring the Armed Conflict and Self-Defence Justifications', 38 William Mitchell L Rev 1655 (2011).

Blank L, and Noone G. *International Law and Armed Conflict: Fundamental Principles and Contemporary Challenges in the Law of War* (Wolters Kluwer, 2013).

Bloom C. 'Square Pegs and Round Holes: Mexico, Drugs, and International Law', 34 Houston J Int'l L 345 (2012).

Blum G, and Heyman P. 'Law and Policy of Targeted Killing', 1 Harv Nat'l Sec J 145 (2010).

Bongard P, and Somer J. 'Monitoring Armed Non-State Actor Compliance with Humanitarian Norms: A Look at International Mechanisms and the Geneva Call Deed of Commitment', 93 IRRC 673 (2011).

Boothby W. ' "And for Such Time As": The Time Dimension to Direct Participation in Hostilities', 42 NYU J Int'l L & Pol 741 (2010).

Boothby W. *The Law of Targeting* (OUP, 2012).

Boothby W. *Conflict Law: The Influence of New Weapons Technology, Human Rights and Emerging Actors* (TMC Asser Press, 2014).

Bosch S. 'Private Security Contractors and International Humanitarian Law' 16 African Sec Rev 34 (2007).

Bothe M, Partsch KJ, and Solf W. *New Rules for Victims of Armed Conflicts: Commentary on the Two 1977 Protocols Additional to the Geneva Conventions of 1949* (Martinus Nijhoff, 1982).

Boyle A, and Chinkin C. *The Making of International Law* (OUP, 2007).

Brands H. 'Crime, Irregular Warfare, and Institutional Failure in Latin America: Guatemala as a Case Study', 34 Studies in Conflict and Terrorism 228 (2011).

Breau S, Aronsson M, and Joyce R. 'Drone Attacks, International Law and the Recording of Civilian Casualties of Armed Conflict', Oxford Research Group Discussion Paper 2 (June 2011).

Bugnion F. *The ICRC and the Protection of War Victims* (ICRC, 2003).

Busch M (trans.). *Bismarck in the Franco-German War 1870–1871* 2 vols (Scribners, 1879).

Cameron L. 'Private Military Companies—Their Status under International Humanitarian Law and its Impact on their Regulation', 88 IRRC 573 (2006).

Cameron L, and Chetail V. *Privatizing War: Private Military and Security Companies under Public International Law* (CUP, 2013).

Camins E. 'The Past as Prologue: The Development of the "Direct Participation" Exception to Civilian Immunity', 90 IRRC 853 (2008).

Carpenter A. 'Beyond Drug War: Transforming Factional Conflict in Mexico', 27 Conflict Resolution Quarterly 401 (2010).

Carr J. *Inside Cyber Warfare* (2nd edn, O'Reilly, 2012).

Carrillo-Suárez A. '*Hors de Logique*: Contemporary Issues in International Humanitarian Law as Applied to Internal Armed Conflict', 15 Am U Int'l L Rev 1 (1999).

Casley-Maslen S (ed.). *The War Report: Armed Conflict in 2013* (OUP, 2014).

Cassese A. 'The Spanish Civil War and the Development of Customary Law Concerning Internal Armed Conflicts', in A Cassese (ed.), *Current Problems of International Law: Essays on UN Law and on the Law of Armed Conflict* (A Guiffrè, 1975).

Cassese A. 'The Status of Rebels Under the 1977 Geneva Protocol on Non-International Armed Conflicts', 30 ICLQ 416 (1981).

Cassese A. 'Wars of National Liberation and Humanitarian Law', in C Swinarski (ed.), *Studies and Essays on International Humanitarian Law and Red Cross Principles in Honour of Jean Pictet* (ICRC, 1984).

Cassese A. 'The Martens Clause: Half a Loaf or Simply Pie in the Sky?', 11 EJIL 187 (2000).

Cassese A. 'On Some Merits of the Israeli Judgment on Targeted Killings', 5 JICJ 339 (2007).

Chesterman S. 'Global Norms, Local Contexts', in S Chesterman (ed.), *Civilians in War* (Lynne Rienner, 2001).

Chinkin C. 'Normative Development in the International Legal System', in D Shelton (ed.), *Commitment and Compliance: The Role of Non-Binding Norms in the International Legal System* (OUP, 2000).

Clarke MHF, Glynn T, and Rogers APV. 'Combatant and Prisoner of War Status', in M Meyer (ed.), *Armed Conflict and the New Law: Aspects of the 1977 Geneva Protocols and the 1981 Weapons Convention* (BIICL, 1989).

Clarke R, and Knake R. *Cyber War: The Next Threat to National Security and What to Do About It* (Harper Collins, 2010).

Corn G. '*Hamdan*, Fundamental Fairness, and the Significance of APII', 8 Army Lawyer 1 (2006).

Corn G. 'Enemy Combatants and Access to Habeas Corpus: Questioning the Validity of the Prisoner of War Analogy', 5 Santa Clara J Int'l L 236 (2007).

Corn G. 'Hamdan, Lebanon, and the Regulation of Hostilities: The Need to Recognise a Hybrid Category of Armed Conflict', 40 Vanderbilt J Transnat'l L 295 (2007).

Corn G. 'Thinking the Unthinkable: Has the Time Come to Offer Combatant Immunity to Non-State Actors?', 22 Stanford LPR 253 (2011).

Corn G. 'Self Defense Targeting: Conflict Classification or Wilful Blindness?', 88 International Law Studies (2012).

Cornell S. 'Narcotics and Armed Conflict: Interaction and Implications', 30 Studies in Conflict and Terrorism 207 (2007).

Crane D. 'Terrorists, Warlords, and Thugs', 21 Am U Int'l L Rev 505 (2005–06).

Crawford E. 'Terrorism and Targeted Killings in International Law', in B Saul (ed.), *Research Handbook on International Law and Terrorism* (Elgar, 2014).

Crawford E. *The Treatment of Combatants and Insurgents* (OUP, 2010).

Cullen A. 'Key Developments Affecting the Scope of Internal Armed Conflict in International Humanitarian Law', 183 Mil L R 66 (2005).

Cullen A. *The Concept of Non-International Armed Conflict in International Humanitarian Law* (CUP, 2010).

Daintith J, and Wright E. *A Dictionary of Computing* (6th edn, OUP, 2008).

d'Aspremont J. *Formalism and the Sources of International Law: A Theory of the Ascertainment of Legal Rules* (OUP, 2011).

David E. *Principes de droit des conflits armés* (2nd edn, Bruylant, 1999).

Deeks A. 'Unwilling or Unable: Toward a Normative Framework for Extra-Territorial Self-Defence', 5 Va J Int'l L 483 (2012).

den Dekker G, and Myjer EPJ. 'The Right to Life and Self-Defence of Private Military and Security Contractors in Armed Conflict', in F Francioni and N Ronzitti (eds), *War by Contract: Human Rights, Humanitarian Law, and Private Contractors* (OUP, 2011).

Department of the Army, *The Law of Land Warfare* (Washington DC, 1956).

Dinstein Y. 'The Distinction between Unlawful Combatants and War Criminals', in Y Dinstein and M Tabory (eds), *International Law at a Time of Perplexity: Essays in Honour of Shabtai Rosenne* (Martinus Nijhoff, 1989).

Dinstein Y. *The Conduct of Hostilities under the Law of International Armed Conflict* (CUP, 2004).

Dörmann K. *Elements of War Crimes under the Rome Statute of the International Criminal Court: Sources and Commentary* (CUP, 2003).

Dörmann K. 'The Legal Situation of "Unlawful/Unprivileged Combatants"', 85 IRRC 45 (2003).

Doswald-Beck L. 'Private Military Companies under IHL', in S Chesterman and C Lehnardt (eds), *From Mercenaries to Market: The Rise and Regulation of Private Military Companies* (OUP, 2007).

Draper GIAD. 'The Interaction of Christianity and Chivalry in the Historical Development of Law of War', 7 IRRC 3 (1965).

Draper GIAD. 'The Status of Combatants and the Question of Guerrilla Warfare', 45 BYBIL 173 (1971).

Draper GIAD. 'Combatant Status: An Historical Perspective', 11 *Revue de Droit Pénal Militaire et de Droit de la Guerre* 135 (1972–73).

Drews I-I. 'Private Military Companies: The New Mercenaries?—An International Law Analysis', in T Jäger and G Kümmel (eds), *Private Military and Security Companies: Chances, Problems, Pitfalls and Prospects* (VS Verlag für Sozialwissenschaften, 2007).

Drumheller T. *On The Brink: An Insider's Account of How the White House Compromised American Intelligence* (Carroll and Graf, 2006).

Dunn Cavelty M. 'Cyberwar', in G Kassimeris and J Buckley (eds), *The Ashgate Research Companion to Modern Warfare* (Ashgate, 2010).

Ellis J. 'Shades of Grey: Soft Law and the Validity of Public International Law', 25 Leiden J Int'l L 313 (2012).

Etter G, and Lehmuth E. 'The Mexican Drug Wars: Organised Crime, Narco-Terrorism, Insurgency or Asymmetric Warfare?', 20 J Gang Research 1 (2013).

Eyffinger A. *The 1899 Hague Peace Conference: 'The Parliament of Man, The Federation of the World'* (Kluwer, 1999).

Eyffinger A, Stephens A, and Muller S (eds). *Self-Defence as a Fundamental Principle* (TMC Asser, 2009).

Faite A. 'Involvement of Private Contractors in Armed Conflict: Implications under International Humanitarian Law', 4 Defence Studies 166 (2004).

Fearon J, and Laitin D. 'Ethnicity, Insurgency and Civil War', 97 American Political Science Review 75 (2003).

Feith D. 'Law in the Service of Terror—The Strange Case of the Additional Protocol', 1 National Interest 36 (1985).

Fellmeth A. 'Questioning Civilian Immunity', 43 Texas Int'l L J 453 (2008).

Fenrick W. 'ICRC Guidance on Direct Participation in Hostilities', 12 YBIHL 287 (2009).

Ferrell W. 'No Shirt, No Shoes, No Status: Uniforms, Distinction and Special Operations in International Armed Conflict', 178 Mil L Rev 94 (2003).

Fleck D (ed.). *The Handbook of International Humanitarian Law* (2nd edn, OUP, 2008).

Fletcher G. 'The Law of War and its Pathologies', 38 Colum Hum Rts L Rev 517 (2007).

Gardam J. *Non-Combatant Immunity as a Norm of International Humanitarian Law* (Martinus Nijhoff, 1993).

Giladi R. 'The Jus Ad Bellum/Jus In Bello Distinction and the Law of Occupation', 41 Israel L Rev 246 (2008).

Gillard E-C. 'Business Goes to War: Private Military/Security Companies and International Humanitarian Law', 88 IRRC 525 (2006).

Gillespie A. *A History of the Law of War: Volume 2—The Customs and Laws of War with Regards to Civilians in Times of Conflict* (Hart, 2011).

Gilmore E, Gleditsch NP, Lujala P, and Rod JK. 'Conflict Diamonds: A New Dataset', 22 Conflict Management and Peace Science 257 (2005).

Gold J. 'Strengthening the Soft International Law of Exchange Arrangements', 77 AJIL 443 (1983).

Goldman M. 'We Need to Cut Off the Head of the King: Past, Present, and Future Approaches to International Soft Law', 25 Leiden J Int'l L 335 (2012).

Green L. 'The Status of Mercenaries in International Law', 8 Israel Yearbook on Human Rights 9 (1978).

Green L. *The Contemporary Law of Armed Conflict* (3rd edn, Juris, 2008).

Greenberg K, and Dratel J (eds). *The Torture Papers: The Road to Abu Ghraib* (CUP, 2005).

Greenwood, C. 'The Laws of War (International Humanitarian Law)', in Malcolm Evans (ed.), *International Law* (OUP, 2003).

Greenwood C. 'War, Terrorism and International Law', 56 Current Legal Problems 505 (2004).

Greenwood C. 'Scope of Application of International Humanitarian Law', in D Fleck (ed.), *The Handbook of International Humanitarian Law* (2nd edn, OUP, 2008).

Grillo I. *El Narco: Inside Mexico's Criminal Insurgency* (Bloomsbury, 2011).

Gross L. 'The Peace of Westphalia 1648–1948', 42 AJIL 20 (1948).

Grotius H. *The Law of War and Peace* (1625), in L Friedman (ed.), *The Law of War: A Documentary History* (Random House, 1972).

Haas P. 'Choosing to Comply: Theorising from International Relations and Comparative Politics', in D Shelton (ed.), *Commitment and Compliance: The Role of Non-Binding Norms in the International Legal System* (OUP, 2000).

Haggenmacher P. 'Self Defence as a General Principle of Law and its Relevance to War', in AS Eyffinger, and S Muller (eds), *Self-Defence as a Fundamental Principle* (TMC Asser, 2009).

Haines S. 'The Nature of War and the Character of Contemporary Armed Conflict', in E Wilmshurst (ed.), *International Law and the Classification of Conflicts* (OUP, 2012).

Harrison Dinniss H, *Cyber Warfare and the Laws of War* (CUP, 2012).

Harrison Dinniss H. 'Cyber Warriors, Patriotic Hackers and the Laws of War', in D Saxon (ed.), *International Humanitarian Law and the Changing Technology of War* (Martinus Nijhoff, 2013).

Hartigan RS. *Lieber's Code and the Law of War* (Precedent, 1983).

Hauck P, and Peterke S. 'Organised Crime and Gang Violence in National and International Law', 92 IRRC 407 (2010).

Hays Parks W, 'Part IX of the ICRC "Direct Participation in Hostilities" Study: No Mandate, No Expertise, and Legally Incorrect', 42 NYU J Int'l L & Pol 769 (2010).

Heller KJ. '"One Hell of a Killing Machine": Signature Strikes and International Law', 11 JICJ 89 (2013).

Henderson I. *The Contemporary Law of Targeting: Military Objectives, Proportionality and Precautions in Attack under Additional Protocol I* (Martinus Nijhoff, 2009).

Heymann P, and Kayyem J. *Protecting Liberty in an Age of Terror* (MIT Press, 2005).

Hill G. 'The Evolution of the UN Standard Minimum Rules for the Treatment of Prisoners', 37 Corrections Compendium 33 (2012).

Hippler T. *Citizens, Soldiers and National Armies: Military Service in France and Germany, 1789–1830* (Routledge, 2008).

Holmes R, Singleton C, and Jones S (eds). *The Oxford Companion to Military History* (OUP, 2001),

Hoisington M. 'Cyberwarfare and the Use of Force Giving Rise to the Right of Self-Defence', 32 BC Int'l & Comp L Rev 439 (2009).

Ipsen K. 'Combatants and Non-Combatants', in D Fleck (ed.), *The Handbook of Humanitarian Law in Armed Conflicts* (3rd edn, OUP, 2013).

Jäger T, and Kümmel G (eds). *Private Military and Security Companies: Chances, Problems, Pitfalls and Prospects* (VS Verlag für Sozialwissenschaften, 2007).

Jensen ET. 'Combatant Status: It is Time for Intermediate Levels of Recognition for Partial Compliance', 46 Va J Int'l L 209 (2005).

Jensen G. 'The Meaning of War in a Technological Age', in G Jensen and A Wiest (eds), *War in the Age of Technology: Myriad Faces of Modern Armed Conflict* (New York University Press, 2001).

Jones A, and Fay G. 'Investigation of Intelligence Activities at Abu Ghraib/ Investigation of the Abu Ghraib Prison and the 205th Military Intelligence Brigade, August 2004', reprinted in K Greenberg and J Dratel (eds), *The Torture Papers: The Road to Abu Ghraib* (CUP, 2005).

Junod S. 'APII: History and Scope', 33 AULR 29 (1983–84).

Kalshoven F. 'Civilian Immunity and the Principle of Distinction', 31 AULR 855 (1981–82).

Kalshoven F, and Zegveld L. *Constraints on the Waging of War: An Introduction to International Humanitarian Law* (4th edn, ICRC, 2011).

Kelsey JTG. 'Hacking into International Law: The Principles of Distinction and Neutrality in the Age of Cyber Warfare', 106 Mich L Rev 1427 (2008)

Kerr C. 'Mexico's Drug War: Is it Really a War?', 54 S Tex L Rev 193 (2012).

Kinsey C. 'Challenging International Law: A Dilemma of Private Security Companies', 5 Conflict, Security and Development 269 (2005).

Kirk-Greene A. *Crisis and Conflict in Nigeria, A Documentary Sourcebook*, vol. I (OUP, 1971).

Klabbers J. 'The Redundancy of Soft Law', 65 Nordic J Int'l L 167 (1996).

Klaidman D. *Kill or Capture: The War on Terror and the Soul of the Obama Presidency* (Houghton Mifflin Harcourt, 2012).

Kleffner J. 'From "Belligerents" to "Fighters" and Civilians Directly Participating in Hostilities—On the Principle of Distinction in Non-International Armed Conflicts One Hundred Years after the Second Hague Peace Conference', 54 Netherlands Int'l L Rev 315 (2007).

Koh H. 'The Obama Administration and International Law', Keynote Address, 104th Annual Meeting of the American Society of International Law—'International Law in a Time of Change', 24–27 March 2010, Washington DC, 104 ASIL Proceedings 207 (2010).

Koninklijke Landmacht. *Militair Juridische Dienst* (The Hague, 2005).

Korns S, and Kastenberg J. 'Georgia's Cyber Left Hook', 38 Parameters 60 (2008–09).

Krahmann E. *States, Citizens and the Privatization of Security* (CUP, 2010).

Kretzmer D. 'Targeted Killing of Suspected Terrorists: Extra-Judicial Executions or Legitimate Means of Defence?', 16 EJIL 171 (2005).

Lanning ML. *Mercenaries: Soldiers of Fortune, From Ancient Greece to Today's Private Military Companies* (Presidio, 2005).

Laqueur W. 'The Origins of Guerrilla Doctrine', 10 Journal of Contemporary History 341 (1975).

Laqueur W. *Guerrilla: A Historical and Critical Study* (Little, Brown and Co., 1976).

Lavaux S. 'Natural Resources and Conflict in Colombia: Complex Dynamics, Narrow Relationships', 62 International Journal 19 (2006).

Leander A. *Global Ungovernance: Mercenaries, States and the Control over Violence*, COPRI Working Paper 4/2002, Copenhagen Peace Research Institute.

Lee S (ed.). *Intervention, Terrorism and Torture: Contemporary Challenges to Just War Theory* (Springer, 2007).

Leverick F. *Killing in Self-Defence* (OUP, 2006).

Lewis M. 'Drones and the Boundaries of the Battlefield', 47 Texas Int'l L J 293 (2011–12).

Lewis M, and Crawford E. 'Drones and Distinction: How IHL Encouraged the Rise of Drones', 44 Georgetown J Int'l L 1127 (2012–13).

MacLaren M, and Schwendimann F. 'The New ICRC Study on Customary International Humanitarian Law as an Exercise in the Development of International Law', 6 German Law Journal 1217 (2005).

Mahken T. *Technology and the American Way of War Since 1945* (Columbia University Press, 2008).

Mallison WT, and Mallison S. 'The Juridical Status of Irregular Combatants under the International Humanitarian Law of Armed Conflict', 9 Case W Res J Int'l L 39 (1977).

Mallison WT, and Mallison S. 'The Juridical Status of Privileged Combatants under the Geneva Protocol of 1977 concerning International Conflicts', 42 Law & Contemp Probs 4 (1978).

March JJ, and Glabe S. 'Time for the United States to Directly Participate', 1 Va J Int'l L Online 13 (2011).

Maxwell MD, and Meyer R. 'The Principle of Distinction: Probing the Limits of its Customariness', 3 Army Lawyer 1 (2007).

Maxwell MD, and Watts S. '"Unlawful Enemy Combatant": Status, Theory of Culpability, or Neither?', 5 JICJ 19 (2007).

Melzer N. *Targeted Killing in International Law* (OUP, 2008).

Melzer N. 'Keeping the Balance between Military Necessity and Humanity: A Response to Four Critiques of the ICRC's Interpretive Guidance on the Notion of Direct Participation in Hostilities', 42 NYU J Int'l L & Pol 831 (2010).

Meron, T. 'The Martens Clause, Principles of Humanity, and the Dictates of Public Conscience', 94 AJIL 78 (2000).

Milanović M. '*Al-Skeini* and *Al-Jedda* in Strasbourg', 23 EJIL 121 (2012).

Ministry of Defence. *British Manual of Military Law* (London, 1958; Swindon, 2004).

Moir L. *The Law of Internal Armed Conflicts* (CUP, 2002).

Morgan R. 'Professional Military Firms under International Law', 9 Chicago J Int'l L 213 (2008).

Murphy R, and Radsan AJ. 'Due Process and Targeted Killing of Terrorists', 31 Cardozo L Rev 405 (2009).

Musah A-F, and Fayemi JK (eds). *Mercenaries: An African Security Dilemma* (Pluto, 2000).

Neuman G. 'Humanitarian Law and Counter-Terrorist Force', 14 EJIL 283 (2003).

Nill Sánchez A. 'Mexico's Drug "War": Drawing a Line between Rhetoric and Reality', 38 Yale J Int'l L 467 (2013).

Nurick L. 'The Distinction between Combatant and Noncombatant in the Law of War', 39 AJIL 680 (1945).

O'Brien K. 'PMCs, Myths, and Mercenaries: The Debate on Private Military Companies', 145 RUSI Journal (2000).

O'Connell ME. 'The Role of Soft Law in a Global Order', in D Shelton (ed.), *Commitment and Compliance: The Role of Non-Binding Norms in the International Legal System* (OUP, 2000).

O'Connell ME. 'Combatants and the Combat Zone', 43 U Rich L Rev 845 (2009).

O'Connell ME. 'Remarks: The Resort to Drones under International Law', 39 Denv J Int'l L & Pol'y 585 (2010–11).

O'Connell ME. 'Unlawful Killing with Combat Drones: A Case Study of Pakistan, 2004–2009', in S Bronitt, M Gani, and S Hufnagel (eds), *Shooting to Kill: Socio-Legal Perspectives on the Use of Lethal Force* (Hart, 2012).

O'Hanlon M. *The Science of War: Defense Budgeting, Military Technology, Logistics, and Combat Outcomes* (Princeton University Press, 2009).

Ohlin JD. 'The Duty to Capture', 97 Minn L Rev 1268 (2013).

Orogun P. '"Blood Diamonds" and Africa's Armed Conflicts in the Post-Cold War Era', 166 World Affairs 151 (2004).

Paust JJ. 'Permissible Self-Defence Targeting and the Death of bin Laden', 39 Denv J Int'l L & Pol'y 569 (2011).

Paust JJ. 'Propriety of Self-Defense Targetings of Members of al-Qaeda and Applicable Principles of Distinction and Proportionality', 18 ILSA J Int'l & Comp L 565 (2012).

Percy S. *Mercenaries: The History of a Norm in International Relations* (OUP, 2007).

Perna L. *The Formation of the Treaty Law of Non-International Armed Conflicts* (Martinus Nijhoff, 2006).

Pfanner T. 'Military Uniforms and the Law of War', 86 IRRC 93 (2004).

Pictet J (ed.). *Commentary to Geneva Convention I for the Amelioration of the Condition of the Wounded and Sick in Armed Forces in the Field* (ICRC, 1952).

Pictet J (ed.). *Commentary to Geneva Convention IV Relative to the Protection of Civilian Persons in Time of War* (ICRC, 1958).

Pictet J (ed.). *Commentary to Geneva Convention II for the Amelioration of the Condition of the Wounded, Sick and Shipwrecked Members of Armed Forces at Sea* (ICRC, 1960).

Pictet J (ed.) *Commentary to Geneva Convention III Relative to the Treatment of Prisoners of War* (ICRC, 1960).

Pictet J. *Humanitarian Law and the Protection of War Victims* (Henry Dunant Institute, 1975).

Pictet J. *Development and Principles of International Humanitarian Law* (Martinus Nijhoff, 1985).

Radsan AJ, and Murphy R. 'Measure Twice, Shoot Once: Higher Care for CIA-Targeted Killing', U Illinois L Rev 1201 (2011).

Reed T. *At The Abyss* (Random House, 2004).

Ricou Heaton, J. 'Civilians at War: Re-examining the Status of Civilians Accompanying the Armed Forces', 57 Air Force L Rev 155 (2005).

Rid T. *Cyber War Will Not Take Place* (Hurst and Company, 2013).

Ridlon D. 'Contractors or Illegal Combatants? The Status of Armed Contractors in Iraq', 62 Air Force L Rev 199 (2008).

Risley J. *The Law of War* (Innes and Co., 1897).

Roberts A, and Sivakumaran S. 'Lawmaking by Nonstate Actors: Engaging Armed Groups in the Creation of International Humanitarian Law', 37 Yale J Int'l L 107 (2012).

Roberts G. 'The New Rules for Waging War: The Case against Ratification of Additional Protocol I', 26 Va J Int'l L 109 (1985–86).

Rodley N, and Pollard M. *The Treatment of Prisoners under International Law* (3rd edn, OUP, 2009).

Rodriguez S. 'The Impotence of Being Earnest: Status of the United States Standard Minimum Rules for the Treatment of Prisoners in Europe and the United States', 33 New Eng J on Crim & Civ Confinement 61 (2007).

Rogers APV. *Law on the Battlefield* (2nd edn, Manchester University Press, 2004).

Rondeau S. 'The Pragmatic Value of Reciprocity: Promoting Respect for International Humanitarian Law among Non-State Armed Groups', in B Perrin (ed.), *Modern Warfare: Armed Groups, Private Militaries, Humanitarian Organisations, and the Law* (UBC Press, 2012).

Rosenblad E. *International Humanitarian Law of Armed Conflict: Some Aspects of the Principle of Distinction and Related Problems* (Henry Dunant Institute, 1979).

Ross M. 'Oil, Drugs, and Diamonds: The Varying Roles of Natural Resources in Civil War', in K Ballentine, and J Sherman (eds), *The Political Economy of Armed Conflict: Beyond Greed and Grievance* (Lynne Rienner, 2003).

Rousseau JJ. *The Social Contract, Or Principles of Political Right* (1762, translated by GDH Cole, available at: <http://www.constitution.org/jjr/socon_01.htm, accessed 30 March 2015).

Salzman Z. 'Private Military Contractors and the Taint of a Mercenary Reputation', 40 NYU J Int'l & Pol 853 (2007–08).

Sandoz Y, Swinarski C, and Zimmerman B (eds). *Commentary on the Additional Protocols of 8 June 1977 to the Geneva Conventions of 12 August 1949* (ICRC, 1987).

Sanger D. *Confront and Conceal: Obama's Secret Wars and Surprising Use of American Power* (Crown, 2012).

Sarkees M. 'The Correlates of War Data on War: An Update to 1997', 18 Conflict Management and Peace Science 123 (2000).

Sarkees MR, and Wayman F. *Resort to War: 1816–2007* (CQ Press, 2010).

Sassóli M. '"Unlawful Combatants": The Law and Whether it Needs to be Revised', 97 ASIL Proceedings 196 (2003).

Sassóli M. 'Use and Abuse of the Laws of War in the "War on Terrorism"', 22 Law & Ineq 195 (2004).

Sassóli M. 'Targeting: The Scope and Utility of the Concept of "Military Objectives" for the Protection of Civilians in Contemporary Armed Conflicts', in D Wippman and M Evangelista (eds), *New Wars, New Laws? Applying the Law of War in 21st Century Conflicts* (Transnational Publishers, 2005).

Sassòli M, Bouvier A, and Quintin A. *How Does Law Protect In War? Cases, Documents and Teaching Materials on Contemporary Practice in International Humanitarian Law* (3rd edn, ICRC, 2011).

Sassòli M, and Olson L. 'The Relationship between International Humanitarian and Human Rights Law Where it Matters Where it Matters: Admissible Killing and Internment of Fighters in Non-International Armed Conflicts', 90 IRRC 599 (2008).

Scahill J. *Dirty Wars: The World is a Battlefield* (London: Serpent's Tail, 2013).

Schaap A. 'Cyber Warfare Operations: Development and Use under International Law', 64 *Air Force L Rev* 121 (2009).

Schabas W. *An Introduction to the International Criminal Court* (4th edn, CUP, 2011).

Schachter O. 'The Twilight Existence of Nonbinding Agreements', 71 AJIL 296 (1977).

Scheimer M. 'Separating Private Military Companies from Illegal Mercenaries in International Law: Proposing an International Convention for Legitimate Military and Security Support that Reflects Customary International Law', 24 Am U Int'l L Rev 609 (2008–09).

Scheipers S. 'Fighting Irregular Fighters: Is the Law of Armed Conflict Outdated?', 43 Parameters 45 (2013).

Schindler D, and Toman J (eds). *The Laws of Armed Conflicts: A Collection of Conventions, Resolutions and Other Documents* (4th edn, Martinus Nijhoff, 2004).

Schmitt M. 'State-Sponsored Assassination in International and Domestic Law', 17 Yale J Int'l L 609 (1992).

Schmitt M. 'Computer Network Attack and the Use of Force in International Law: Thoughts on a Normative Framework', 37 Colum J Transnat'l L 885 (1999).

Schmitt M. 'Computer Network Attack: The Normative Software', 4 YBIHL 53 (2001).

Schmitt M. 'Wired Warfare: Computer Network Attack and the *Jus in Bello*', in M Schmitt and B O'Donnell (eds), *Computer Network Attack and International Law*, 76 International Law Studies (2002).

Schmitt M. 'Armed Conflict and Law in this Century', 30 Human Rights 3 (2003).

Schmitt M. '"Direct Participation in Hostilities" and 21st Century Armed Conflict', in H Fischer (ed.), *Krisensicherung und humanitärer Schutz/Crisis Management and Humanitarian Protection: Festschrift für Dieter Fleck* (BWV, 2004).

Schmitt M. 'Humanitarian Law and Direct Participation in Hostilities by Private Contractors or Civilian Employees', 5 Chicago J Int'l L 511 (2005).

Schmitt M. 'Precision Attack and International Humanitarian Law', 87 IRRC 445 (2005).

Schmitt M. 'Human Shields in International Humanitarian Law', 38 Israel Yearbook on Human Rights 17 (2008).

Schmitt M. 'Targeting Narcoinsurgents in Afghanistan: The Limits of International Humanitarian Law', 12 YBIHL 301 (2009).

Schmitt M. 'Drone Attacks under the Jus ad Bellum and Jus in Bello: Clearing the "Fog of Law"', 13 YBIHL 311 (2010).

Schmitt M. 'The Interpretive Guidance on the Notion of Direct Participation in Hostilities: A Critical Analysis', 1 Harvard National Security Journal 5 (2010).

Schmitt M. 'Discriminate Warfare: The Military Necessity-Humanity Dialectic of International Humanitarian Law', in D Lovell and I Primoratz (eds), *Protecting Civilians During Violent Conflict: Theoretical and Practical Issues for the 21st Century* (Ashgate, 2012).

Schmitt M. 'Extraterritorial Lethal Targeting: Deconstructing the Logic of International Law', 52 Colum J Transnt'l L 79 (2013).

Schondorf R. 'The Targeted Killings Judgment: A Preliminary Assessment', 5 JICJ 301 (2007).

Schwebel S. 'Wars of Liberation—as Fought in UN Organs', in JN Moore (ed.), *Law and Civil War in the Modern World* (Johns Hopkins Press, 1974).

Scott J (ed.). *The Reports to the Hague Conferences of 1899 and 1907* (Clarendon Press, 1917).

Scott J (ed.). *The Proceedings of the Hague Peace Conference: The Conference of 1907, Vol. I* (Clarendon Press, 1920).

Shakarian P, Shakarian J, and Ruef A. *Introduction to Cyber-Warfare: A Multi-Disciplinary Approach* (Elsevier/Syngress, 2013).

Singer P. *Corporate Warriors: The Rise of the Privatized Military Industry* (Cornell University Press, 2003).

Singer P. 'Outsourcing War', 84 Foreign Affairs 119 (2005).

Sivakumaran S. *The Law of Non-International Armed Conflict* (OUP, 2012).

Sivakumaran S. 'The Ownership of International Humanitarian Law: Non-State Armed Groups and the Formation of Enforcement of IHL Rules', in B Perrin (ed.), *Modern Warfare: Armed Groups, Private Militaries, Humanitarian Organisations, and the Law* (UBC Press, 2012).

Skoler D. 'World Implementation of the United Nations Standard Minimum Rules for Treatment of Prisoners', 10 J Int'l L & Econ 453 (1975).

Sofaer A. 'Terrorism and the Law', 64 Foreign Affairs 901 (1985–86).

Solf W. 'Commentary: Non-International Armed Conflicts', 31 AULR 927 (1981–82).

Solf W. 'Problems with the Application of Norms Governing Interstate Armed Conflict to Non-International Armed Conflict', 13 Ga J Int'l & Comp L 291 (1983).

Solf W. 'The Status of Combatants in Non-International Armed Conflicts under Domestic Law and Transnational Practice', 33 AULR 53 (1983–84).

Solf W. 'A Response to Douglas J Feith's "Law in the Service of Terror—The Strange Case of the Additional Protocol"', 20 Akron L R 261 (1986–87).

Solf W. *The Law of Armed Conflict: International Humanitarian Law* (CUP, 2010).

Solis G. 'Targeted Killing and the Law of Armed Conflict', 60 Naval War College Review 127 (2007).

Sood A, and Enbody R. *Targeted Cyber Attacks: Multi-staged Attacks Driven by Exploits and Malware* (Syngress, 2014).

Spaight JM. *War Rights on Land* (Macmillan, 1911).

Spaight JM. *Air Power and War Rights* (Longmans Green, 1924).

Spaight JM. 'Legitimate Objectives in Air Warfare', 21 BYIL 158 (1944).

Stepanova E. 'Armed Conflict, Crime and Criminal Violence', 41 SIPRI Yearbook 38 (2010).

Stephens D, and Lewis A. 'The Targeting of Civilian Contractors in Armed Conflict', 9 YBIHL 25 (2006).

Stuart S. 'War as Metaphor and the Rule of Law in Crisis: The Lessons We Should Have Learned from the War on Drugs', 36 Southern Illinois U L J 1 (2011).

Sullivan J, and Elkus A. 'Plazas for Profit: Mexico's Criminal Insurgency', Small Wars Journal (26 April 2009).

Suter K. *An International Law of Guerrilla Warfare* (St Martin's Press, 1984).

Szesnat F, and Bird A. 'Colombia', in E Wilmshurst (ed.), *International Law and the Classification of Conflicts* (OUP, 2012).

Taber R. *The War of the Flea: A Study of Guerrilla Warfare Theory and Practice* (Paladin, 1970).

Terry J. 'The Lawfulness of Attacking Computer Networks in Armed Conflict and in Self-Defence in Periods Short of Armed Conflict: What are the Targeting Constraints?', 169 Mil L Rev 70 (2001).

Ticehurst R. 'The Martens Clause and the Laws of Armed Conflict', 317 IRRC 125 (1997).

Tonkin H. *State Control over Private Military and Security Companies in Armed Conflict* (CUP, 2013).

Trainin IP. 'Questions of Guerrilla Warfare and the Law of War', 40 AJIL 534 (1946).

Trundle M. *Greek Mercenaries: From the Late Archaic Period to Alexander* (Routledge, 2004).

Turns D. 'Cyber Warfare and the Notion of Direct Participation in Hostilities', 17 J Conflict & Sec L (2012).

van Creveld M. *Technology and War from 2000 B.C. to the Present* (Brassey's Defence Publishers, 1991)

van Engeland A. *Civilian or Combatant? A Challenge for the 21st Century* (OUP, 2011).

Vogel R. 'Drone Warfare and the Law of Armed Conflict', 39 Denv J Int'l L & Pol'y 101 (2010–11).

Watkin K. 'Controlling the Use of Force: A Role for Human Rights Norms in Contemporary Armed Conflict', 98 AJIL 1 (2004).

Watkin K. 'Opportunity Lost: Organised Armed Groups and the ICRC "Direct Participation in Hostilities Interpretive Guidance"', 42 NYU J Int'l L and Pol 641 (2010).

Watts S. 'Combatant Status and Computer Network Attack', 50 Va J Int'l L 391 (2010).

Weber M. *Political Writings*, P Lassman and R Speirs (eds) (CUP, 1994).

Wedgwood R. 'Proportionality, Cyberwar and the Law of War', 76 Int'l L Stud 219 (2000).

Weiner A. 'Law, Just War, and the International Fight Against Terrorism: Is It War?', in S Lee (ed.), *Intervention, Terrorism and Torture: Contemporary Challenges to Just War Theory* (Springer, 2007).

Wheaton H. *Elements of International Law*, R Dana (ed.) (Clarendon Press, 1936).

White M. *The Fruits of War: How Military Conflict Accelerates Technology* (Pocket Books, 2007).

Williams BG. *Afghanistan Declassified: A Guide to America's Longest War* (University of Pennsylvania Press, 2012).

Wilmshurst, E (ed.), *International Law and the Classification of Conflicts* (OUP, 2012).

Wilson H. *International Law and the Use of Force by National Liberation Movements* (Clarendon Press, 1988).

Wood S. 'Uniforms', in R Holmes, C Singleton, and S Jones (eds), *The Oxford Companion to Military History* (OUP, 2001),

Woodward R. *Bush at War* (Simon and Schuster, 2002).

Zarate JC. 'The Emergence of a New Dog of War: Private International Security Companies, International Law, and the New World Disorder', 35 Stanford J Int'l L 75 (1998).

Index

The manufacturer's authorised representative in the EU for product safety is Oxford University Press España S.A. of el Parque Empresarial San Fernando de Henares, Avenida de Castilla, 2 – 28830 Madrid (www.oup.es/en or product.safety@oup.com). OUP España S.A. also acts as importer into Spain of products made by the manufacturer.

www.ingramcontent.com/pod-product-compliance
Lightning Source LLC
LaVergne TN
LVHW011753200926
848484LV00003B/688
9780199678495